They Who Endure to the End

They Who Endure to the End

A Primer on Perseverance

EVERETT BERRY

WIPF & STOCK · Eugene, Oregon

THEY WHO ENDURE TO THE END
A Primer on Perseverance

Copyright © 2020 Everett Berry. All rights reserved. Except for brief quotations in critical publications or reviews, no part of this book may be reproduced in any manner without prior written permission from the publisher. Write: Permissions, Wipf and Stock Publishers, 199 W. 8th Ave., Suite 3, Eugene, OR 97401.

Wipf & Stock
An Imprint of Wipf and Stock Publishers
199 W. 8th Ave., Suite 3
Eugene, OR 97401

www.wipfandstock.com

PAPERBACK ISBN: 978-1-4982-3968-4
HARDCOVER ISBN: 978-1-4982-3970-7
EBOOK ISBN: 978-1-4982-3969-1

Manufactured in the U.S.A.   07/27/20

To my wife, Tabitha

Contents

Preface	xi
Introduction	xiii
What is the Biblical Basis for Asking Questions About Perseverance	xv
Charting the Outline of the Book	xvi
Chapter 1: Perseverance in the Old Testament	1
1. The Creation of Humanity and the First Act of Apostasy	4
2. Defining the People of God as a Remnant Within a Community	7
3. The Covenants of the Old Testament	10
4. Understanding Apostasy in Relationship to the Biblical Covenants	19
5. The Work of the Spirit Under the Old Covenant	25
6. Conclusions	28
Chapter 2: Perseverance in the Gospels	31
1. Perseverance in the Synoptic Gospels	32
2. Perseverance in John's Gospel	44
3. Conclusions	50
Chapter 3: Perseverance in the Letters of Paul	52
1. Perseverance in Romans	54
2. Perseverance in Galatians	60
3. Perseverance in the Letters to the Corinthians	63
4. Perseverance in the Letters to the Thessalonians	67
5. Perseverance in the Prison Epistles	71
6. Perseverance in the Pastoral Epistles	75
7. Conclusions	81
Chapter 4: Perseverance in Acts, the General Epistles, and Revelation	84
1. Perseverance in Acts	85
2. Perseverance in Hebrews	89
3. Perseverance in James and Jude	94

4. Perseverance in the Letters of Peter	98
5. Perseverance in the Letters of John	102
6. Perseverance in Revelation	106
7. Conclusions	110

Chapter 5: Perseverance in the Post-Apostolic Church — 113
1. Perseverance in the Apostolic Fathers — 114
2. Perseverance in Early Christian Apologists and Leaders — 118
3. Early Christian Deliberations on Apostasy: The Novatian Schism — 124
4. Conclusions on the Early Church's View of Perseverance — 132

Chapter 6: Augustine, Pelagianism, and Perseverance — 134
1. The Pelagian Controversy — 135
2. Augustine's Understanding of Sin, Salvation, and Election — 142
3. Augustine on Perseverance — 146
4. Conclusions about Augustine's View of Perseverance — 148

Chapter 7: The Reformation, Early Protestants, and Perseverance — 150
1. Luther, Lutheranism, and Perseverance — 152
2. Calvin, the Reformed Tradition, and Perseverance — 156
3. Anglicanism and Perseverance — 161
4. Anabaptists and Perseverance — 163
5. Roman Catholicism, the Council of Trent, and Perseverance — 167
6. Conclusions — 170

Chapter 8: Perseverance in the Classical Arminian and Wesleyan Traditions — 172
1. Setting the Stage for the Arminian View(s) of Perseverance — 174
2. Key Facets in Jacob Arminius' Soteriology — 176
3. The Clash Between the Remonstrants and the Synod of Dort — 182
4. Arminian Theology Transitions: Wesleyan Views on Perseverance — 186
5. Conclusion: Arminianism in Subsequent Protestant Traditions — 192

Chapter 9: Perseverance and the Modern Lordship Salvation Debate — 194
1. Theological Factors Involved in the Debate — 195
2. Precursors to the Lordship Salvation Debate — 198
3. The Beginning of the Lordship Controversy — 202
4. The Lordship Debate Erupts: MacArthur, His Critics & His Responses — 206
5. Conclusions on How the Lordship Debate Impacts Evangelical Views of Perseverance — 211

Chapter 10: Final Thoughts on the Doctrine of Perseverance — 213
1. Putting Together a Theology of Perseverance — 214

2. Developing a Biblical-Theological Understanding of Perseverance   223
  3. What are the Grounds and Means of Having Personal
     Assurance of Salvation?   237
  4. Final Conclusion   245

Bibliography   247

Author Index   277

Subject Index   279

Scripture and Ancient Documents Index   283

Preface

I HAVE EXPRESSED INTEREST in the doctrine of perseverance for quite some time. One reason being that it raises some weighty questions with which all believers struggle at one time or another. How do professing believers know if their conversion experiences are genuine? Can someone lose their salvation? Can believers sin to such an extent that they forfeit their salvation? Can an unbroken chain of unrepentant, chronic sin be proof that one is not a true believer? Inquiries like these raise significant concerns and searching for answers can be quite perplexing at times. For instance, I can recall several occasions as a pastor when congregants, guests, and even other pastors would want to discuss these matters. Sometimes these conversations were casual while others occasionally exuded a bit of theological friction. Also, there were encounters when people were not wanting to dialogue about the nuanced complexities of this subject. Rather they were struggling with their own faith and wanted to find some sort of assurance that could ground them amid their various doubts. These same scenarios emerged over the years since I have been a professor as well. I have visited with students who expressed uncertainty about their faith. I have met with some who wanted to know why Christian traditions disagree so strongly over this doctrine. And I have counseled some who almost abandoned their faith. Sadly, I have even met with a few who had already chosen to do so.

In addition to these many concerns that believers face on their spiritual pilgrimages, the doctrine of perseverance has become even more intriguing to me in the last few years because of recent scholarly discussions about the nature of faith, justification, and final judgment. Historically, the mainstay Catholic and Protestant answers to questions about apostasy and the nature of endurance in one's personal faith are well established. But ongoing developments in Pauline scholarship and studies on the nature of biblical apocalyptic have created new conversations that have persuaded some in evangelical guilds to revisit major biblical concepts including those related to perseverance and apostasy.

These factors are primarily why I want to produce a concise primer on this topic. Yet I must acknowledge that any successful attempt to complete a book requires one to stand on the shoulders of many people, including family, friends, colleagues, and other fellow scholars. This project is no different. I want to express gratitude, first of all, to my beloved wife, Tabitha, as well as our daughter, Elaina, and our son, Brian. There were many evenings where most of my time was consumed with reading books and typing on a laptop. I could not have invested this time without their love and support. I also want to thank Criswell College, which is the institution where I have taught for the past fifteen years. They provided me with a sabbatical that allowed me to do most of my research and writing. Finally, I want to give thanks to several scholars and editors who agreed to review various chapters of this book, including Alan Streett, Andrew Streett, Christopher Graham, David Brooks, Matthew Pinson, Russell Meek, Patrick Schreiner, and Ken Yates. Their input was invaluable to the development of the following chapters. I only hope that now this labor of love can be an encouragement to readers who wrestle with this doctrine and informative to those who want to learn more about it.

Introduction

THERE ARE MOMENTS IN the lives of many people where they truly come to grips with their condition outside of Christ. They begin to consider the demands that he makes upon their lives and eventually one pressing question demands an answer; what must one do to be saved? We see this pattern in various forms throughout the New Testament (hereafter NT). We read about a rich young ruler who thought he was abiding by all the expectations of the law since his youth but still wanted to ask Jesus if there was something else he needed to do to inherit eternal life (cf. Matt 19:16–30; Mark 10:17–31; Luke 18:18–30). We hear of a healed blind man asking Jesus who the Son of Man was so that he might believe in him (John 9:35–36); a dying criminal asking Jesus for mercy before his impending death (Luke 23:39–43); a massive Jewish crowd at Pentecost wanting to know what they should do after hearing Peter's convicting sermon about the resurrection and exaltation of Jesus as the Christ (Acts 2:37); and a pagan jailer in the city of Philippi desperate for direction from Paul and Silas when he was considering ending his own life (Acts 16:29–30). No matter the circumstances, despite the different backgrounds of the inquirers, their concern remained the same, which was how one could receive God's salvific mercy.

The fact that this request is repeated so often in biblical accounts lets us know how important it is. Understandably, this is why one's experience of believing in Christ, or as we would say, being converted (or saved), is so foundational to the Christian faith. It is why key terms such as regeneration, conversion, justification, and sanctification have received such significant attention in the history of the church. They are all connected to the simple yet profound question of how one comes to a saving knowledge of Christ, thereby becoming a citizen of his kingdom. However, another related concern that is just as crucial and has received an equal amount of attention from Christian thinkers over the centuries is whether someone who has experienced conversion can somehow become an unbeliever once again, or more specifically, can true saints forfeit their status in Christ? Do all believers ultimately persevere in their faith or can they, for one reason or another, abandon their faith and become apostates?

No doubt, this has been one of the most hotly disputed conundrums in Christian theology. The reason being that it touches upon so many issues that are all related to one's understanding of salvation as a whole. Matthew Pinson has summarized this well by stating,

> Besides the subject's long history and integral connection with Christian spirituality, the doctrine of perseverance serves as a handy gauge of one's theological vantage point. Perseverance touches so many other doctrinal themes—free will, grace, predestination, atonement, justification, sanctification, spirituality. Thus, the way people handle this subject tells a great deal about where they locate themselves on the theological spectrum.[1]

This point is well taken. If one thinks that people experience something *irreversible* when they come to Christ via the inward work of the Spirit and the external expressions of repentance and faith, then that is an outflow of several other distinct doctrinal commitments. But for others who are convinced that people can be born of the Spirit and still somehow lapse back into an unconverted state, this belief is linked to other theological inclinations as well.

On a bit more practical note, we can clarify the perplexity that this subject instills by offering a scenario. Let's say that a young man confesses faith in Christ at an early age. He becomes part of a church family. He grows in his knowledge of the Lord. He worships, prays, shares his faith, maybe even mentors other young believers periodically. Then at some later point in his life, for whatever reasons, he renounces his faith, becoming an atheist. The looming question now is how does one define his present condition in light of his past. Was he a believer who later apostatized, a false believer who showed his true colors, or the infamous backsliding carnal Christian who is just going through a radical phase of rebellion? Or even more intriguing, what if he were to come back to the faith later in life. Does this mean he was a genuine convert for a while, then an unbeliever when he renounced his faith, and finally a believer once more when he recanted his prior renouncement? Or was he merely an AWOL believer while professing atheism and later became an active one once more?

---

1 Pinson, introduction to *Four Views*, 7.

Finding satisfactory answers here can be challenging, but before one is tempted to dismiss this as a mere hypothetical case, the reality is that these kinds of situations do take place. And even more unsettling is this concern. What is the difference between the faith of a person who will eventually apostatize and your own faith at this moment (if you as a reader profess to be a believer)? How do you know you will never apostatize? How can you presently show without any doubt that your faith is any different experientially from other professing believers who just have not reached the point of becoming an apostate yet? These are the kinds of soul-searching questions that make the subject of perseverance so pertinent to Christian thought. It not only pertains to questions about how one can know if someone else is a believer. It forces one to ask how they can have assurance of their own personal salvation.

WHAT IS THE BIBLICAL BASIS FOR ASKING QUESTIONS ABOUT PERSEVERANCE

It is no secret that Christians over the ages have strongly disagreed on how to resolve matters related to perseverance and apostasy. In fact, I would say that when it comes to the doctrine of salvation, perseverance would be the most controversial subject of all if it did not always take a back seat to the doctrine of election, which always takes first place (even though they are related topics). Be that as it may, the reason there is such polarized disagreement is the same as it is for any other doctrinal dispute. Christian thinkers clash because there is lack of consensus on how certain biblical texts should be interpreted individually (i.e., textually) and then understood collectively as a whole (i.e., intertextually). This dual challenge emerges when discussing this particular issue because of two major themes that emerge within the NT.

One motif that we notice in many passages is what one may call the permanency of salvation. Relevant texts regarding this idea are well known by those familiar with this debate. For example, we read Jesus' words where he promised that all who believed in him would be changed in such a way that it would last forever. He assured his followers that they would receive eternal life which is qualitative (*a new kind of life for the age to come*) and quantitative (*life without end because the age to come will be eternal*, John 3:15–16; 4:13–14; 5:24; 6:35, 51; 11:25–26). This is why Jesus claimed that those who believed in him would never be lost (Luke 22:31–32a; John 6:37–39; 10:27–29). Likewise, Paul on occasion claims that believers have currently received the Holy Spirit as a guarantee that they will receive final salvation in the future (2 Cor 1:22; 5:5; Eph 1:14). He expresses this confidence elsewhere when he periodically assures his readers that God would bring their salvation to completion (1 Cor 1:4–9; Rom 8:29–39; Phil 1:6; 2 Tim 1:12; 4:18). Also in this vein, the idea of permanency appears to be highlighted by the writer of Hebrews who claims that Christ acts as the high priest for all believers because he continually intercedes on their behalf (Heb 4:14–16; 7:25) and cleanses them from all their sins (Heb 9:24–26; also see 1 Pet 1:18–19). In accordance with these promises, other NT writers allude to the idea that God will be protect and preserve believers in their salvation to the end (1 Pet 1:3–5; Jude 24–25).

Admittedly, if we stopped there, it would appear that the debate over perseverance would be quite short. This is not the case, however, because there is another emphasis throughout the NT. We discover just as many texts, if not more, that link believers' final eschatological salvation to their perseverance in faith. For instance, we read consistent warnings that many will apostatize from the faith (Matt 10:21–22; 24:10–13; 2 Thess 2:3–5; 2 Tim 4:1–3); there are continual admonitions for believers to persevere in their faith (Acts 14:21–22; Col 1:22–23; 2 Cor 13:5; Heb 3:14; 2 Pet 1:10; 2 John 9); and more emphatically, there are some sobering commands to persevere which entail promises of eternal judgment if disobeyed (Rom 11:17–20; 2 Tim 2:11–13; Heb 2:1; 3:6, 12–14; 4:14; 6:1–6; 10:36–39; Rev 2:10–11; 3:5; 22:19). At a more practical level, we often see constant contrasts between the way believers are to live and how the world conducts itself. Believers are to adopt attitudes and lifestyles that are different from the unbelieving world (John 15:1–6; Rom 6:1–2; 1 Cor 6:9–11; Gal 5:19–21; Eph 5:11–13; Rev 22:14–15). Those who fall into sinful patterns are to be confronted so they can be brought to repentance and the purity of the church can be protected (Matt 18:15–20; 1 Cor 5:3–5, 9–13; 2 Thess 3:14–15). Likewise, conduct is treated with the upmost importance because believers are determined to be authentic by how they live their lives for the Lord (Matt 25:31–36; John 13:35; 15:16; Gal 5:6; Jas 2:18; 1 John 2:3–4; 4:20–21). Their conduct also shows that they are prepared for Christ's return as opposed to those who will not. Those who are oblivious to the Second Advent reveal such ignorance by their reckless living (Matt 24:23–24; 25:1–13; 1 Thess 5:4–6; Heb 9:28; 2 Pet 3:11–13).

CHARTING THE OUTLINE OF THE BOOK

Now what becomes emphatically clear when we compare all of these texts is that there are serious exegetical and theological issues warranting attention.

Hence, the purpose of this book. We want this volume to serve as a fresh primer on the doctrine of perseverance that hopefully achieves two primary goals. One is to provide a concise synopsis of alternative answers that many Christian interpreters have offered in their attempts to wrestle with this doctrine.[2] The reason for this is simple. Part of understanding the reasons why someone takes a particular view on issues of apostasy and perseverance is being able to navigate the potential components in the history of Christian thought that may be influencing one's theological dispositions. No one reads Scripture, interprets select passages, or advocates certain doctrinal positions in a vacuum. Everyone takes a position in light of their acceptance and/or rejection of an assortment of theological commitments. Thus, it is critical to have at least some awareness of the spectrum of positions on this subject so one can understand why various interpreters espouse conflicting viewpoints.

Alongside this task, the other objective of this volume is to engage the corpus of relevant biblical material and make the case that the NT emphasizes two truths about perseverance that must be equally maintained. On the one hand, Scripture does often highlight the security that believers have in their relationship to Christ while on the other, it consistently expresses real warnings of final eschatological judgment for those who do not endure in their faith. We will argue that the tension between these two realities can be alleviated when we recognize that the NT is often trying to do different things when engaging its first-century readers. Sometimes biblical writers stress the theological realities that define who believers are because of their new union with Christ, his kingdom, and his church. This kind of encouragement usually happens when writers want to comfort believers who are already faithfully enduring hardship. Yet these same authors sometimes discuss the fact that a believer's initial conversion is just a prologue to a larger experience which is still to culminate in their future vindication at the final judgment. This is why frequent warnings are mentioned because those who are now believers are expected to exhibit the reality of the indwelling Spirit through persevering faith. These conversations usually occur in situations where believers are either in rebellion or possibly on the threshold of apostatizing.

In the end, then, the NT offers the promise of security to believers who are looking to Christ and counsels those who are not to repent. So when it comes to the age old question of whether "believers" can "lose" their

---

2 This volume will not provide a comprehensive or exhaustive survey of all views of perseverance. For instance, detailed analysis of traditional Catholic or Orthodox views will not be provided. Rather, the lion's share of attention will be given to Protestant evangelical views.

salvation, the main conclusion or thesis of this book will be that the modern way of asking this question can sometimes cause one to lose sight of how the NT approaches the matter. The NT admonishes believers to persevere with promises of eternal life to those who do and warnings of divine judgment to those who do not. Or put another way, *while the NT teaches that it is theologically certain that all true believers will inherit all the blessings of the age to come, it is practically uncertain as to whether all professing believers will persevere. This means we must concede to the fact that the NT contains a tension which includes both of these realities.*[3] Obviously, this thesis needs to be fleshed out in more detail and indeed it will be.

So with these objectives being stated, this book will provide ten chapters that are broken down into three major sections. Chapters 1–4 make up the first segment which assesses the bulk of biblical material pertinent to perseverance and apostasy. Chapter 1 begins with an examination of relevant topics in the OT. Here, the discussion will focus primarily upon the theological implications of what it means to be part of "God's people" under the old covenant. There are complexities with such a treatment because as we shall see, being a part of the covenant community (i.e., the people of Israel) did not necessarily mean everyone was an actual believer. Some were not at all whereas others were. Israel was a mixed community. This means that defining the nature of faith, perseverance, and apostasy has to be done carefully because of the covenantal nuances that were intrinsic to the Mosaic economy. Relatedly, attention will be given to the nature of salvation prior to the coming of Christ and the new work of the Spirit. This will require that we address several matters such as the role of blessings and curses in the Mosaic covenantal agreement with Israel; the exact meaning behind the concepts of being "cut off" from Israel because of disobedience or ceremonial uncleanness; and the function of the Spirit whereby he would temporarily empower individuals, only to sometimes abandon them because of moral failures (e.g., Samson, King Saul).

Subsequently, chapters 2–4 transition to examine how the idea of perseverance emerges in the NT. The analysis provided includes a treatment of how concepts such as faith, discipleship, and eternal life are used throughout the gospels. We will argue that the evangelists describe faith as an act of trust that results in allegiance to Christ and his kingdom, thereby eliminating any distinction between a believer and a follower. We will then cover numerous passages in Paul's writings as well as the general epistles where believers are admonished to endure in their faith with some of these accounts warning

---

3 In making this statement, it should be said for transparency's sake that to a degree, the author is defending a Reformed perspective of soteriology, but without the ecclesiological commitments to covenant theology.

them of impending judgment if they do not. As we engage these passages, we will see that these texts sometimes express confidence that the readers will persevere because of God's providential enablement while others convey a tone of contingency because the emphasis is placed on the audience's responsibility to heed the warnings.

From here, chapters 5–9 serve as the second major section of the book. The focus here will be upon how beliefs about perseverance and apostasy developed throughout the history of Christian thought. This survey begins in chapter 5 with a treatment of how early Christian writers addressed the possibility of apostasy. In the latter half of the chapter, we will then look at the third-century Novatian controversy which centered upon the question of whether or not believers who had recanted their faith because of Roman persecution (i.e., the lapsed) should be permitted to return to the fellowship of the church. Chapter 6 moves forward to examine the fifth-century Pelagian controversy because it set the backdrop for the influential Augustine of Hippo to articulate his view of perseverance. The combination of his sacramental views of baptism and justification with his view of election led him to deduce that people could indeed be saints without being part of God's elect. The reason is that only saints who were given the gift of persevering faith were the elect ones. Therefore, it will be argued that Augustine believed in the perseverance of the elect, but not the saints because not all saints persevere. We will also show how this Augustinian distinction set the theological trajectory for how many Catholics and Protestants would address this doctrine for centuries (even to this very day).

Chapter 7 builds on this contention by leaping forward to the Reformation and surveying several of the perspectives that major Protestant traditions embraced. Specific attention is given to the views of Lutherans, the Reformed tradition, Anglicans, the Anabaptists, and the Catholic response via the Council of Trent to show how they each approached the idea of perseverance. Chapter 8 will shift gears to describe how the theological divide between the Reformed tradition and Arminianism emerged regarding to the concept of apostasy. We will begin with an assessment of James Arminius' work, thereby setting the backdrop for examining the opinions of his later Dutch successors who drafted the well-known Five Articles of Remonstrance. At this point, we will move to the later great awakenings of the eighteenth and nineteenth to discuss how the classical Arminian view of apostasy morphed somewhat via the theology of John Wesley. Here, we will address his views of conversion and the idea that salvation is "amissible." Likewise, it will be shown how both strands of Arminian thought continue to be advocated in an assortment of Protestant traditions today.

Chapter 9 continues this survey by discussing one last subject, which is the development of a mediating position between Reformed and Arminian thought known today as "eternal security." Though this idea began to surface in various strands of Free Church traditions, its influence grew significantly in the late twentieth-century rift in the United States popularly known as the "Lordship Salvation Debate." The item of most interest in this theological divide was the upsurge caused by Pastor John MacArthur's book *The Gospel according to Jesus* and his interactions with two specific opponents, those being Charles Ryrie and Zane Hodges. It will be shown how these arguments for the "No Lordship" view helped solidify a nominal Arminian view that some evangelicals embrace today known as the "Free Grace" position.

Finally, with all of this biblical and historical content about perseverance in place, chapter 10 serves as the last section of the book. It will bring our discussion full circle and show how the idea of perseverance relates to other doctrinal matters. We will illustrate this by initially giving attention to how one's view of perseverance is indicative of one's theological method, or more specifically, how one believes biblical passages interrelate. Then we will offer some further clarifications to the general thesis, which again is that while the New Testament does emphasize the permanency of a believer's salvation, it never allows one to foster a presumptuous attitude of disobedience because saving faith is an enduring faith. Moreover, while I have no delusions that this contention will resolve all of centuries of debate on this topic, I do hope this volume can open a few new doors of dialogue between Christian traditions. Perhaps it can even provide a helpful introduction to the subject that curious readers can consult for years to come.

Chapter 1

Perseverance in the Old Testament

THE OT IS WHERE we begin our inquiry into the subjects of apostasy and perseverance because this is where the story line of Scripture is born.[1]

[1]. We retain the designation "Old Testament" for referring to the Hebrew Bible throughout this book given its widespread use among Protestants. Likewise, the approach we take in developing our conclusions about apostasy and perseverance begins with the affirmation that the sixty-six books of the Bible form one book (or library of books) that tells one unified narrative. This is why we will often use the word "Scripture" throughout this work to refer to the OT as well as the NT both at the micro level—i.e., specified texts—and at the macro level—i.e., individual books and the canon as a whole. Together as a corpus of sacred divinely-inspired texts, we affirm that these accounts retain a theological symmetry that bequeaths revelatory information for believers to receive. Therefore, for any doctrinal conclusion to be tenable, it must maintain a balance between the diverse ideas that are found in the biblical canon and the ways in which those ideas complement each other. We want to see how biblical texts are individually unique while at the same time identifying how they interconnect together rather than allegedly contradicting or competing against each other. The reason these points are so important to mention at the outset is various guilds of biblical scholarship possess an underlying assumption that to describe biblical writings with terminology like "canon" or "inspired" is to engage in problematic anachronisms. But for our purposes, we mention our perspective at the outset so readers can be aware of our convictions regarding theological method. Furthermore, our intention for using "story line" here is not a subtle way of pitting the concept of narrative against the historicity of biblical accounts or downplaying the belief that biblical revelation entails propositional content that can be restated accurately in contemporary language. Rather, we are emphasizing that the theological truths of Scripture emerge within the contours of redemptive history. One could say the Bible is God's story about God's story. In other words, the Bible speaks about how God intervenes in history to perform various acts such as creation, redemption and judgment (i.e., the story). But it does not stop there. It also tells us how we should understand the significance of these actions (i.e., the story about the story). So

The OT opens with the Genesis account of creation and the tragic fall of humanity. Then it chronicles how God promised to heal this fallen world by initially forming a nation, the people of Israel, through whom a redeemer would come to bring salvation to all peoples. And it is the recounting of these events that serves as the theological ground zero for all biblical doctrines. Every major Christian belief is rooted in the themes, events, and hopes of the OT narrative. We do confess, however, that trying to encapsulate everything the OT contributes to the topics under investigation is daunting. This is why we will only focus on certain themes that we feel are the most pressing.

Specifically, there are three that provide an optimal amount of insight. One is what it means to be part of God's people. How the OT defines the people of God necessarily entails questions about who is "in" and who is "out," how one can become a part of God's people, or how one can possibly part ways from the group. Second, the very phrase "people of God" emerges from the context of a set of covenants that the Israelites received from the Lord at various stages of their history. Collectively these sacred agreements helped form the theological matrix of Israel's religious convictions, including their views of sin, righteousness, and yes, apostasy. So understanding the nature of these covenants can shed significant light on what it means in the OT for one to turn away from or rebel against the Lord. Finally, a third factor warranting attention is how individuals personally experienced salvation prior to the coming of Christ and the new work of the Spirit.

Together these features can help us conceptualize how the OT approaches apostasy and perseverance. But before we begin examining this material, one important qualifier should be mentioned. Believers during the OT era understood their experience of God's mercy in ways that were unique to that specific period. This is not to imply that there are multiple ways of receiving salvation. Scripture is clear that one can only obtain peace with God through faithful trust in whatever provisions he puts in place and/or promises he extends. Even so, the outworking of this truth varied depending on the amount of revelation that had been disclosed or redemptive acts that the Lord had performed up to a given point in biblical history. For instance, the ancient Israelites who came out of Egypt understood their national deliverance and standing before God in terms of the divine promises received by Abraham, the legal instructions given by Moses for the Passover,

---

for example, the account of the exodus tells us both what God did to deliver Israel from Egypt as well as how we should interpret its significance in Israel's history. Probably the most pronounced evangelical scholar who continues to highlight the importance of this fact when dealing with any Christian doctrine is Kevin Vanhoozer. See especially his works *Drama of Doctrine* and *Biblical Authority after Babel*.

and their eyewitness accounts of God's judgment upon their oppressors through the great plagues and the Red Sea event. However, centuries later, some NT writers who looked back on these events through typological and christological lenses were able to flesh out an understanding of a new exodus from the satanic tyranny of sin and death.[2] They reflected on events like the Passover or the Red Sea miracle and saw significant connections since Christ had accomplished a greater victory.[3]

These kinds of developments and parallels are critical to note because they apply to all theological topics. They are part of what we typically call progressive revelation. No doctrine is fully treated in any one biblical text. Clusters of texts introduce various subjects in rudimentary form, gradually taking on more texture as redemptive history unfolds. Then they take on even richer layers of meaning after the coming of Christ and the highly anticipated ministry of the Spirit. As it pertains to concepts like perseverance and apostasy, NT teaching on these subjects does not contradict what the OT proposes. Yet later revelation can say more than what earlier revelation disclosed. This means we must show caution in our investigation of OT views of apostasy and perseverance because, as I. Howard Marshall observes, "Any conclusions which may be drawn from the OT about the relation of the community of God must accordingly be applied with caution to the position of the individual under the New Covenant."[4] Consequently, we acknowledge that the OT does provide instruction on how covenant faithfulness and apostates were perceived by the Israelites.[5] And it also helps set the stage for our subsequent discussions about how the NT treats these matters as well. What needs to be conceded then is that while OT and NT

---

2. One obvious parallel between Christ's work and the original exodus of OT Israel can be seen in the gospel accounts of the Mount of Transfiguration. All three Synoptic Gospels mention that Elijah and Moses appear with Jesus on the mountain but Luke is the only one who describes their subject of discussion, namely Jesus' upcoming death, or his departure (i.e., his exodus or *exodon*). See Vanhoozer's discussion in "Ascending the Mountain, Singing the Rock," 794–95.

3. E.g., Paul sees a theological correspondence between Israel's first Passover and the responsibility of God's people, the church, to remain morally pure as a community of faith (1 Cor 5:6–8); and he views the concept of baptism as somehow prefigured in Israel's identification with Moses in their deliverance at the Red Sea (1 Cor 10:1–3).

4. Marshall, *Kept by the Power of God*, 29. The reason for this is not because the teachings are incorrect, but rather because the OT parallels on their own are incomplete.

5. Also, various traditions in second temple Judaism have much to say about apostasy as well. Cf. observations by Marshall, *Kept by the Power of God*, 38–50; Oropeza, *In the Footsteps of Judas*, 3–5; Oropeza, *Churches Under Siege*, 101–2; Bryan, *Jesus and Israel's Traditions of Judgment and Restoration*, 70–72; Schremer, "Thinking about Belonging," 249–75; and Stern, *Jewish Identity in Early Rabbinic Writings*.

views of perseverance have many points that overlap, there are some areas where the NT adds further input.

1. THE CREATION OF HUMANITY AND THE FIRST ACT OF APOSTASY

With these preliminary observations in place, some initial remarks need to be made regarding Adam's sin since it introduced an apostate-like act to creation. Even though Christian traditions disagree on whether genuine believers can lose their salvation through disobedience or apostasy, none deny that the Genesis account of Adam's fall from a state of innocence is the place where sin entered the human race.[6] Not only that, *in a qualified sense* it is not off the mark to say that the first turning away from the Lord occurred in the creation story. This tragedy comes on the heels of the first two chapters of Genesis, where we see a clear emphasis placed upon humankind as the crown jewel of creation. The account in Genesis 1 omits any detailed discussion about the Lord creating angels, the planets, the galaxies, or any extensive list of species of animals. Instead, it summarizes the creation week, which culminates with the making of human beings, Adam and Eve. This first couple is created in God's "image and likeness" (Gen 1:26–27), meaning at the very least that they served as delegated vice regents on earth since they were given a stewardship to exercise dominion over it (cf. Gen 1:28; 2:19–20).[7] Part of their task included a command to spread the divine image by procreation (Gen 1:28).[8] Similarly, Genesis 2 emphasizes the uniqueness of Adam and Eve within the rest of creation as well.

---

6. This is not to deny the ongoing discussions about the historicity of Adam and current tensions over the potential interplay between the Genesis account of creation and scientific theories of origins. The simple point here is that the history of Christian thought shows a consistent commitment to the Genesis account as a theological description of sin entering the human race, regardless of the historical details. However, it is safe to say that most trajectories in Christian theology align with a commitment to the historical nature of Adam's fall.

7. An excellent synopsis of the ancient Near Eastern dynamics that are packed into such a concept as the imago can be seen in Middleton's *Liberating Image*, 93–234; and Lints, *Identity and Idolatry*, 43–56.

8. Like ancient kings of that time who identified their kingdoms by placing their replica on key items (e.g., temples, coins, statues) to mark their territories, God wanted to mark the earth with his created image-bearers. See Middleton, *Liberating Image*, 93–146. So God did not place Adam and Eve in the garden of Eden only to tend to the garden—he wanted their offspring to eventually reign over the entire earth.

1.1 Adam Defies God's Authority

Now it is critical at this point to observe that Adam and Eve stood in moral harmony with the Lord. They were innocent creatures delegated to reign over his creation. But these privileges entailed certain stipulations. Alongside their responsibilities and privileges were further instructions to care for the earth, or the garden, in which they were placed (Gen 2:15), and they were given a prohibition not to eat from one tree in the garden that Genesis calls "the tree of the knowledge of good and evil" (Gen 2:16–17a).[9] They were told that if they ate from this tree, the consequence would be death (Gen 2:17b).[10] From here, though, we know that Adam and Eve did not heed the Lord's warning. They chose to misuse their position as stewards over the earth, thereby fracturing the goodness of Genesis 1 and 2. Their demise began when Eve was deceived by Satan who took the form of a serpent (cf. Gen 3:1a, 15; Rom 16:20; Rev 12:9; 20:2). He tempted her to question the Lord's motives for excluding access to the one forbidden tree and doubt his warnings about possible death (Gen 3:1b, 4–5).[11] The serpent twisted the words of God just enough so she would fall for a lie. He told her that God did not want her to be like him and so, tragically, she ate of the fruit. Then she gave some of the forbidden fruit to Adam.

This act of defiance immediately plunged Adam and Eve into a cycle of spiritual entropy, robbing them of their dignity. They became aware of their exposed vulnerability, which compelled them to collect fig leaves in a pitiful attempt to cover their nakedness (Gen 3:7). The scene gets even worse when

---

9. The title does not intend to describe anything intrinsic to the tree itself as if its fruit contained some sort of ingredient that made one good or evil. Most likely it is that this tree is designated by God as off limits so a moral context could be established whereby obedience could be rewarded and rebellion could be judged.

10. Some believe that the language used here in Genesis to describe God's commands is covenantal in nature. The primary source for this view comes from the Reformed tradition. The idea is that an Adamic covenant (of works) was initially established before the later covenant of grace was needed to remedy Adam's fall. The basis for this is the instruction on what they are to do and the warning of judgment if they violate the one prohibition. Those who advocate this idea think that the possible divine intent was to place Adam and Eve on a kind of probationary period to see if they would obey God's commands. If they did, they would be allowed to eat of the tree of life and be confirmed in their innocent state. Though there is obvious debate about this, the suggested idea that Adam was under a probationary status does make some sense of the narrative. A good concise summary of this view can be found in McComiskey, *Covenants of Promise*, 213–21; and Williamson, *Sealed with an Oath*, 52–58.

11. When comparing the layers of biblical revelation, we come to know that the serpent is being controlled by Satan. See an important discussion of this point in light of how ancient stories sometimes spoke of similar events in Chisholm, "Etiology and Its Implications," 43–50.

the Lord eventually made his presence known.[12] They hid in the garden only to be discovered and confronted (Gen 3:8). Knowing they had nowhere else to run, they shamefully admitted their guilt, albeit with excuses and blame shifting. The Lord subsequently announced certain curses that were to come upon them and creation itself. Their fate then ended in banishment as they were cast out of the Lord's presence in the garden. One could say they were exiled from the garden that they were originally allowed to tend as well as the divine presence itself.[13] Subsequently, a spiral of judgment continued as the story of humanity became riddled with death, immorality, deception, violence, and idolatry.[14]

1.2 Defining Adam's Fall as a Qualified Version of Apostasy

Moving forward from here, it must be conceded that labeling Adam's fall as the first act of "apostasy" can only be done in a qualified sense. The reason is apostates are usually identified as those who convert to a faith (or at least outwardly others think they do) only to later renounce their confession so they can either return to their previous way of thinking (or living) or perhaps adopt something altogether different that is still antithetical to the faith they are now choosing to deny. So strictly speaking, Adam's sin was not an explicit act of apostasy because he was not returning to a previous way of sinful living or thinking. Nor did he abandon the Lord altogether and cease to worship him. Likewise, he was not a fallen creature who was

---

12. The real tragedy of apostasy or sin is not just that one abandons the Lord. It is that one must eventually face God outside of his covenantal provisions.

13. This banishment is later replicated by Israel itself. After their repeated and unrepentant disobedience, the people were exiled from the land of promise. This thematic connection, which has been emphasized in numerous works, begins with the divine presence in Eden being lost; regained through the establishment of the tabernacle/temple; lost again through the breaking of the covenant; and finally received in its full form through Christ and the Spirit via the ratification of the new covenant. Two works that highlight this strand well are Heiser, *Unseen Realm*, 23–72; and Alexander, *From Eden to the New Jerusalem*, 13–73.

14. This is not to say this was the whole story. The Genesis account also shares the Lord's promise that through the seed of a woman (Gen 3:15), a serpent-crushing victor would come who is later identified as Christ, the messianic King who would one day rule over the earth with his people as Adam and Eve were originally delegated to do (e.g., Jer 23:5; Zech 9:9–13). Also the narrative contains many other instances of God's grace such as his provision to cover Adam and Eve's shame with animal skins, the miraculous taking of one man named Enoch who later walked with God, the salvation of Noah and his family from the future flood, and after dividing the nations at the tower of Babel, the Lord chose one man who would help form one group to be the eventual avenue of blessing.

redeemed and later became fallen once more. He was created with no need for forgiveness. It was only when he defied God's authority that he incurred the new experience of a fallen state. His sin was not technically returning to a set of lies that he had affirmed at one time. His lapse was unique in that all he knew was truth until he decided to embrace the serpent's words, which in reality turned out to be well-camouflaged half-truth.[15]

At the same time, Adam's failure does set a moral trajectory that would lead others to commit acts of apostasy. One could say that his lapse serves as a precursor to an assortment of apostate acts that people would commit. Here Israel is a perfect example. Just as Adam received a qualified type of covenantal agreement, or at least divine instructions that included delegated tasks and warnings of judgment, so would the nation of Israel later receive divine promises that entailed blessings and curses.[16] And similar to Adam who was expelled from his home in the garden of Eden, the severest judgment that the Hebrew people would experience was ejection from their sacred location, the land of promise. Granted, Adam's situation was unique because the expectations placed upon him had nothing to do with receiving forgiveness, atonement for sin, or geographical restoration while Israel's covenantal parameters did (as we shall discuss shortly). But we can say that Israel acted as a corporate replica of Adam. They followed in his footsteps by often failing to abide by the Lord's directives.[17] Thus, Adam's fall does give us a bit of insight on the subject of apostasy since it began a pattern that his progeny would emulate.

2. DEFINING THE PEOPLE OF GOD AS A REMNANT WITHIN A COMMUNITY

Thankfully the story of Adam's fall does not end in judgment. God's acts of condemnation were laced with divine acts of grace as well. While the Lord did declare curses upon humanity and the earth, we read that he also covered the first couple's shame with animal skins and declared that he would

15. See discussion on the serpent's temptation in Walton, *Genesis*, 170–72.

16. This parallel is not a concession to the covenantal view that Adam was under a covenant of works whereas Israel was under the preliminary form of the covenant of grace. Rather the point is based on comments like that of the Prophet Hosea who laments that just as Adam defied the Lord's command, so has Israel rebelled against him by violating their covenantal obligations as his people (Hos 6:7).

17. At the same time, positively, they are a replica of Adam because they receive promises of salvation. Just as Adam failed and was still promised that the deceiving serpent would be crushed, when Israel failed, they were still promised that a deliverer would restore them.

defeat the lying serpent by crushing its head through an agent identified as the seed of a woman (Gen 3:15). This seed is eventually revealed to be Christ himself. Yet his identity as the one who would overthrow the cataclysmic effects of Satan's activity and sin's corruptive power cannot be separated from the fact that he would be a progeny of a particular people.[18] One Savior would come through one people to redeem all peoples. The OT comes to identify this group as the "sons of Israel" or the Israelites who were the physical descendants of Jacob, the son of Isaac and grandson of Abraham. They are ultimately called the people of God, a phrase deeply grounded in the language of a sacred bond, or covenant. One could say that the bestowal of this phrase carries similar overtones to the announcement of a couple who become "husband and wife."

The concept was born out of a promissory agreement that the Lord made with Israel through their mediator Moses after their deliverance from Egyptian bondage in the exodus event. The Lord stated that "I will be their God and they will be my people" (e.g., Exod 6:6–7; 19:5; Lev 26:9–14; Deut 9:10; 10:4; 18:16). This claim meant the people would become a special possession of the Lord, elected heirs of special blessings and bearers of significant responsibilities.[19] It also included that the Lord, being "their God," would tangibly abide in their midst, whether it was through theophanies like a pillar of fire or a cloud during the exodus, through his special presence with the ark of the covenant, or the holy of holies in the tabernacle/temple.[20] And because such a weighty agreement was ratified by the Lord himself, he was obligated to keep whatever promises he made with Israel, whether for blessings or judgment.

Now this title, "the people of God," has great bearing upon apostasy and perseverance because of how it applies to Israel throughout her history. The label of "God's people" can apply generally to the Israelites in a corporate manner as a collective nation or in a restrictive sense to a select remnant of committed Israelite believers.[21] In the latter case, this remnant

---

18. Gerald McDermott summarizes this point well by observing that the story line of Scripture consistently begins with God choosing something particular (e.g., Abraham, Israel, Christ the Messiah) to bring blessings to broader or universal recipients (e.g., the nations or the world). See McDermott, *Israel Matters*, 46–47.

19. This did not mean that people outside of Israel could not receive divine favor. It just meant that they must follow the God *of Israel* to experience it.

20. Through these mediums, the presence of the Lord that Adam and Eve lost in Eden was regained to a degree. Cf. observations here by Beale, *Temple and the Church's Mission*, 31–38; Heiser, *Unseen Realm*, 44–55.

21. For our purposes, we are focusing on these two usages because of the theological import they bring to the subjects of apostasy and perseverance. For passages that focus on the concept of a remnant within Israel, cf., e.g., 1 Kgs 19; Isa 10:20–21; Jer 42;

is sometimes described as a group that existed within the nation at a given time, one that would be delivered in the near future, or vindicated eschatologically. Consequently, while the covenantal promises made with Israel were directed at the nation as a whole, this did not mean every Israelite would be a direct recipient of its blessings. The nation was a community within a community. There was the general population of Jews who were born in the line of Jacob with each boy receiving the Abrahamic sign of circumcision. Yet as Israel's history reveals, many of them, often even the majority, did not remain committed to the Lord.

Some were spurious in their commitment to the Lord even though they were externally a "part" of the nation. We read of the exodus generation, for instance, where every Hebrew obeyed the instructions to escape the impending tenth plague of Egypt through the Passover event and then crossed the Red Sea with Moses. However, many of them died in the wilderness after they failed to enter the promised land due to their unbelief.[22] Only Joshua, Caleb (who actually was not an Israelite), their families, the younger generation of children and a designated cluster of others (e.g., the Levites), were permitted to enter.[23] We read of numerous other stories in a similar vein like the accounts in the book of Judges where the nation was in a constant cycle of idolatry, conflict, and restoration. We learn about the highs and lows in Israel's monarchy where the nation split in two and many of the kings served other deities, or at least practiced a syncretistic piety. Both the northern and southern kingdoms became so corrupt that they were taken away into exile. Still, throughout these dark periods, there were those committed to the Lord during the times of the judges as well as the era of the monarchy. There were faithful remnants such as the one that the Lord had in the days of the Prophet Elijah despite the loyalty to Baal among the Israelite masses (1 Kgs 19:15–18) and others who would repent of their rebellion after they received various oracles from the prophets.

The point to see is that the Israelite nation as "God's people" was a complex conglomerate in which only some were truly his followers. Some

---

Zech 8:11–12; Zeph 3:13. The concept of a remnant within Israel is important to the Apostle Paul as well, see his discussion of this matter in Rom 9:27–29; 11:1–5.

22. Again, the unbelieving generation is not described as dying off so they could experience eternal punishment. They died so that they could not inherit the land.

23. Cf. the allowances for various groups to enter Canaan in Num 1:1–4, 44–46, 47–50; and 14:28–30. Also, Caleb's participation in Israel's experience of Abrahamic blessings was a prelude to others such as Ruth who would become part of the nation because of their faith in the covenant God of Israel. One thinks of Isa 56:3–8 where the prophet proclaims that foreigners who keep the Lord's covenant will be welcomed into his house and holy mountain.

were fickle henotheists, sporadically committed to the Lord at best.[24] Others fell into idolatry or egregious sins for a time but later repented. And then there were those, despite their shortcomings, who followed their ancestor Abraham in keeping their faith in the Lord. So what we learn is that the inner-workings of being part of "God's people" within the economy of the old covenant entailed an underlying distinction between those who were believers (i.e., the faithful remnant within the nation) and those most likely who were not, or at least refused to remain in the community (i.e., people who were mere citizens of the nation).[25] This factor has huge implications for understanding the nature of apostasy and perseverance in the OT. However, its full significance can only be understood in light of the covenantal obligations that Israel was expected to follow and it is to this component that we now turn.

3. THE COVENANTS OF THE OLD TESTAMENT

We have already mentioned that Israel's identity as God's people in the OT is tethered to a series of covenants that God established with them.[26] This network of promises encompasses several agreements that prescribe how the Lord would use Israel to bring salvation to the nations and how the people could interact with him as a sacred community of worshippers. They begin with several pledges that set the stage for how the nation would be formed. Then an official constitution was later enacted that included stipulations which Israel had to follow if the people wanted to experience God's favor and avoid his discipline. Later during the early stages of Israel's monarchy, the Lord promised one king that his line would produce a descendant who would establish an everlasting kingdom so that righteousness could flow from Israel to all the earth. And finally, another set of promissory

---

24. As opposed to "monotheists" who affirm the sole existence of one God or "polytheists" who affirm the existence of many gods, a "henotheist" is someone who believes in many deities but gives allegiance to only one. An excellent discussion of how these ideas circulate in the Old Testament can be seen in Heiser, "Monotheism, Polytheism, Monolatry, or Henotheism?," 1–30.

25. This comment creates friction with some theological traditions mainly because of significant disagreement on whether this dynamic is perpetuated under the ramifications of the new covenant. Is the church a mixed community of believers and unbelievers? This is a matter that will be addressed later.

26. This kind of agreement between parties was a common practice in the ancient Near East. Today we have nearly sixty of these treaties. See Walton, *Ancient Near Eastern Thought*, 69; and Walton, *Ancient Israelite Literature*, 95–107. Also, for an extensive treatment on the function and roles of treaties in ancient cultures, see Kitchens and Larence, *Treaty, Law, and Covenant*.

declarations were made in which the Lord assured Israel that they would receive salvation, forgiveness of their sins, and even resurrection from the dead. The issue that concerns us, however, is how these covenants contribute to our understanding of perseverance and apostasy in the OT. To answer such questions, we need to examine these covenants in more detail.

3.1 The Abrahamic Covenant

Summarizing how the ramifications of Israel's covenants were to guide their conduct as God's people requires us to look at the initial one God made with Abram, or Abraham (cf. Gen 12:1; 17:5). This agreement served as the missional blueprint for how the Lord would restore his rule on the earth, one that promised one man that he would father one nation, which would bring healing and favor to others.[27] The early stages of this covenant begin to unfold following the Lord's promise to never destroy the earth again by a flood (Gen 9:11). In time after the Lord scattered the nations because of their collective rebellion at the Tower of Babel (Gen 11:1–19), he selected Abram from the land of Ur of the Chaldeans who had been living in Haran. He commanded him to take his family and leave everything, including his relatives and homeland (cf. Gen 12:1a; Acts 7:2–4).[28] The Lord promised Abram that if he embarked on this pilgrimage, he would be given a land and become the source of a great nation that would be the channel of blessings to all the other nations (Gen 12:1b–2).

The Lord later sealed the covenant with a ritual of sacrifice (Gen 15:7–17) in which he further promised Abraham that he would have a son through whom his descendants would eventually multiply to an innumerable degree (Gen 15:1–6). He was also reminded that his line would

---

27. For sake of time, we are not giving attention to what is called the Noahic covenant. Nevertheless, we should make mention that the Lord's promise to never destroy the world by a flood is significant because it showed that mankind's corruption would not prevent the Lord from keeping his promise to overcome the work of the serpent (i.e., Satan). Likewise, all the subsequent promises of how this would be accomplished were an outflow of the promise to Noah that worldwide deluge would never wipe out the nations again. This is partly why after the flood is over, some of the creation language of Genesis 1 is replicated in the description of the flood waters receding (cf. Gen 8:1–19; Sarna, *Genesis*, 49–50) and the Lord gives immediate instructions on how humanity is to enforce justice upon the earth (cf. Gen 9:5–6; VanDrunen, "Protectionist Purpose of the Law," 103).

28. In ancient Mesopotamia, the southern region of Sumer was known as Chaldea and Ur was located along the western side of the Euphrates River. His father, Terah, had already moved the family from Ur to Haran, a region northwest of Ur and directly north of Canaan. It should be noted that today, the specific location is disputed.

eventually inherit a specified area of land some four generations in the future (Gen 15:18–19). Eventually this covenantal bond was marked by a custom of remembrance via the practice of circumcision because the promise of blessing started with Abraham's seed (Gen 17:11–14).[29] From here, we then discover that the lineage of Abrahamic promise expanded to twelve sons who were born to Abraham's grandson Jacob (Gen 29:31–30:24). And in time the family made their way to Egypt because of providential dealings in the life of Joseph (Gen 37–47), which, in years to come, led to future generations becoming enslaved to Egyptian tyrants (Exod 1:7–14).

3.2 The Mosaic Covenant

This predicament set the stage for the exodus event where the Lord displayed his superiority over Egypt by rescuing Israel from bondage (Exod 12:12; Num 33:4).[30] After these dramatic events, the people began their long journey to the Abrahamic land of promise, and it was during this sojourn that they received the bonding title of God's people (Exod 6:6–7; 19:5). This honor occurred when Israel gathered at the region of Mt. Sinai to meet with the Lord in a ceremony where they could receive their new constitution.[31] From the outset, Moses served as the mediator on behalf of the people. As such, once he received the Lord's instructions, he recorded the specific code for living, again known as the law. It encapsulated legal, economic, social, personal, and liturgical guidelines which the people were to follow as priestly representatives and set-apart citizens of a newly established kingdom of which the Lord was king (Exod 19:6). This covenant promised blessings

---

29. What is interesting about this covenant (as well as the others) is that mainstay arguments on whether the promises to Abraham are unconditional or conditional can reach a fever pitch among various Christian traditions. What is interesting is that many scholars concede that such a dichotomy is perhaps wrongheaded. Some argue that perhaps the covenantal relationship between Yahweh and Abraham/Israel is in some ways conditional because the divine promises entail intentions that are only fulfilled in congruence with devout obedience and in other ways unconditional because the Lord is utterly committed to ensuring that the promises eventually come to pass. See Willis's helpful overview of this point in "Mediating Conditional & Unconditional Promises," 39–47; Waltke's older discussion in "Phenomenon of Conditionality," 123–39; and Smith, "Doctrine of the Future," 138–41.

30. It was God's defeat of these alleged deities that would make apostasy all the more egregious. Many Israelites pined over returning to Egypt and even thought the gods/forces of the Canaanites were insurmountable.

31. By constitution, we mean that the Mosaic code expressed the parameters that Israel was to follow as a theocratically governed people. The blessings or curses that came upon Israel because of their obedience or disobedience was enforced by the Lord himself. This was true even when the monarchy was established.

if it was obeyed and curses if it was violated (Exod 20:1–21; Lev 26; Deut 4:26–27, 36–38; 5:2–5). It should be noted, as well, that part of the reason this covenant was established was to continue the faithful outworking of the promises made to Abraham. But it created a new theological wrinkle. Obedience to the law's stipulations had to be followed if Israel wanted to experience them. Or put another way, the Abrahamic promises would only be realized when Israel remained committed to the Mosaic agreement.

These demands applied corporately to the people as well as any potential rulers of Israel, which would become a reality in Israel's later history. Furthermore, defiance against the law or moral collapse into unrepentant idolatry affected the entire nation, which sometimes included those who may have still remained loyal to the Lord. This means that any time Israel as a whole "turned away" from the Lord, we cannot assume that meant every individual Israelite abandoned their personal faith. The reason this is important is because minorities of faithful Israelites sometimes experienced the consequences of covenant violation if the nation as a whole suffered defeat from a rival pagan nation or worse, went into exile.[32] And even when national Israel did suffer consequences for covenant violations, the group still retained the title of God's people even though many of them did not worship him.[33] Thus, the way(s) in which the OT assesses the dynamics of apostasy are complicated because they do not perfectly overlap symmetrically with the later covenantal parameters in Christ. The reason being that the OT sometimes maintains a fine line between the acts of individuals and the overall condition of the nation as a whole.[34]

---

32. E.g., Joshua and Caleb had to wander the wilderness along with the rebellious generation until they died off. Also believing Jews went into exile along with the apostate idolaters. This is quite an important theme in the OT, that being specific times when some must suffer because of the failures of others. In some contexts, God promises that people will not be put to death for the sins of their children or their fathers (cf. Deut 24:16; 2 Kgs 14:6; Jer 31:30; Ezek 18:19–20). But there many other passages that speak of the sins of the fathers visiting the children of later generations (cf. Exod 34:7; Num 14:18; Deut 5:9). Most likely, the way of balancing these passages properly is to see the former set as speaking of legal judgment of the Mosaic code—i.e., one can be cut off from the community only because of their own covenantal violations. However, with regard to the other passages, the sins of parents can replicate themselves in the proclivities of their children and result in a pattern of disobedience and divine judgment.

33. As we shall see, even times where the Lord declares separation from Israel such as in the divorce language used by Jeremiah, the instance where Hosea refers to Israel as "not my people," or in the passage in Haggai where the Lord calls Israel "this people," the point always has the intent of achieving restoration, not condemning Israel for all time.

34. Marshall, *Kept by the Power of God*, 29.

Another way these complexities can be seen is in the sacrificial system that was put in place to make provision for sins committed under the Mosaic economy. There were certain ceremonies that were performed so atonement could be made for the sins of the whole nation while others were practiced by individual Israelites so they could receive personal forgiveness.[35] The most well-known corporate ritual was the Day of Atonement, which is documented in Lev 16. The purpose of this annual event was to sustain a kind of spiritual cleanness so that the people could remain in covenantal harmony with the Lord. Leviticus presents the idea that the sinful condition of the people had detrimental effects on everything around them.[36] One could say that the sinful fallenness of people contaminated their surroundings. So the sacrifices on this day temporarily eliminated the defilement of the tabernacle and surrounding areas since they were constantly inhabited by sinners (Lev 16:16).[37] Likewise, the actions performed by the priests on this day applied to the people themselves because the animals used in the ceremony served as substitutes who incurred the cursedness and judgment that the people deserved. In both of these cases, the condition of the people as a whole was in constant need of being addressed. If they did not abide by these guidelines, the Lord could abandon the tabernacle (or the temple) which would ultimately lead to the people being defenseless against the surrounding nations.

Along with this annual ceremony were also other designated sacrifices and offerings that people could offer on behalf of different kinds of sins. The law prescribed some that dealt with what we can call sins of ignorance, or unwitting infractions.[38] Examples include mishaps in following certain cultic regulations in the law or instances where one wronged another in various monetary cases.[39] There are many other instances, though, where sins were considered outright defiant. These kinds of sins were given no means of atonement. If an Israelite chose to act recklessly against the Lord

---

35. The Day of Atonement dealt annually with the *corporate* weight of Israel's sin while the many other prescribed sacrifices addressed the *personal daily* sins of individuals. While the Day of Atonement covered the penalty for the Israelites' sins each year, the people were still affected by sins they committed each day after the Day of Atonement. We also see that sacrifices were offered for different purposes, including cultic purity, declaring sacred vows, or attaining ceremonial cleanness after incurring various maladies.

36. See Morrow, *Introduction to Biblical Law*, 138–60; Maccoby, *Ritual & Morality*.

37. For more discussion about the concepts of ritual uncleanness and defilement, see Sprinkle, "Rationale of the Laws of Clean and Unclean," 637–57; Averbeck, "Clean and Unclean," 4:477–86; Milgrom, "Rationale for Cultic Law," 103–9.

38. E.g., Lev 4:2, 22, 27; 5:17–18; Num 15:22–41.

39. Marshall, *Kept by the Power of God*, 35.

on clear-cut issues of morality, then they could be excommunicated from the community or even experience capital punishment. However, what is interesting to note is that there are times where people committed such sins and later desired to return to the Lord through confession and repentance.[40] What this tells us is that while the law prescribed official ways in which Israelites could address all kinds of sinful behavior, there appears to be an underlying consciousness embedded in the OT that even sin worthy of death or excommunication could possibly be forgiven if one truly expressed a broken and contrite spirit.[41]

So what conclusions can we make regarding the Mosaic covenant and its prescribed system of atonement? First, we see that the OT sacrifices were made so that relational harmony with the Lord could be sustained. They appeased the Lord so his wrath could be deterred, the people's guilt could be expiated, their worship could be accepted, they could avoid some of the consequences of their sins such as excommunication or death, and they could live peacefully with each other in the Abrahamic land of promise with the divine presence in their midst. Second, the law set the parameters for experiencing divine blessings as well as judgments at both corporate and individual levels. In the former case, the people as a whole could be overrun by enemies who would take them away in exile if they remained in unrepentant idolatry. And in the latter, individual Israelites could be cut off from the community of Israel because of various sins, which usually meant they could no longer receive covenantal privileges and in some cases, die a premature death.[42] Third, there appears to be a certain between-the-lines assumption that those who were in covenant identity with the Lord could possibly be forgiven of heinous sins through genuine repentance even when sacrifices were not explicitly prescribed. Beyond these points, however,

---

40. An insightful discussion of the development of repentance in biblical history can be found in Lambert, *How Repentance Became Biblical*, esp. 71–142.

41. Samson and David are good examples here.

42. Texts like Exod 31:14–15; Lev 23:29–30; 1 Kgs 14:10 imply that being "cut off" means dying a premature death. Yet texts such as Judg 21:6 and 2 Chr 26:21 convey the idea of being excommunicated from the sacred community or nation. One can see a vacillation between these two ideas in Deut 13 where the law addresses the matter of false prophets. Israel is instructed to *put to death* any false prophet who entices an Israelite to turn to other gods (Deut 13:5a). In doing so, the evil within the camp is *put away* (13:5b). The same language is repeated to any family member (13:6–11) or any Israelite within a city (13:12–18). The emphases are upon the capital punishment of false teachers and their status as being accursed, or cast, outside the camp of the people. To maintain the covenantal blessings of the Mosaic covenant, the purity of the community was to be protected. However, questions about whether any devout Israelites could apostatize or whether a defector was condemned to eternal judgment is not the focus here. Rather it is the capacity to experience the blessings of the Mosaic agreement.

trying to extrapolate on the question of whether an Israelite who was a genuine follower of Yahweh could lose out on being in the Lord's presence after death is a much more difficult enterprise. Much more information is needed before one can possibly address such concerns.

3.3 The Davidic Covenant

After the Mosaic economy recalibrated the means for experiencing the hopes of the Abrahamic promise, another covenantal feature was integrated when God established a royal line from which a ruler over Israel would emerge.[43] This process was initiated when the Israelites expressed a desire to have a king because they wanted to be like their surrounding nations. An arbitration ensued between the elders of the nation and the Prophet Samuel, who was helping guide Israel at the time. The end result was the selection of Israel's first king, Saul, which ended in disaster. During the tragic end of Saul's forty-year reign, the Lord selected a new king whom we know to be David. David was anointed by Samuel when he was young and Saul was still ruling (1 Sam 26). He did not officially become king over all the regions of Israel until after Saul's death (2 Sam 5:1–4). But when all the dust finally settled, King David galvanized the morale of the people by bringing the ark of the covenant back to Jerusalem (2 Sam 6:12–23). Ironically, though, doing this actually troubled David at one point because he became displeased that the Lord's special presence in the ark was relegated to a lowly tent (2 Sam 7:1–3).

David expressed his desire to build a special building for the Lord's presence, which then elicited a response from the Lord. Through the Prophet Nathan, God said that instead of David building a temple, he would build David a house. This set the stage for the declaration of a new promissory covenant (cf. 2 Sam 7:12–16; 1 Chr 17:11–14). The agreement was that David's lineage would become a dynasty which would produce a ruler who would extend the Abrahamic blessings to Israel as well as other nations who would submit to this royal seed. This is why the Lord spoke of adopting David's male descendants. Consequently, just like Israel was known as "God's son" by covenant (Exod 4:22–23), David's regal posterity would be "God's son" too (cf. 2 Sam 7:14a; 1 Chr 28:6). Likewise, resembling the Mosaic language of blessings and curses, the Lord promised to judge David's sons if they fell into disobedience and bless them if they followed his law. Yet unlike

---

43. While literature on the Davidic covenant is vast, some excellent treatments can be found in Steinmann, "What Did David Understand," 19–29; Grisanti, "Davidic Covenant," 233–50; and Dempster, *Dominion and Dynasty*, 138–47.

Saul, one key difference was that the Lord promised not to withdraw his covenant love from David's line (2 Sam 7:14b–15; 1 Chr 17:13).[44]

In the end then, this covenant clarified the focus of the Abrahamic hope a bit more because the seed of blessing that would come through the great patriarch was now identified specifically as Davidic (cf. Gen 3:15; 18:18; 22:18; 26:4; 28:14; 35:11; 38:49; 49:10; Ruth 4:18–22). A descendant of both Abraham and David would be a king who would reign on a throne over an Israel-centric kingdom in the land of promise with the overflow of this reign bringing blessings to all other nations. Simple enough.

The problem was that like Israel as a whole, the Davidic line did not always follow the Mosaic stipulations of covenant faithfulness. Most of the time they did not. Still, the consequences for breaking kingly obligations did not necessarily define the salvific status of the various kings or everyone in the kingdom(s). Kings like David or Solomon willfully violated divine instructions on numerous occasions while their identity as genuine believers never came into question.[45] However, numerous other kings never showed any concern for the Mosaic covenant, proving to be unbelievers from the outset. In each of these cases, though, regardless of the moral fiber of individual kings, the newly ascribed covenantal expectations placed upon the Davidic line described how rulers could be potentially disciplined for acts of disobedience and how their faithfulness could result in national peace for the people of Israel. Thus, to try and determine the spiritual identity of Israel's kings by only examining the regulations of the Davidic covenant is extremely difficult because they did not prescribe criteria for one's status as a believer in Yahweh. Rather they set the standards for how kings could be successful as Israel's political leaders.

3.4 The New Covenant

Finally, whether one reads about Israel's history immediately after the exodus, during the times of the judges, or throughout times of the monarchy, the glaring truth is that the nation never owned up to the demands of the Mosaic agreement. Israel's story is one consistent trajectory of covenant breaking.

---

44. Note here that God's covenant loyalty to David did not mean that all of his descendants would be believers or that the kingdom could not fall because his later successors broke the Mosaic covenant. Indeed many of the later kings were moral disasters, which ultimately led to the temple being destroyed and Israel being taken into captivity. What the Lord never said to any Davidic descendant was that the kingdom would be taken away from the family altogether the way it was from Saul.

45. Although it is troubling to read of Solomon's affection for his wives and their gods in 1 Kgs 11:1–2.

This is why the nation experienced a consistent barrage of curses as prescribed in the law. To make matters worse, the later disobedience of many of the Davidic kings and the idolatry of the nation led to the apex of Mosaic curses, which, again, was exile (Deut 28–30). This judgment proved to be the hardest to swallow because it shook Israel's hopes in the Lord's covenantal promises (see Lam 5:21–22). They were no longer in their land, they had no temple of worship, and no Davidic king to follow. Even worse, it had become crystal clear that the expectations of the Abrahamic and Davidic covenants were being hamstrung by the litany of Mosaic violations, which meant there was a systemic problem in need of resolution. The law, as good and righteous as it was, could not enact the Mosaic blessings because Israel, as a whole, never fostered a heart for the Lord. This is why the Lord eventually promised to establish a final covenant with his people wherein his law would be written on their hearts.[46] They would be forgiven of their sins, inherit eternal life, and be resurrected from the dead both nationally as well as bodily.[47] They also would be restored to their land, never fall into the hands of any enemies, and be protected by the Lord himself (cf. Jer 31:33–34; Ezek 11:19–20; 36:25–27; 37:1–23; Dan 12:1–2). So essentially, this new (or some would say *renewed*) covenant would bridge the gap between Israel and the law by changing the hearts of the people so that they would follow the Lord fully. Likewise, such a miracle would eliminate any need for a distinction between the remnant of true followers and the nation where the majority were not. The remnant would become the entire community.

---

46. When referencing the later prophets' proclamations about the new covenant, questions often arise regarding the meaning of Moses' earlier comments in Deuteronomy regarding the law being written on Israel's heart (30:14). There are many who see this passage as alluding to the future when the new covenant would result in God's commands being placed on their renewed hearts (e.g., Sailhammer, *Pentateuch as Narrative*, 473; Coxhead, "Deuteronomy 30:11–14," 305–20) whereas others see the comments in 30:11–14 as commissioning the new generation of Israelites who are about to enter Canaan to accept their obligations to the Mosaic covenant (e.g., Moo, *Romans*, 652; Schreiner, *Romans*, 558). One thing that is for certain is that Paul believed Moses' comments did ultimately interrelate to the work of Christ (Rom 10:6–8). And unquestionably, such a connection elicits fascinating questions about how Paul understood this text. See many of these interpretive complexities in Bekken, *Word Is Near You*, 1–24.

47. The concept of resurrection in relation to national restoration can be seen in the classic vision that Ezekiel had of the dry bones being raised from the dead (Ezek 37:1–14). And the most well-known promise of a literal resurrection from the dead for Israel can be found in Daniel's proclamation that the eternal kingdom of the Son of Man will include vindication from death (Dan 12:1–3).

4. UNDERSTANDING APOSTASY IN RELATIONSHIP TO THE BIBLICAL COVENANTS

Now in reflection, it is imperative to highlight certain interconnections between these covenants because they serve as a kind of theological matrix that can help us conceptualize how the ideas of apostasy and perseverance emerge. When we do this, we discover that acts of faithful endurance in following the Lord versus the abandonment of his covenantal requirements are addressed in several different contexts. One venue that emerges frequently entails defiant sinfulness expressed by those who are outside Israel's covenants altogether. These instances technically do not fall under the category of apostasy because they pertain to actions committed by individuals or nations who were always devoted to other deities or their own base natures (or both). People under these circumstances pledged no allegiance to the God of Israel. They remained steeped in their own forms of idolatry and moral debauchery. When their wickedness reached a certain level of intensity, we see the Lord declaring swift retribution to end their streaks of wickedness. Some of the most prominent examples of such accounts include Noah's flood, the destruction of Sodom and Gomorrah, and the demise of ancient kingdoms like Egypt, Assyria, and Babylon. Sometimes, the Lord gave these parties opportunities to repent, such as in Noah's day when he warned people of the impending deluge or various prophets who warned nations to turn from their sin, like Jonah who preached at Nineveh.[48] Occasionally people chose to obey the Lord like Rahab before the destruction of Jericho or turn from their wickedness like many of the Ninevites. Most of the time, unfortunately, nations refused to change their ways and were judged accordingly. But as often as these events occurred in the OT, it is two other scenarios that have more to bear on questions about whether believers can apostatize.

---

48. In Jonah's case, the Ninevites experienced the exact mercy that the Lord had originally extended to Israel after the golden calf incident. One can see this in the fact that part of the language of God's gracious forgiveness as depicted in Exod 34 is applied to non-Israelites. So the Lord is willing to forgive all kinds of repentant peoples just as he granted mercy to Israel because of Moses' intercession. See Timmer, "Jonah's Theology of the Nations," 5–6. This means that those within Israel's boundaries as well as those beyond them can experience the blessings of God. One might say in this qualified sense that an ancient who followed after the Lord would qualify as a part of God's people more than an unbelieving Israelite.

4.1 Disobedience and Divine Discipline

A second set of situations that are important to this discussion are times when individuals within Israel were disciplined for various acts of disobedience, whether they be explicit violations of the law or failure to follow other instructions that the Lord periodically gave. The OT is full such instances, especially among Israel's leaders. We read of Moses disobeying the Lord's instruction to speak to a rock so water would miraculously come out for the people; Uzzah, out of good intentions, touching the ark of the covenant in an unauthorized way; King Saul directly disobeying two specific commands that the Lord had given him during is tenure; King David committing adultery and conspiracy to murder; King Solomon permitting idolatry to spread throughout the land of Israel; and King Uzziah presuming that he could overtake the priestly role of approaching the divine presence. In all of these instances, individuals sinned and experienced subsequent consequences. Moses was forbidden to lead the second generation of Israelites into the promised land. Uzzah was immediately struck dead. Saul was eventually ejected as Israel's first king. The child produced from David's affair with Bathsheba died and his family went through waves of turmoil until his death. The Lord promised that the kingdom of Israel would be split in two after Solomon's reign ended. And Uzziah was struck with leprosy, thereby becoming ceremonially unclean, unable to approach the Lord's sacred presence again.

These events reveal ample evidence of old-covenant characters who committed egregious sins that resulted in severe discipline from the Lord.[49] Still, none of these failures warrant the conclusion that any of them were believers who committed apostasy.[50] So there is substantial justification in the OT to speak of people exhibiting various levels of moral failure while

---

49. In none of these cases do we read about the condemnation of someone's soul that resulted in any eternal judgment after death (though some might argue that Saul was never a true believer). These individuals usually incur consequences of their sin within their lifetimes, except for Solomon whose sin is judged after his death when Israel's kingdom splits during his son's reign. Also, to be fair, the true spiritual condition of every Israelite is not always explicitly defined.

50. One could say that each of these accounts of disobedience entailed either violations of certain covenantal responsibilities (e.g., Uzzah, David, Solomon, Uzziah) or spontaneous failures while one was filling the role of a leader (e.g., Moses). But none of their actions were defined in terms of apostasy although Solomon's failure indeed permitted others to turn their hearts to other deities. His shortcomings in the latter years of his rule definitely pushed him to the precipice of apostasy but the OT never says he completely abandoned the Lord of Israel. Complexities regarding the question of Solomon's failure can be seen in Begg, "Solomon's Apostasy," 294–313; and Brindle, "Causes of the Division," 230–33.

not forfeiting their faith. Furthermore, some were given the opportunity to repent and receive forgiveness even when experiencing the consequences of their sin.[51]

4.2 Apostasy and Divine Judgment

The most dire complications about apostasy in the OT come with a third set of concerns that relate to Israel's constant abandonment of their covenantal obligations to the Lord. We read about Israel's failures at Mt. Sinai where they forsook the Lord in idolatry on the cusp of Moses' return to deliver God's covenant with them; their subsequent wilderness wanderings after the exodus from Egypt because of their refusal to trust the Lord in entering the promised land; the cycle of following after other gods and ignoring the Mosaic covenant during the times of the judges; and the later corruption that eroded the northern and southern kingdoms so much that both settlements were led into exile.[52] All of these failures were simply different expressions of their resistance to the Lord and his promises. That is why the OT uses a variety of terms to describe their sins, such as forsaking, turning aside, wandering, and rebelling.[53] The nation's reputation became so tragic that the prophets sometimes compared their proclivity to commit idolatry to the shame of prostitution (Jer 3:6; Hos 4:12; 9:1) or an unfaithful spouse (Isa 57:7–8; Ezek 16:31–34).[54] Such imagery encapsulated the overall narrative of Israel—a chosen nation that frequently failed to abide by the Lord's standards during the Mosaic economy. In these instances, one could say that apostate acts entailed a radical reversal from devotion to Yahweh to an unrepentant, unrelenting love for other deities; a kind of anti-conversion, if you will.[55]

---

51. Even Samson, amid all his rebellion and debauchery, was allowed to repent and later be listed in the Hall of Faith in Heb 11.

52. Often we discover that in Israel's history, their spiritual deficiency was henotheism in that they still believed in Yahweh but they cast their affections upon other deities so they could live in ways that aligned with their corrupt desires instead of the "moral rigidity" of the law. One could say that many within Israel frequently thought it was much more fulfilling to live in adultery with other gods than be committed to the expectations of the covenant(s) that Yahweh made with them.

53. Ortlund, "Apostasy," 383.

54. Ortlund, *Whoredome*, 47–75.

55. Ortlund, "Apostasy," 384. Or in the case of old-covenant Israel, we use the word "conversion" in the sense of being in covenant loyalty to Yahweh and then turning away from the covenant to follow other gods.

The looming question then is how Israel's history of apostate actions should be understood theologically in relationship to the larger issue of salvation in Christ. Is this elect nation's pathological forsaking of the Lord indicative of the fact that new-covenant believers can do the same today? This is indeed a valid concern. *The first thing to say in response is, again, that ancient Israel's acts of faithlessness were expressed by the nation as a whole, not every individual person.* No doubt in almost every case, many Israelites did follow the spiral into idolatry. Yet there was always a group that did not (or some who did but eventually repented). The exodus generation had Joshua and Caleb, a remnant lived in the days of Elijah, and there were exiles like Daniel who followed the Lord even when the nation was exiled. Therefore, one cannot extrapolate that when apostate Israel experienced judgment, it necessarily meant every Israelite was apostate.

Second, even when Israel did suffer the consequences of their rebellion, their identity as God's chosen people was never forfeited. True, the Lord did claim at times that if Israel forsook him, then he would forsake them (see Deut 31:6, 8, 16–17). However, this warning had to do with the Lord's hand of protection and blessing on the people in the land of promise. If they abided by the parameters of the Mosaic covenant, then they would experience the Lord's presence and provision, which again included fruitful harvests and peace with the surrounding nations. But when they fell into unrepentant idolatry and corruption, the Lord brought severe curses upon them as a result, thereby forsaking them in the sense of letting them suffer because of their covenant-breaking sin(s). There are even instances where the prophets use strong separation language to convey the Lord's disfavor with Israel's ways. We read Jeremiah who speaks of the Lord issuing a bill of divorce against Israel (Jer 3:8) and Hosea who was commanded to name one of his children Lo-Ammi, or "not my people," as an act indicative of God's judgment upon Israel (Hos 1:9). The Prophet Haggai does the same thing by claiming that the Lord saw them as "this people" instead of "his people" because at that time, they were refusing to show corporate devotion by rebuilding the temple (Hag 1:3–4).

On the one hand, these sobering claims are made in light of the Lord's obligation to be true to his word; if they forsake him, he will abandon them. Still, on the other hand, the Lord never allows these charges to be the last word. He always tempers such oracles with the assurance of restoration. We see the same Jeremiah who said the Lord would divorce Israel also claiming the people would be judged only temporarily because they would eventually be restored to their land (Jer 29:10). Hosea prophesies that the same Lord who disclaims Israel will also one day be betrothed to her forever (Hos 2:18–20). And Haggai promises that the glory of the previous temple would be nothing compared to the Lord's presence in Israel's midst in the future (Hag 2:4–9). So OT judgment language of apostate Israel cannot be used to deduce that the nation as a whole is forgotten permanently. Why? Because the only thing that rivals Israel's resume of apostasy and the divine discipline that they incurred is the Lord's unrelenting faithfulness to forgive and restore them.

This truth leads to a third component that is critical to understanding the nature of apostasy in the OT. *When the law and the prophets spoke about the consequences of Israel's rebellious actions as well as their restoration, the focus was often upon how the people could experience God's blessings in the land of promise, not necessarily how they could enter the Lord's presence after death.* This is not to imply that the OT denies the concept of an intermediate state. To the contrary, there are occasional references to believer's confidence in entering the Lord's presence after death (cf. Gen 5:24; 2 Kgs 2:11; Job 19:25–27; Pss 23:6; 73:24).[56] Nevertheless, the primary emphasis in much of the OT is upon a restored creation in which Israel will receive the blessings of the new covenant. The point here is simply that apostasy and faithfulness on old-covenant terms are usually discussed in terms of who experiences the blessings of the Mosaic covenant versus those who lose out. The only other alternative that the OT focuses upon regarding the problem of apostasy is that it will be fully remedied when the Lord ratifies the new covenant. The inauguration of this act will ensure that the faithful remnant will encompass the entire "nation" of God's people.

4.3 The Focus of Apostasy in the Old Testament

One set of passages that illustrates these points about the old covenant is found in Ezekiel. In 3:16–21, the prophet's divine commission is likened to that of an ancient watchman.[57] His task is to forewarn people of potential judgment that could come upon them if they chose not to repent. Ezekiel is charged with warning those who are "wicked," or had no regard for Yahweh whatsoever, and those who were righteous that for whatever reason chose

---

56. No question, OT support for an intermediate state (or postmortem pre-resurrection existence) is disputed heavily in much of biblical scholarship. Nevertheless, the point here is that the dominant OT theme of how sin impacts one's life before and leading up to death does not mitigate against the possibility that some texts can describe, even if in vague form, human life after death. Cf., e.g., treatments of this subject by Johnston, *Shades of Sheol*, 2002; Levenson, *Resurrection and the Restoration of Israel*, 35–66; Routledge, "Death and Afterlife in the Old Testament," 22–39; and Williamson, *Death and the Afterlife*, 38–44, 163–70.

57. Similar language is used later in Ezek 18:19–32 and 33:1–11.

to lapse into sinful behavior. Ezekiel informs both groups, who were both in the covenant community of Israel, that if they do not repent, they will die in their sins.[58] Some interpreters view the death language here as a reference to postmortem judgment that unbelievers and backsliders alike experience if they choose not to repent. This is often supported with the point that physical death comes to everyone regardless of whether they are righteous or wicked due to the impact of Adam's sin upon humanity. Hence, something more severe is being described here.

We propose another reading of this passage, which sees it as harkening back to the Mosaic language of forfeiting the opportunity to experience divine blessings in this life. For the unbeliever, or the wicked, the point is that if they choose to continue in their unbelief and rebellion, impending death would come upon them. Their lives would be cut short. And as a matter of fact, if too many of them were corrupt, the entire nation would be judged.

Though not an exact parallel because other nations were not in a covenantal bond with Yahweh, an example that somewhat pictures Ezekiel's warning here is the story of Jonah. Nineveh was on the precipice of being wiped out as a national superpower. But once the people listened to Jonah's message of judgment, they repented and the city was spared. They did not "die" because of their debauchery at that time.[59] Likewise, a similar point is being made for the righteous who rebel, or turn away from the Lord. Their former covenant keeping cannot and will not be grounds for excusing any current sinfulness. No matter how devout they have been in their service and worship of Yahweh throughout their lifetimes, if the righteous fall into an unrepentant state of disobedience, the Lord can bring judgment through impending death. Such a warning comes up again several times in Ezekiel (14:9; 18:20) with the point being that Israelites should never develop an attitude of presumption regarding their enjoyment of the Lord's provisions. If they fell into sin, their covenant breaking could lead to death if they chose to continue down that path without repenting. The point was that it is not only important how one starts in their walk with the Lord, but also how they finish.[60]

Consequently, we see that the OT includes warnings against outright sin because it can lead to physical death with no further opportunity for

---

58. See Block's discussion here in *Ezekiel*, 139–50.

59. Granted, if the Ninevites had ignored Jonah's message and died, we can deduce from passages elsewhere that they would have entered Sheol to face the Lord in judgment as unbelievers. But the primary impetus of the prophet's warnings as well as Ezekiel's was that if repentance was not expressed, the wicked would soon experience death so their evil would be removed from the earth.

60. See Block, *Ezekiel*, 149.

restoration to the covenant community. Yet beyond this general point, it is difficult to discern any compelling evidence supporting the idea that genuine believers, or Yahweh-following Israelites, can somehow fail to enter the Lord's presence when they face the jaws of Sheol. Can they lose communal identity by being excommunicated from the nation? Yes.[61] Can they fall into patterns of sin and later repent after certain Mosaic curses are enacted? Yes. Can the Lord even bring swift death upon one who chooses to continue in sin? Absolutely. But again, questions about whether believers can possibly lose out on a heavenly destination are quite difficult to address in the OT alone. This is important to note because the OT indeed functions as a major source upon which the NT builds its theological perspectives on perseverance and apostasy. However, as we shall see in upcoming chapters, the connections that writers make are not always straightforward. Sometimes they are typological; other times they are analogical; and in some instances, they are rather direct depending on the point an author is trying to make. And the reason for these diverse ways of interpreting the OT is because the issues of perseverance and apostasy take on new layers of complexity in light of the realization of the new covenant.

5. THE WORK OF THE SPIRIT UNDER THE OLD COVENANT

A final component that needs to be addressed briefly when evaluating the subject of apostasy in the OT is the ministry of the Spirit in the lives of believers prior to the establishment of the new covenant. This feature is so important to our discussion because it highlights a crucial difference

---

61. A classic and difficult passage that highlights this point well can be found in Deut 13. The first section of this chapter gives instruction on how to deal with a false prophet (1–5); the second addresses defective family members who try to drag others into paganism and idolatry (6–11); and the third segment speaks about dealing with entire cities that are corrupted by idolatry (12–18). In each of these instances, capital punishment is prescribed and what is interesting is early on, the author states that one of the reasons these circumstances may occur is so the Lord can test whether one genuinely loves him or not (13:3). One could possibly deduce from this statement that if some do embrace another god, perhaps their love for Yahweh was dubious or never existed at all. And a fellow Israelite's faithfulness to resist such tendencies shows that their covenant loyalty is steadfast. Furthermore, the emphasis even here is not upon the eternal destiny of the defectors or the exact nature of their apostasy, specifically as it pertains to whether they were genuine believers or not. The focus is upon their expulsion from the community and certain death that would obviously exclude them from experiencing the Mosaic blessings in the land of promise. Thus, whether an Israelite could "lose" their salvific identity is not the emphasis here as much as their communal identity within the covenant group as a whole.

between the work of the Spirit in the lives of ancient believers and those of the new-covenant age. As we have already argued, the ancient nation of Israel was a mixed community made up of Jews whose commitment to the Lord was spurious or altogether absent and a remnant of true committed followers. Combined with this dynamic is the fact that the divine presence of the Holy Spirit was not even experienced equally by all of those who were part of the faithful remnant.[62] Typically the OT speaks of the divine presence with Israel under the old covenant in terms of being localized in a designated area, initially through theophanies like the storm atop Mt. Sinai, then later within the tabernacle, and finally in the temple.[63]

Still, as it pertains to the presence of the Spirit upon or within members of God's people, several further considerations should be mentioned. One is that the OT does mention occasions where the Spirit was with select individuals in some unique way. Figures like Joseph (Gen 41:38), Joshua (Num 27:18), and Daniel (Dan 4:8; 5:11–14) are examples of believers who are described as being indwelled by the Spirit in some way. Second, in other instances the OT attests that the Spirit came upon, or empowered, individuals so they could engage in certain tasks. Such instances echo the language of Gen 1:2 where the breath of God hovered over the waters at the beginning of creation. Just as the power of the Spirit was expressed through the divine speech that produced creation, so do people supernaturally receive the ability to perform certain actions. We read of various judges like Samson (Judg 14:19), workers on the tabernacle like Bezalel (Exod 31:3; 35:31), and kings like Saul and David having the Spirit come upon them at different moments (cf. 1 Sam 11:6; 16:13).

At the same time, the Spirit's empowering presence could also leave. Samson, for example, lost the presence of the Spirit because of his rebellion (Judg 16:20), as did Saul because he forfeited his role as king when he refused to follow the Lord's instructions (2 Sam 16:14). Such an experience was so sobering that David apparently remembered the effects it had on Saul because later in the Psalms, he prays as the king that the Lord would forgive him of his sins and not take his Spirit away (Ps 51:11).[64]

Third, the fact that the Spirit did not come upon or indwell every single believer under the old-covenant era (cf. Num 11:29) is a difficult theological

62. A helpful survey of Old Testament texts that shows clear support for this idea can be found in Hamilton, *God's Indwelling Presence*, 25–55.

63. One of the most recent works to trace this theme within the OT at an exceptional level is Heiser's, *Unseen Realm*, esp. 23–68.

64. Even here, the point is not that David is afraid he will lose his relationship with the Lord altogether. It appears he is concerned about losing the Lord's empowerment to fill the role as King that had been promised to him.

reality to apply to believers under the new covenant. Whereas under the former economy, the Spirit empowered or indwelled believers in a selective fashion and the divine presence was fixated to a specified location such as the tabernacle and/or temple, the NT is clear that the Spirit's residence is no longer identified with a building or miraculous act of nature.[65] Rather the Spirit now indwells all believers collectively as well as individually. Another related contrast is that while Israel related to the Lord through faith and obedience to the law, these dynamics were not conjoined to the concept of regeneration, or the new birth as prescribed by new-covenant promises because this act of the Spirit was to be something that would occur when the Messiah arrived.[66]

Unquestionably, there were some qualified means of sanctifying grace that the Lord bestowed to people. There were the hopes instilled by his covenantal promises, the prophetic word heralded by ordained messengers, the preliminary work of the Spirit upon anointed servants, and redemptive acts in history that spurred people unto faith and obedience. Still, each of these instances were preliminary means that collectively set a trajectory for a future hope. One that looked to a time when the Spirit would perform an inward spiritual surgery upon all those who would be part of God's people, starting with Jews and extending to the Gentiles, whereby the law would be written on their hearts so they could remain within the fold of his flock forever. And relatedly, this pneumatic transformation would be linked to the very renewal of creation itself.[67]

All of these variables show that a significant transition took place between the work of the Spirit in OT history and the ministry inaugurated by Christ and the new covenant, which in turn, helps shape our understanding of apostasy. Under OT terms, only a minority remnant expressed true faith in the Lord and even they were not equal partakers of the Spirit's presence. It would only be in the NT economy that the entire community would be made up of people equally indwelled by Spirit. The relevance this distinction has for the subject of apostasy is that those in the OT era who rejected the Lord as well as those who remained loyal were never permanently indwelled by the Spirit. However, under the new covenant, if one thinks a

---

65. This is not to imply that the divine presence could not still be manifested in supernatural ways as seen in the coming of the Spirit like a mighty rushing wind at Pentecost and the tongues of fire that fell upon the early disciples (Acts 2:2–3).

66. This a delicate point to make because one does not want to fall prey to any form of pelagianism, which would deny the inward work of grace that empowers people to express faith in God's promises. However, the further theological complexities of this question go beyond the scope of our discussion here.

67. Goldsworthy, "Regeneration," 722.

genuine believer in Christ can apostatize, that would necessarily mean the Spirit's life-giving presence can be forfeited just as the Lord's presence was lost in the temple when Israel refused to repent. The problem with such a deduction is that the very fiber of the new covenant seems to entail the hope that such an event will be eradicated.

6. CONCLUSIONS

We now want to bring this part of our journey to a close by reviewing our findings thus far and then offer just a few remarks about how the OT's conception of apostasy expands once the context of the NT begins to develop. *The first feature to revisit is that God's covenant people under the Mosaic economy were a mixed community.*[68] As we have argued, the entire nation of Israel was identified as God's elect even though many of them were often not necessarily devout followers. So when the OT recounts numerous times where Israel strayed from the Lord, one is forced to ask if the majority of these Hebrews were believers at all—or two other options are, again, whether they were apostates or simply rebellious people in need of discipline.

Such questions arise, for example, when examining the exodus generation. The liberated Hebrews followed the instructions given in the Passover so they could escape the tenth plague against Egypt and then went with Moses to the land of promise. We know that later most of them rebelled at Sinai, subsequently refusing to believe God could give them victory over the inhabitants of Canaan, which resulted in their inability to enter the land. But this tragedy did not mean the Lord abandoned them altogether. Even though virtually all of the unbelieving generation died in the wilderness, their needs were still met and the Lord's presence remained among them via the tabernacle. Were these Hebrews who fell short of the land of promise unbelievers, apostate believers, or believers who were severely disciplined? Indeed questions like this make it difficult to argue conclusively from the OT that we have clear examples of true believers who later forsook their faith in the Lord to the extent that they were ultimately sent to eternal damnation.

This challenge is exacerbated even further by a second dynamic we have covered, namely that *the covenants made with Israel focus mainly on how they can experience the Lord's blessings, favor, and acceptance in land promised to Abraham.* Though each individual Israelite's faith in the Lord was expressed in the context of his covenantal promises, the focus of these agreements was upon the nation's capacity to receive its earthly

---

68. A helpful discussion here on how the covenants contrast each other is by Carson, "Reflections on Assurance," 394–95.

land-and-kingdom blessings, not upon whether defiant Jews would fall under permanent final judgment after death. When Israel was disciplined, the consequences that are discussed in the OT usually pertain to national hardships and military oppression. Likewise, the third feature that contributes a theological wrinkle to the issue of apostasy is that *very few Israelites were indwelled or empowered by the Spirit*. This is why the expectations of the new covenant were so high. The law would be written on the hearts of all those who would be part of God's people. Everyone would be a Spirit-recipient. The remnant would be the sum total of the nation.

Thus, the question still stares us in the face—does the OT support the idea that believers can lose their salvation? What we can say is that Israel could clearly forfeit her covenantal blessings if she chose to follow the trail of unrepentant sin. The people could be ejected from their land, the Lord's presence could depart from the temple, and they could suffer defeat at the hands of their enemies. While the nation could not forfeit its identity as God's people, Israel could lose out on experiencing the temporal and physical blessings of the Abrahamic covenant when they were enforced under the Mosaic economy. Also, with regard to individual Israelites, there were many situations where they could be cut off from the community if they fell into certain patterns of unrepentant sinful behavior or committed specified sins. Yet as it pertains specifically to whether someone could be a genuine follower of Yahweh and later renounce their faith altogether, this is a different matter. We conclude, although it is heavily disputed in biblical scholarship, that there is no compelling data to say that such an event could occur. *The stress of the OT is upon faithful trust in the Lord that leads to covenantal blessings, not whether the inconsistency of one's faith can end in eternal punishment.* The reason we make this conclusion is because the OT does not explicitly equate an Israelite's experience of retribution under Mosaic guidelines with their soul being judged for all time.

Finally, in light of these deductions, one last observation should be mentioned to begin building a bridge to upcoming material in the following chapters. That point is the NT often appeals to stories of Israel's failures as theological points of reference for instructing believers in Christ about the dangers of apostasy. This occurs when various authors see Israel's apostate actions as foreshadowing potential moral hazards to which NT believers can be susceptible. Paul does this, for example, when he talks about the exodus generation having multiple provisions given to them during their wilderness wanderings and still most of them died short of the promised land because of their unbelief. He appeals to this narrative to warn his readers that just as many Israelites fell short of their Abrahamic inheritance, so would any believer who succumbed to temptations without repentance potentially fall as well (1 Cor 10:11–12). The same kind of thinking is echoed in the book of Hebrews where the author contends that just as many in Israel did not enter their "rest" in the land, so could the audience of Hebrews not inherit their eschatological Sabbath rest if they turned away from Christ (Heb 4:1–11).

What is important to see in these instances is that the general motivation for appealing to Israel's shortcomings is not to make a parallel between the eternal destiny of *both* the ancient Israelites and Christian audiences. The connection is that just as many Israelites failed to inherit the land of promise because of their acts of unbelief, so can professing believers fall short of inheriting the blessings of the age to come if they renounce their faith in Christ. This creates an interesting dynamic because what we discover is that the OT concept of apostasy often takes a bit of a turn in portions of the NT. As opposed to the loss of earthly Abrahamic blessings through the lenses of the Mosaic and Davidic covenants, now the stakes are, in fact, directed at the ultimate end of all these covenants, which is salvation in Christ. And such a focus does pertain to one's eternal destiny.[69] Therefore, this compels us to move on to the specifics of how this transition affects the ideas of apostasy in the New Testament.

---

69. There are some OT allusions where the language does go in this direction. For instance, Jude warns his audience about the dangers of false teachers by comparing their plight and all those who follow them to that of the generation who did not believe after being delivered in the exodus (Jude 5). Jude says they were destroyed, or died in the wilderness, and then he mentions other examples of rebellion, including the sins of certain angels and the wickedness of Sodom and Gomorrah (Jude 6–8). In all these cases, the parties experienced assorted forms of divine judgment because of their rebellion and Jude is warning his readers that if they succumb to false teaching, they could experience final eschatological wrath.

Chapter 2

Perseverance in the Gospels

We now move from our preliminary discussion about the concepts of perseverance and apostasy in the OT to a more detailed treatment of how they further develop in portions of the NT. This chapter will limit its survey to pertinent texts found in all four of the gospel accounts.[1] We will then examine the writings of Paul in the following chapter and finally conclude this first section of the book in chapter 4 with a treatment of select passages found in the book of Acts, the General Epistles, and the book of Revelation.

Hopefully, by the time we complete this part of our study, we will have achieved three goals. One is to highlight some of the basic complexities that these texts pose for articulating a holistic definition of what perseverance is exactly. What we will discover is that there are many facets to this subject which various passages address. But none of them explain it exhaustively. That is what makes this doctrine such a knotty one hermeneutically. No one passage can serve as some sort of "silver bullet" proof text that shores up every concern because each one must be understood both in its own context and in light of numerous others. Of course, this goes to the heart of the matter because the theological wedge that exists in Christian theology over the nature of perseverance is indicative not only of what individual texts possibly mean. It is also derivative of differences on how all of the relevant texts

---

1. In dealing with the content of the Synoptics and John's account together, we will not be encumbered with long-standing debates concerning the authorship of these books. Nor will we do so in the subsequent chapters on other NT books (e.g., the Pastorals, 2 Peter, Hebrews, etc.).

should be understood as a canonical whole.² Second, this overview will help set the backdrop for the next major section of the book, which summarizes some of the most significant moments in the historical development of the doctrine of perseverance. It will be much easier to see where thinkers are coming from theologically if one is privy to the collection of texts they are attempting to interpret and synthesize. Third, our survey of these texts will finally provide the basis for the conclusions that will be made in the last chapter. My intent is to provide a framework that can possibly move in a direction that helps balance all of these passages without cherry-picking any favorites or downplaying certain others.

1. PERSEVERANCE IN THE SYNOPTIC GOSPELS

Our treatment of how the NT broaches the subject of perseverance starts with a journey through portions of Jesus' teachings in the gospel accounts because they are so instrumental in shaping the beliefs of the early church.³ Likewise, subsequent NT authors often based their ideas and exhortations directly upon claims that Jesus originally made. Or in many other instances when they engaged areas of concern that he did not address directly, they still never strayed from the theological boundaries that he set in place. These connections between Jesus and NT writers are especially seen in how the subjects of perseverance, apostasy, and faith are fleshed out. The various ways in which Jesus approached these subjects helped set the trajectory for further claims that other inspired authors would make on these matters. So with that being said, the outline for this portion of our investigation will be as follows: (1) we will first examine relevant data found in Synoptic Gospels,

---

2. Often the fact that Scripture approaches the subject of perseverance from so many angles causes many interpreters to be suspicious of attempts to synthesize or form a cohesive, or "biblical," understanding of the topic. The reason being that if one tries to harmonize all the viewpoints of the various NT authors, one is inevitably forced to view one set of texts, or a writer's theological categories, as having some sort of hermeneutical precedence over others. As we shall see, there is some validity to this critique. However, the fact that this error can be committed does not militate against the possibility of finding a theological harmony that allows every NT voice to describe various facets of this doctrine in complementary rather than competing ways. One can see how evangelicals on the theological left and right debate this dynamic in Enns, *Inspiration and Incarnation*, 107–11; Sparks, *God's Word in Human Words*, 279–328; Meadors, *Four Views*.

3. See the discussion of how Jesus' traditions developed historically both in the works of the evangelists themselves as well as other NT writers in Bird, *Gospel of the Lord*, 74–112; Gamble, *Books and Readers in the Early Church*, 28–30; Schweizer, "Testimony of Jesus," 86–98.

including parables he told, direct teachings he shared, and specific predictions he made about the reality of apostasy; (2) and subsequently we will look at similar material from John's gospel where Jesus provides insights on the nature of belief and eternal life.

1.1 The Parables of Jesus in the Synoptics

The parables that Jesus shared had various purposes depending on what effect he wanted to have on an audience at a given moment.[4] Among the many that we have recorded are some that have content bearing upon the nature of faith, unbelief, and spiritual endurance. One that immediately stands out is about the sower who scattered seeds that fell on four kinds of surfaces or soils (Matt 13:1–23; Mark 4:1–20; Luke 8:4–15). Jesus said that some fell "beside the road" where the ground was hard and dry. They had no chance of sprouting and ended up being eaten up by hungry birds. Other seeds fell on rocky surfaces that had little if any soil at all. Having no chance of taking root, they were scorched by the sun and withered away. Some fell on soil that was infested with thorns. So while they were able to grow initially, the thorns choked the life out of them. Finally, some seeds fell on good soil that was not dried out or hindered by rocks and thorns. They were able to take root, grow, and produce various portions of crops. After Jesus finished speaking, the disciples later approached him privately to ask what the parable meant. Following a brief discussion about the underlying prophetic agenda of his parabolic teachings, Jesus explained the gist of the story. He said that the seed represents the words he spoke (Mark 4:15), which were words from God (Luke 8:11) that encapsulated the message of the kingdom which he was proclaiming (Matt 13:19). When this seed is spread over the "soil" of the various hearers, there are four different responses that can occur. The hard ground represents those who have hearts so blinded by sin that when they hear the word, they do not understand it

---

4. Snodgrass wades through the currents of debate on how the parables are to be interpreted, concisely highlighting what many scholars have conceded that Jesus told them "to confront people with the character of God's kingdom and to invite them to participate in it and to live in accordance with it." See Snodgrass, "Parables," 596–97; and cf. his comments in Snodgrass, *Stories with Intent*, 25–31. We would add that part of the way in which parables often confronted people was by initially causing them to let their mental and emotional guards down. As they listened to a given story, often they may become so enthralled in how it was unfolding that they were caught off guard when Jesus concluded with a given point of conviction. A perfect example of this strategy in the OT can be seen in the parabolic account that the Prophet Nathan tells King David. After becoming so distraught with the injustice of the story, David inadvertently indicts himself (2 Sam 12).

and Satan comes to ensure that they remain in their hardened condition by snatching the message (seed) away. The stony ground symbolizes those who embrace (or in Luke's rendition, believe) the message enthusiastically at the outset.[5] But later when temptations, afflictions, or persecution come their direction, they fall away. The thorny ground pictures those who hear the message but the competing voices of the world's luxuries drown it out. Finally, those whose hearts are depicted as good ground receive the word and allow it to achieve its ultimate end which is to produce the fruit of salvation.[6] The element of this story that is most pertinent to concerns about perseverance is the condition of the second soil, which again entails someone who believes *for a time* only to fall away later.[7] Usually there are no significant disputes focusing on the identities of the first, third, or fourth soils because they seem clear enough when read at face value. The disagreements emerge when inquiring as to whether the second-soil is speaking of someone who genuinely believes for a while, a type of "carnal" immature believer, or an unbeliever who is exposed when their commitment is tested.[8] What should be said amid this discussion is that any potential resolution has to concede a few items. One is that if the "second soil response" represents a real believer who apostatizes, then theoretically a person can exercise a saving faith in the gospel that eventually fades because of external or internal pressures. In addition, this same person can be a believer who produces no spiritual fruit whatsoever. One cannot avoid this latter conclusion because clearly the fourth soil is the only one that does. Yet such a deduction goes against the very nature of discipleship as Jesus describes it.[9] Consequently, when

---

5. Luke explains that those who endure for a while are those who believe only for a while. See comments here by Schreiner and Caneday, *Race Set Before Us*, 220.

6. Some evangelical interpreters fear that this parable could be construed as advocating some type of salvation by works. However, the point of the parable is not that fruit bearing substantiates some sort of merit for those who believe and endure. The focus is that those who receive the seed of the word of the kingdom in a way that germinates unto salvation will bear fruit. Or from another angle, the parable is primarily describing the variating nature of unbelief. Some reject the message outright, others misunderstand it, and others accept it temporarily until it demands too much. Cf. Kingsbury, *Matthew 13*, 31; Davies and Allison, *Matthew 8–18*, 402–3; Turner, *Matthew*, 341–42.

7. The term translated as "falling away" is used again in Mark, for example, to describe the disciples when they "abandoned" Jesus at his arrest. See Oropeza, *In the Footsteps of Judas*, 28.

8. Regarding the carnal believer, this soil illustrates the fact that some believers do not persevere. Some go as far as to say that someone can be a type of "apostate" Christian. Cf. comments by Wilkin, *Confident in Christ*, 37–40, 174–75; Hodges, *Gospel Under Siege*, 78.

9. Affirming the message of the kingdom and producing the results go together in

comparing the synoptic portrayals of this parable, the point here is that unbelief can sometimes be expressed through a spurious form of belief that eventually defects.

We quickly discover that this kind of distinction between faith that is transitory versus a kind that is enduring is also substantiated in many other parables that Jesus told. Some often depict the nature of true faith in terms of the relationship between trust in Jesus' promises and obedience to the ethical demands that his promises entail. A good example can be seen in the parables that he shares concerning his coming as the Son of Man to judge the earth. While the earliest Christian communities most likely had a different perception of these accounts than the original hearers because of initial confusion about the concept of the Messiah coming twice, the moral ramifications of these parables could be clearly seen by both.

For instance, in Matthew 25, Jesus tells three parables on the heels of the Olivet Discourse in ch. 24 that emphasize the importance of being ready for his return.[10] In the first two, he speaks of ten virgins waiting for a coming bridegroom (Matt 25:1–13) and three servants who were given an assortment of talents by which they would be audited when their master returned from a trip (Matt 25:14–30). Both accounts speak about the difference between people who are ready for their Lord's return and those who are not. The first story says that five of the ten virgins were excluded from the wedding celebration because they were not present when the bridegroom approached. Apparently, their lamps ran out of oil during the night because his coming took longer than they anticipated and so they missed his arrival while they were out trying to gather more. Similarly, one of the servants is deemed unfaithful by his master because he wasted his talent and is therefore cast out into outer darkness where there is weeping and gnashing of teeth (note that Jesus sometimes used the latter phrase to describe *gehenna*).[11] So five unprepared virgins and one unwise servant were excluded from their Lord's favor.

---

this parable. Granted, the "amount of fruit" can vary from hearer to hearer. But the seed that falls on good soil, which is indicative of one who expresses enduring belief, bears fruit. A similar point is made with other parables where two servants receive various returns on their faithfulness (Matt 25:15–17). See France, *Matthew*, 522.

10. Most likely, Matthew 25 is a continuation of the Olivet Discourse in ch. 24 where Jesus warns his disciples that his return will be like the flood that caught Noah's generation by surprise (24:38–39), a thief whose appearance catches people off guard (24:43), or servants who live carelessly only to be judged when their master returns unexpectedly (24:45–51).

11. Jesus uses the phrase outer darkness three times in Matthew's gospel (Matt 8:12; 22:13; 25:30). Some contend that this language alludes to the possibility of believers being rebuked when they are judged. Cf. Sapaugh, "Call to the Wedding Celebration,"

Some deduce, at this point, that these parables support the idea that a genuine believer can ultimately fall short of inheriting salvation because all of these characters are initially identified in the same way, whether it be a virgin or servant. However, the intent of these parables is to identify true followers as those who are ready, not distinguish between followers who are and some who are not. This can be supported by a helpful clarification that comes in the third account (which is not a parable strictly speaking) where Jesus compares the final judgment of the nations to a shepherd's separation of sheep from goats (Matt 25:31–46). The story describes the Son of Man coming in all his glory to distinguish his people, who will inherit life in the age to come, from the wicked, who will suffer eternal punishment. The criteria for distinguishing the two is that the sheep showed kindness and mercy to Jesus' brothers (or followers) whereas the goats ignored them to focus only on their own needs.[12] There is no discussion of some sheep who started off as such only to later defect and join the opposing team of goats. Said another way, there is no distinction between faithful and unfaithful sheep. One is either a sheep or a goat. They are identified as such when the bridegroom arrives, the master shows up, or the Son of Man returns. The overall point, then, is that the unexpected nature of the coming kingdom, which is the hope of Jesus' followers, entails an ethic to be ready whereby those who follow it are the ones who are true believers, the prepared virgins, wise stewards, or beloved sheep (or in the case of the parable of the sewer, those who bear fruit).[13]

Other parables in the corpus can cause a bit more consternation for some theological perspectives. Some emphasize various ethical imperatives with an uncomfortable bite to them because they include certain contingencies that some interpreters find disconcerting. One example can be seen in a parable that emphasizes the importance of forgiveness and how one must

---

10–34; Huber, "'Outer Darkness' in Matthew," 10–25; and Hodges and Wilkin, *What Is the Outer Darkness?* In context, a stronger case can be made that these specific uses are being directed at Israel's religious leaders (and anyone else committing their error) who were opposing his messianic mission. See Tanner, "'Outer Darkness' in Matthew's Gospel," 445–59.

12. In Matthew, the concept of Jesus' true family and little ones is directly linked to those who do the will of his Father, which, in essence, means obeying his instructions (cf. 12:48–50; 25:38–40, 44–45). This is how Jesus' Father is described as the Father of all his disciples. Hagner, *Matthew 1–13*, 360.

13. The same thing could be said about the parallels made at the end of Matt 24. Because no one knows when the Son of Man will return, many will be unprepared and taken away in judgment like the generation in Noah's day (24:36–39). The servant who is prepared when his master returns will receive reward but the one who is not will be judged and, again, allotted to a place where there will be weeping and gnashing of teeth (Matt 24:45–51).

exhibit the same kind of compassion to others that one has received from heaven (Matt 18:23–35).[14] This account entails a story where a king becomes outraged when a servant, who he had forgiven of a great debt, later refused to forgive a peer of a much lesser amount. The ruler turned this servant over to the jailers, or torturers, until he repaid the debt of which he was originally cleared. Jesus then applies a warning to his disciples in kind. The point of this story is not only that one forgives because they have been forgiven. This is indeed part of the parable's rhetorical punch. But Jesus mentions another angle which is that only those who choose to forgive are the ones who will not be held liable for their own heavenly debts.[15]

Similarly, another set of parables indict the hard-hearts of Jewish leaders in Jesus' day who refused to redirect their faith toward him, thereby being cut off from the fast-approaching blessings of the new covenant (e.g., Matt 21:33–43; Luke 20:9–18). Some of them deconstruct the dangers of unbelief and presumption. A prime example of this can be found in the parable that Jesus told about a king's wedding feast for his son (Matt 22:1–14; modified form in Luke 14:16–24). He spoke of a king who sent his servants out to invite all his expected guests (i.e., comparatively the Jewish leaders and surrounding cities that rejected Jesus' authority). Each of them had different excuses as to why they could not attend. This led the king to send his servants out and invite the general public (i.e., seemingly directed at Jews and Gentiles who were believing in Jesus) so that the wedding hall would be filled.

This is where one might expect the story to end because the parallel is straightforward. Just like the original guests missed out on the wedding feast, the Jewish leaders were going to lose the ultimate blessing promised to the house of Israel, namely the visitation of the messianic bridegroom. Yet the parable continues. When the king entered the dining hall, he saw a guest who was not wearing the proper attire. He was subsequently thrown out of the hall into the outer darkness. The parable finally concludes with the sobering statement that many are called but few are chosen. The twist then is not simply that unbelief is condemned. Rather it is that accepting the invitation necessarily entails obedience to the parameters that the king sets in place.[16]

14. While one does not want to build entire doctrines on a parable, what we find in this story is that if God's mercy does not take root in one's heart, then it has not been experienced. Forgiveness that is not shown externally is not known personally. See Snodgrass, *Stories with Intent*, 75.

15. The parable is not trying to navigate the theological complexities of justification or post-Reformation issues concerning faith vs. works. The thrust of the story is that forgiveness cannot be claimed if it is not extended. Thus, the implications seem to relate to receiving forgiveness in the age to come. See Turner, *Matthew*, 452.

16. See the excellent discussion of this point in Bauckham, "Parable of the Royal Wedding Feast," 471–88.

Jesus' parables, therefore, exhibit an unmistakable conditional element that makes demands upon the hearers who want to inherit the coming kingdom.[17] The point is not that works are the basis for a believer's salvation. Rather, it is that the experience of salvation cannot be constrained to the boundaries of only one context. Sometimes it is described as a gift that believers can possess in the present age whereas at other times it is described as a destination that one reaches after completing the pilgrimage of discipleship.[18]

1.2 The Teachings of Jesus in the Synoptics

While the parables of Jesus contain unavoidable tensions when it comes to the relationship between faith and perseverance, his teachings also provide a minefield for debate on matters like eternal life, unbelief, and sinful conduct. A prime example is the well-known discussion about the unpardonable sin (Matt 12:31–32; Mark 3:22–30). In an interchange with the Pharisees and scribes, Jesus is provoked by their accusation that he had cast out demons by the power of Beelzebul, the ruler of demons (or for short, Satan).[19] He responds with a biting rebuke that if they speak against him or commit other sins, they can still potentially receive forgiveness. But if they blaspheme the Spirit, it would not be forgiven in the present age nor the one to come.

In one sense, this kind of claim about a no-turning-back sort of sin, though rare, was not unique. The law itself occasionally deemed certain sins in this category (Num 15:30–31; Deut 29:18–20).[20] However, this does not really offer much aid in deciphering the exact nature of what Jesus is describing. That is why there is a long history of conjecture about what this act may be as well as whether it can still be committed by people today.[21] Most proposals equate it with either rejecting the gospel or some kind of

17. In the story, the one who enters the feast with soiled clothes shows just as much contempt for the event as the ones who refuse to come at all. So not only do those who spurn the Father's invitation miss the kingdom of heaven. Those who appear to accept it but reject what it really represents will not receive it either. Bauckham, "Parable of the Royal Wedding Feast," 487–88.

18. If this is the case, one could also say that the gospels present the ideas of being a believer and a follower interchangeably.

19. For treatments on this term as it relates to the devil or Satan, see Maclaurin, "Beelzeboul," 156–60; Twelftree, "Demon, Devil, Satan," 164; Gaston, "Beelzebub," 18:247–55.

20. One might mention Heb 6:6 here but this will be discussed in the next chapter. See Hagner, *Matthew*, 323.

21. A good engagement of this question can be found in Litfin, "Revisiting the Unpardonable Sin," 713–32.

egregious sin after conversion. The problem is that both of these alternatives entail troublesome dilemmas. If the sin is unbelief, how does this harmonize with the fact that many eventually received forgiveness for their previous hatred of Christ when they were later converted. Or if it is some kind of sin after conversion, how is it that someone who has been quickened by the Spirit and confessed allegiance to Christ can later blaspheme the Spirit so heinously. Most likely the most sound deduction to make concerning this sin is that it should be confined to the redemptive-historical moment in which it is committed.[22] The context pertains to the Jewish leaders' portrayal of Jesus' messianic activity empowered by the Spirit as actually being demonically derived.[23] So it would seem prudent to see its replication as questionable. Nevertheless, it is still sobering because Jesus claimed that there are such things as lines that should never be crossed.

Another severe warning that Jesus makes can be found in the Sermon on the Mount. In a segment related to false teachers, Jesus claims that on the last day, many will want to enter the kingdom of heaven on the basis of self-acclaimed miracles they had allegedly performed in his name. They will rehash their entire resume of prophesying and casting out demons as grounds for being admitted. Yet as the judge of the earth, Jesus says he will not be fooled. He will not be swayed by their claims to fame. Instead he will express his awareness of their true works which are lawless and wicked. That is why he will say to them that he never knew them as his people. It is not that he knew them temporarily until they defected. No, the response is much more riveting. He never knew them at all. Moreover, what should be noticed in these two cases, again those being the unpardonable sin and the rejection of false teachers, is that conduct and belief are inextricably linked to heavenly citizenship. If the unpardonable sin is committed, as many of the Jewish leaders of Jesus' day were guilty of doing, or if false teachers live in debauchery and try to negotiate with the Lord at his return, the same result ensues, which is eschatological judgment.

We should also be mindful that this kind of connection is not restricted to these two subjects alone. Jesus uses this kind of language throughout the gospels when referring to all sorts of vices. For instance, he taught that if one

22. Some argue that the situation can be applied today. It is said that if someone sees God's work and attributes it to Satan for whatever reason, then that is equivalent to rejecting Christ, thereby being unforgiveable. However, this kind of direct application is difficult "because no contemporary persons have access to the maximum revelatory light God afforded the Pharisees, neither can they be guilty of its maximum rejection." Litfin, "Revisiting the Unpardonable Sin," 732.

23. They were completely convoluting the basis of spiritual values, of good and evil, God and Satan. They were attributing the work of the Spirit to heaven's ultimate nemesis, the devil. See France, *Gospel according to Matthew*, 482.

does not aggressively deal with sinful actions, one can end up in *gehenna* (Matt 5:29–30). He warned that if someone were to lead one of his young impressionable followers (i.e., little ones) astray, it would be better to drown in a watery abyss than to face the awaiting judgment (Matt 18:6; Luke 17:2). He demanded that anyone who wants to find life (that is in the age to come) must be willing to lose their lives—meaning they must be willing to deny themselves even to the point of literal death (Matt 16:25; Luke 9:24).[24] All followers must see the kingdom as so valuable that they are willing to give up everything else to possess it (Matt 13:44–45). He even makes the bold claim that anyone who is ashamed of him before the world will be shamed by him in the presence of his Father (Matt 10:32–33; Mark 8:38; Luke 12:8–9). Or hearkening back to the parable about forgiveness, Jesus says elsewhere that anyone who is unwilling to give forgiveness will not receive any from his Father (Matt 6:14; 11:26).

In all of these sayings, the message is convicting but clear. Being a follower not only entails a confession of allegiance to who Jesus is as Israel's Messiah and the savior of the world (or the nations). This declaration must be coupled with a willingness to follow the path of discipleship if one expects to be vindicated on the final day of judgment.[25] Any other conclusion seems to convolute the overall message of the kingdom that Jesus proclaimed.[26]

1.3 The Predictions of Jesus in the Synoptics

Another portion of information that is pertinent to the subject of perseverance are claims Jesus made about people who would forsake their faith

---

24. This language is a major factor in how early Christian interpreters would understand the link between discipleship and martyrdom. See Chapman, *Ancient Jewish and Christian Perceptions of Crucifixion*, 255.

25. This is partly why the gospels include accounts where Jesus warns about the dangers of looking back once one decides to follow him (e.g., Luke 9:62), especially in example of Lot's wife (Luke 17:32).

26. One important clarification to make here is that how the gospels present Jesus' preaching of the kingdom and how to become a citizen, or heir, of its benefits do not always address the same kind of issues that Paul engages when speaking about the issue of justification. Sometimes the concerns do overlap in the sense that both Jesus and Paul emphasize the dire need that humanity has to receive forgiveness of sin and be delivered from divine condemnation as well as satanic oppression. These mutual emphases sometimes converge with an invitation to give one's allegiance to Christ's kingdom. But in other ways, there are other dynamics that Paul has to address because of the post-Pentecost work of the Spirit and the newly formed body of Christ that allows Jews and Gentiles to equally be part of God's people. Matthew Bates wrestles with some of these issues in Bates, *Salvation by Allegiance*, 77–100, 165–94.

commitments. Here we are able to observe Jesus' own descriptions of those who defect in their loyalty to him and his message. Two examples that immediately come to mind are Simon Peter and Judas Iscariot.[27] Peter's lapse was predicted right after Jesus spoke of Judas' impending actions and the fact that the rest of the disciples were going to desert him.[28] On the heels of the shock caused by such remarks, the disciples wondered who would be the traitor and Luke adds a further element to the drama. He mentions that Jesus said directly to Peter that Satan wanted to attack him. Fortunately, this message was tempered with grace because Jesus added that he had prayed for him so that he would overcome his upcoming trial and eventually strengthen his brothers (Luke 22:31–32). Peter impetuously responds that he will not forsake the Lord even if it requires death, which then elicits Jesus' chilling prophecy that Peter would deny that he even knew him three different times before morning. As we then follow the story of Jesus' prayerful struggle in Gethsemane to his arrest and trial before the Sanhedrin, we read that Peter did deny his affiliation with Jesus just as predicted. Afterward, he went out and wept bitterly but his story does not end there. Jesus was not only correct that Peter would fail. He was also right that Peter would be restored.

Jesus himself was the one who later encouraged Peter privately after the resurrection. This encounter empowered Peter to become the great apostle that Jesus claimed he would be (cf. Matt 16:17–19; John 21:15–17).[29] So one feature that we see from this account is that a faith which may experience a temporary lapse is not always evidence that it is automatically dubious. This is why Jesus prayed that Peter's faith would not fail. The misfortune that Jesus addressed in his intercession was not Peter's denials themselves. Rather it was the spiritual hangover that could follow such a blunder. Were these denials going to be the final word in Peter's life? That is what Jesus desired Peter to overcome and indeed he did. Why? Because Jesus' heavenly petition was the difference maker. His effectual prayer preserved Peter just as it is later argued that Christ intercedes for his people as a faithful high priest of the new covenant (cf. Heb 4:14; 7:25).[30]

---

27. While the Synoptics all mention the fact that Judas betrayed Jesus, (Matt 26:14–16, 47–48; Mark 14:17, 43–45; Luke 22:3–6, 47–48), the Gospel of John provides some unique features. Our treatment of his actions will be in the next section.

28. The latter event would serve as a life-action parallel to Zechariah's prophetic utterance about a shepherd being struck and his sheep being scattered (cf. Zech 13:7; Matt 26:41; Mark 14:27).

29. Just as Peter denied the Lord three times, the resurrected Christ later allowed Peter to reaffirm his love and devotion three times as well (John 21:15–19).

30. Jesus also prayed for all who would believe just prior to his impending death on their behalf (John 17).

Alongside this test case in Peter's life are even more sobering accounts where Jesus spoke about apostasy on a much larger scale. Such claims are found in eschatological texts where he spoke of history culminating on the day of resurrection and final judgment. For instance in the famous Olivet Discourse, Jesus warned his disciples about the impending destruction of the temple, the inevitable reality of persecution, and gradual build-up to the climactic intervention of the heavenly Son of Man.[31] Amid the details, Jesus said that many would fall away, betray one another, be deceived by false teachers, and the love of many would grow cold (Matt 24:9–12). He warned that some personalities would be so persuasive through their words and deeds that if it were possible, they could deceive even the elect (Matt 24:24; Mark 13:22). Declarations like this cause a certain amount of tension in discussions about perseverance for obvious reasons. Jesus is telling his disciples that they need to be prepared for upcoming attacks because they will cause some, in fact many, to defect. We even find Jesus lamenting elsewhere as to whether the Son of Man will find any faith on earth when he comes (Luke 18:8).

Usually at this juncture many evangelicals will take one of two routes. Some advocate that being part of the elect does not guarantee everyone in the group will receive final vindication because as Jesus later concludes, only those who endure to the end will be saved (Matt 24:13; Mark 13:13; Luke 21:19). As B. J. Oropeza says regarding Matthew's rendition of this statement, being a part of the elect community does not guarantee one's individual salvation.[32] One can defect even if they are part of the divinely favored group. Or to state the point in more Arminian terminology—if one is volitionally free to become part of God's people by faith, then they are also free to possibly abandon this status by renouncing their faith. Because belief is freely initiated by the human will, it can be freely continued or extinguished by the will as well.[33] On the opposite end of the spectrum, Reformed evangelicals see these warnings as the divine means of weeding out those who are not truly converted. Every true convert in the elect group will persevere while those who are not eventually fall away. This leads to an

---

31. Regardless of one's specific interpretation about the details of the Olivet Discourse (i.e., Dispensational Futurist, [Partial] Preterist, Historicist, etc.), the warnings about apostasy still have to be addressed.

32. Oropeza, *In the Footsteps*, 96.

33. The will, however, is empowered by prevenient grace so it can potentially believe. One could say that people are drawn by the Spirit so they can cooperate with grace and potentially believe. Likewise, those who embrace a position of belief can choose to endure and reach final salvation or freely turn away because of the lure of false teaching or the pressures of persecution. See Ashby, "Reformed Arminian View," 159.

implicit reversal of Jesus' words with the assumption being that those who are truly saved will endure to the end.[34]

These proposals notwithstanding, we would point out two concerns. One is that limiting the concept of election to only a corporate sphere in this particular instance is problematic because in the context of the Olivet Discourse, Jesus is initially speaking to his twelve disciples who he personally selected or at least approved (Judas as a special exception will be discussed later). Here one cannot say that the group is elected but each individual is not, regardless of one's beliefs about the relationship between grace and free will. The group, as encapsulated here by the twelve, are made up of chosen individuals.[35]

If this is the case, though, how does one deduce that the elect will be saved on the last day if some who are part of the group may not? If the group entails all the chosen ones but some who are genuinely part of the group do not endure, then technically that means that only some of the elect will inherit eternal life. There is an elect within the elect, one could say. If this is the way of things, how are we to interpret Jesus' claim that future false teachers could *possibly* deceive the elect. Jesus asserts that if divine help does not step in during these perilous times, the elect might be deceived, even destroyed. Yet clearly that will not happen because the Son of Man will intervene. It appears, then, there is an underlying assumption that the elect will withstand the upcoming onslaught that Jesus is describing while many others will wilt away for various reasons. Therefore, all of the elect, not some, will endure to the end.

At the same time, we should be careful and not interpret Jesus' words that "those who endure will be saved" to simple mean "those who are saved

---

34. To avoid both of these alternatives, some dispensational interpreters argue that Jesus' language here pertains only to physical preservation of those who remain faithful during a future eschatological Tribulation period. At the end of the age, faithful believers will be delivered from martyrdom and persecution via the return of Christ. Cf. Walvoord, "Christ's Olivet Discourse," 213, Wilkin, "Christians Will Be Judged," 34–35. However, other dispensationalists such as Darrell Bock observes that Jesus' remark would be a mere tautology if all he meant was that those who endure to the end will be still be alive. Bock, *Luke*, 2:1674. The point to see is that Jesus has a dual focus—he assures the elect that they will be saved while at the same time claiming that only those who endure are the elect.

35. Some might quickly appeal to the fact that Israel was God's elect nation which included believers, unbelievers, and apostates. But the key here is that Jesus is calling the twelve to reconfigure Israel under an upcoming new covenant wherein the distinction between the elect nation and the believing remnant will be abolished. They will now be one in the same. The disciples are to be the new rulers of Israel under Jesus as their king and the Gentiles are now part of the new exodus that Jesus will ratify with his death and resurrection.

will endure." It is not because the point is necessarily untrue but because it is simply not what Jesus is saying. He is not identifying the inevitable result of what the true elect will do. He is telling the disciples, as the elect, what they must do to be gathered by the Son of Man at his coming.[36] That is why he is describing all these things ahead of time so the disciples can be ready. Just as Peter was restored because of Christ's prayers, all the disciples will be prepared for future turmoil because of Christ's words; and we know that they were because they endured even unto their deaths.

Now undoubtedly a strong tension emerges here. Christ sees the elect as those who will heed his warnings but still says that if they pay him no mind, they will not inherit his kingdom. This is a delicate yet essential balance to maintain. Still, the most defensible concession is that while Jesus is confident that all his elect will be saved, they will not inherit salvation unless they endure. While it is certain what will happen in theory, it is uncertain in terms of practical outcome in the minds of Jesus' disciples at that time. All his followers must be ready and indeed all of them shall be. However, exactly who will be ready is still unsettled until the final day occurs. The theological truth is in place but who will receive its benefits is still to be determined by who heeds the warnings (and all the elect indeed will).[37]

2. PERSEVERANCE IN JOHN'S GOSPEL

Coupled with the rich material and theological nuances that the Synoptic Gospels provide on the importance of enduring faith is the additional emphases that we find in John's gospel on the role of *belief* in salvation. This feature is important to our discussion because, as we will see, John describes how different people "believe" in Jesus for all sorts of reasons. And sometimes when their perceptions of Jesus' identity and mission were misguided, their shallow belief would melt away as their shortsighted expectations were not met. But in many other cases, many would believe unto salvation and be committed to Christ. This emphasis on the nature of "belief" surfaces immediately after the majestic prologue when John introduces John the

---

36. This is why, for example, in Mark's rendition of Jesus' claim about the Son of Man gathering his elect, one must keep his earlier contrasting statements in mind about how the Son of Man will be ashamed of the adulterous and sinful generation that does not believe in him when he comes in the glory of his angels. See discussion in Stein, *Jesus, the Temple, and the Coming of the Son of Man*, 113–14.

37. While there are texts that can be used to support the idea that true believers are supernaturally preserved and enabled to endure, passages like the one here in the Olivet Discourse alternate the emphasis. The point is that only those who endure are believers. See Schreiner and Caneday, *Race Set Before Us*, 151.

Baptist as one who came to be a witness about the light (i.e., the Savior) so that all might believe (John 1:7). John subsequently structures his account to include seven miracles that Jesus performed along with several major discourses with each event mentioning the idea of believing. He also highlights several conversations that Jesus had with people like the Pharisee Nicodemus, a Samaritan woman living in adultery, Mary and Martha who were the sisters of his close friend Lazarus, and the farewell discourse he shared with his disciples prior to his arrest and death (John 3:1–21; 4:1–38; 11:1–45;14–16). In these encounters, Jesus described "belief" in various ways such as being born again, or by the Spirit; looking to him for help as the Israelites looked upon a bronze serpent to escape death; taking a drink from a well of water of which one would never thirst again; having confidence that he was the means of resurrection even in face of someone's death; and entrusting oneself to his plan even though it was going to include him leaving for a time.

Likewise, John records many strong claims that Jesus made about the people that the Father had given him. They are drawn by the Spirit so they can eventually be raised on the last day as his faithful sheep. They are his people for whom he lays down his life and no one will be able to steal any of them from his fold (John 10:11–15, 25–29). They were the ones for whom he prayed as he approached the precipice of his death (John 17:9). Then finally toward the end, John reveals his underlying purpose for writing. He wanted readers to believe that Jesus was the Christ, the Son of God, and thereby have eternal life (John 20:30–31).

2.1 Belief Can Be Temporary

All of these grand promises in John are legendary. But we would be too hasty if we deduced from these texts that John restricted the idea of belief to the cognitive affirmation of facts about the identity of Jesus that may or may not lead to repentance and discipleship.[38] This would be premature because

---

38. Some argue that John does not mention the concept of repentance but rather solely focuses upon the importance of believing as the means of experiencing personal salvation. See, e.g., no-Lordship advocates such as Ryrie, *So Great a Salvation*, 97–98, and Hodges, *Absolutely Free*, 146–47. However, both repentance and believing are actions that can be found in John's descriptions of how people receive the gospel. David Crouteau has provided a helpful case in showing how repentance is a part of John's gospel. He shows that John presents the idea that those who do not believe continue to dwell in darkness or engage in "evil deeds" whereas those who do believe cease from partaking of evil so they can exhibit works wrought from God. See Crouteau, "Repentance Found?," 97–123 (114).

John's descriptions of believing are much more nuanced than that. The kind of belief that leads to life in the age to come, or eternal life, is something that entails a significant transformation in the one believing.

This is an important qualification to consider because there are instances where a person's belief can be off course. It is almost as if John expresses his awareness of the parable of the sower because of how he describes some people who believe for a time but eventually turn away. Only instead of recounting the parable itself, John illustrates it with a real-life situation.[39] We see this in the portion where John writes that early on in Jesus' ministry, some observed the miraculous signs that he performed and "believed" (John 2:23). Ironically, though, Jesus does not respond in kind. He did not compel them to "follow him" like he did with the disciples. Rather he did not commit himself to them because he knew their hearts (John 2:24). One could say that while the crowd was believing in him, he was not believing in them.[40] Or put in other terms, their belief was not an act of submissive trust to Jesus' authority. It was a fickle hope that he would meet their agenda on their terms, not his.

Later Jesus' concerns are validated when he rebuked a group of followers because he knew that many of them were just pursuing him so they could witness his next miraculous feat and hopefully see him fulfill their preconceived notions of what the Messiah should do. Jesus confronts their attitudes with difficult sayings that were so hard to accept that these fickle followers turned away and followed him no more (John 6:66). They had been enjoying the show until it made certain demands. Jesus was now speaking about things not to their liking, which exposed their superficial commitment. So what we see here is that belief can be something that is driven by misconstrued perceptions or misplaced hopes. When this happens, the "belief" turns sour because the expected outcomes never materialize.

2.2 True Belief Can Be Absent in Those Who Appear to Follow Jesus

Another factor that highlights some of the nuances regarding the nature of "belief" is John's discussion about one who was a "follower" of Jesus but in actuality was not a believer at all. This individual was Judas of course. John informs us early on that Jesus was well aware of what Judas was going to do (John 6:64). This is why he claims that he chose all of the twelve to be his

---

39. See some helpful parallels in Choi, "I Am the Vine," 51–75.

40. Said another way, Jesus was looking for signs of genuine conversion and mere enthusiasm for the spectacular was not one. Morris, *Gospel according to John*, 182.

disciples while knowing that Judas was ultimately going to be an instrument of Satan (John 6:70). Then as we approach the event of the last supper, John mentions that the OT spoke of the Messiah being betrayed by a friend (cf. Ps 41:9; John 13:18). Jesus even identifies Judas as the culprit when John asked who the defector would be (John 13:21, 26). Jesus also labels Judas as the son of perdition, possibly alluding to Daniel's vision of the abomination of desolation who defiles Israel's temple.[41] The connection is that Judas is now going to betray the incarnate temple, the Messiah himself (John 17:12).[42] Nevertheless, Judas' prophetic role as a traitor would not prevent Jesus from preserving the rest of the disciples. What we learn from this scenario is that unlike Peter who was a believer that failed temporarily and was restored, there can be others like Judas who seem to be part of the group. They are along for the ride until a better offer comes their way. And sometimes such individuals can even be sorrowful for their actions while still not expressing true repentance that leads unto reconciliation.

2.3 Belief That Endures

What we begin to see here regarding John's presentation of the nature of "belief" is that it is not monolithic. It can be observed from several different angles. It can be seen as an act of confession that is evidence of the work of the Spirit in the human heart or an act of trust that embraces Jesus' claims about himself. It can sometimes be described in terms that are temporary or unstable because a person's belief can be shallow or confused only to be exposed when situations do not meet the standards of the one believing. Or belief can be something that is completely absent in the lives of some who outwardly appear to be among those following Christ just like Judas.

This last point is further punctuated by John's emphasis upon the link between belief in Christ unto salvation and abiding in, or obediently following, him. A passage that emphasizes this connection well is in John 15:1–6 where Jesus compares himself to a vine that gives life to connecting branches, which are his disciples. They are identified as such because they had already expressed their belief through their willingness to abandon

---

41. The idea here is that Judas is the foreknown one for apostasy. For John here as well as his later writings, it is possible that Judas is serving as a model of numerous apostates who often are initially part of a believing community but in time eventually defect. See discussion in Keener, *Gospel of John*, 2:1058–159.

42. This wording is also used by Paul to describe a lawless one who will defile the temple (2 Thess 2:7) and John later uses the image to describe the devastation that false teachers can have on early Christian communities (1 John 2:18–19). Cf. Beasley-Murray, *John*, 273; Carson, *Gospel according to John*, 563; and Oropeza, *In the Footsteps*, 183–84.

their former lives and follow him. However, part of Jesus' discussion entails a warning that if they do not bear fruit, then they will be cut off and, just like fruitless branches, be thrown into a fire for burning. Stated another way, if they do not reveal the life-giving power of the vine, then the vinedresser (the Father) will remove them. The question is whether Jesus' point is that disciples, or believers, can be legitimately incorporated into his "circle" only to be later "cut off" because of spiritual apathy.

At least two points deserve more attention in this regard. First, it is difficult to interpret the "cutting off" imagery as something other than divine judgment.[43] The vine-branch symbolism heavily reflects OT allusions to Israel as a vine or a vineyard that bears no fruit and so God brings judgment upon the people whether it be exile or death (e.g., Isa 5:1–7; Jer 2:19–21; Ezek 15:1–8; Hos 10:1–2).[44] John the Baptist also spoke of the Messiah coming and anyone in Israel who was not prepared would be like a tree with no fruit that would be cut down to be cast into the fire of judgment (cf. Matt 3:7–10; John 1:22–23). This imagery overlaps with what Jesus is saying in John 15. He is now the vine that provides life to the branches connected to him and those who choose not to bear fruit will be judged accordingly.[45] He is telling his disciples that to be part of him entails that they do what the unbelieving Jewish leaders and spurious enthusiasts were unwilling to do, namely stay with or abide in him.

The second consideration to mention is that after this warning, Jesus tells the disciples that they were chosen specifically so they would bear fruit after he was gone (John 15:16).[46] This is why he was now sharing these final words of instruction so they would be prepared for the upcoming times of persecution coming their way. They would be strengthened by his words and kept from stumbling (John 16:1–3). Thus, Jesus knew his disciples would indeed bear fruit, similar to his additives in the Olivet Discourse.

---

43. See discussion in Harrison, "Vine," 4:986; cf. refutation by Carson, *Gospel according to John*, 518–19; and Köstenberger's point that there is most likely an antithetical parallelism being used whereby Judas pictures those who are cut off whereas Peter illustrates those who are pruned. See Köstenberger, "John," 492.

44. See discussion of this image in the OT by Caragounis, "Vine, Vineyard, Israel, and Jesus," 201–14.

45. Similarly, one thinks of the barren fig tree that Jesus curses as a parabolic act that pictures the divine condemnation to come upon apostate Israel and the obstinate religious leaders (Matt 21:18–22; Mark 11:12–14, 20–25). Though they were heirs to the covenants of promise, they would be cut off because of their refusal to repent.

46. What the fruit is exactly is disputed and is not our primary concern here. A concise overview of various proposals can be found in Bolt, "What Fruit Does the Vine Bear," 11–19.

Still, for any potential branch that did not, a question arises as to whether the life of the vine was pulsating through it—and the implied answer is "no."

But again, how can there be branches connected to the vine that bear no fruit. Questions like this have helped create the theological minefield which currently exists in discussions about perseverance. Some say these branches represent believers who apostatize; others contend that they represent false professors of faith; and some argue that the "cutting off" language refers to disciplinary measures that the Lord uses to chastise rebellious believers.[47] While each of these proposals have strengths and weaknesses, we would offer somewhat of an alternative proposal. Since Jesus calls the disciples clean because of the earlier words he had shared with them, there could be a possible distinction being made here between the eleven and Judas as well as the other Jews who were temporarily captivated with his messianic authority.[48] So on the one hand, there are those who embrace the demands of Jesus through belief and strive to walk in obedience to his commands (or abide in him). They are the ones who bear fruit. On the other hand, there are those who appear linked externally to the vine of God's covenant people but conceal corrupt intentions like Judas or are apathetic toward obedience like Jesus' spectators. In either of these cases, such parties have no vine-life flowing through them, thus being discarded.[49]

---

47. Again, some argue that the verb translated "cut off" should actually be rendered as "to lift up." See, e.g., Dillow, "Abiding Is Remaining in Fellowship," 51–52. The reason is so that the branch can be nurtured and bear fruit later. The problem is that Jesus says the fruitless branches are eventually cast into a fire, which is not something that is done to branches intended to be used later. Branches that are useless because they are cut off and dead have no further purpose. That is why they are burned. Carson, *Gospel according to John*, 517. Some even argue that there also possible linguistic parallels between this imagery and other accounts in the Synoptics where Jesus speaks to the Jews as they are "in" the covenant fold but will be rejected, or cut off, if they reject the Messiah. See Choi, "I Am the Vine," 51–75.

48. This is reinforced by the later language Jesus uses when he tells the disciples that he is instructing them and promising that the Spirit will come so they will not fall from the faith when persecution eventually comes their way (John 15:26–16:4). We later see that Peter and the rest of the disciples did endure such events successfully whereas Judas betrayed the Son of Man, thereby performing a pinnacle act showing that the life-giving power of the vine was not in him. So in the end, he was judged. We could say that the vine and branch imagery was a parabolic expression describing what was about to happen among the twelve.

49. The same idea is echoed by Paul in Romans where he argues that Gentiles who are in the vine but fail to exhibit enduring faith are likewise cut off (Rom 11:17–22).

3. CONCLUSIONS

As we come to the end of this part of our journey through the New Testament's descriptions of perseverance and apostasy, two major factors must be kept in mind as we move forward. First, being a true believer is normally substantiated over the long haul, not in the short term. This is not to say that people cannot be converted and immediately express the handiwork of the Lord in their lives. Look at the thief on the cross who asks to be remembered in the heavenly kingdom. But the general assumption that emerges from Jesus' teachings is that any initial confession needs time to grow so it can be discerned whether one's faith is genuine.

Second, the gospels have no problem speaking of salvation in one of two ways; as a gift or treasure that believers already have or as something that believers are pursuing (not earning). Admittedly, this can be an uncomfortable union because of post-Reformation phobias against any compromise to the idea of justification by faith alone or the mainstay theological distinction between justification and sanctification. These concerns indeed have their place. Nonetheless, we cannot ignore the consistent dual emphasis that the gospels make between people's faith/trust in Christ to make them heavenly citizens and the fact that his cross and empty tomb mark the pathway of discipleship that one must travel to enter his kingdom.[50] The cross does

---

50. We have already alluded to some evangelicals who baulk at such claims and we will have more to say as to why in chapter 9. The problem is that some want to maintain an unfortunate distinction, which we mentioned earlier, between people who are believers and others who are followers. While all followers of Christ (or disciples) are believers, not all believers are necessarily followers. The problem is that such a notion is foreign to how the gospels present the teachings of Jesus. The evangelists do not portray Jesus' personal encounters, parables, or discourses in ways that treat belief as an isolated act of affirmation. Those who "believe" do cast themselves on the mercies of Christ and depend on his capacity to forgive them of their sins. Yet those who express belief unto salvation do so with the simultaneous acknowledgment that they no longer belong to themselves. They have believed so that they may now follow. Another way this could be stated would be to say that expressing faith, or belief, in Jesus as the Messiah entails two things. First, it includes a confessional affirmation of his true identity as the heavenly Savior of the nations. And second, such an act of trust is a declaration of allegiance whereby a "believer" comes into solidarity with the Messiah and his mission. This means a believer is a benefactor of Christ's redemptive work as well as a participant in it. They experience the blessings of his victory over death as well as the suffering and rejection by the world that hated him. So while believers will inherit the earth in the future, they must also endure rejection and persecution in the present as they follow after Christ. As Brant Pitre states in addressing Dale Allison's assessment of how Jesus understood his mission, "Jesus both anticipated his own death and understood it in terms of the Jewish category of the established eschatological tribulation that would precede the coming kingdom of God." Cf. Allison, *End of the Ages*, 139; Pitre, *Jesus, the Tribulation, and the End of Exile*, 17. Pitre deduces from this that Jesus saw his ministry as inaugurating the promised

nothing *for* someone if it does not do something *to* them as well. And to try to explain this tension away may be theologically convenient, but such attempts miss a major impetus in the teachings of Jesus.

Tribulation period that would culminate in the restoration of Israel and the healing of the nations. Just as he experienced the brunt of this reality via his betrayal, trial, and crucifixion, so will all those who become his people encounter similar opposition, Pitre, *Jesus, the Tribulation, and the End of Exile*, 18–40. Regardless of one's eschatological convictions on this matter, the overarching point is what Christ came to do for sinners not only provided salvific benefits. It trailblazed a path upon which all believers must now embark. We can illustrate our point with the act of becoming a citizen of a given country. Once one officially becomes a part of one, they incur the benefits that the country offers. Similarly, when one believes upon Christ, by grace they receive the salvific mercies that he provides. But those who receive these gifts automatically receive the moral demands as well as the cultural scourge that this kingdom incurs in the present age due to its conflict with the powers of darkness. Consequently, the point to see in all of this is that the NT simply leaves no room for the notion of a believer who is not a follower. Though they are distinct, they cannot be separated.

Chapter 3

Perseverance in the Letters of Paul

WE NOW MOVE FROM our assessment of the gospels to discuss major points about apostasy and perseverance that the Apostle Paul bequeaths in his writings. Much of the debate between Christian traditions today regarding these subjects is fueled by relevant claims that Paul makes in his cluster of letters. One major reason for this is the fact that he fluctuates between two ideas on these matters. On the one hand, he fills his letters with encouraging words that remind believers of their identity in Christ, their heavenly inheritance, and the assurance that their suffering will one day be vindicated on the day of resurrection. Yet on the other hand, when he addresses all kinds of problems caused by strife, immorality, or false teaching, he frequently reminds his readers that any unwillingness to make things right or follow the ethical expectations of the gospel he preached could result in the Lord's providential discipline, or even worse in some cases, final eschatological judgment.[1] Said another way, Paul often reminds his readers that the means of securing one's justification before God in Christ is by faith while also arguing in many other

---

1. What is interesting is that in some cases, Paul actually allows for the possibility that Satan himself can be used by the Lord in disciplinary situations. Cf. discussions of this perplexity in Thornton, "Satan as Adversary and Ally," 137–51; Page, "Satan: God's Servant," 449–65; Moses, "Physical and/or Spiritual Exclusion," 172–91; and Phillip, "Delivery into the Hands of Satan," 45–60. For believers in Christian communities who refuse to repent of open immorality, Paul says their choices are either to be cast out so satanic oppression can be used as divinely sanctioned means of discipline or be judged at the eschaton.

instances that believers will only be vindicated at the final judgment if they have evidenced their faith through works of obedience.

The looming question is how this tension in Paul's thought should be understood. Did Paul warn believers because he believed some genuine converts could potentially apostatize or did he think such a tone would act as a means of deciphering the remnant from those who were not truly regenerate.[2] Some say neither of these options are acceptable, proposing instead that Paul's warnings are about a potential loss of rewards in the coming kingdom, thereby having no bearing on the salvific status of a wayward believer.[3] Or aside from these long-standing debates, many deem these kinds of proposals as short-sighted because they neglect the ways in which Paul's conceptualization of perseverance may be derivative of certain social and theological perceptions of apostasy that emerged out of Second Temple Judaism.[4] In any case, the point here is that an examination of Paul's writings is needed because it is a significant challenge to navigate his words of assurance alongside his warnings against defection.

---

2. We will argue that Paul warns all members of his congregations that perseverance is an intrinsic part of the nature of saving faith and that while he is certain all believers will heed the warning, he is not certain that everyone is a genuine convert because of the various vices that some of them were embracing. See important discussion of this point in Thomas, *Case for Mixed-Audience*, 232–52.

3. It is feasible that one could make a considerable case for this idea in some of Paul's writings such as his comments in 1 Cor 3:10–15. Some contend that Paul is discussing the ways in which believers may possibly lose rewards when their works are divinely audited at the judgment. Cf. Cox, "The 'Straw' in the Believer," 34–38; Rosscup, "New Look at 1 Corinthians 3:12," 33–51; and Fee's excellent summary of options in Fee, *First Epistle to the Corinthians*, 144–45. Others, interestingly enough, interpret Paul's treatment here as pertaining to God's judgment of the validity of the apostolic ministry to the church, see, e.g., Evans, "How Are the Apostles Judged?," 149–50. Aside from this text and an assortment of others, however, there are numerous other passages where Paul's words regarding the potential loss that can be experienced goes beyond rewards.

4. The possible overlap of these two trajectories is initially due to the now famous endeavors of E. P. Sanders where he defends the idea that in Jewish (as well as Paul's) views of inheriting salvation as a part of God's people, while the initial reception is by grace, works are the condition that one must maintain to stay in the community that experiences that grace. See Sanders, *Palestinian Judaism*, 543. Also Judith M. Gundry-Volf saw the impact of this thesis some twenty-six years ago in her important study on Paul's view of perseverance in Gundry-Volf, *Paul and Perseverance*, 1. Many nuanced alternatives have been formed since the pioneering studies of Sanders which have created a host of implications for all traditional views of Paul's soteriology in general or his views of perseverance in particular. One need only consult James Dunn's proposals for example in Dunn, *Theology of Paul*, 494–98; or Wright's, *Paul*, 57–58, to see how Paul's understanding of perseverance is approached in various ways.

1. PERSEVERANCE IN ROMANS

We begin our tour of Paul by examining his most monumental letter, the book of Romans. Its theological content and influence have enthralled, dare we say sometimes even perplexed, Christian thinkers for two millennia. That is why the amount of attention given to this NT epistle is so copious to say the least.[5] Even today scholars continue to hash out the technical exegetical nuances of Paul's thought as it is portrayed in these sixteen chapters. There is no end in sight when it comes to the unrelenting barrage of new voluminous commentaries and monographs being produced on Romans (and justifiably so).[6] But amid the flurry of discussion, we want to highlight a few of Paul's concerns regarding perseverance that emerge in this letter because they touch upon both themes of security in Christ and the necessity of faithfulness to Christ.

One important factor surfaces early on in the famous introduction where Paul claims that he is not ashamed of the gospel which he had been commissioned to preach because it is the means of rescuing any Jew or Greek who believes (Rom 1:16).[7] He deduces in 1:17 that God's *saving* righteousness was being revealed for those "righteous one(s) who would live by faith."[8] The general thrust of Paul's point harkens back to the Prophet Habakkuk's decision that he would trust the Lord despite the fact that the Chaldeans (or Babylonians) were going to invade Israel as a means of judgment. Similarly, Paul states that those who escape God's judgment are those who believe the gospel promises found in Christ. In Habakkuk's case as well as Paul's, faith is something that confidently *rests* in God's covenantal trustworthiness despite any impending events and *responds* accordingly in a steadfast way of life. Thus, for Paul (and Habakkuk), faith and faithfulness are not polarized

---

5. A good survey of the general spectrum of thought in Christian history on the book of Romans can be found in Greenman and Larsen, *Reading Romans through the Centuries*; and a helpful primer on the breadth of prolegomena to the study of Romans is provided by Longenecker, *Introducing Romans*.

6. Commentaries continue to be produced with some significant ones including Longnecker, *Epistle to the Romans* (2016); Hahn, *Romans* (2017); Harvey, *Romans* (2017); Schreiner, *Romans* (2018); and Bird, *Romans* (2016).

7. This is contra Campbell's recent formidable argument that Paul is describing an inferior thesis in chs. 1–4 that he corrects in the second half of the letter. See his work *Deliverance of God*.

8. This is a quotation from the LXX's version of Hab 2:4, which has some linguistic variations within its own textual versions as well as differences against the Masoretic Text that scholars have highlighted. See a short synopsis of the textual issues in Oropeza, *Jews, Gentiles, and the Opponents of Paul*, 146–47. Some even argue that the statement should read as "those who have faith will live," or literally will live again in the resurrection from the dead, e.g., Kirk, *Unlocking Romans*, 8, 44–55.

either-or features. Paul, instead, sees a connection between *faith* as an act of belief in what Christ does on a sinner's behalf, and a life of *faithfulness* that is empowered by the Spirit which Christ gives to all of those who believe.[9]

Paul begins to flesh out this point when he discusses humanity's condition before God. He argues that Gentiles stand in God's sight as unequivocally condemned because they "idolatrize" his creation instead of worshipping him as the one true God. And Jews are all indicted under the law because they commit sins in secret that they openly condemn others of doing. They are all guilty, none are righteous. However, in the middle of this discussion, Paul adds a certain component that sparks robust debate. He claims in Rom 2:12–16 that only doers of the law will be justified when God judges the secrets of men but then at the end of his synopsis of humankind, he says no one will be justified by the works of the law (Rom 3:20). Tensions exist today on how to reconcile these claims. Some, who espouse Lutheran or Reformed views of justification, often argue that Paul's claim in 2:13 is hypothetical because the law exposes everyone as incapable of meetings its standards, which in turn, sets the stage for Christ to step in via substitutionary atonement (Rom 3:21–31).[10] Many who are not convinced of this idea and are sympathetic to New Perspective(s) on Paul tend to see his initial comment as a prelude to those in Christ who will be enabled to keep the law's expectations because of the indwelling Spirit (8:2–4).[11] Regardless of how one fits these points together, Paul does argue that believer and unbeliever alike will be judged by their works (cf. Rom 14:4, 7–12).[12]

This comparison between divine righteousness and humanity's sin picks up steam when Paul begins to discuss the way in which a sinner's standing before God can be changed. He argues that anyone who exercises

---

9. There is quite a stir caused by this language, especially in light of debates caused by the New Perspective(s) on Paul in NT studies. Thinkers such as Wright have caused controversy by describing the experience of justification in seemingly provisionary terms as if it is only validated once a believer is judged by their works. My point is not that believers can only find full assurance of their salvation once they have "passed" the final judgment. It is that for Paul, faith not only connects believers to Christ. It also enables them to live by the Spirit.

10. See survey of alternative views on this in Snodgrass, "Justification by Grace," 87–93; and Schreiner, "Did Paul Believe in Justification by Works?," 131–58.

11. Cf. Dunn, *Romans 1–8*, 97–98; Wright, *Justification*, 189–91.

12. Granted, a person judged by their works on their own merit will only lead to eschatological doom in Paul's mind. However, a believer's obedience to God that is wrought by the work of Christ by the Spirit is the by-product of justification's work. The issue here is not merit, it is new-covenant validation. I would argue that this commitment fits perfectly with Jesus' teachings about believers being ready for the coming of the Son of Man, especially in light of parables like the sheep and the goats and the unforgiving servant.

faith in the death and resurrection of Christ will have their sins atoned and thereby escape the wrath of God (Rom ch. 3). Like Abraham, they can place their trust in the Lord's promises and receive a right relational (or covenantal) standing (Rom ch. 4). Paul also argues that Christ's work solves a redemptive-historical dilemma caused by humanity's incapacity to keep the law. His actions result in the law's demands being met and its purpose realized. Not only that, his atoning sacrifice initiates an exchange of a believer's identity in the first Adam for a new one in another Adam, who is none other than Christ himself (Rom ch. 5). The transaction highlights the fact that Christ's death and resurrection are a kind of mystical simulation into which every believer is incorporated.[13] This means that just as he died, so also have believers died. Just as he was resurrected, so likewise are believers already raised (and waiting for a bodily resurrection).

Consequently, the moral repercussion of these theological realities is that believers are dead to sin—crucified to the world—and alive unto God—raised to life. And the connective that tethers these dynamics together is the indwelling Holy Spirit (Rom chs. 6–7). He is the agent that unites believers and now mounts an assault on all sinful proclivities so believers can walk in new resurrection life (Rom 8:3–4). Likewise, the indwelling Spirit marks believers as God's family (or Christ's brothers, heirs) from which there is no means of being disinherited. He supports this by arguing that all of those who are called to the gospel and are justified are also seen as already glorified, even though this last component pertains to the future resurrection at the renewal of creation (cf. Rom 8:22–23, 30). This kind of language makes sense for Paul because he couches all these actions in God's act of predestination. God chose to initiate a relationship with believers, or foreknow them, whereby he then determines to conform them into the image of his

---

13. Such a concept does not dispense with the concept of forensic justification. It compliments it. Both are actions based on God's grace. They are induced by the Spirit with the by-product being faith that leads to salvation. We could say that while justification is legal in nature, this "mystical" union is more organic. The former results in a sinner being declared righteous and the latter brings one into a supernatural union with Christ's actual death and resurrection. This occurs because the same work of the Spirit that brought Christ back from the dead now works in the hearts of believers (Rom 8). This is why Paul thinks of believers not just as being righteous forensically. In his mind, they are also raised-from-the-dead creatures who ironically await a literal bodily raising on the last day. This is because becoming like Christ entails being like him as a glorified resurrected human. As an aside, this is also why the concept of theosis needs more attention in some Protestant regions of soteriological thought. Helpful contributions, though problematic in some ways, that have moved this conversation forward include works from Gorman, *Cruciformity*; Gorman, *Inhabiting the Cruciform God*; and Blackwell, *Christosis*.

Son.[14] Those who receive such promises are called, justified, and thereby glorified. These points then reach a crescendo where Paul concludes that there is nothing that can place a wedge between believers and their new solidarity in Christ (Rom 8:31–39). Just as those outside of the gospel cannot escape the wrath of God, those who take sanctuary within it can never be condemned.[15]

Now up to this point we can step back to see how Paul couples the security that the gospel brings with the ethic that it expects. Believers are justified, or deemed, righteous through the exercising of faith in God's promises, similar to their new forefather Abraham and they are no longer viewed as guilty like their former forefather Adam. They can rest assured that their new covenantal bond with Christ can never be severed by any external forces. But since they are also indwelled by the same Spirit that brought Christ back from the dead, they are commanded to walk, or live, according to the will of the Spirit because they are now dead to who they used to be. Believers are assured of their position and also admonished to live in a way that reflects it (just as Jesus does in the gospels). As Paul says in ch. 8, believers can be certain that their glorification awaits them because they are called, chosen, indwelled by the Spirit, and justified. Yet such assurance should never be assumed apart from embracing the moral imperative that believers are heirs of God and coheirs with Christ in the future if they suffer with him in the present. Both features are true and this kind of reciprocation is stressed even more when Paul transitions to his discussion about Israel in Rom chs. 9–11.

How the Jewish people fit into the Christ-event is a significant challenge for Paul because it creates a huge storm cloud over what he has argued thus far.[16] The dilemma is essentially this. How can one be sure that all the

14. Many contend that the word "foreknow" here should be understood of temporal terms—i.e., that God knew ahead of time who would believe. Even if this is the case, Paul's point would still stand that those he knew would believe ahead of time are predetermined to be sanctified, justified, and glorified. So one is exegetically tied to some form of determinism (there would be serious quibbles from Arminian interpreters on this point, both classical and Wesleyan alike). The question is just whether one thinks Paul sees "foreknowing" as predetermining activities before or after belief. Cf. discussions regarding the complexities that this point raises in Baugh, "Meaning of Foreknowledge," 183–200; McCall, "S. M. Baugh and the Meaning of Foreknowledge," 19–31.

15. However, one question that is often raised concerning this passage is whether a person can choose to deny their faith and thereby separate themselves from Christ. This is especially pertinent in light of Paul's comments in ch. 11 regarding a warning of potentially being "cut off" if one falls into unbelief.

16. The transition in Paul's argument to a discussion about Israel and the nations is not parenthetical, it is pivotal. If Paul is going to claim that no one or nothing can sever a believer's covenantal standing in Christ (Rom 8:31–39), then how does one

promises found in Christ are truly reliable when it appears that God failed in his dealings with Israel, the nation that was supposed to be first in line to receive them. If the Lord failed in keeping his promissory obligations to the Jews, how can we know for certain that things will go well for those who are now following Christ. Paul considers this question to be a high priority not only because of the theological ramifications involved but also because it is extremely personal since it pertains to his own people (Rom 9:1–5).

Paul begins to answer this sensitive issue by saying that God's promises to Israel were not intended for every single solitary Jew (Rom 9:6). To use his own words, not all of Israel (i.e., the Jews as a whole) were Israel (i.e., Jews who would receive the promises).[17] The covenantal heritage was to be bestowed on those whom God selects. Divine favor was not placed upon every physical descendant of Abraham, only the ones who would receive the promises. Paul illustrates this dynamic by describing how God chose Isaac through Sarah and Jacob instead of Esau. Furthermore, for anyone who would object to such "favoritism," Paul retorts that God expressed the same kind of divine prerogative when he used Moses while hardening Pharaoh—the idea being that election is an action that God performs of which there is no higher arbiter to which he is accountable. Such choosing also applies to the fact that only some Jews are called because God wants to include many Gentiles as well. And for such a plan to unfold, Paul says that currently the majority of Israel are being hardened (like Pharaoh of old) so that Gentiles can now become part of the covenant people. Likewise, a Jewish remnant is being redeemed now until this hardening is relented when the fullness of the Gentiles has come in (Rom 11:25).[18]

---

reconcile that with the fact that most of the Jewish people were outside of the covenant because of their predominate rejection of the Messiah. Such a theological conundrum warrants serious attention and is a critical part of Paul's discussion. It is not an on-the-fly sidebar. One could say that the question of covenantal fidelity is not just a matter of confidence in God's power to save. It pertains to the whole scope of redemptive history. Cf. insights here by Longenecker, "Different Answers," 95–123; and Ticciati, "Future of Biblical Israel," 497–518. Also, since Paul began the letter with a treatment of how Jews and Gentiles are equally condemned under sin and now justified through Christ, it would only make sense for the apostle to address this historical elephant in the room, namely that the Jewish people for the most part are now outside the covenant. Finally, it should be noted that the nature of the discussion regarding Israel and the Gentiles can often be eclipsed by debates about divine sovereignty, especially in light of Paul's comments in ch. 9. For an overview of the interpretive history in this regard, see Taylor, "Freedom of God," 25–41.

17. Again, as we have argued, under the old covenant, one could be part of the "elect" nation without being a specific benefactor of salvation.

18. Paul says that after the hardening is repreived, all Israel will be saved (Rom 11:26). But because the debate about what this means is so vast, it would take us in

This line of reasoning results in a powder keg of implications, especially for election and eschatology. Still, Paul then adds a stern warning that raises serious questions about the idea of perseverance. We see it when Paul anticipates a question as to whether God is finished with the Jewish people (Rom 11:1). His response is simply, "No, just look at me." God's present-day faithfulness to Israel is exhibited in the fact that some Jews are still embracing the Messiah. And again, the fact that the majority of the nation was in denial still substantiated God's providence over history because it simply opened the door for the gospel inclusion of other nations. The problem, however, was that any expression of divine favor could potentially tempt one to become arrogant. Originally this was already the case because many Jews looked down on the Gentiles because they were outside the covenant group. Now that the tables were turned, Paul did not want believing Gentiles emulating the same attitude toward others. So he warns them by using an analogy of an olive tree (Rom 11:17–24).

He describes believing Gentiles as wild branches that have been grafted into the olive tree of salvific blessings (whether the tree represents Christ, the covenant people, or the elect is debatable).[19] He says that some natural branches (i.e., Jews) were broken off, meaning that they are no longer under the umbrella of divine favor because they chose to remain in unbelief, or reject the Messiah. In similar fashion, he finally applies the same plight to the believing Gentiles if they should not abide in faith. He argues that just as Jews who were originally part of the covenant people are now separated because they have rejected the Messiah, so will current believers be "cut off" as well if they do not remain steadfast in their faith. This is a remarkable claim in light of Paul's emphatic predestinarian language in ch. 9. Apparently, Paul had no problem whatsoever in acknowledging that while the Lord sovereignly determines the life-outcomes of human beings, such a reality does not circumvent the mandate that the elect have to endure in faith if they expect to inherit salvation.[20] Therefore, this warning sounds much like Jesus' prior caution that being a soil that embraces the message of the kingdom or a branch that is truly in the vine must produce fruit. Paul

---

directions that we need to avoid for the moment. For an excellent survey views on the meaning of "all Israel being saved," see Zacolli's "And So All Israel Will Be Saved," 289–318; and Staples, "What Do the Gentiles Have to Do with 'Israel'?," 371–90.

19. This has tremendous implications for Paul's views on ecclesiology. Cf. Kim, *God, Israel, and the Gentiles*; Gadenz, *Called from the Jews and from the Gentiles*; and Zerbe, "Jews and Gentiles as People of the Covenant," 20–28.

20. Barclay goes as far as to say that this language calls into question any Augustinian (or Reformed) perspective of perseverance, Barclay, *Paul and the Gift*, 557.

just expresses this point in covenantal terms. One who is in Messiah abides by a faith that endures, not a temporal faith that lapses back into unbelief.[21]

Romans leaves us then with some critical components regarding Paul's thoughts on perseverance. One is that while all humanity will be judged by their works, one must choose whether one wants to be judged by God's standards on their own or with Christ as their advocate. Coupled with this initial point is the fact that all of those who believe are incorporated into Christ and become part of a new humanity of which they cannot be separated. We could say that whereas everyone is naturally linked to Adam because of their shared status of guilt and corruption, that condition can be changed by inheriting the blessings of Christ, the new Adam.[22] Nevertheless, Paul makes no hesitation in echoing the warnings of Jesus concerning branches in the vine that bare no fruit or seeds that start off well but die out in time. He will simply not allow anyone to find solace in the promises of security if they want to become arrogant, presumptuous, or lax in their conduct. So as it pertains to perseverance, Romans highlights through a long prolonged argument that believers are brought into a right relationship through faith in Christ and then exhibit the reality of that experience through faithfulness (i.e., the pursuit of holiness).

2. PERSEVERANCE IN GALATIANS

Anyone familiar with the book of Galatians knows that it has significant overlap with much of the content found in the Letter to the Romans. In both epistles, Paul addresses the nature of justification, the struggle to shun the works of the flesh in the power of the Spirit, and the new bond that Christ establishes between believing Jews and Gentiles. What makes Galatians unique, and has direct bearing upon our concerns about perseverance, is Paul's well-known polemics against aberrant conceptions of what it meant to be part of the new messianic community known as the church.

---

21. One could say that just as all Jews are not recipients of covenantal salvific blessings, nor will any belief-professing Gentile (or Jew) who does not endure in their faith receive eschatological vindication. Despite any reading of this warning, whether it be Arminian, Reformed, or otherwise, it is clear that is written to the Roman Christians as a sober reminder. See Schreiner, *Romans*, 609; Moo, *Romans*, 707. Interestingly enough, Moo also highlights Volf's contention that even if one were "cut off," they could potentially be grafted in once again, Volf, *Paul and Perseverance*, 198–99.

22. In all fairness, some respond to this point by arguing that none of Paul's points here prohibit the possibility that someone can separate themselves from Christ through apostasy. It is that nothing external to a believer's faith or lack thereof can separate them.

More specifically, a party of "Judaizers" were applying external pressures to the Galatian congregations by demanding that Gentile converts only be accepted into the fold if they complied with the Jewish rite of circumcision.[23] Paul was incensed at such a notion and after initially defending the legitimacy of his divine calling to be an apostle, he argues that the Judaizers' proposal went against the very nature of the new covenant itself. The reason being that its arrival meant that previous ways of demarcating God's people had been abrogated. Relatedly, Paul expresses his thoughts about the ethical standards that the Galatian Christians needed to follow.[24] And intermixed with these topics are a few points where questions about perseverance emerge. The most pertinent ones include the ultimate end of false teachers, how imperative it was to uphold the gospel that Paul preached, and the importance of walking in the power of the Spirit so one can inherit the coming kingdom of God.

The first concern pertains to the identity of the Judaizers who Paul opposed. From the outset of the letter, he is emphatically clear that these antagonists are false teachers who oppose the very gospel that the Galatians had originally embraced. He claims that the "gospel" they proclaim is not the same one that he preached and so it is really a "different" one entirely, which means it is not the gospel at all (Gal 1:6–7). This is why Paul says this party is comprised of individuals who are "accursed," meaning they are outcasts who are not part of the community of faith. They are designated for divine judgment unless they repent.[25] What Paul is saying with this indictment is that the Galatian believers should not view themselves as second-class converts unless they follow the demands of the Judaizers. Instead, they should acknowledge that the Judaizers are not part of God's people at all. They are false brethren (Gal 2:4) whose plea for Gentile circumcision is a smokescreen or a hoax. Their real agenda is to avoid the social scourge that comes upon anyone who embraces the scandal of the cross and even

---

23. Discussions about the specific reasons for the circumcision question in this letter as well as how it relates to Paul's larger discussion about justification are legion today because of the debates triggered by the New Perspective(s) on Paul. Was circumcision a matter of legalistic torah compliance, Jewish ethnocentrism, or a combination of these issues and several others. Cf. analysis here in Deenick, *Righteous by Promise*, 185–210; Smit, "In Search of Real Circumcision," 79–83; and Schreiner, "Circumcision," 138–39.

24. This has perplexed interpreters of Galatians for quite some time. How should one understand the moral impetus in the latter part of the letter in light of all the previous discussions about justification and Gentile identity in Christ apart from the law. See Barclay's treatment here in Barclay, *Obeying the Truth*, esp. introduction, 1–35.

25. This term (anathema), which is used five times in the NT, conveys the idea of being delivered over to divine wrath. Cf. Fung, "Curse, Cursed, Anathema," 200; Berthelot, "Notion of Anathema," 35–52.

worse, persuade the Galatians to their camp as a means of bolstering their own reputation (Gal 6:11–12). They did not have the Galatians' best interests at heart. They were only concerned about themselves and how others perceived them. What causes a bit of dismay in this discussion is whether these Judaizers were professing believers originally who later defected into this sectarian teaching. It is difficult to discern whether or not this was the case because Paul's letter omits any helpful clues.[26] But clearly he did view them as false teachers who were outside of Christ, which leads to the second question regarding the potential status of the Galatian believers to whom Paul was writing.

There is no question that Paul saw his audience as made up of genuine believers who had embraced the gospel that he had preached. Yet it is equally clear that he was afraid some of them were on the precipice of affirming the teachings of the Judaizers, which meant they would be abandoning their faith in the sufficiency of Christ's death and resurrection. They were being duped, deceived, or bewitched (cf. Gal 1:6; 3:1) into thinking that their newly found faith in Christ had to be merged somehow with certain forms of torah compliance. Paul warns them that just as they had begun in the Spirit, the only way they could complete their journey of faith was if they continued in the Spirit (Gal 3:1–5). This was another way of saying that if the ramifications of the new covenant brought one into this new relationship with Christ, they would also be the only means whereby one could inherit the blessings of the age to come. Paul argues that the Mosaic economy, which included the function of the law, had experienced a significant transition because of Christ. He is the promised seed that brought all the original hopes of Abraham together, which retires the law of its custodial function in redemptive history (Gal 3:15–22).[27] This is why Paul says that if a professing believer, whether they be a Jew or Gentile, were to lapse back into dogmatic observance of Jewish religious days, festivals, and years, it would be equivalent to becoming a slave to a previous master (Gal 4:8–11). Paul essentially is telling the Galatians that if they try to define who they are in terms of the

---

26. One thing that is certain is that Paul knew himself to be a believer. But he includes himself in his early warning about being accursed. He said that if "we," or an angel were to proclaim another gospel, let them be damned, or cursed.

27. One could say that the cross and resurrection nullified the role of the Levitical priesthood and temple. So if one wanted to lapse back into some form of Judaism and be circumcised, then one would also have to follow the whole law (Gal 5:2–3), only this time without any means of atonement. Paul's conclusion is that this kind of strategy leads to a dead end. The "works of the law" cannot be sustained after Christ's redemptive work because the sacrificial system as well as the priestly sanctions that were established to provide maintenance are now nullified. One must now be changed by the Spirit through faith in Christ.

law *in addition to Christ*, it would be akin to a former unbeliever lapsing back into a version of idolatry because the Mosaic economy is now nullified. To try and go back to it would be equivalent to returning to functions that are now out of business. This is why Paul tells the Galatians that if they choose to be circumcised for the theological reasons posed by the Judaizers, then they are abandoning their position in Christ (Gal 5:3–4).

Not only that, Paul reminds his readers that even though they are no longer under the regulations of the law, this fact must not be misconstrued to mean that they have no ethical obligations whatsoever.[28] Paul tells them that Christ has set them free from sin and the law so that they might be empowered by the Spirit to love one another (Gal 5:13–14). Thus, not only are they in danger of judgment if they deny the authority of Christ over the law. They can also miss their inheritance in the age to come if they should choose to be consumed by the works of the flesh (Gal 5:21b). *What we discover from this discussion then is that for Paul, the Galatians' initial identity in Christ had to be coupled with fidelity to the ethics of the kingdom if justification was to result in eternal life in the age to come.* This idea has been highlighted by numerous scholars in recent years, but B. J. Oropeza highlights the tension well when he says that for Paul (in Galatians as well as Romans), "a distinction should be made between justification in the present (initial justification/righteousness) and justification on judgment day (final justification/righteousness). For the believer, perseverance bridges the gap between the two."[29] Put another way, anyone who affirmed what the "accursed" Judaizers were teaching regardless of their previous profession would be accursed as well. Paul even says the same thing about himself if he were to preach another gospel. A faith induced by the power of the Spirit ultimately clings to Christ, not any other rite or false teaching.

3. PERSEVERANCE IN THE LETTERS TO THE CORINTHIANS

Paul reveals some other interesting thoughts about perseverance and apostasy in the two letters that he wrote to the Corinthians.[30] One major feature

---

28. As Barclay argues, while Paul does not view a believer's works as a means of *earning* God's grace, he does believe that eschatological judgment will take account of their works. See Barclay, *Obeying the Truth*, 229–30.

29. Oropeza, *Jews, Gentiles, and the Opponents of Paul*, 10.

30. We acknowledge the fact that what we call 1 Corinthians is at least Paul's second letter to this church while the epistle we call 2 Corinthians is probably Paul's fourth letter to these believers.

that stands out in the first epistle is Paul's assumption that a congregant's lapse into sinful behavior does not necessarily mean they are automatically on the road to final eschatological doom. Sometimes Paul believes that wrong conduct may induce immediate discipline from the Lord which can result in believers forfeiting their opportunity to receive certain heavenly reward or even experience a premature death.[31] But in either case, they still remain in the family of faith. Paul initially expresses such an attitude when he opens the letter with concerns about unfortunate factions that existed. Some of the people were favoring different leaders such as Apollos, Peter, and even Paul himself (1 Cor 1:12–13; 3:3–4). He tells the Corinthians that the gospel compels them to abandon such petty attitudes. They should exhibit humility toward one another because all believers are servants of the same Christ—and no one can be an elitist whose salvation is bound to a cross. Paul warns that if they continue to serve the Lord trivially or without unity, then their efforts will be deemed worthless at the final judgment (1 Cor 3:10–15). However, the language here does not lean toward the idea of being judged as an unbeliever. It appears to describe something short of such an end.[32]

Another example of this kind of language occurs when Paul addresses a situation involving the scandalous behavior of a Corinthian believer who was having a scandalous relationship with his step-mother (1 Cor 5:1). Paul instructs the church to disallow the man from being part of the church's fellowship. They are to do this so that if he is a genuine believer, the Lord would turn him over to Satan so he could experience some unspecified kind of discipline while still retaining his life for the day of judgment (1 Cor 5:5).[33] At the same time, Paul does express a bit of consternation on the

---

31. Certain elements of these warnings read as if they parallel various OT covenantal venues. For example, a Corinthian member is *cast out* or *cut off* from the believing because of his defiant immorality and other members lost their lives because they shamelessly defamed the Lord's table. Both of these instances carry OT overtones of being separated from the nation or being judged suddenly regardless of one's previous record of faithfulness.

32. Fee is correct that the emphasis is not so much on all believers individually as much as to the leadership who are responsible for "building" up the body of Christ (*First Epistle to the Corinthians*, 145). See also Thiselton, *First Epistle to the Corinthians*, 313–15. Herms argues that much of Paul's language here overlaps with other intertestamental literature such as 1 Enoch 50, which speaks of eschatological judgment for leaders that may lead to significant loss even though they will still receive final salvation. Herms, "Being Saved without Honor," 187–205.

33. The implication is that if one is going to act in ways contrary to the moral parameters of the Christian community, they should experience the full onslaught of consequences, including being relinquished to Satan's realm so they will either repent and/or the church's purity will be upheld. Cf. Phillip, "Delivery into the Hands of Satan,"

matter because he reminds the Corinthians that they are to avoid fellowship with any sexually immoral person who claims to be "a brother," or part of God's people (1 Cor 5:9–13). The reason being that the church is to hold its members morally accountable because God will do the same when he judges the world.

Finally, Paul makes a similar assessment when he speaks about matters related to the Lord's Supper. Some Corinthian believers were acting inappropriately because they were getting drunk during the meal and others were somehow neglecting the needs of less fortunate members. Paul instructs them on how to rectify these matters by first letting the church know that the Lord was already intervening to a degree because some of these disorderly members were sick and others had even died (1 Cor 11:30). Again, though, Paul does not seem to view such circumstances as indicative of the fact that these believers were complete apostates. Instead they were divinely expelled because of their presumption at the Lord's table, which could contaminate the church as a whole if left unchecked. Paul says that they were judged by the Lord so they would not be condemned with the world (1 Cor 11:32). Thus, we see once more that Paul does believe some form of temporal judgment can occur in the lives of disorderly believers.

In several other instances, however, Paul uses a more serious tone (such as in Romans and Galatians) when he thinks members are possibly on the precipice of experiencing eschatological judgment if they do not repent. One example arises after Paul finishes talking about the unrepentant member who must be cast out of the church. He speaks about the kind of character that the Corinthians should exhibit and before he specifically addresses the subject of sexual purity, he reminds them that people who are committed to all kinds of wrongdoing will not inherit the kingdom of God (1 Cor 6:9–10). He asserts that the Corinthians used to live accordingly but now they have been set apart in Christ Jesus to behave otherwise. The implication being that if their lives lapsed back into an unrepentant lifestyle or they did not experience the Lord's chastening, they would be reflecting the lives of wrongdoers who will not inherit the kingdom and they were apparently on the dangerous cusp of joining their fate.[34]

45–60; Hayes, *1 Corinthians*, 84–86; and Collins, "Function of 'Excommunication' in Paul," 251–63.

34. There are assorted interpretations of this passage which all revolve around the question as to whether Paul is warning the Corinthians about behaviors that can lead to apostasy or simply encouraging them to shun sinful conduct so they can avoid potential divine discipline. We would argue the most compelling reading is that he is admonishing them to avoid this list of vices because they are indicative of how unbelievers live. However, the underlying implication is that emulating these kinds of lifestyles has the same consequence for those who avidly express their unbelief as well as any Corinthian

Another scenario where Paul uses such severe language is when he discusses the influence that mature believers can have on novices. The context pertains to the practice of eating meat sacrificed to idols. Some of the new Corinthian converts who came from idolatrous pagan backgrounds were confused about whether they should partake of such food. They apparently thought they should abstain because they still had hazy views of God and the spiritual realm. Paul instructs the seasoned believers, who ate such meat because they knew pagan practices were mere superstitions, that they should be willing to limit their liberties if it meant the betterment of their fellow brethren in Christ. He makes this admonishment in hopes of ensuring that the young believers not potentially turn back to their previous way of life and miss their full inheritance in the kingdom. Paul says that if this were to happen, they would be repeating the sad heritage of many Israelites who left Egypt, yet never reached the promised land (1 Cor 10:1–13).[35]

Likewise, a third instance where Paul expresses concern over the eternal destiny of the Corinthians is when he discusses the matter of the resurrection in ch. 15. Scholars speculate on the specific reason why some of the Corinthians were denying a future bodily resurrection of believers.[36] Whatever the reason was specifically, Paul tells them that a repudiation of a future resurrection necessitates a denial of Christ's resurrection. Such logic nullifies their faith not only because they would still be in their sins if Christ did not conquer death. Their faith would also be utterly worthless because they would be denying a central tenet of the gospel that Paul preached to them (1 Cor 15:2, 17). So what we see in the end is that Paul treats various situations in context-specific ways because he does not see all misconduct or faulty thinking as automatically requiring preemptive instruction on the dangers of apostasy. Sometimes believers simply need a reprimand while at other times, they do need a reminder about the final destination of those who refuse to repent altogether or defect from the fundamentals of the gospel's message.

From here, as time transpired and we come to the writing of 2 Corinthians a year or so later, most of Paul's reasons for writing had changed.[37]

---

congregant who claims to be a believer. A good discussion of views on this text is provided by López, "Does the Vice List," 59–73.

35. See the probing treatment of this text by Oropeza, *Paul and Apostasy*, esp. chs. 3 and 4, 69–190.

36. While dated, cf. discussions of this question by Dykstra, "1 Corinthians 15:20–28," 196–204; Wedderburn, "Problem of the Denial of the Resurrection," 229–41; and Wilson, "Corinthians Who Say There Is No Resurrection," 90–107.

37. See full discussions by Martin, *2 Corinthians*, xlvi–lxi; and Harris, *Second Epistle to the Corinthians*, 51–100.

The main reason for this epistle was in response to a series of events that had transpired wherein a group of unidentified leaders were questioning the legitimacy of Paul's apostolic relationship with the Corinthian church. Paul sees these teachers in a negative light, calling them false apostles, potential agents of Satan (2 Cor 11:2–6), and implies that they may be in the "ministry" just for profit (2 Cor 2:17). He also recounts some of the loving devotion that he had showed to the Corinthians during his ministry there (2 Cor chs. 6–7). He counters that if these so-called teachers want to brag about their giftedness, he will only speak ever so reluctantly about the hardships he has suffered for the sake of the gospel (2 Cor 11:21–33). Furthermore, he mentions that they will all stand before Christ in judgment one day. And if they choose to question, or even worse, abandon the gospel that Paul preached in exchange for what these teachers were offering, then they will have failed the test set before them (cf. 2 Cor 6:1–2; 13:5–6).[38]

4. PERSEVERANCE IN THE LETTERS TO THE THESSALONIANS

Paul's letters to the Thessalonians maintain strong continuity with his thoughts on perseverance that we have seen thus far.[39] This makes perfect sense especially in light of the fact that these are probably some of the earliest epistles that he wrote. What makes them unique is that much of what he says to the Thessalonians regarding this subject is interrelated with certain theological viewpoints that he expresses about the return of Christ. This is not to say that eschatology is not pertinent to Paul's view of perseverance elsewhere. Indeed it is. We have seen already that he consistently connects the importance of persevering in one's faith to inheriting the kingdom of God and experiencing the resurrection unto eternal life in the age to come. The added nuance in these letters is that Paul gives much more attention to the events surrounding Christ's return and the moral imperative that believers must heed to be prepared for his arrival.

---

38. While some of the theological parameters need a bit of attention, Oropeza is on to something when he says that Paul sees faith "as not only a commitment to Christ but also as the ability to sustain the tension of the present status of the 'now' and 'not yet.' Paul believed the Corinthian congregation must live out that tension in perseverance until the end of their natural lives." Oropeza, *Paul and Apostasy*, 178. This point derives from a conflation of theological points made by Beker and Ladd; cf., respectively, Beker, *Paul the Apostle*, 356; and Ladd, *Theology of the New Testament*, 566.

39. There is some debate as to whether the letter we call 1 Thessalonians was written after 2 Thessalonians. Cf. Wanamaker, *Epistles to the Thessalonians*, 37–45; Foster, "Who Wrote 2 Thessalonians?," 150–75.

We discover in the first letter that this church was predominately made up of Gentiles who were former idol worshippers (cf. Acts 17:4; 1 Thess 1:9; 2:14). Their service for Christ had become a great personal encouragement to Paul as well as other believers who lived in the surrounding Macedonian regions (1 Thess 1:2–9). Paul also had a special affection for these people because of the time he spent with them when their church was first getting started. And now he longed to see them again because they were enduring persecution. They were being oppressed by their fellow countrymen who were possibly an unidentified group of pagan Gentiles.[40] This was a common trend in the first century because converting to Christ meant that one repudiated the cultural milieu of pagan deities and idols. This usually created a huge upsurge of resistance because such an attitude disrupted the harmony among family members who worshipped various deities and hurt economies that were sometimes largely driven by the sustaining of temples, idols, and pagan festivals. For whatever the reason, Paul says they were emulating the experience of churches in Judea who had suffered at the hands of unbelieving Jews (1 Thess 2:13–16). He then reminds them that he had prepared them for such circumstances. This is partly why he mentions the fact that he had sent Timothy to visit them earlier. Timothy was to remind the Thessalonians that Paul had told them such things would most likely happen and report back to him about how they were doing (1 Thess 3:1–5).

Paul was equally concerned about their everyday conduct. He was well aware that the pressures of external hardships could possibly lead some to succumb to luring temptations. And he knew that a major way to gauge whether these believers were possibly doing so was if their conduct was slowly becoming indistinguishable from those around them. So he warns them about some of the moral pitfalls that the Thessalonians commonly faced in their surrounding environment. A major one was the strong draw of sexual immorality. This vice was rampant in the Roman Empire, especially in light of the fact that it was frequently promoted by prostitution and sometimes linked to the worship of various deities.[41] Paul points out that sexual purity is a hallmark of Christian discipleship because one's body is a vessel that is to be used for Christ's service, not lustful passions (1 Thess 4:3–4). This is why anyone who ignores this command is potentially defrauding their fellow spiritual brethren as well as defying God's authority over their lives. In addition, it would be impossible to follow his later admonition to

---

40. Theories abound here; cf. surveys of views by Bruce, *1 & 2 Thessalonians*, 44–49; Wanamaker, *Thessalonians*, 114–19; Fee, *First and Second Letters to the Thessalonians*, 89–100.

41. Cf. discussions by Glancy and Moore, "How Typical," 555–60; McGinn, *Economy of Prostitution*, 14–110; McGinn, *Prostitution, Sexuality, and the Law*, 23–43.

continue loving one another and maintain a good testimony among unbelieving Gentiles if one was involved in immoral behavior (1 Thess 4:9-12).

All of these points then transition to one final set of concerns that pertain to the Thessalonians' conduct in light of the coming return of Christ and the related (and mysterious) Day of the Lord (DOL).[42] The shift begins with Paul addressing an apparent uncertainty that the people had about fellow Thessalonian believers who had died. There was some sort of ambiguity regarding their understanding of how their reunion with these loved ones coincided with the return of Christ. Paul clarifies the matter by describing how both dead believers and believers who are alive at his coming will be glorified and caught up to meet the Lord at his return (1 Thess 4:13-18). Such a wonderful promise is to serve as a means of comfort for the Thessalonians during their times of grief. Yet in lieu of this assurance, Paul further mentions that Christ's heavenly descent to summon his people entails the impending drama of judgment. In other words, Christ does not arrive just to save his people. He comes to judge those who are not.

It is here where Paul makes a correlation between the assurance believers have that their hopes will be culminated with Christ's return and the responsibility they have to always be ready because they are unaware of the specific time in which it will occur. Paul fleshes this point out in 1 Thess 5 by contrasting the attitudes that unbelievers and believers have about the coming DOL. Unbelievers think their lives will continue indefinitely without any divine intervention. They live as drunks who wallow in their stupor or sluggards who sleep because they enjoy the dark (1 Thess 5:3a, 7). Believers are to be just the opposite. They know that the DOL will come unexpectedly, catching the unbelieving world off guard just like birth contractions on a pregnant mother or a thief who comes at night. This is why they are to be sober minded, alert, living carefully as if it is daytime because they know that God's wrath, from which they are exempt, is coming upon those who reject the gospel (1 Thess 5:2, 3b-6a).[43] Paul then ends this discussion with

---

42. The OT develops this idea of the *Day of the Lord* as a given time when God directly intervenes in history to either judge a given people, which sometimes may be a foreign nation or Israel, or deliver his people from impending peril. It is also used periodically throughout portions of intertestamental literature (e.g., 1 Enoch, 4 Ezra, 2 Baruch) and is later conflated in the gospels with the coming of the Son of Man. See Kreitzer, "Eschatology," 259. In Paul's writings in particular, Day of the Lord language is used on occasion (e.g., 1 Thess 5:2; 2 Thess 2:2) but in some instances, he modifies the phrase by referring to the Day of the Lord Jesus Christ. For further discussion here, see Vander Hart, "Transition of the Old Testament Day of the Lord," 3-25.

43. Regardless of how one parses the eschatological details here in Paul's discussion about the coming of the Lord Jesus, it is clear that he is linking the Thessalonians' readiness for Christ's return to the reality of their conversion. One could say Paul is arguing

an intriguing promise where he states that whether the Thessalonians were awake or asleep, they will ultimately live together with Christ. The question that arises is whether this awake-sleep language means dead or alive, which would fit nicely with the language he just used at the end of ch. 4 regarding Christ's return. Or in light of the most immediate remarks about being awake for the Lord's return as opposed to sleeping as unbelievers do, some deduce that Paul means believers will be with Christ regardless of whether they are ready for his return or not.[44]

The most likely option is the former for two reasons. One is that Paul ends the discussion again with the same tone as he did at the end of ch. 4 where he tells the Thessalonians to encourage one another with these words (1 Thess 5:11). Just as they should comfort one another because they know they will be reunited with their beloved dead at Christ's return, they should build one another up in the faith because they know that they will be part of it regardless of whether they are dead or alive (i.e., physically). Second, this idea is the best option because Paul says destruction and judgment will come upon all of those who are not ready. His point is not that there are three kinds of people: (1) unbelievers who are asleep, or not ready for Christ's return; (2) believers who are awake, or ready for Christ's return; and (3) believers who are asleep, or not ready for Christ's return. Paul is not admonishing these believers to be ready because regardless of whether they are, they will be united to Christ. No, his point is that if all of them are ready when Christ comes back, they can be assured that their faith will become sight regardless of whether they experience death beforehand.[45]

Paul fleshes out the believer's responsibility to be ready for Christ's return even more in his Second Letter to the Thessalonians. The epistle opens with a promise of vindication if his readers faithfully withstand the onslaught of persecution. Paul assures them that all those who harm Christ's people will receive divine affliction at the Lord's return (2 Thess 1:6–10). Then the discussion takes an interesting turn that plagues interpreters because there are several key gaps in the discussion of which we are not privy. Paul opens this section with the claim that he is aware the Thessalonians

---

that those who live in the day, or are prepared for the *parousia*, are those who have been brought into the light. But those who are not ready because they live in the dark are the unbelievers who will be caught off guard and judged.

44. Cf. support for this view, see Thomas, "1 Thessalonians," 285–86; Edgar, "Meaning of 'Sleep,'" 345–49. Also see a direct critique by Weima, *1–2 Thessalonians*, 368–71.

45. As David Williams states, "It is inconceivable that Paul should suggest that whether we are morally alert or moribund will make no difference in the end," Williams, *1 and 2 Thessalonians*, 91. Also Fee observes that "awake" language is shorthand for Paul's way of describing the Thessalonians who might be living at the Parousia (Fee, *Letters to the Thessalonians*, 199).

were dismayed because of a message from some unspecified source that said the DOL had come (2 Thess 2:1–2). Immediately disputes emerge today regarding speculations about the identity of this source, whether the coming of Christ and the believers' gathering to him mentioned in 2:1 are referring to the same event, and what affairs does Paul include in his understanding of the DOL. Be this as it may, the issue of perseverance arises when Paul mentions that the DOL had not come yet because the man of lawlessness had not arrived nor had a great apostasy occurred.[46] These comments sound like the ones Jesus made in the Olivet Discourse about the rise of false teachers, the deception of many, and the rise of the abomination of desolation. It should be recalled, however, that Jesus' observation about many being deceived must be understood in light of his other claim that the elect will be spared. The same point can be seen here in Paul's treatment. He warns the Thessalonians of what is to come when, or before, the DOL transpires. At the same time, his deferral to the fact that an apostasy will occur does not include any explicit assumptions about true believers defecting.[47] Actually he says that those who do not receive the truth are deceived by the powers of this "lawless man," not the elect. Still, to be fair, it is clear that anyone, including any member of the Thessalonian church, that follows the teachings of the lawless one will share in his fate, which is final eschatological judgment initiated by Christ himself (2 Thess 2:8).

5. PERSEVERANCE IN THE PRISON EPISTLES

The four smaller letters that scholars traditionally recognize as the prison epistles add some significant features to our understanding of Paul's views of apostasy and perseverance. Three of the four, Ephesians, Philippians, and Colossians, are similar in content because they are all written to predominately Gentile congregations that are wrestling through the implications of being part of a largely "Jewish" movement as well as trying to withstand the negative influences of rival teachers. In his correspondence with the

---

46. Though many would quibble about his conclusions, see a general overview of the complexities related to "man of lawlessness" feature in Johnson, "Paul's 'Anti-Christology,'" 125–43; Riddlebarger, *Man of Sin*, 117–34; and Morris, "Man of Lawlessness," 592–94.

47. In fact, Paul's language here almost mimics Jesus prediction exactly about the coming abomination of desolation and the defamation of the temple. And as previously discussed, Jesus said the elect could not be deceived. In all likelihood, then, Paul is following this pattern of prophetic expectation because he has the same conviction. Those who are Christ's will resist the strong temptation to apostatize. Cf. Weima, *1–2 Thessalonians*, 510–42; Green, *Letters to the Thessalonians*, 300–330.

Ephesians, Paul does not focus so much on this latter problem. He devotes most of his attention to the new relationship between believing Jews and Gentiles. He begins by opening the letter with some of his strongest predestinarian language where he describes the Ephesian believers as chosen, or elected, in Christ before the foundation of the world to be holy, blameless, and receive an eternal inheritance.[48]

He adds that these believers have been given the Spirit as a seal or divine marker so that they are guaranteed to receive the full benefits of salvation because they are God's possession. In other words, the Spirit is an irreversible sign of things to come (Eph 1:13–14). Consequently, because these blessings belong to everyone in Christ, Paul argues that a new humanity has been formed where Gentiles, who were originally alienated from the promises of Israel, are now part of a new household, or temple, in which the Spirit dwells. He then continues this discussion by speaking about his stewardship as an apostle to preach this message, the importance of unity among the Ephesian churches, and the ethical mandates that come with such a high calling in Christ. Regarding the latter point, he highlights the proper manner in which they should speak. He reminds them of how they should treat one another as well as the need to avoid all forms of immorality. He also stays true to form during these discussions by reminding

---

48. There is little doubt that Paul's "election" language here is strongly tied to Israel's identity as God's chosen people. Only now in Christ, Jew and Gentile are linked together as his new-covenant citizenry, a newly "selected" people. See O'Brien, *Ephesians*, 98–99. At the same time, what needs to be kept mind is the fact that the people of Israel's selection was based on God's choice to place his favor on them. And in this case in Ephesians, Paul links the concept of being elected to one's experience of salvation, not just being part of a redemptive-historical group. While one cannot necessarily show that this passage carries the weight of what one might call "double predestination" (see Hoehner, *Ephesians*, 175), what can be stated is that all believers are "predetermined" to receive all the blessings of the new covenant in Christ. In Newman's words, "The death and resurrection of Jesus, as a prolepsis of the eschaton, a down-payment of the future, enabled Paul to speak of God, his purposes, and the mysterious past." See Newman, "Election and Predestination in Ephesians," 243. But extending Newman's point a bit further than he would concede, the certainty of the future is based on God's choosing those who receive the Spirit, namely believers. Where controversy emerges is when one asks the exegetical question as to whether Ephesians 1 is claiming that God chooses who believes as well. When Paul says God chose us "in him (Christ)," some argue that the election is a predetermination to redeem all those "in Christ" whereas others contend that he chooses who will in fact be identified "in Christ." Literature here is astronomical but a recent source that can be consulted to see the vast difference of opinion here is by Thornhill, *Chosen People*, 186–253. Furthermore, the issue of whether God merely chooses believers or chooses who believes has even become somewhat complicated within certain pockets of modern Reformed thought since the christocentric view of Karl Barth has been added to the theological scene. See discussion of this complication in Crisp, "Election of Jesus Christ," 131–50.

the Ephesians that those who practice all forms of debauchery have no inheritance in the coming kingdom (Eph 5:3–5) just as he told the Corinthians and Galatians.

Paul's Letter to the Philippians echoes some of these same emphases. He speaks about his commission to preach the gospel and admonishes these believers to live in a way that reflects the nobility of being called saints, or holy ones (cf. Phil 1:12–18, 27).[49] However, unlike Ephesians, Paul devotes some of his time in this epistle to problems with false teachers who once again were apparently some kind of Judaizing sect. He warns the Philippians not to fall for these advocates of pseudo-circumcision as some sort of supplement to the new work of the Spirit in Christ (Phil 3:1–3). They should shun these theological peddlers because they are actually enemies of the cross whose end is destruction and eternal judgment, with the implication being that anyone who follows them will suffer the same fate (Phil 3:17–19). Likewise, we see Paul once again coupling his assurance that he will be with Christ either in life or death with his constant pursuit of reaching the finish line of life so he can experience this hope. While he is confident that to live is Christ and to die is gain (Phil 1:21), he knows that he must count his former life as vanity so he can chase after Christ to lay hold of his ultimate goal (Phil 3:7–14). And for the record, he expects the Philippians to follow his lead by adopting the exact same mindset. This is why he admonishes them to work out their own salvation because it is their efforts to strive after their eternal prize that are the very evidence of God's presence within them (Phil 2:12–13).[50] In fact, this is why he expresses confidence that the Lord will lead them all to a final vindication (Phil 1:6).[51]

---

49. A saint is a holy one who inherits the earth when the Son of Man comes to reign over it. They are to live by the Spirit now in a way that reflects the righteousness that will cover the earth in its fullness in the eschaton. See a critical discussion about this idea of a "saint" in Heiser, *Unseen Realm*, 255–58.

50. Paul sees God's activity in the lives of the Philippians as incentive for them to pursue Christ in sanctification. See Carson, *Basics for Believers*, 62. And as they do so, they exhibit the divine interworking of the Spirit that led them to faith in Christ at the outset. Cf. Silva, *Philippians*, 140; Murray, *Redemption*, 148–49. Contra this view, some argue that Paul's admonition here as pertaining to a striving that needed to be exerted so the health of the Philippian congregation as a whole could be protected. Hawthorne, "Letter to the Philippians," 712–13.

51. Paul's hope at this early point in the letter is linked to the Philippians receiving the culmination of their faith on the "Day of Christ." This expectation is common to many of Paul's letters as we see on some occasions where he is confident that some churches are awaiting that day faithfully, like the Thessalonians. But there are other instances like the congregations in Galatia where Paul was concerned that they were getting off course theologically and placing themselves in jeopardy in light of that day.

Paul similarly deals with this list of concerns in his Letter to the Colossians. One clear example is his discussion about the dangers of following false teachers even though in this epistle, he does not disclose their identity. Paul warns the Colossian believers about the hazards of following empty Christless philosophies, arbitrary demands to observe certain religious days and festivals, or abiding by random food restrictions (Col 2:8, 16–17, 20–21). Paul makes the point that they must stay the course to receive the inheritance they have in Christ and remain in the faith, not being moved from the gospel that they had believed (Col 1:21–23).[52] He also devotes much of the letter to describing the kind of conduct that reflects the high calling that the Colossians have received as citizens of heaven. Moreover, the letter carries the same kind of tone as Ephesians and Philippians in that while Paul assumes these Gentile believers have embraced the gospel that he preaches, he does treat such a certainty as mitigating against their responsibility to avoid aberrant ideologies and pursue Christ until he comes (Col 3:1–2).

This Pauline balance between confidently resting in Christ and ardently striving after him are further exemplified in Paul's Letter to Philemon. This entire epistle pertains to a request that Philemon forgive someone named Onesimus. What is interesting about how Paul approaches the matter is that he really gives Philemon no choice in the situation. He opens with a stellar commendation for the wonderful accounts that he has received from others about Philemon's commitment to Christ and serving others. He then asks Philemon to forgive Onesimus and receive him as a new brother in Christ. As he does, Paul says that if he can be released from prison and pay Philemon a visit, he will repay any debt that Onesimus may owe (while at the same time reminding Philemon that he is already indebted to Paul for his own life). He also assumes that Philemon will do more than what he is asking. So much so that he cannot wait to come with his constituents to see how well they are getting along as newly reconciled brothers. Thus, in the end, Paul's unequivocal assumption is that Philemon will forgive Onesimus. The main reason he does is because he is confident that Philemon will be faithful to the gracious witness he has exhibited thus far. Furthermore, the major contribution that this letter makes to the discussion of perseverance is that Paul echoes the teachings of Jesus by making the case that forgiveness

---

52. Murray Harris provides an expanded paraphrase of this passage and 23a states, "But this will occur only if you continue to exercise faith, the faith in which you were once firmly founded and now should be steadfast . . ." Harris, *Colossians and Philemon*, 62. Or as King argues, Paul's wording extends an attitude of courteous confidence that the Colossians will remain devoted to Christ but at the same time, such assurance does not mitigate against a warning so that they do not develop a false sense of security. King, *Exegetical Summary of Colossians*, 76–77; cf. O'Brien, *Colossians, Philemon*, 69.

is a nonnegotiable practice that Philemon, or any believer, must practice if they expect to maintain their testimony as a follower of Christ and be forgiven by the Father.[53]

6. PERSEVERANCE IN THE PASTORAL EPISTLES

The last set of letters that need to be engaged are those that the apostle wrote to two of his young sons, or protégés, in the ministry, Timothy and Titus.[54] These epistles reflect many of the same concerns that Paul expresses elsewhere. The major difference is that instead of being written to an individual church or churches in a given region, they were addressed to young leaders that Paul had trained. One was written to a worker named Titus who evidently Paul had commissioned to the island of Crete to provide some leadership in the churches spread throughout the city regions (Titus 1). The other two were written to Timothy, a mainstay partner of Paul's who joined him on his second missionary journey with Silas (Acts 16:1–20). The first was written after he had become a resident in Ephesus at Paul's request so he could provide pastoral guidance of a congregation there. The second was written to Timothy (and possibly the church as well) for at least two reasons. One was to provide more instruction regarding some pastoral issues Timothy was facing and the other was to ask him to pay one last personal visit because Paul thought his demise was probably imminent. Altogether, these letters offer some critical input on the issues of perseverance and apostasy because both Timothy and Titus had to deal with the potential dangers of false teaching that were leading some people astray.[55]

---

53. One can quickly surmise after reading the letter that Philemon has no choice but to forgive Onesimus. Paul's appeal is expressed so masterfully. He closes by saying that he cannot wait to visit them both to see how well they are getting along. He is so hopeful that he has even informed many of his missionary colleagues about the situation, including Timothy, Epaphras, Mark, Aristarchus, Demas, and Luke (cf. Phlm 1:1, 23–24). The obvious implication being that they support the appeal for Onesimus to be restored as well. See Fitzmyer, *Letter to Philemon*, 125.

54. As with the treatment of other parts of the NT thus far, we are assuming Pauline authorship of these books even though these are the most disputed letters within the apostle's corpus. For assessments of the vast literature on this issue, though, see Marshall, "Recent Study of the Pastoral Epistles," 3–29; and Bumgardner, "Paul's Letters to Timothy and Titus," 77–116.

55. Cf. assessments by Fee *1 and 2 Timothy*, 7–12; Mounce, *Pastoral Epistles*, lxix–lxxvi.

6.1 1 Timothy

We see such problems arising in 1 Timothy where Paul spends much of his time talking about some in the Ephesian church who were either questioning certain tenets that believers were to affirm or were involved in sinful conduct that contradicted how the people of faith were to behave. Examples of the former concern include a certain number of members who were apparently entangled in bizarre theological speculations about old Jewish traditions, ancient folklore, and eccentric genealogical conjectures. They were so convinced of their conceived notions that they believed themselves to be credentialed teachers of the law even though Paul said they had no idea that the implications of their teachings were theologically catastrophic.

Two such individuals who were possibly spearheading this faction are mentioned by Paul, Hymenaeus and Alexander. He says they had shipwrecked their faith, along with others, and that he had turned them over to Satan so they could experience divinely sanctioned discipline or perhaps even worse.[56] Also, there was the possibility that some women in the church were involved in malicious gossiping to the point that Paul said they had fallen under satanic influence. And whether the false teachers previously mentioned were guilty of this act or not, Paul says that some wanted to instill conflict among believing communities for the sake of personal financial gain, which is the context for the famous statement that the love of money is the root of all kinds of evil. Furthermore, Paul thought all these trends were merely proofs of the Spirit's declaration and Jesus' early predictions that as the last days commenced, many would turn from the faith to listen to liars who would be controlled by demonic forces.

Along with these issues are a few instances where Paul mentions various patterns of sin that were indicative of unbelief rather than faith. Some include profane lawlessness, sexual immorality, lying, being a sluggard who does not provide for their family, or spreading slander within the church. Each of these actions are directly contrary to God's law, and even worse, they go against the teaching of Christ which always leads to godliness. With each of these trends in mind, Paul consistently encourages Timothy to

---

56. Similar to the situation in Corinth, Paul sees a role for Satan in disciplining wayward congregants. The idea is that they must be excommunicated from the fellowship of the church so that they can be vulnerable to a full satanic assault. They must be relinquished to the full landscape of the present age over which Satan holds sway. Cf. Thornton, "Satan as Adversary," 149; Marshall, *Pastoral Epistles*, 414–15. However, the purpose of such an act was not to treat defectors like a cancer that needed to be cut out only for the benefit of the rest of the body. Rather they were to be cast off into the sea so they could fully see its dangers and want to regain the benefits of being on the ship. Towner, *1, 2 Timothy, and Titus*, 59–60.

exercise the gifts that God has given him and remain committed to the faith both personally and doctrinally. He makes it clear to Timothy that part of his pastoral responsibilities entails an unflinching commitment to doctrinal purity because it is part of the means that the Spirit uses to grow the faith of the people.[57] What the Ephesian believers have in Christ is preserved by God's power through the means of sound doctrine which in this case was to be provided by Timothy both in his character as well as his teaching. Thus, Paul sees Timothy's perseverance as a faithful minister to be an ordained part of how the Lord would ensure that the Ephesian saints reached the goal of eschatological salvation.[58]

6.2 2 Timothy

In like manner, 2 Timothy expresses many of these same concerns. Paul begins this letter with a heartfelt greeting because he was aware that Timothy longed to see him. He knew about Timothy's tears. He was reminded of his dear grandmother and mother because their faith was now being replicated in him. This is why Paul assures Timothy of his confidence that the Lord will bring his faith and ministry to its rightful end all the way up to the day of redemption. But in the meantime, he admonishes Timothy to stay on his course as a minister of the gospel. One reason Paul does this is because he mentions some who had abandoned him. Phygelus and Hermogenes had left him while he was in Asia and Demas forsook him to go to Thessalonica. Tragically, the trend for some to lapse into theological error was still on the rise as well. Paul mentions two individuals, Hymenaeus and Philetus, who had concluded that the resurrection of believers had already taken place.[59] Although we are not told what line of thought they had em-

---

57. In looking at 4:15–16, one can conclude that part of the means whereby a believer's individual faith reaches its culmination on the day of Christ (as Paul expressed in Phil 1:6) is by being nurtured by the faithful work of pastoral ministry. Or said another way, "The NT speaks of human agents in addition to the ultimate and absolute source, God himself." Knight, *Commentary on the Pastoral Epistles*, 212.

58. Faithful confession to the gospel tradition that Paul passed on to Timothy as well as the practical outworking of it in everyday life are evidence of the Spirit's work in the lives of the Ephesian believers. And, again, Paul views Timothy's faithfulness to his mission as a catalyst that God would use to achieve this goal. Timothy was to preach sound doctrine as well as exemplify it so the people could understand the implications of the gospel both audibly and visibly. See Mounce, *Pastoral Epistles*, 264–65; Marshall, *Pastoral Epistles*, 565–71.

59. It appears that this kind of over-realized eschatology had become a trending problem; just revisit Paul's letters to the Thessalonians and Corinthians. Fee, *1 and 2 Timothy, Titus*, 256.

braced to reach such a conclusion, Paul says their words were spreading like gangrene among some. Their actions fell in line with a long sad pedigree of false teachers who, Paul claims, will always try to exploit those who are vulnerable to deception. They were like the infamous Egyptian magicians, Jannes and Jambres, who tried to counterfeit the power of God that Moses displayed. Their antics were impressive initially until they were ultimately thwarted and exposed as imposters. So will it be for false teachers. People will be deceived by their lies but still receive judgment if they do not repent. This is why Paul continually encourages Timothy throughout the letter not to fall prey to the sad end of the defectors. He should rather follow Paul as he pursued Christ. He tells Timothy not to be ashamed of his current situation but to link arms with him as a co-laborer and co-sufferer in the gospel. Timothy is instructed to put away fear, exhibit the strength of a soldier, the discipline of an athlete, and the grit of a farmer because if he did so, he would fulfill the ministry that God had given him.

Likewise, as Timothy listens to Paul's counsel, there are two major promises that he receives. One emerges within a rather controversial saying that Paul offers. While speaking about the sacrifices that Paul had made so he could serve God's people, he tells Timothy that the motivation for such commitment can be summarized in a trustworthy saying (or possibly an ancient hymn). It states that if one dies with Christ, they will live with him; if one endures for Christ, they will reign with him; if one denies Christ, then they will be rejected as well; but if one is faithless, Christ will remain faithful.

Exegetical questions usually come up regarding this last line. The reason being that in the first two, death leads to life and endurance leads to reward. Then in the third, denial of Christ leads to Christ denying the denier. So does the symmetrical flow of the quote require that faithlessness result in Christ being faithful to judge the faithless.[60] Some think this is the proper interpretation while others contend that it contradicts numerous other passages where Paul emphasizes Christ's love for people even when they temporarily fall into temptation.[61] Part of the issue here is whether syntax is the all-determining factor. Some contend that a grammatical case can be made for the idea that Christ will faithfully judge those who prove to be faithless. However, one can argue that these undefined acts of unfaithfulness are distinct from the concept of denying Christ that is referenced in the

---

60. See Oropeza's discussion of this view and survey of sympathetic commentators in *Jews, Gentiles, and the Opponents of Paul*, 281–82; and Marshall, *Pastoral Epistles*, 741–42.

61. One might think of the restoration of John Mark or in the gospels, the Apostle Peter.

previous line. The meaning could be that even when one fails on occasion or experiences a lack of faith, they can be assured that Christ will be faithful to them.[62] Such a meaning does have some support as the rest of the letter unfolds and such a promise would be an encouragement to Timothy in light of his pastoral struggles.

Along with this assurance, Paul tells Timothy that even though some within the church will embrace false doctrines and/or sinful behavior with no intent of repenting, the Lord will still preserve those who are his (2 Tim 2:19—3:5), or keep them to the eschatological end. Paul supports this point by initially appealing to the story of Korah where the Lord confronted his rebellion and let Israel know that he knew who truly belonged to the Aaronic priesthood versus those who were trying to organize a mutiny. Paul subsequently alludes to the command that the faithful within Israel must abstain from wickedness. So just as the book of Numbers emphasizes God's sovereignty in protecting his people without negating their responsibility to pursue holiness, Paul lets Timothy know that the same truths apply now. God's work of salvation will be done and those who are to be saved must pursue holiness. One truth does not contradict the other. One empowers the other.

6.3 Titus

Now in accordance with the thoughts that Paul shares with Timothy, he similarly reminds Titus that to be a faithful pastor, elders must be well grounded in their faith so that they can know what the truth is, be equipped to communicate it effectively, and able to discern error when, not if, it rears its ugly head. Crete was like Ephesus in that it had no shortage of false teachers. Paul says that there were some who were openly rebellious with the sole intent of willfully deceiving unsuspecting families. Yet unlike the letters to Timothy, it is somewhat difficult to determine if these teachers were defectors from within the Cretan churches or problem-making Judaizers who entered the churches to proselytize Christian converts.[63] One thing they shared in common with the Ephesian detractors was a fascination with Jewish traditions and eccentric interpretations of the law. In any case, the

62. Mounce contends that this "faithful saying" is trying to cover the basic spectrum of Christian experience; e.g., death, life, apostasy, and temporal failure. Yet if the last strophe is another warning like the one given in the third, then it is redundant. Mounce, *Pastoral Epistles*, 518.

63. Wieland provides a helpful discussion about how various aspects of Cretan religions correspond to specific points that Paul makes in instructing Titus in Wieland, "Roman Crete," 338–54.

end-all was that they were deceiving vulnerable households for the purposes of financial exploitation and to build their own constituencies.

Paul says they exhibited the universal mark of all false teachers, namely they exhibited the appearance of knowledge about God but their actions proved otherwise. So tragically whether one followed their teachings or their immoral lifestyle, divine judgment would be the ultimate destination. This is why Paul admonishes Titus to make sure that believers are instructed on how to conduct their lives in ways that reflect the truthfulness of "sound doctrine." Though their salvation is based upon God's mercy as displayed in the renewing power of the Spirit, anyone who truly believes the gospel is to be careful in engaging in good deeds.[64] And when facing the opposition of the false teachers, Titus was instructed to avoid unhelpful debates about spurious issues concerning the law. Instead, he should offer correction first and if an opponent was unwilling to comply, they were to be rejected, or even excommunicated so they could possibly face divine judgment.

Altogether then, we are left with several important facets of Paul's thought on perseverance and apostasy in these letters. The most dominant feature entails some important insights into how Paul thought the church should respond to the impact that false teaching could potentially have on congregations. We see for starters that Paul was confident that the Lord would bring his people to the eschatological culmination of their faith.[65] This was not simply a theological axiom he preached. It was personal. He was assured that he would reach the final lap of his own race of faith so he could be graciously rewarded at the coming of the Lord. He also assured Timothy that God would preserve his elect unto salvation as well. Nevertheless, this promise did not mitigate against the possibility that believers could struggle and temporarily falter. This was why Paul saw Timothy and Titus' leadership roles as being so crucial. God's protection of his chosen ones was to be fulfilled in part through the faithful ministry of the church's elder/pastors. This was the case because one of the means whereby the faith of the elect was enabled to persevere was through the continual reception of sound doctrine and the spiritual fiber exemplified by their leaders.

Juxtaposed to their example, Paul equally addresses those within the community who could embrace false teaching and even subvert the faith

---

64. Reciprocation is important in Paul's ethic but not in any way that entails notions of merit or some absurd way of trying to "pay God back." For Paul, God has elected a people to become a new-covenant community and with such blessings come kingdom responsibilities. Believers are now to exhibit by the power of the Spirit both in what they affirm (orthodoxy) and how they live (orthopraxy).

65. Again, this echoes his sentiments elsewhere as we saw in his Letter to the Philippians for example.

of some. The key point to keep in mind is that in these letters, Paul applies a binary set of theological insights because of the possibility that defectors could repent. On the one hand, he describes them as following a path that would lead to final judgment. The ideas they were advocating and the damage they were causing to some in the church were marks of false teachers who Paul had once described one time as wolves in sheep's clothing (Acts 29–30). Yet on the other hand, he extends a ray of hope by giving these defectors over to Satan either to be judged or chastised to the point that they may return in repentance. If the latter was the case, then obviously they could be restored to the faith. But if they continued down the path they were taking, Paul believed they would be living illustrations of the prophetic message given by the Spirit that many would express temporal faith for a while only to turn away to their own devices and cling to teachers who would tell them what they wanted to hear instead of what they needed to hear.

7. CONCLUSIONS

We now want to close this part of our study with a few remarks that can hopefully synthesize the spectrum of ideas that we have surveyed regarding Paul's views on perseverance. One observation to make at the outset is that Paul interprets the Christian life through a pair of theological spectacles, so to speak.[66] One lens represents his understanding of conversion.[67] Here we often see Paul talking about the many theological realities that one receives when expressing faith in Christ. And coupled with this is the other lens that entails Paul's beliefs about the church's ultimate hope, the day of resurrection when Christ returns to judge his enemies and vindicate his people. Together, these two emphases form the grid through which he writes about the importance of spiritual endurance. Because a believer has experienced

---

66. Admittedly, we would argue that these spectacles could be categorized in terms of inaugurated eschatology, one lens being the past and the other being the future. Paul interprets a believer's present status in light of the past event of Christ's death and resurrection as well as the future reality of the new creation that is certain because of what Christ achieved. So his moral admonitions are grounded in the historical landmark of the Christ events of the past and the bless hope to come. As Anthony Hoekema has succinctly surmised, "The believer . . . , is already in the eschatological era spoken of by the OT prophets, but he is not in the final state." Hoekema, *The Bible and the Future*, 68. Thus, believers' lives are now to be a visible precursor, no matter how flawed they may be, of the future before it arrives in its glorious fullness. Also, I have written elsewhere about the importance of inaugurated eschatology and its importance to the overall doctrine of sanctification in "How Can the Theological Construct," 109–11.

67. One can interrelate his teachings on repentance, faith, and justification in this category as well.

the resurrection power of the Spirit when they came to faith in Christ (Rom 8) and they are promised to receive a new body empowered by the Spirit (1 Cor 15) when all things are made new, Paul thought one undeniable implication of such events was that a believer is enabled by the Spirit to persevere in faith until death or Christ's return, which ever came first. *Furthermore, he does not see this imperative as in any way compromising his view of justification because a believer's ability to persevere is as much a divine work of grace as repentance or faith.*

Another way to summarize this point would be to say that Paul looked at salvation in terms of an already / not yet tension. Believers *have already* received an initial foretaste of the glorious age to come that Christ inaugurated via his resurrection.[68] They have forgiveness of sin, the indwelling Spirit, and eternal life. Yet the full realization of Christ's triumph over death *has not been realized*. While believers experience the power of Christ in the present, they still wrestle with sin and temptation until the final day of redemption. And it is this tension between a believer's new identity as a citizen of Christ's heavenly kingdom and their struggling condition with sin that creates the backdrop for the importance of perseverance. *A believer's faith in Christ, which is initiated by the work of the Spirit, is something that is shown to be genuine not by its perfection, but by its endurance.* This does not mean believers cannot fall into deep sin or embrace bad ideas doctrinally. Indeed, Paul on occasion had to address such situations, as we have seen. Sometimes the situations were so dire that Paul had to intervene, or he occasionally instructed churches to hold believers accountable, and in other instances, the Lord himself enacted severe discipline. But even in these circumstances, Paul was always quick to remind his readers that if they were who they claimed to be, then they must repent, embrace sound doctrine, and finish their race of faith.

Still, the question remains as to whether Paul thought a believer could fall short of obtaining the final inheritance in the age to come. We would begin by saying Paul clearly believed the only faith that will receive vindication at Christ's return is one that endures. Again, this does not mean believers must maintain perfect obedience or walk the straight and narrow without fail. Rather, Paul himself as well as those to whom he ministered were to struggle well and direct their faith toward Christ. They had been given the Spirit not only in conversion and as a firstfruit promise pointing to the power of resurrection. They had also been empowered to finish their

---

68. This reality is expressed in believers both individually and corporately. All have received the same Spirit that raised Christ from the dead and now that same Spirit indwells each one as well as each local body expressed in distinct congregations. Cf. Paul's comments in Rom 8:11; 1 Cor 3:9; 6:19; 2 Cor 6:16.

life of faith whether it may end prematurely in divine discipline, in death to meet Christ in the intermediate state, or to be resurrected at his return. Consequently, it is not cliché to say Paul believed true faith that leads to salvation is one that endures, not one that starts well but ends in disbelief or apostate conduct. Faith that justifies a sinner legally before God's divine court is a faith that is proven to endure when it is audited eschatologically at the final judgment.

Chapter 4

Perseverance in Acts, the General Epistles, and Revelation

OUR TOUR THROUGH BIBLICAL texts that touch upon the doctrine of perseverance finally comes to a close with this chapter. Thus far, we have surveyed ways in which it emerges in portions of the Old Testament, the teachings of Christ, and the writings of Paul. Now we want to engage the remaining parts of the New Testament, including the book of Acts, the General Epistles (i.e., Hebrews, James, 1 & 2 Peter, Jude, 1–3 John), and Revelation. We shall see that these writings give significant attention to points of emphasis that have been raised already. The authors fluctuate between concerns about being deceived by false teachers, apostatizing in the face of persecution, and the peril of moral collapse. But there are also new wrinkles that appear as well. While authors such as Luke, James, Jude, John, and Peter, do sometimes appeal to similar concepts or common problems that Jesus and Paul engaged, there are some added situations where they provide new layers of perspective and offer nuances that need explanation. What we discover is that while their perceptions of why and how believers should persevere do not contradict the sources we have covered, they do offer further insights that compliment them.

1. PERSEVERANCE IN ACTS

We begin with the book of Acts, a second volume in Luke's work to Theophilus (cf. Luke 1:3; Acts 1:1) that picks up where his gospel ends with the ascension of Christ. It chronicles one of the most significant transitions in redemptive history, that being the establishment of the new-covenant community known as the church. This shift meant that the people of God were now being expanded to include both Jews as well as Gentiles on a grander scale.[1] Such a change meant that many questions required serious attention. For one, how were believing Jews supposed to understand their previous commitments to the law of Moses in light of their new confession that Christ was Israel's Messiah. Not only that, how should Gentiles who believed in Christ relate to this movement that was, in a sense, a newly revised Jewish religion. These were the kinds of questions that set the stage for much of the early deliberations in the early church.[2] But amid the growing pains that came with such concerns were also instances where the Lord enacted judgment on wayward believers and the dangers of apostasy had to be addressed.

There are two cases where we see divine discipline being enacted upon people within the ranks of the church who acted disobediently. One involved a married couple, Ananias and Sapphira, who chose to participate in a surge of generosity that was sweeping through the church in Jerusalem (Acts 5:1-11). Many members were freely liquidating assets, if you will, so the apostles could use the proceeds to take care of the needs of others who were struggling. They wanted to be part of the effort not because of their concern for the poor but simply so they could be perceived as benevolent.

---

1. This has proven to be controversial over the centuries because some biblical interpreters have had a tendency to use it as a means of supporting various forms of supersessionism (i.e., the idea that the new-covenant church replaces national Israel in the unfolding of redemptive history), or worse, anti-Semitic sentiments. See survey of these ordeals in Hedrick, "Fewer Answers and Further Questions," 294–305; Tannehill "Israel in Luke-Acts," 69–85; and Soulen, *God of Israel*, 168–74.

2. As Dum states, "The relation of Christianity to Judaism is at the heart of Christianity." Dunn, *Neither Jew Nor Greek*, 12. The reason this is the case is because the OT writings, the core of Jewish identity with all of its covenantal expectations, messianic hopes, and legal prescriptions, found their culmination in the ministry and work of Christ. And because the early church was predominately Jewish at the outset, it was only natural that questions about torah compliance would arise once many Gentiles began to believe in Christ with little or no familiarity with the Jewish roots of the gospel message. Because of the discussions prompted by these questions, the book of Acts reciprocates back and forth between how the spread of the gospel impacted both groups. Even the end of Acts focuses upon how the message of Christ would potentially continue to spread to more audiences. See Palmer, "Mission to Jews and Gentiles," 62–73.

Their strategy was to sell a piece of property and only give part of the revenue, hoping everyone would think they offered all of it. The plan failed when Ananias offered the gift because Peter was privy to his deception. He immediately confronted Ananias for intentionally withholding part of the profits that he had accrued, charging him with being used by Satan himself, which is a similar accusation that Jesus had made against Judas.[3] Then his wife was indicted shortly afterward for putting the Spirit to the test. We read that the Lord struck them dead, which in turn, sparked fear in the hearts of the people.

Such an account leaves us with a host of questions, especially as to whether this couple were believers who were severely disciplined, believers who were judged as apostates, or unbelievers who showed their true colors through their deception. This is difficult to discern because the text makes no explicit claims one way or the other. We know they were part of the church fellowship, which would lead us to think they had at least expressed faith in Christ and been baptized. Beyond this, however, we can only speculate. The satanic influence is not conclusive because this happened to Judas, who was not a believer, and Peter as well, who obviously was a genuine follower of Christ. Possibly the safest deduction is to see this story as a prelude to the later instructions on church discipline that Paul would put in place later in response to the Corinthian congregation that was abusing the Lord's supper.[4]

Another account is given later regarding a man named Simon Magus (Acts 8:4–24). As the church spread to other regions when a persecution broke out in Jerusalem, a believer introduced earlier in Acts named Philip visited the city of Samaria. He began preaching the gospel, casting out unclean spirits, and healing various ailments just as Jesus and some of the apostles had done. These activities sparked tremendous interest from the people. So much so that some believed in Christ, including a former sorcerer named Simon. He, along with these other Samaritans, were convinced that the authority of Christ's kingdom, as seen in the miracles that Philip performed, was greater than any mysticism or cheap tricks. Eventually after these events, a report was sent to the Jerusalem church about the Samaritan reception of the gospel. And it was decided that Peter and John should visit to lay hands on these new believers so they could receive the

---

3. McCabe, *How to Kill Things with Words*, 200–17. Also, how the ancient context of oath keeping and vow breaking helps color the context of this account is discussed quite well in Harrill, "Divine Judgment against Ananias and Sapphira," 351–69.

4. Readers can also be reminded of Uzzah's sudden death for inadvertent disobedience (2 Sam 6:6–7) or the immediate incineration of Aaron's two sons Nadab and Abihu because of their carelessness in fulfilling their priestly duties (Lev 10:1–2).

Spirit. Upon their arrival, they prayed over the Samaritan brethren and they were empowered by the same Spirit that the Jewish believers had received at Pentecost.

Afterward, this miracle impressed Simon in an adverse way. He asked Peter if he could buy this kind of power.[5] Peter quickly rebuked him for such a request, saying that he needed to repent immediately in hopes that he could be forgiven. Simon responded with a seemingly penitent attitude by asking Peter to intercede for his reconciliation. Like the previous story, we are prone to ask whether Simon was a genuine believer or not. It is reasonable to think that perhaps he was a brand new follower of Christ who was falling prey to a form of syncretism wherein he wrongfully thought his former way of looking at the world through the lenses of power and money could somehow converge with the power of God.[6] This is probably a viable option since Simon immediately shows remorse when Peter confronts his misguided request. At the same time, there is still tension because if he chose not to repent, it is difficult to avoid concluding that either he would have experienced some immediate discipline from the Lord or perhaps even be in danger of being indicted with the rest of the unbelieving world.

Beyond these accounts where individuals faced immediate confrontations because of their actions, the rest of the book of Acts focuses more upon members of the early church who were willing to endure in their faith even if it meant becoming a martyr, as we see in the cases of James and Stephen.[7] The reason for this is because Acts describes the gradual surge of opposition that many unbelieving Jews and pagan Gentiles expressed toward the spread of the gospel message. This clash, again, jump-started in Jerusalem because of tensions primarily between the apostles who preached in the name of Jesus and antagonistic Jewish authorities, only to later intensify with the

---

5. While certainly not justified, such an attitude by a "possible" new convert would be understandable since magic and sorcery had been such an ingrained part of his life. In fact, magic, divination, and a fixation with mystic activity permeated much of the ancient world, the Roman Empire being no exception. Cf. Yamauchi, "Magic in the Biblical World," 169–200; Ferguson, *Religions of the Roman Empire*, 157–58; and Aune, *Apocalypticism, Prophecy, and Magic*, 369–420.

6. Larkin, *Acts*, 129. Also, offering payment for religious functions was typically something that Gentiles would engage in, perhaps to attain cultic favors or purchase magical secrets. Cf. Bock, *Acts*, 333; Derrett, "Simon Magus," 52–68. Such an unthinkable act made quite an impression on Christian thought, so much so that the word "simony" (named after Simon) eventually was coined for describing the unlawful practice of selling church offices or positions. Likewise, this initial scene in Acts became an important feature in Christian thought, art, and the overall telling of the early church's story. See a fascinating survey by Ferreiro, *Simon Magus*.

7. Oropeza rightly highlights this in Acts and gives further details in Oropeza, *In the Footsteps of Judas*, 133–34.

aid of Saul (or Paul) of Tarsus before his conversion. After he had his Damascus Road experience, we then see a consistent pattern in his missionary journeys. There were always those who believed the gospel message that he preached while many others passively rejected, some mocked, aggressively resisted, and at times outright attacked him and/or his new converts.

This is why Paul came to warn new believers that their endurance in the faith was crucial because the path that led to Christ's kingdom would entail hardships, or tribulations (Acts 14:22).[8] Like Paul, they should expect them if they are going to follow Christ faithfully. Paul also warns that another set of difficulties could potentially blindside the church. Believers might be anticipating opposition from unbelievers when the gospel began to take spiritual ground in the Roman empire. Yet what would happen if resistance came from leaders in churches. We see that Paul mentions this reality just before he left Ephesus to visit Jerusalem. Before his departure, he met with the elders of the Ephesian church and echoed the words of Jesus himself from the Olivet Discourse, which we discussed earlier. He spoke of false teachers who would deceive many and in similar fashion, Paul warns the Ephesian elders that savage wolves would come into their flock in attempts to lead as many astray as possible. He reminds them that one of the reasons he stayed with them for so long was so he could prepare them for any future influences that could potentially dupe them into false doctrine (Acts 20:28–32).[9] What we see then is that Acts alludes to the importance of perseverance in the face of persecution and false teaching as well as the possibility that believers who sin brashly can face severe discipline in their lifetimes.

---

8. Some argue that the use of the term "tribulation" (Grk. *thlipsis*) is sometimes used not only to describe everyday persecution against followers of Christ. It can carry eschatological overtones as well. The sufferings, or tribulations, that believers face in the present age are indicative of the events that will immediately precede the full arrival of the age to come. In other words, the unjust suffering that believers endure now reflects the same kind of hatred that Jesus himself faced and such ordeals will continue until the kingdom of God comes in its fulness. Cf. Mattill, "Way of Tribulation," 531–46; Pitre, *Jesus, the Tribulation, and the End of Exile*, 1–9, 509–14.

9. This goes hand in hand with Jesus' warnings against false Christs who will deceive many, except for the elect, and Paul's comments elsewhere regarding false teachers (e.g., 1 Tim 1:3; 2 Tim 1:15). In addition, Paul's connection between the overseers responsibility to protect the Ephesian flock from the predatorial false teachers fits perfectly with his admonitions to Timothy to guard his own ministry so he can feed the people and help them reach the final culmination of their faith (1 Tim 4:16). These admonitions proved to be timely because by the end of the second century, Asia had become a seedbed for Christian heresy. See Polhill, *Acts*, 428.

2. PERSEVERANCE IN HEBREWS

The attention given to apostasy in Acts is clearly exceeded in the Epistle to the Hebrews. This letter, in fact, stands as one of the most controversial in all the New Testament because it raises a host of questions about the relationship between perseverance and final salvation.[10] These concerns emerge primarily because of several explicit warnings (five to be exact) that the author directs at his audience.[11] These passages have become exegetical land mines over the centuries for several reasons. One is the long-standing impasse between Reformed and Arminian interpretations of these texts. Reformed readers typically argue that Hebrews must be read in light of other NT teachings on the nature of election, justification, and glorification. Since all those who are called unto salvation are also justified and guaranteed to be glorified, the warnings in Hebrews must be either hypothetical in some way or be a means of weeding out those who are not really regenerate.[12] Arminian proponents are quick to counter that the warnings in Hebrews are actually congruent with many other instances in the NT that clearly allow for the genuine possibility of believers apostatizing.[13] So they argue that Calvinist readings not only misrepresent the warnings of Hebrews. They also must explain away other NT cautions against apostasy as well. Added to this polarization is the fact that there are larger questions regarding the letter that also have fostered robust debates. The author of the book is essentially unknown, the audience is not specifically identified, and many details surrounding the reason(s) for letter are relegated to the inaccessible archives of history.[14] Thus, any interpretation of Hebrews as a whole is always based on an assortment of disputed proposals that attempt to fill in the historical gaps regarding the background of the letter itself.

10. Without getting distracted by questions of authorship, the canonization of Hebrews ultimately was sealed because it was finally included within the Pauline corpus. See discussion by Ellingworth, *Commentary on Hebrews*, 34–36.

11. Though there is some scholarly squabbling over the details, the passages generally include 2:1–4; 3:7–4:13; 5:11–6:12; 10:19–39; and 12:25–29.

12. For overviews of the competing views of these passages, cf. McKnight, "Warning Passages of Hebrews," 21–59; Oropeza, "Warning Passages in Hebrews," 81–100; and Thomas, *Case for Mixed-Audience*, 25–96.

13. Dale Moody argues that understanding the warning passages in Hebrews is a good prerequisite to understanding other warnings in other parts of the NT. See Moody, *Word of Truth*, 352. Also see Ashby's use of Moody in his treatment of "Reformed Arminian View," 171.

14. Here Herbert W. Bateman IV in his introduction to Hebrews is on target in summarizing the frustration when he quotes Philip Hughes, who said, "Its author unknown, its occasion unstated, and its destination disputed." Cf. Bateman, "Introducing the Warning Passage," 24; Hughes, *Commentary on the Epistle to the Hebrews*, 1.

That being said, at bare minimum the author was most likely writing either to a group of Jewish believers, some former Gentile proselytes, or a possible mixture of both.[15] Whoever they were, some in the group were apparently on the precipice of renouncing their faith in Christ and lapsing back into some previously held form of Judaism.[16] These believers had suffered a significant level of persecution to the point that some had been publicly ostracized, others had their properties confiscated, and several had perhaps even been put in prison (cf. Heb 10:32–34; 13:3, 23). Such external pressures were taking their toll on these believers because some had begun to stall in their spiritual growth and become lax in their interaction with fellow believers in their representative congregations (cf. Heb 5:11–12; 10:25). These problems were nothing unique in the first century. And the author of Hebrews (AOH) was well aware that such symptoms could be precursors to abandoning one's faith if the situation was not put in check. This is why the AOH presses these believers to consider the repercussions of such a lapse in judgment. Likewise, he wants to encourage them amid their hardships by reminding them of what they have in Christ as well as what awaits them in the age to come.

The book's strategy for accomplishing this goal is to describe how Christ and the new covenant that he has ratified are superior to the former era of provisions in the Mosaic economy. Hence the periodic warnings to not turn back to Judaism because it is now a system that offers no hope. The AOH makes his case by first discussing the exalted status of Christ over all the angels since they were highly regarded in Judaism because of their function as God's emissaries. This leads to the first warning passage in which the author says that if one perished on the basis of ignoring an angel's message, how much more disastrous would it be to neglect the salvation that Christ now provides (Heb 2:1–4).[17]

---

15. Some argue that the audience was possibly a group that were on the verge of leaving Judaism and embracing the gospel message, but were on the fence at the moment, see, e.g., Hill, "Use of Perfection Language," 727–42.

16. Again, there are numerous proposals on who the audience is exactly and the situation(s) that precipitated the need for the letter itself. Any good commentary will provide the reader with insightful overviews on these matters. One helpful place to start is with Bateman, *Four Views of the Book of Hebrews*. The main reason most concede that the audience had some sort of Jewish element is because of the constant emphasis on Jewish rites and traditions. For technical discussions about OT and other Jewish backgrounds pertinent to Hebrews, see Hurst, *Epistle to the Hebrews*; Docherty, *Use of the Old Testament in Hebrews*; and Walser, *OT Quotations in Hebrews*.

17. The OT recounts several occasions where angels were sent to bring divine judgment upon Israel's enemies and, obviously, resistance was futile. So if ancient powerhouse nations could be defeated by the heavenly hosts at the Lord's bidding, how much more extreme will eschatological judgment be upon those who turn away from the one

From here, the AOH returns to the discussion about how Christ is above the angels and then mentions that he became a human being so he might serve as a qualified high priest who identifies with his people. In so doing, Christ proved himself to be better than Moses because of the greater household that he establishes. Such a comparison leads to the second longer warning in Heb 3:7—4:13 where the author uses the OT narrative of Israel's initial failure to enter the promised land as an illustration of what could happen to his audience if they should turn from Christ. Just as the majority of the exodus-generation Israelites failed to enter the promised land because of unbelief (clearly Moses' restriction was for a different reason), the AOH makes the parallel that some of his audience could fail to enter the eschatological Sabbath rest if they do not remain steadfast in their faith.[18] To encourage them in hopes of avoiding such a tragedy, the author returns to his description of Christ's role as a priest who identifies with them in their suffering. Subsequently, he pauses his discussion because he knows he cannot provide too many more details. His readers had become stunted in their spiritual growth. This results in a short rebuke because they should already have reached a point where they can be exposed to more fruitful content. Instead, they are in need of being reminded of the fundamentals. Their condition leads the author to confront them with the third and most perplexing warning in the book, which spans Heb 5:11—6:12.[19] Here the readers are

---

who has all authority over the angelic hosts? Note as well that however one chooses to read this kind of language, it cannot be legitimately interpreted to allude to believers losing rewards because the contrast is between degrees of destruction (angels bringing judgment vs. the Son), not levels of possible commendation.

18. Some disagree with this reading because they think it implies that these Israelites possibly "missed heaven" because of their lapse at Kadesh-Barnea. See, e.g., Allen, *Hebrews*, 292–93. But the eternal destination of the ancient Israelites is not the concern of the AOH. His focus is upon the condition of his readers. The implicit logic being used is a parallel between the OT recounting of the failure to enter the physical land of Canaan and the potential for some in the AOH's audience to fall short of their eschatological inheritance because of the same kind of unbelief. Just as the Israelites who were initially delivered in the exodus still had to faithfully endure so they could eventually enter the promised land, so would all within the sound of the AOH have to remain steadfast in their faith if they expected to enter the rest of the new creation. See Thomas, *Case for Mixed-Audience*, 221–22. Said another way, as opposed to being tempted to mimic the unfaithfulness of the wilderness generation, the AOH admonishes his readers to follow Christ's example who faced his temptations and emerged victorious (Heb 4:14–17). The point then is that the AOH is speaking of salvation as a future inheritance that is received after perseverance, not just a forensic event that is declared in God's court via the act of justification.

19. Scholars acknowledge close to twenty different interpretations of this passage. Wilson concedes that there are at least eighteen while Sauer identifies fifteen distinct proposals and Eaton claims there are sixteen. Cf. Wilson, "Hebrews 3:6B and

warned that even though they have been exposed to numerous benefits of the age to come via the Lord's message (i.e., word of God) and the ministry of the Spirit, there will be no means of returning to Christ if they fall away because no other means of salvation will be provided.[20] They will face the consequences of their sin without a mediator. It should be noted that again just like Jesus and Paul, what we see here is yet another example of a NT speaker who thinks that any kind of faith that turns away from the Lord is not the kind that leads to salvation.[21] Only a faith that does not drift away is one that leads to inheriting the eschatological "rest" of the age to come.

The letter then transitions back to a discussion about Christ as a gracious high priest who serves as a kingly priest like the ancient character known as Melchizedek. This parallel allows the author to argue that Christ culminates the hopes of Judaism by offering the salvific benefits of the new covenant. The basis of these provisions is his vicarious death and if anyone chooses to repudiate this sacrifice, their inevitable end will be eschatological judgment. This is the gist of the fourth warning found in Heb 10:19–39. The author argues that only those who hold fast to their confession and faithfully endure the reproach of Christ will inherit the promises that the coming kingdom extends.[22] This charge is then illustrated by discussing examples of such faithfulness. The great characters of the OT collectively serve as a cloud of witnesses along with Christ himself in awaiting the completion of every saints' race of faith. Finally, this exhortation leads to the last warning found in Heb 12:14–29 where the author reminds the readers that they must not neglect the Lord's promises because if Israel was judged when they ignored divine mandates in Moses' day, what will be their end if they now turn from Christ.[23]

3:14 Revisited," 248; Sauer, "Critical and Exegetical Re-examination"; and Eaton, *No Condemnation*.

20. The language that the AOH uses in 6:4–5 to describe certain ones in his audience who might turn away reflects the same point that Jesus makes in the parable of the sower where the seed, or word/message, of the kingdom comes to some who "believe" for a while. This is confirmed in 6:7–8 where the AOH compares two soils, one that provides vegetation and the other that only provides thorns and thistles. This accords with Jesus' other point that while some believe for an indefinite period, others believe to the point of producing various levels of fruit. See Thomas, *Case for a Mixed-Audience*, 253.

21. As the AOH says in 3:6b and 3:14, we (including himself) are part of God's household and partners with Christ "if" they stay steadfast to the end.

22. Moving past the contrast between the lethal power of angels and the greater authority that Christ will one day exhibit, the AOH goes further by stating that if people previously rejected the law of Moses in certain ways that warranted the death penalty, what greater consequence awaits those who abandon the community that is based on the covenant ratified by Christ and applied by the Spirit. Again, this is judgment language in sobering form.

23. In this passage, the eschatological nature of what is at stake is clear. What the

Now even though there no way to resolve the endless debates over what these warnings in Hebrews mean to every Christian tradition's satisfaction, several observations still deserve mentioning. First, we contend that the audience is being addressed as if it is a mixed community—this is to say there are those who are enduring well versus others who are possibly on the cusp of renouncing Christ. And like other instances in the NT, the AOH is unsure as to what the latter group's decision will be.[24] What is intriguing to note at this point is that the author includes himself in the warnings that he gives to his audience. He sees himself as a mutual follower of Christ and still, he believes that he, along with his readers, must persevere if they expect any inheritance in the kingdom age to come. So the question surfacing throughout the letter is which group the readers want to be part of, the one that leads to final eschatological salvation or the one that ends in judgment.

Second, the final inheritance, completeness, or eternal destination as described throughout the letter can be missed by those in the audience who choose to defect.[25] Though the AOH is certain that those who maintain their faith in Christ will be reach the final goal of salvation, he is not privy to which individuals in his reading audience are being tempted to defect. So this helps create the literary tension that pervades all warnings within the book.

Third, the alternative to not attaining this goal is eternal judgment, not simply a loss of rewards. The language that the author uses is far too severe and explicit to mean forfeiting some desired rank in heaven. He claims that

---

audience of Hebrews chooses to do with the AOH's warnings will set the tone for how they face God on the last day. Cf. Thomas, *Case for Mixed-Audience*, 267; Peterson, *Hebrews and Perfection*, 160; and Toussaint, "Eschatology of the Warning Passages," 67–80.

24. More interpreters are conceding that the audience of Hebrew is made up entirely of genuine believers. See Allen's summary here in *Hebrews*, 357–59. Interestingly enough, some Calvinists are taking this route, like Schreiner and Caneday, who argue that the warnings in Hebrews are to believers so that they can serve as the divine means of enabling them to persevere. This means the warnings against apostasy are describing perceivable stakes, not because they want to foster uncertainty about the future. Rather they are like road signs that caution against conceivable consequences, not probable ones. *Race Set Before Us*, 207–8. However, the problem with this argument is that it renders the warnings as merely hypothetical. The warnings to avoid apostasy here and elsewhere in the NT are given because people were either on the verge of defecting and/or some had already. Or put another way in response to Schreiner's and Caneday's analogy, road signs are posted not because of potential hazards, but to prevent certain disasters that can and do in fact happen. See Thomas, *Case for Mixed-Audience*, 81–82.

25. This is why some interpreters who find Reformed and Arminian interpretations unsatisfactory opt for a loss of rewards or eternal inheritance view. Salvation cannot be lost but rank in the future kingdom can. Cf. Eaton, *No Condemnation*, 214–17; Kendell, *Once Saved, Always Saved*, 175–82; and Oberholtzer, "Warning Passages," 319–28.

there remains no sacrifice for sins and that only destruction awaits those who turn back.[26]

Fourth, the author views any such act of apostasy as a no-turning-back decision for which there is no remedy. In his own words, it is impossible to renew such a one to repentance. Now altogether, trying to answer the questions that these warnings elicit puts interpreters in a bind. Often one is forced to make the warnings say things that they were not intended to mean in order to make them harmonize with what one thinks about other passages that affirm the security of the believer. Or others sometimes interpret other NT passages that emphasize the permanency of salvation in ways that coincide with the assumption that Hebrews teaches a contrary idea.

The dilemma is in trying to let these texts express their individual parts while at the same time discovering their harmony with the rest of Scripture.[27] What can be said at this point is that Hebrews expects believers who have saving faith to endure external pressures and persecution just as Jesus and OT saints did so they can inherit the unseen realm that will one day become seen. Therefore, the fifth and final point we would emphasize is that the AOH only thinks the faith of his readers is saving if it perseveres. The "salvation" that is already theirs because of their confession (cf. Heb 3:6, 14) is only a reality if they believe in Christ to their deaths just as previous saints have done before them.

3. PERSEVERANCE IN JAMES AND JUDE

Two other letters that offer important insights into the idea of perseverance come from two half-brothers of Jesus, James and Jude. James stands out a bit more in NT history because he was not only part of Jesus' natural family. The book of Acts tells that he was an important spokesperson in the early Jerusalem church.[28] In the letter that bears his name, James says he is writing to

---

26. Though his conclusion is disputable regarding the possibility of genuine believers being able to apostatize, McAffee does make a strong case that much of the wording used in the warning passages reflects the blessing and cursing language that was indicative of the Mosaic code. The conclusion being that defectors (again their specific identity being debatable) can be excluded from the community. And in the case of Hebrews, being set outside the new-covenant community results in eschatological judgment with the world, not a mere demotion in the coming kingdom. See McAffee, "Covenant and the Warnings of Hebrews," 537–53.

27. Fanning is refreshingly candid about this struggle when he says that "every interpreter must adjust the straightforward reading of one of the elements from these warnings." See "Classical Reformed View," 218.

28. The name James occurs forty-two times in the NT and we discover that there are at least four men with this name—James the brother of John who was one of the twelve,

the twelve tribes who were dispersed throughout the Roman world. This is most likely an allusion to what one might call messianic congregations that were struggling throughout the various regions of the empire.[29] The epistle provides instruction on how to exhibit wisdom and character in everyday situations. This is why it is often so beloved by modern readers. James uses a plainspoken style and addresses extremely practical topics. One factor, in particular, that James speaks to quite a bit is the importance of successfully enduring trials because of the character they can instill.[30] He goes as far as to say that believers should consider them as joyous occasions not because of the suffering or discomfort they bring. Rather believers should see them as the means of developing spiritual maturity (Jas 1:2–4). Not only that, James later observes that perseverance has an eschatological component as well. He argues that enduring hardship is indicative of every disciple because, like Job and the prophets, the Lord vindicates those who patiently wait for his justice.[31] And for James' audience, this would happen at the coming of the Lord (cf. Jas 1:12; 5:7).

A natural question that arises from this discussion is whether James sees failure to endure trials as necessarily resulting in apostasy or maybe just temporal divine discipline. This is difficult to ascertain but it is clear he

---

James the half-brother of Jesus, James the son of Alphaeus, and the father of Judas (not Iscariot). Several circumstances have been used over the centuries to deduce that Jesus' half-brother James is the author. But this traditional view has been seriously questioned over the last two centuries. For discussions of these matters, see Moo, *James*, 9–22; Martin, *James*, xxxi–lxxvii; 1–7; Johnson, *Letter of James*, 3–164; and Stevens, "Does Neglect Mean Rejection," 767–80.

29. Some in critical scholarship see such an introduction as dubious, see assessment in Llewelyn, "Prescript in James," 385–93. Nevertheless, the language of the "twelve tribes" is an occasional phrase in the NT that refers to the Jewish people, or Israel in a corporate sense (cf. Matt 19:28; Luke 22:30; also Rev 7:5–8; 21:12 use the phrase but its exact referent is disputed because of its apocalyptic overtones). Also, for James to refer to the tribes scattered, or dispersed, is to highlight that they are not where they belong. Just as ethnic Jews had been dispersed throughout the Roman Empire and did not live in the land of promise any longer, now James evidently is applying the idea to Jewish followers of Jesus to say that they are dispersed among the nations. See Moo, *James*, 49–50; Blomberg and Kamell, *James*, 28–29. Now they were awaiting the final eschatological ingathering of God's people.

30. It is interesting that James and Peter are the two NT authors who write to believers scattered throughout different regions. Both have much to say about the importance of endurance and how it is the only means whereby faith concludes with eschatological salvation. See Kovalishyn, "Endurance unto Salvation," 231–40.

31. Similarly, just as Job desired the Lord's vindication, so did Israel yearn for her deliverance from "dispersion" in the exile because of their covenantal infidelity. In both cases, Job awaited the Lord's response and Israel endured a seventy-year captivity before traveling back to Canaan. Likewise, now the Jewish believers needed to exhibit patience in enduring their trials because their faith would be rewarded.

does treat the subject with a serious tone. He argues that trials can either be opportunities to grow or sin since they can simultaneously be tests from the Lord and temptations from the devil (Jas 1:12–13). Likewise, he speaks about how sin leads to death, which could be interpreted as referring to either practical or perhaps eschatological consequences.[32] It is, again, a challenge to decipher the exact end to which this kind of sin can lead. In either case, James makes it clear that unchecked sin or failure to endure trials can create a competitive allegiance in one's heart between the world and the Lord. This can ultimately lead one down a path that gradually makes one an enemy of God and if any believer helps another avoid such a temptation, they have helped rescue them from a plight that possibly teetered on the edge of apostasy (Jas 5:19–20).[33]

It is in light of such dangers that James also addresses how important it is that believers use their speech to build one another up instead of breeding conflict. The external pressures of persecution and sin's inward pull are enough to withstand without having to endure the evil lashing of a fellow believer's tongue. Joined with these admonitions are James' related correctives about favoritism. He instructs his readers on the matter of riches and power by telling them that they should never exonerate anyone in their midst simply because of their economic or social status while shamefully discarding those who are poor because they may be unappealing. Such antics are what the unbelieving world does. Moreover, James' treatment of these matters are simply an outflow of his view of works and faith. He contends that one's faith is seen not merely in affirming a proposition such as "there is a God." Instead, it is seen as trusting in God's promises to such an extent that it results in actions like feeding a brother who is in need. And if one's faith does not result in such an outcome, it may be many things but it is not saving (Jas 2:14–26). Or said more emphatically, James argues that one is justified by works and not faith alone (Jas 2:24), meaning that saving faith shows itself to be alive by exhibiting action.[34]

---

32. The idea of death here is connected to a matrix of allusions. One is reminded of what happened to Adam and Eve. When they disobeyed God, they died, or began the long painful process of dying. Additionally, James' words have overtones of wisdom literature that speak of being lured into temptation thinking that one will indulge in pleasure only to discover that it takes one's very life. Moo, *James*, 76.

33. The language here does possibly allude to the danger of apostasy, see discussions in Martin, *James*, 218; Davids, *James*, 125–26; McCartney, *James*, 263–64.

34. The historical archives of hermeneutical debates over how to reconcile this claim with Paul's polemics on justification are well known. The discussions' most volatile impasse initially emerged during the Reformation via the Protestant divide with traditional Roman Catholic ideas of sacramentalism. Then later the discussions took on new layers of complexity when post-Enlightenment critical scholarship posed various theories that

We find a bit of contrast with the letter provided by James' brother Jude. As opposed to James, who does speak about restoring those who may fall into sinful conduct, Jude focuses upon the matter of resisting the allure of spiritual cons, or apostate leaders. He writes to an undesignated group of believers, or churches, who were probably Jewish for the most part. Many scholars think as much because of Jude's constant appeal to OT narratives and traditions.[35] He pleads with them as God's beloved ones to fight for the deposit of truth that has been placed in their care (Jude 1b-3). They must always recall the words they have received from Christ's apostles and be true to them by building each other up, remaining steadfast in prayer, and being willing to confront others who may go astray (Jude 17, 22-23). The main reason for these admonitions was that apparently some false teachers had made a good impression with some of these believers. They used flattering speech and were gradually allowed to attend the churches' communal meals, or love feasts, with the concealed purpose of exploiting undiscerning believers (cf. Jude 4, 12, 16).

Jude has no shortage of referents to describe these individuals, including ungodly intruders, those marked out for condemnation from of old, deniers of Christ, defilers of the flesh, and rejecters of authority. He says that these teachers are like the Israelites who refused to enter the promised land because they lacked faith. They are like defiant fallen angels because they indulge in shameful acts and are not like the holy angels, such as Michael, because they respect no authority, thinking that they answer to no one. They are reckless like Cain, self-deceived like Balaam, and defiant like Korah.[36]

---

disallowed any real harmony between the authors. And in recent decades, the issues are even more complex because of the famous New Perspective critique on previous Protestant readings of Paul. Cf. discussions by Laato, "Justification according to James," 43–84; Popkes, "Two Interpretations," 129–46. We would argue that Paul speaks about how sinners, whether they be Jew or Gentile, can receive a right standing before God without the law because of the new-covenant work of Christ. It is by faith without efforts to stay faithful to the Mosaic economy (or by works). The works that "merit" salvation are those committed by Jesus, not his people. James' point, on the other hand, is that a faith that saves is not merely cheap talk or mere affirmation of certain realities. It is a trust that performs action. This means his point aligns with Paul because a faith's work does not accrue merit. Rather it is that the only way to know if faith "has breath" is if it exudes signs of life, or namely works. So before God's tribunal, Paul argues that faith without works (or earned merit) justifies while James quickly qualifies that faith is not alive or saving unless it is animated by obedience.

35. Cf., e.g., Schreiner, *1, 2 Peter and Jude*, 410; Eybers, "Background of the Letter of Jude," 114; Wolthuis, "Jude and Jewish Traditions," 21–41; and Dunnett, "Hermeneutics of Jude and 2 Peter," 287–92.

36. Just as divine judgment fell upon each of these characters in a variety of ways, Jude combines them to form a prophetic woe oracle against the false teachers that were troubling these churches. Bauckham, *Jude, 2 Peter*, 91–92.

Because of their lack of character, their words may be eloquent, but they can never deliver because they are empty like clouds without rain or trees without fruit. And at the end of day, even the ancient character Enoch predicted their end when he said that the Lord will come with his holy ones to judge the ungodly (Jude 14–15). Whether these teachers were former professing believers who defected or had always been promoting their deceitful doctrines is uncertain when reading this letter in and of itself. Yet two truths are clear in Jude's mind. One is that if these teachers repented, they could be forgiven. The other is that anyone who followed their teachings indefinitely would be judged as an unbeliever along with the false teachers themselves.

4. PERSEVERANCE IN THE LETTERS OF PETER

Another set of epistles that contribute to our understanding of perseverance are those written by the Apostle Peter.[37] The first letter was sent to believers who Peter describes as aliens, or foreign sojourners, scattered throughout regions of Asia Minor.[38] They are depicted this way not so much for their cultural status even though most of them were probably at the lower end of the social pecking order. They were outsiders because they were displaced as believers in Christ who lived in a pagan empire that was devoid of godliness or concern for any kingdom except its own.[39] This kind of climate can often breed persecution, which was exactly what these believers were experiencing, thereby giving warrant for Peter to provide this letter. Some were being falsely accused as evil doers, others possibly enduring physical harm, and all of them were socially ostracized in one way or another (cf. 1 Pet 2:12; 3:13–14; 4:16). Peter says that none of these matters are reasons for discouragement because if they were suffering for righteousness' sake as opposed to sinful conduct, then they were following the very road that Jesus trail blazed himself (1 Pet 2:21–22). Furthermore, the intensity of their hardships could actually be used by God to purify their character so that they may be rewarded at the eschatological revelation of Christ (1 Pet 4:12–13).

---

37. The authorship of 2 Peter is one of the most disputed questions regarding this letter. But again, we are choosing to avoid this debate for the sake of our discussion. One can see variety of opinions in Bauckham, *Jude, 2 Peter*, 158–63; Schreiner, *1, 2 Peter, Jude*, 255–74; Hillyer, *1 and 2 Peter, Jude*, 9–11; Guthrie, *New Testament Introduction*, 820–24, 1011–24.

38. Scholars go back and forth in their dialogue about whether the readers were predominately Jews or Gentiles. Arguably, it was at least a mixture of the two, though most likely predominately Jewish. Discussions of this matter are standard in most commentaries but one in particular that is quite helpful is Jobes, *1 Peter*, 23–41.

39. Oropeza, *Churches Under Siege*, 110.

In the meantime, as these believers eagerly awaited this moment, Peter informs them that the way they live must remain noticeably distinct from the world around them. One way they were to do this was by shunning the immoral vices that once consumed them. They were exhorted to resist lustful passions and not join the unbelieving world in its debauchery. Granted, this kind of faithfulness would result in unbelievers rejecting them. Yet it would also serve as an open indictment against their antagonists on the day of resurrection (1 Pet 4:1–5). Likewise, their natural impulses to resent their oppressors must be abandoned as well. They must exhibit an attitude of kindness that seeks to live at harmony with as many unbelievers as possible, whether they be governmental authorities, masters, critics, or even antagonistic spouses.

Knowing that such a goal is daunting, Peter is quick to remind these believers of the promise that they are protected by God's power so that they will be saved on the last day (1 Pet 1:5; 5:10). These admonitions are tied together by Peter partly through the lens of the exodus-wilderness plight that Israel originally experienced. He sees them as "the prophetic diaspora and sojourners making their way through the metaphorical desert to the final eschaton."[40] It should be added, though, that while these believers have security in Christ because they have been born again with his imperishable blood, Peter says in the same breath that his audience must live with godly fear because the Lord will judge everyone according to their works (1 Pet 1:17–19). The point here is not that his readers should be paralyzed with uncertainty because of the potential for failure. Rather it is simply that no believer should see the work of Christ on their behalf in a presumptuous way that plays down the gravity of their calling, especially in the face of persecution.[41]

Coupled with these important points are some other crucial observations that Peter makes in his second epistle. While it is similar to his first letter in that there is serious debate about the makeup of his audience, he writes this piece for several clear reasons. One is to fan the flame of devotion to the Lord in the hearts of these believers. He does so by first reminding them of the divine power they have in Christ and then stressing the virtues they should emulate as they pursue his eternal kingdom (2 Pet 1:3–11). Relatedly, Peter writes to reassure these believers that the apostolic witness

---

40. Oropeza, *Churches Under Siege*, 130.

41. No matter how high a cost they might pay, Peter's message to his readers is that "the evil that Christ redeemed them from at the highest cost of his own life is nothing other than the evil of their former way of life" (Jobes, *1 Peter*, 116). Therefore, they are to live in a way that reflects the fact that they have been redeemed, or bought. They are now to imitate the character of their new master.

they had embraced was trustworthy. He does this by first appealing to the mount of transfiguration where he was an actual eyewitness to Christ's heavenly glory firsthand. Peter's point is that the message he proclaimed was not based on cunning rhetoric or fascinating myths. It derived from a real person that they followed, engaged, and in this case, beheld in a supernatural encounter.

What is even more interesting at this point is that Peter does not stop with an argument about empirical verification. He claims that this event, as overwhelming as it was, aligned perfectly with a more definitive source of authority, which was the written testimony of the prophets. From here, Peter deduces that if his readers could be certain that their faith was based on a sound foundation, they could be confident that it will one day become sight. This will occur when history culminates at the return of Christ despite the naysayers who think its delay is indicative of the fact that it will never come (cf. 2 Pet 1:16–21; 3:1–10). Believers should never be discouraged by the existence of such mockers because God's timetable is not the same as man's. What some might construe as a hoax is actually a sign of God's mercy because the longer the interim between Christ's first advent and his return, the more time people have to repent.

Along with these exhortations is one other serious matter that Peter addresses. Apparently, tensions were rising among these communities of believers because a group of false teachers infiltrated their ranks. Some scholars question whether Peter is possibly addressing the same opponents that Jude confronted, because they use a similar cluster of images to describe them.[42] Peter alludes to similar kinds of immoral activities that Jude mentions. Just like Jude, he also tells his readers that the impending judgment of these teachers is just as certain as the doom that came upon rebellious angels and the immoral cities of Sodom and Gomorrah. He even echoes Jude in how he talks about the emptiness of their claims, their lack of respect for any kind of authority, and how they replicate the antics of the Prophet Balaam, who led Israel astray.

Nevertheless, one factor that is unique to Peter's treatment of these opponents is that he says they were originally part of these Christian communities before they defected. Peter says that just as Israel sometimes had false prophets who emerged from their own camp, so did these false teachers arise out of these churches (2 Pet 2:1).[43] So the pressing question is whether

---

42. Part of the reason for this is because of the numerous parallels in both epistles. But generally speaking, it is difficult to pin down any air-tight case for who Peter's opponents were exactly. See discussions of this matter in Schreiner, *1, 2 Peter, Jude*, 277–80; and Cavallin, "False Teachers of 2 Peter," 263–70.

43. They were acting like counter leaders who were teaching ideas that were directly

Peter saw these opponents as believers who had apostatized. There is no doubt that he now views them as deceivers who will fall under eschatological judgment if they do not repent. The crux of the issue, however, is how should his descriptions of their former selves be understood. The least one can say is that they were perceived by others as being believers.[44]

Tragically, though, they were now seen as being in a worse condition than they were before because they had been overtaken by the vices that they had previously repudiated. They were like dogs returning to their own vomit, or pigs returning to their muddy slop. Some argue that these metaphors are being used in terms of *as-if* lingo, meaning that these false teachers only seemed as if they were genuinely converted at one time.[45] Others contend that these references portray an undeniable treatment of how believers can revert back to an unconverted state.[46] In response to this impasse, it does appear that these false teachers were perceived to be believers by the churches before their defection. However, the language of "dogs" or "pigs" returning to their natural inclinations can legitimately be understood as conveying the idea that these false teachers were revealing their base natures once again, thereby implying that they had never really experienced inward transformation.[47] They exposed their true inclinations by eventually returning to the corruption they once enjoyed.

---

opposed to the message given by the apostles. Bauckham, *Jude, 2 Peter*, 239.

44. Because Christ is described elsewhere in NT writings as giving himself for his people (barring atonement debates), the idea is carried over here to describe these Petrine communities as being purchased by Christ. These former members had become false teachers who denied their former identity with believers. Some interpret this language to be emphasizing the universality of the atonement rather the potential that a believer has to apostatize, cf. Alford, *Greek New Testament*, 4:402; Hiebert, "Portrayal of False Teachers," 259–60. We would simply say that this language (i.e., denying the Lord who bought them) is couching the gravity of apostasy in covenantal terms. That is to say that these false teachers initially became part of a community for whom Christ gave his life only to deny solidarity with them in the end, thereby renouncing their allegiance to the one who died for the group.

45. Schreiner argues that the language of "being bought" in 2 Pet 2:1 and the pig/dog imagery are being used phenomenologically to describe the defectors in terms "as if" they were believers when in reality they truly were not (*1, 2 Peter, Jude*, 331, 364). We would argue that this description is on the right track. We would simply add that these depictions are, again, using covenantal terms. They essentially were renouncing their vows, which in turn, exposed the fact that their initial oath was suspect.

46. E.g., Bauckham, *Jude, 2 Peter*, 240.

47. We would argue that the pig/dog language reflects the same idea that Jesus spoke of in the parable of the feast. A man accepted the invitation to a king's banquet but did not wear the proper attire. He thought he could join the attendants on his own terms but quickly discovered otherwise. Likewise, these false teachers accepted the invitation early on but did not take on the proper attire because they eventually

5. PERSEVERANCE IN THE LETTERS OF JOHN

The three small letters that come from the hand of John the apostle have much to say about the concept of perseverance. The most pertinent insights are found in the first epistle where he admonishes believers to remain, or continually abide, in Christ and gives his own theological assessment about who apostates really are. The impetus for these discussions came in lieu of a high Christology that John expected his readers to affirm. He establishes this standard in the prologue where he claims to have been an eyewitness of the ministry of the Messiah (he echoes the language of his gospel by referring to him as the Word of life). He lived a portion of his life with Christ as one of his disciples. He then adds the declaration that Jesus is in fact the Messiah, the Son of the heavenly Father (1 John 1:1–3).[48] And it was this solemn confession that bound John to his audience. They had believed his testimony by choosing to follow the Son who was the Father's emissary on their behalf. They had now received forgiveness of their sins. They were now in solidarity together as God's people.

The problem, however, was that this community of believers was being disrupted because of the influence of some false teachers who arose from within the group. John makes the strong charge that these individuals were actual replicas of the antichrist, or antichrists, because they were originally part of this assembly but chose to defect, thereby proving that they were never true believers at all (1 John 2:18–19).[49] This is a critical observation on John's part because he is explicitly saying that some were a part of the community who expressed compelling features of discipleship. Yet in time, their defection exposed their true character or lack thereof. Their choice to reject Jesus as the Messiah was evidence that they had never experienced any real inward transformation.

---

repudiated their allegiance to Jesus. Hence, there is a difference between a dog or pig getting a temporary bath and having their true natures changed so that vomit or mud are no longer desirable.

48. One major dispute within scholarship on 1 John is the exact identity of the false teachers and/or defectors within the Johannine communities. One major view that numerous commentators espouse is that they were early gnostics who abandoned John's churches because they embraced faulty versions of christological ontology. However, another competing view that offers an alternative reading of these opponents is that they were defectors who repudiated their initial confession of Jesus as the Messiah in exchange for possible reacceptance into Judaism. See a recent defense of this thesis in Streett, *They Went Out from Us*, esp. 142–72.

49. Said another way, the defectors' external act of leaving was the means of revealing their lack of inward transformation. See Kruse, *Letters of John*, 102–3.

Notably, it is difficult to read John's comments and not think of his experience with Judas. John saw a fellow disciple who heard everything he heard, experienced practically everything he had experienced with a few exceptions, and on the surface, appeared to be as committed as he was. But eventually Judas' true character emerged as the "son of perdition." So, even here, there were some who were part of these communities who had now revealed their true spiritual colors. They denied the identity of the Son, even questioning whether Christ had come in the flesh,[50] and to make matters worse, they intended to deceive others with their lies (cf. 1 John 2:22–23, 26; 4:2–3).

Amid John's various responses to this heretical sect, certain interpretive challenges arise. Specifically, there are questions on how to understand several contrasts he makes between certain features that should be emulated by his readers, or "his children," as opposed to the antics being expressed by the defectors. John mentions numerous character traits that believers are to exhibit so they can be encouraged that they have eternal life. The looming concern is how such texts should be read. One in particular that causes some exegetical consternation is how to reconcile the claim that John makes regarding the fact that those born of God do not sin (1 John 3:9) with his point elsewhere that anyone who denies they have any sin does not have the truth in them (1 John 1:8). How can both of these claims be true? Numerous theories have been proposed but one in particular seems to be the most viable. John's comment that those born of God "do not sin" can be understood in terms of practicing sin with an unrelenting, unrepentant attitude. This is partly why some translations render John's language as "he who sins" while others provide the reading "he who practices sin"—the point being that one who abides in Christ and his teachings cannot do so while sinning continually without either repenting or experiencing divine discipline.[51] However, even if the language here is making an intentional contrast of extremes—i.e., believers do not sin but must admit that they do—the point still stands that

---

50. Like Judas, they voluntarily withdrew from the community and revealed that their entire time with the Christ and his people was dubious. See Smalley, *1, 2, 3 John*, 96–98.

51. Some argue that interpreting John's language about "not sinning" in a durative fashion proves problematic grammatically if one tries to apply it consistently throughout the entire letter. See, e.g., Kubo, "1 John 3:9," 47–56. The case is made that John speaks in terms of believers "not sinning" while at the same time "having sin" because he is emphasizing a dualistic polarity. One end upholds absolute idealism (i.e., those born of God, or of the age to come, do not sin) while the other concedes to practical realism (i.e., believers still are in the present age, therefore they still sin). In this interpretation, John is critiquing the defectors who have rejected Christ and are making misguided ethical claims. John uses this contrasting language to exploit them because they are sinning while they are claiming that they do not. Kubo, "1 John 3:9," 55–56.

willful unrepentant sinning and/or denial of being guilty of sin are evidence that one is not born from above.

Another point that John makes in this letter serves as one of the most difficult passages in all of the NT. It is found in 1 John 5:16 where he alludes to "a sin unto death." He speaks of a contrast between a sin(s) that does not lead to death and others, or at least one, that does. Three obvious questions arise regarding this claim: (1) what this sin is exactly; (2) what kind of death is experienced if the sin is committed; (3) and can believers commit it so as to forfeit their salvation. All kinds of interpretations have been offered in the attempt to deal with these concerns.[52]

We would argue that in response to the first question, the sin unto death at least reflects the defection that the false teachers had expressed. They were part of the group that had sealed their fate by denying the Lord.[53] Second, when looking at John's language throughout the letter, it makes the best sense to interpret "death" in terms of eternal judgment.[54] Therefore, John believes that this sin(s) can end in eschatological irreversible death. And third, as it pertains to whether John's audience could commit this act, his point seems to accord with the many other contrasts he has made in the letter. Thus, the argument is not just that a certain sin leads to eternal death while others do not. The distinction is between *believers* who can commit various sins that do not necessarily lead to final judgment as opposed to *unbelievers*, including the spiritual posers who turned out to be false teachers, who can decry any allegiance to Christ and ultimately face the eternal consequences.[55]

This is partly why earlier in the letter John admonishes his audience to abide in Christ so they will not be ashamed at his coming (1 John 2:28). Those who might choose to ignore such a warning would prove to be like

---

52. Such an idea is not novel in and of itself. The OT describes certain sins that warrant punishment by death; e.g., Num 15:30–31; 18:22; Ps 19:13. And we have seen several examples in the NT, including Ananias and Sapphira (Acts 5:1–10) and those who ate the Lord's Supper in an unworthy manner (1 Cor 11). One key difference, though, is that all of these examples identify the specific sins that could lead to one's demise. In John's case, it is not. See Busenitz, "Sin unto Death," 17–18; and much more detail by Brown, *Epistles of John*, 612–22.

53. It is likely that at a minimum, John has the sin of the defectors in mind. Kruse, *Letters of John*, 192.

54. It is difficult not to see John's emphasis here as something beyond physical death. While it is true that the OT and other Jewish literature leave room for certain sins that lead to death, it is always described as physical in nature. Yet John's language throughout parts of the epistle imply that he has something more severe in mind. Smalley, *1, 2, 3 John*, 284.

55. See Davis, "Sin Unto Death," 262–63.

the other defectors and inherit judgment instead of eternal life. So our proposal aligns with the view that John is distinguishing between two kinds of sinners, those being believers who sin in ways that can be forgiven because they have not denied their advocate Jesus Christ and John's opponents who have denied the Savior and await death.[56] What we see is that unfortunately sometimes the children of Satan can coexist in Christian communities for a time until eventually their true nature is revealed by their conduct.

These theological perspectives are repeated later in John's second and third epistles. In 2 John, for example, he encourages the readers to abide by the commandments of Jesus which in many ways can be encapsulated by loving fellow believers (vv 2 John 5–6).[57] He gives this admonition because he wants his audience to be aware that there are many deceivers, again identified as antichrists, who deny that Christ came in the flesh. John claims that they should be vigilant so they are not duped by these false teachers. Those who do continue to abide in Christ's teachings are those who have the Father and the Son, which implies that any who may defect do not. Likewise, such detractors who refuse to repent are to be shunned by the church so that no one is tempted to participate in their deception.

In 3 John, the apostle applies this outlook to a peculiar situation in another church wherein an apparent leader named Diotrephes was causing significant turmoil within the congregation, even making false accusations against John himself. John says that Diotrephes is sinning recklessly, which most likely means at best that he was a possible leader who had disqualified himself through dishonorable conduct, or at worst, he was an evil doer who did not know the Lord.[58] He contrasts Diotrephes' conduct with another servant named Demetrius who retained a good testimony among the people, loved the truth, and was in good standing in John's estimation. He was everything that Diotrephes was not. Therefore, once again, John applies the theology of his first letter to other practical situations in his other two

---

56. A major reason for this categorizing in the letter is because it marks out God's people as distinct in the present age. They are the ones who embrace who Jesus is and do not follow the way of the world, which is marked by those who repudiate Jesus' message and claims to messiahship.

57. Yarbrough explains that a chiasm is used in vv. 5–6 to emphasize that the command to love is non-negotiable. See *1–3 John*, 341–42.

58. Historical questions pertaining to the exact nature of the tension between "the elder" and Diotrephes has caused the most controversy in interpreting the epistle. See survey and critique of the early historical-critical nuances of this debate in Mitchell, "Diotrephes Does Not Receive Us," 299–320; and for a review of the issues revolving around authorship, see Schnackenburg, *Johannine Epistles*, 267–73. Also, Campbell makes a strong case for Diotrephes being confronted as an elder who had fallen into disobedience. Campbell, "Honor, Hospitality, and Hautiness," 321–41.

smaller epistles. What we discover is that John only has theological room for two categories of people—there are believers who abide in Christ by remaining in his teachings and enduring in their faith until his return whereas unbelievers, who can even sometimes affiliate with Christian communities, reject Christ, and bring final judgment upon their souls. Therefore, the theological wrinkle here in John's letters is that sometimes unbelievers can bond with churches by expressing a short-term untested form of faith or belief that eventually becomes exposed through either unrepentant sinful behavior or doctrinal defection.[59]

6. PERSEVERANCE IN REVELATION

It should be observed at the outset that perseverance is a central theme in John's Apocalypse. The reason being that much of the book focuses upon encouraging believers to endure potential persecution faithfully so they can be vindicated in the resurrection when Christ returns. This indeed is a significant promise. That is why John provides his credentials early on. He declares that he has been given a revelation, or unveiling, of Jesus Christ through a collection of visions mediated through an angel and that all those who hear and keep what is written will be blessed (Rev 1:1–3). After identifying his audience to be seven churches throughout Asia Minor, he informs them that he is commissioned to share this revelation because it discloses how history will culminate with Christ coming to enact retribution on the earth (Rev 1:7).[60] From here, John expresses solidarity with these churches by describing himself as a fellow brother who is participating in the same kind of sufferings that some of them are enduring as citizens of Christ's kingdom. And he claims that the initial source from whom he is

---

59. Again, there are strong typological and eschatological components at work here. In John, apostasy is indicative of the present age, especially in light of the world's disdain for Christ and his kingdom. His presence in his first coming exposed the powers of darkness and the corruption of humanity to the point that he was executed. His subsequent defeat over death heralded the fact that now the present age is on borrowed time. So those who hate Christ and his people, regardless of whether they never associate with believers at all or do so temporarily only to defect in time, will always exist. They are replicas of the son of perdition, Judas, and are present-day antichrists. Yet those who remain faithful are born of the Spirit, or from above, and are awaiting the age to come. See how Schuchard ties these themes together in discussing 1 John 2:18–29 in Schuchard, *1–3 John*, 261–87.

60. This claim is a quotation from Daniel 7 about the coming Son of Man. Just as Daniel was admonishing the remnant of Jews in exile to be faithful until God delivered them, so likewise were followers of Christ to endure until they were exonerated at their king's return. See Beale, *Use of Daniel*, 154–77; Shepherd, "Daniel 7:13," 110–11.

receiving his prophecies is the risen, glorified Christ himself. He appears to John as a divine figure who walks amid the seven churches just like a priest walks within the tabernacle surrounded by candlesticks (Rev 1:12–20). He inspects them, gives encouragement, offers instruction, and if necessary, expresses warnings.

This is the very point where we begin to see the idea of perseverance taking shape. Christ first commends each of these churches for areas where they were being obedient and enduring hardships. He then transitions to address specific problems that the congregations were apparently ignoring. When he does, we see that Christ never overlooks any moral or theological shortcomings simply because the churches were doing some things well. Five of the seven churches receive serious rebukes, including the ones in Ephesus, Pergamum, Thyatira, Sardis, and Laodicea. After expressing words of approval on some things, Christ consistently says to them, "but I have this against you." However, after expressing his grievances, he would always conclude with the assurance that they would partake of an eternal inheritance if they repented. Those at Ephesus are promised that they will have access to the tree of life in the coming heavenly paradise; those in Pergamum are assured to receive heavenly rewards; believers in Thyatira will have messianic-delegated authority over the nations in the coming kingdom; saints in Sardis will be clothed in righteousness and not be blotted out of the book of life; and finally those in Laodicea who overcome will sit with Christ in victory just as Christ endured and the Father awarded him.[61]

What complicates these promises is that they are contingent upon the church's willingness to change. If they refuse his admonitions, Christ says there will be dire consequences. For example, he tells the Ephesians if they do not repent, he will remove their lampstand, which at least means the church will cease to exist.[62] He says to those in Pergamum that he will come and make war with them using the sword of his mouth, which is exactly

---

61. All of these promises describe experiences that are related to the culminating moment in Revelation when all things are made new. The heavenly abode, which is depicted as a New Jerusalem, comes to take up residence upon the earth itself, thereby resulting in a new heaven and a new earth. The believers in these churches are promised that if they listen to what the Spirit says, they will partake of those blessings. Moreover, the promises to the church at Sardis include the statement that "those who are victorious will, like them, be dressed in white" (Rev 3:5). Thus, the implication is that the believers in all the churches as well as those who read the prophecies can be overcomers who receive these rewards as well. Fee, *Revelation*, 23. But there is a further implication that should not be missed, namely that those who refuse to heed the warnings will be judged.

62. Cf. Aune, *Revelation 1–5*, 147; Beale, *Book of Revelation*, 232; and the interaction with competing views of the "lampstand removal" phrasing by Osborne, *Revelation*, 116–18.

the same means that he later uses to judge the nations at his return. The believers in Thyatira are warned that if any of them stay aligned with a false prophetess who was leading some astray, they will be judged along with her. The church at Sardis is told that if some do not repent, they will be caught off guard because Christ will come judge them unexpectedly like a thief. And Christ tells the church at Laodicea that if they choose to remain lukewarm, they will be cast out of God's mouth. Now obviously we ask what to make of all this. There is no question that Christ is talking to churches as a whole. He clearly refers to everyone and the rewards that he offers are mostly allusions to what the saints inherit in the coming kingdom described toward the end of Revelation. The challenge is that some of these warnings could possibly be references to temporal judgments similar to what Paul describes in the situation pertaining to the Corinthians who abused the Lord's supper. But some of them use language that is much stronger. Some, such as ones posed to the church at Pergamum and Sardis, reflect the same language that Christ uses elsewhere to describe the final doom of unbelievers.[63]

Only two of the seven churches, Smyrna and Philadelphia, receive commendation without any added rebukes. Yet even this achievement does not exclude them from being told like the others to continue in their faith so they can receive the blessings of the coming kingdom. In fact, both congregations are encouraged to remain unmoved in their commitment because they are about to experience even more persecution. The believers at Smyrna are told that some of them are going to be cast in prison and be under tribulation for ten days (Rev 2:10). Similarly, the believers at Philadelphia are instructed that because of their perseverance, they will be spared from a time (or hour) of trial that is about to come upon the whole earth and test the earth-dwellers. Most likely, this language alludes to an upcoming period where severe oppression was going to take place among the nations throughout the Roman Empire.[64]

---

63. Again, Christ says to Pergamum that if they refuse to repent, he will make war against them with the sword of his mouth and in ch. 19, this is exactly what he does when he judges the unbelieving nations along with the Beast and False Prophet. Then to Sardis, he promises that those who persevere will have their names in the book of life, which is an essential component to escaping the Lake of Fire at the final judgment in Revelation.

64. Cf. Oropeza, *Churches under Siege*, 218; Brown, "Hour of Trial," 308–14; Blount, *Revelation*, 76–77; and Beale, *Book of Revelation*, 289–92. To see this language in Rev 3:10 as referring to some kind of end-time event that just precedes the *parousia* is difficult to discern because on the one hand, the subsequent series of visions do speak of eschatological woes that will come upon the earth that lead up to Christ's judgment of the nations and the renewal of all things. On the other hand, there is a bit of hermeneutical complexity because we have to ask how such an admonition could make any sense when all of these early Christians died centuries before any such event occurred.

Nevertheless, in both of these church's cases, Christ views the believer's endurance as a prerequisite to entering his kingdom and receiving vindication. He tells the church at Smyrna that those who endure will receive the crown of life (or life itself) and that those who overcome will not be affected by the second death, which is later identified to be final judgment that results in being cast into the Lake of Fire. He similarly informs the Philadelphian believers that they must remain steadfast so they do not lose their crown. They must show themselves to be overcomers so they can be identified with the heavenly city of Jerusalem, which again is imagery representing the coming new creation where heaven and earth become one. So even though they are exempt from the critiques that Christ makes against the other five churches, they are equally expected to endure if they desire to be vindicated in resurrection and rule with Christ.[65]

This theme of the necessity of faithfulness to Christ continues throughout the rest of the book. Beginning in ch. 4, John utilizes visionary imagery from various traditions to describe a cosmic antithesis between God's people and the satanic powers. These evil forces are expressed on the earth through the Roman imperial cult and possibly the bankrupt religion of Christ-rejecting Judaism.[66] John describes this clash with a series of visions so he can convey a theological interpretation of history and the future.

It is rather difficult to see Christ admonishing the Philadelphian believers to be ready for a coming worldwide trial that really transpires millennia later in the future. Dispensational interpreters often go even further by making the case that this promise entails an actual removal of believers just prior to a worldwide series of apocalyptic judgments that will come upon the earth, otherwise known as a rapture before an impending Tribulation period. For a succinct survey of interpreters who take this stance on Rev 3:10 by a dispensationalist who actually questions this reading, see Svigel, "Apocalypse of John," 26–28. Still, regardless of one's eschatological interpretation of this tribulation language, every interpreter has to wrestle with the fact that Jesus ties these believers' endurance to their inheritance of the heavenly kingdom.

65. One can see this in the fact that Christ says to the Philadelphians that they will become pillars in the temple of God and the divine name as well as the name of the new city will be written upon them. Essentially, they will become part of the final eschatological residence of the divine presence in the new creation. Those who overcome will be part of the new earth that the heavenly realm will establish. For more on the background to this language, see Wong, "The Pillar and the Throne," 297–307.

66. For important input on Roman imperialism and its relationship to the Apocalypse, cf. Howard-Brook and Gwyther, *Unveiling Empire*, 87–119; Thompson, *Book of Revelation*, 171–200; Friesen, *Imperial Cults*, 122–30, 210–18; Hays and Alkier, *Revelation and the Politics of Apocalyptic Interpretation*; Bauckham, *Bible in Politics*, 85–102; and Zerbe, "Revelation's Exposé of Two Cities," 52–53. And for a succinct treatment on whether John's depiction of Babylon is imagery describing apostate Jerusalem, see Biguzzi, "Is the Babylon of Revelation Rome or Jerusalem?," 373–86; and Beagley, "Babylon," 111–12.

He does so because he wants his audience to be assured that they can overcome Satan through their faithful testimony to Christ, even if it results in martyrdom. Why? Because whether it be God's people in the past or in the future, it is the faithful ones who will be raised from the dead so they can reign over a new earth.

Consequently, the book of Revelation's dramatic portrayal of the conflict between the present age and the age to come includes a key idea in developing a theology of perseverance. Just as Christ overcame the evil powers and tribulation by becoming the victorious sacrificial lamb who the Father vindicated in resurrection, so likewise must his people follow him to reach the moment of vindication as well. If they face such odds, John says they will live in the heavenly Jerusalem, an apocalyptic image of the very abode of God in heaven that is to take up a new address on a newly redeemed earth. But if they do not, John claims that they will join the unbelieving nations in judgment and inherit nothing in the coming kingdom (Rev 21:7–8).[67]

7. CONCLUSIONS

In retrospect, there are several important ideas that these NT authors share in common regarding the importance of perseverance and the dangers of apostasy. Two, in particular, stand out the most. The first is that portions of the book of Acts and general epistles view a believer's *past* conversion, their *present* blessings and responsibilities as Christ followers, and their *future* inheritance in the age to come as overlapping realities, not neatly separated categories. This is not to say that these dynamics are never discussed or treated individually. Sometimes they are. Still, the fact remains that what has happened when someone becomes a believer and what has not happened yet because they await Christ's return are inseparably linked to what must happen in their present-day experience, which is faithful endurance.

Theologically speaking, we can state the point this way. *The grace that secures a believer's position in Christ when they are born again and that will one day be displayed when they are raised from the dead is the same divine power that enables them to persevere in the present.* Or put another way, the

---

67. Interestingly enough, John lumps those who are cowardly and unbelieving with murderers, the immoral, sorcerers, idolaters, liars, and everyone else who experiences the second death. Quite strong language indeed. It should further be seen that there is no distinction between believers who overcome and those who do not. Those who do not receive eschatological judgment. The language here echoes covenantal oath bonding that goes all the way back to Exod 6:7 where God promised to be with the people and he would be there God. So here in Rev 21:7, those who overcome will be his sons and he will be their God. Dempsey, "Revelation 21:1–8," 402.

grace that is expressed in regeneration and glorification is to be realized in the process of sanctification through one's clinging to Christ, albeit how imperfect it may be. Furthermore, in response to Protestant concerns about blurring the lines between justification and sanctification, it would appear that these NT writers have no problem in arguing that the work of grace that changes the heart of a sinner to exercise faith in Christ also enables that person to love Christ even unto death.[68] They offer comfort and assurance to those who are in Christ while at the same time motivating them to perseverance so the full inheritance of resurrection and new creation can be received in the eschaton.

Another notable point that these authors share with each other as well as Paul and the even the gospel writers is a common concern for certain pitfalls that believers must avoid in their pursuit of Christ-likeness. One is, again, the danger of false teachers and their abilities to deceive. Acts speaks of wolves that will enter churches in hopes of ravaging the sheep; Peter, Jude, and John have much to say about the ugliness of false teachers and prophets; and James speaks about the severity of being a teacher because of the pressing responsibility it entails. Another frequently mentioned temptation is the potential for sinful behavior that remains unchecked. These writers mention all kinds of vices that are common to those who live in rebellion against God, showing devotion for their own appetites and passions. They warn readers that struggles with sin that do not include confession and repentance can be indicative of the fact that one's faith is not altogether genuine. And, finally, another common thread that we see in minds of these writers

---

68. One must be careful here because we do want to convolute the concepts of regeneration, justification, and sanctification. To be ambiguous on such matters, especially sanctification or what one might call Christian spirituality, can easily erode into notions of works righteousness or legalism. Cf. Porter, "Renewal of Interest in the Doctrine of Sanctification," 416; and Carson, "When Is Spirituality Spiritual?," 381–94. While these matters are indeed interrelated because one necessarily leads to another, they are still distinct dynamics of the salvation experience. A believer's initial justification is based on the righteousness of Christ that is afforded to those who exercise saving faith, which is the fruit of the work of the Spirit who produces the new birth, or regeneration. (This Protestant mainstay view of justification has come under serious fire in recent decades, so see a formidable and clear defense of imputation in Fesko, *Death in Adam, Life in Christ*; and the theological implications of Christ being the second Adam in Crowe, *Last Adam*, 199–216.) In contrast, the changed status of a sinner who believes leads to a subsequent process of being conformed to the image of Christ practically via the work of the Spirit. Whereas regeneration and justification are events, or moments, sanctification is an ongoing series of experiences. At the same time, though, these distinct realities are seen as necessarily linked together. This is partly why we see consistent admonitions in the NT for believers to act (to live) like what they are (i.e., saints, righteous) even unto death just as Jesus did as our example. He trusted the Father even unto death and waited to be vindicated in his timing. Therefore, all of his people are expected to do the same.

are their sensitivity to the stresses of persecution. We read about the first martyrs in Acts, the pressures being experienced by new believers in Hebrews and Peter's first letter, and the attacks of Satan himself against God's people in the Revelation. Yet just as Christ entrusted himself to his Father even when his enemies ultimately murdered him, so must his people walk in obedience to the mandate of the gospel by entering the straight gate to the heavenly kingdom even if one is surrounded by mockers and naysayers, and yes, sometimes, even executioners. In James' words, faith that saves is faith that is put in action.

Along with these commonly shared points are also certain nuances that are unique to some of these writers. One important example can be seen in how these authors talk about the true nature of apostates who sometimes became false teachers. We saw in John's first epistle that he described them as former members of a community, or church, who eventually revealed they were truly unregenerate from the start. Writers like Peter and Jude talk about clusters of false teachers in other ways. Jude talks about a certain group who were always rotten to the core. They entered communities of believers in stealth mode with sinister intents from the outset. However, in Peter's account in his second letter, he speaks of false teachers in similar fashion to John in that he says they were originally part of a believing community. But instead of making the direct claim that John does about their inward natures lacking the work of the Spirit, Peter uses the imagery of unclean animals to imply what John says explicitly. The false teachers he addressed were those who knew the truth and were thought by others, including Peter, to have embraced it. Sadly, like dogs or pigs who cannot deny their instinctive traits, these defectors turned from the truth when their base natures resurfaced.

In conjunction with this feature, a final wrinkle that the book of Acts and James highlight is the idea that while believers must endure hardship to inherit Christ's kingdom, it is possible that the Lord can use death as a disciplinary measure at his discretion when his children commit certain sins and harden their hearts toward repentance.[69] This is an important feature because it shows that while the sin of unbelief can lead to eternal death, a defiant heart in a believer can lead to physical death if the Lord sees fit.

---

69. This theme also accords well with Paul's occasional strategy to hand unrepentant members of local churches to the domain of Satan in hopes that the providential use of his attacks can motivate such people to repent and receive restoration.

Chapter 5

Perseverance in the Post-Apostolic Church

So far, we have spent the first four chapters surveying biblical texts that are most pertinent to the doctrine of perseverance. Now we want to spend the next five examining some critical points in Christian history where the subject receives serious attention. This will help us understand how Christian thinkers in the past have wrestled with this topic's complexities and why they sometimes came to such conflicting conclusions. As we begin, it is important to remember from our earlier investigation that NT authors spoke of at least three threats that could potentially lure believers into the dangers of apostasy. They include (1) the persistent draw of everyday temptations to a lifestyle of unrepentant sin, (2) the ongoing pressures of religious persecution, and (3) the rhetorical appeal of false teachers who could potentially deceive one into renouncing their allegiance to Christ.[1] These ordeals did not fade away once the first-century church passed off the scene. They only intensified. This is why they continued to be addressed in numerous parts of early Christian literature. Documents provided by the Apostolic Fathers, early apologists, and other Christian thinkers all contain admonitions for believers to persevere in their faith by avoiding the very temptations that NT audiences were originally commanded to resist. Consequently, it is this connection

---

1. Or as Oropeza has summarized, early Christian communities were endangered by temptations, deceptions, and persecutions. See Oropeza, *Paul and Apostasy*, 2.

that launches our examination into how second- and third-century believers approached the subject of perseverance.[2]

1. PERSEVERANCE IN THE APOSTOLIC FATHERS

Historians recognize a collection of writings recorded roughly between AD 90 and 150 during what is called the post-apostolic period, or the immediate decades after all the apostles were gone. This corpus was recorded by an unknown number of writers who are normally called the "Apostolic Fathers." This phrase was first used by a French scholar named J. B. Cotelier who in 1672 labeled a section of early Christian literature as being written by "the Fathers of the Apostolic Period."[3] The basis for using this phrase was the belief that the authors most likely either knew one or more of the original apostles or at least had received instruction from a disciple of the apostles. Even though some of the works were authored by individuals who remain anonymous, a select amount of their entries are sufficient for us to see some ways in which the idea of perseverance was conceptualized in early Christian thought.[4]

1.1 1 and 2 Clement

A good place to start is with segments of pastoral exhortations for believers to endure in their faith. We see, for instance, in the famous letter known as 1 Clement that the author is giving instructions to the church at Corinth.[5] Clement, at one juncture, discusses the hope of the resurrection and he encourages the readers to "remain bound to the one who is faithful in his promises."[6] As they await that glorious day, he along with the Corinthian

---

2. Many of the passages we will discuss have been neatly categorized for reference purposes in Bercot, *Dictionary of Early Christian Beliefs*. And we are being extremely selective in our treatment because an exhaustive account of patristic quotes on perseverance would require an entire monograph, perhaps even several.

3. See Holmes, introduction to *Apostolic Fathers*, 5; and Jefford, *Reading the Apostolic Fathers*, 1–10.

4. The portions of the collection that we will cover include material in *1* and *2 Clement*, the *Letters of Ignatius*, the *Didache*, the *Epistle of Barnabas*, and the *Shepherd of Hermas*. Other writings not directly addressed include a *Letter of Polycarp*, a *Letter of Diognetus*, the *Martyrdom of Polycarp*, and the *Letters of Papias*.

5. Earliest records designate Clement as the third bishop of Rome. This is disputed, but if tradition is correct, then this pastor is writing to these believers about some sort of schism between members and their leaders.

6. *1 Clement*, 27.1.

believers must fear the Lord, forsaking all lusts so they can be protected from his coming judgments.[7] Clement goes on to argue that faithfulness is really the only option for a believer because no one can flee from the Lord. He poses a rhetorical question that since the Lord knows all things and that his presence cannot be escaped, is there any doubt what would happen to any who tried to desert him.[8] The implied answer is that only final judgment awaits such individuals.

A similar line of reasoning can be found in the subsequent letter known as 2 Clement. Though written much later by an unknown presbyter, this shorter homily echoes a similar exhortation. The author speaks about the coming resurrection as a reward for God's people and claims, "Let us, therefore, practice righteousness, so that we may be saved in the end. Blessed are those who obey these injunctions; though they may endure affliction for a little while in the world, they will gather the immortal fruit of the resurrection."[9] What is important to notice is that both of these documents only apply the eschatological vindication of resurrection to those who endure in their faith. We could say that these sources have no theological problem in saying that a believer's obedience to the moral demands of discipleship are part of the road that must be taken to experience life in the age to come.

1.2 Ignatius of Antioch & the Didache

There are also other pastoral instructions regarding the importance of enduring faith that we find in the Apostolic Fathers, which focus more upon the dangers of false teachers. Their ability to sway believers with ideas that were contrary to the original gospel preached by Christ and his apostles was a threat that had to be resisted at all costs. We see such concern, for example, in some of the letters that Ignatius, the bishop of Antioch, wrote to several churches as he was being deported to Rome for execution. In writing to the Ephesians, he claims that those who corrupt households with the stench of false teaching will not inherit the kingdom of God. Likewise, anyone who pollutes himself by following any wolf in sheep's clothing will experience the judgment of unquenchable fire as well.[10] He makes similar comments in several other letters, including the one to the Philadelphians where he sternly warns them that any who are misled and follow any schismatic will

---

7. *1 Clement*, 28.1.
8. *1 Clement*, 28.2–4.
9. *2 Clement*, 19.3.
10. Ignatius, *To the Ephesians*, 16.2.

not inherit the kingdom.[11] Similarly, in the anonymously written corpus known as the Didache, we find an admonition that conflates apocalyptic overtones from the Olivet Discourse, Paul's letters to the Thessalonians, and the book of Revelation. Believers are to be vigilant because false teachers will lead many astray in the last days and all humankind will be put to the test. Many will fall away and perish while those who endure will be saved.[12]

1.3 The Epistle of Barnabas and the Shepherd of Hermas

Alongside these incentives are other parts of the Apostolic Fathers that employ other kinds of warnings against apostasy. Two sources that provide clear examples can be found in the Epistle of Barnabas and the Shepherd of Hermas (SOH).[13] The piece that bears Barnabas' name primarily focuses on how early Christians should understand the Old Testament and the related tradition of Judaism in light of their newly found faith. Periodically throughout the discussion we discover directives on being prepared for the coming last days which will culminate with the final judgment. The writer at one point urges his readers to

> never fall asleep in our sins, as if being "called" were an excuse to rest, lest the evil ruler gain power over us and thrust us out of the kingdom of the Lord. Moreover, consider this as well, my brothers and sisters; when you see that after such extraordinary signs and wonders were done in Israel, even then they were abandoned, let us be on guard lest we should be found to be, as it is written, "many called, but few chosen."[14]

Note that this claim aligns with the previous point in 1 and 2 Clement because it identifies spiritual vigilance as a hallmark of God's people. Yet instead of connecting it to the future resurrection, this writer appeals to the history of Israel as a test case. His argument is that just because the Jewish people witnessed all sorts of divine miracles, it did not guarantee that all of them automatically inherited God's promises. Israel was called as a special nation to experience God's manifest witness in history but not many of the Jews were chosen to be his heirs because they eventually turned from the Lord. The writer's point is that this tragedy can still be replicated by those

---

11. Ignatius, *To the Philadelphians*, 3.3.
12. *Didache*, 16.5.
13. These sources are similar to *2 Clement* and the *Didache* in that their authors are unknown.
14. *Epistle of Barnabas*, 4.13–14.

"who genuinely receive the knowledge of the way of righteousness only to ensnare themselves once again in darkness."[15] One can be part of the called group yet still prove not to be a chosen heir.

The SOH uses similar language to stir his audience to obedience. Sometimes he reflects the same kind of eschatological focus by stressing the importance of endurance so that one can enter the coming kingdom. An example of this can be seen where he exhorts his readers to

> not be double-minded, in order that you may gain entrance with the holy angels. Blessed are those of you who patiently endure the coming tribulation and who will not deny their life. For the Lord has sworn by his Son that those who have denied their Lord have been rejected from their life, that is, those who now are about to deny him in the coming days. But to those who formerly denied him, mercy has been granted because of his great compassion.[16]

This quote comes in the middle of SOH's commission to warn some of God's elect who had fallen into serious rebellion. They are told that God provides a limited period of time for them to be forgiven, but after it is over, there will be no other opportunity. So it is imperative that they return while they still can.

Later the SOH recounts a vision in which an angelic figure instructs him on matters that partly pertain to the nature of apostates. He asks, "Sir, now explain to me . . . , what kind of person each of them is, and where they live, in order that when those who have believed and have received the seal and have broken it and have not kept it sound hear this, they may recognize what they are doing."[17] The messenger responds by saying that apostates and traitors to the church will utterly perish if they do not repent.[18] The idea then is that the Lord will forgive spiritual turncoats who return to the fold but judge anyone who refuses.

Matters become a bit more complex in another part of the SOH's teachings when a question is posed on whether forgiveness is possible for sins committed after one's baptism.[19] The angelic messenger tells him that a person may have post-baptismal restoration once, "but if that one sins repeatedly and repents, it is of no use for such a person, for that person will

15. *Epistle of Barnabas*, 5.4.
16. Shepherd of Hermas, *Vision*, 2.2, 6.7–8.
17. Shepherd of Hermas, *Parable*, 8.6, 72.3.
18. Shepherd of Hermas, *Parable*, 72.4–6.
19. Shepherd of Hermas, *Commandment*, 4.3, 31.1–7.

scarcely live."[20] Such a reply highlights a bit of tension in the SOH's visions over the extent to which apostates may be forgiven. The apparent idea is that they could be forgiven only one time if they repented before a divinely delegated probationary period expired. But this related question about the status of sins after baptism lingered on for quite some time. Many Christians eventually concluded that such sins could receive no remission. That is why some became convinced that, if possible, baptism should be delayed until someone was on the brink of death.[21]

2. PERSEVERANCE IN EARLY CHRISTIAN APOLOGISTS AND LEADERS

Beyond these sporadic comments about perseverance in the corpus of the Apostolic Fathers, there are many other treatments that we see in the treatises, letters, and homilies of early church fathers. Some of their concerns overlap with previous points we have seen so far. Nevertheless, as we explore the later second and early third centuries, more situations arose that required Christian scholars to clarify the idea of perseverance even further. Increasing persecutions began to break out that would compel many to recant their faith. And more false teachings with sophisticated arguments emerged which influenced pockets of believers to join dubious sects. Such increasing predicaments forced Christian thinkers to make theological sense out of growing scenarios where converts were, for whatever reasons, abandoning the church.

2.1 Justin Martyr

One initial source who offers some insight on this growing question is the famous apologist Justin Martyr. Justin was originally a Gentile who was born in the Roman colony of Neapolis, which was located in Samaria. Early on, he embraced a career in philosophy until he later converted to Christianity. He then became an avid defender of the faith and eventually made his way to Rome where he spent his career teaching. Among his works that we have access to today, one is entitled a *Dialogue with Trypho*. This piece was intended to provide an interchange with a party named Trypho

---

20. Shepherd of Hermas, *Commandment*, 4.3, 31.1–7. This discussion also offered some of the rudimentary elements that would go into the fully orbed distinction between venial and mortal sins.

21. Allison, *Historical Theology*, 545; Ferguson, *Baptism in the Early Church*, 216–17.

(whether he is a real person or a hypothetical character used for rhetorical interaction is debated). The discussion centers around major theological differences between Christianity and Judaism. At one major point, we see Justin making an important qualification regarding the gravity of committing apostasy. The context is an inquiry that Trypho makes about Christians who are tempted to lapse back into Judaism and view torah compliance as normative for everyday life. Justin shows tolerance for those who may want to practice parts of the Mosaic law in conjunction with their faith in Christ. However, he adds the qualification that "such as have confessed and known this man to be Christ, yet who have gone back from some cause to the legal dispensation, and have denied that this man is Christ, and have repented not before death, shall by no means be saved."[22] He even appeals to the Prophet Ezekiel to argue that the Lord "reckons sinful, unrighteous, and impious the man who falls away from piety and righteousness to unrighteousness and ungodliness."[23] So Justin's point is that if someone claims allegiance to Christ at one time only to later defect into Judaism because they no longer see Christ as the Messiah, they are to be treated as unbelievers—that is unless they repent.

2.2 Irenaeus of Lyons

Another early source who provides some important commentary on the ideas of apostasy and perseverance is the great second-century bishop of Lyons, Irenaeus. We find some pertinent comments in book 4 of his classic work *Against Heresies*. Much of this section is spent defending the idea, contra various gnostic teachings, that the God of the Christian faith is the same over both testaments. The God of the Patriarchs and the prophets is the same Father who sent his Son, Jesus Christ, to bring salvation to all believing Jews and Gentiles.[24] Therefore, believers should shun false teachers and heed the teachings of reliable presbyters because they give witness to the fact that Christ is the ultimate treasure hidden within all the Scripture.[25]

From here, Irenaeus expresses some of his pastoral wisdom because he knows that admonitions to remain steadfast in and of themselves do not ensure that congregants will heed them. This leads him to do what many NT writers did, namely warn them of presumptuous sin. He alludes to the OT accounts of David and Solomon's moral failures to remind his readers that if

22. Justin Martyr, *Dialogue with Trypho*, ch. 47.
23. Justin Martyr, *Dialogue with Trypho*, 1.219.
24. Irenaeus, *Against Heresies*, 4.21–25.
25. Irenaeus, *Against Heresies*, 4.26.1–5.

God judged them for their sins, what will happen to those who sin without repentance now that Christ has come. Here Irenaeus echoes the language of Hebrews when he says,

> And truly, the death of the Lord brought healing and remission of sins to the former. However, Christ will not die again on behalf of those who now commit sin. . . . Rather, we should fear ourselves, least perchance, after [we have come to] the knowledge of Christ, if we do things displeasing to God, we obtain no further forgiveness of sins and be shut out of his kingdom.[26]

Then for stronger emphasis, he appeals to Paul's warning in Rom 11 that if God did not spare natural branches, neither would he spare wild ones that had been grafted in.[27]

Irenaeus continues to reference Paul by later reflecting on his famous words to the Corinthians about not making the same mistakes that Israel did in the wilderness wanderings. Just as many Israelites died and fell short of the promised land because of their rebellion, so should believers be careful not to fall. They should never lapse back into their former ways of living because as Paul says elsewhere, those who do so reflect the habits of those who will be judged. Irenaeus is quick to point out here that Paul did not say these things to people outside the faith "but to us, lest we should be cast forth from the kingdom of God, by doing any such thing, he proceeds to say 'And such indeed were you; but you are washed, but you are sanctified in the name of the Lord Jesus Christ, and by the Spirit of God.'"[28]

These kinds of warnings are taken up again later in the last chapter of book 4 where Irenaeus speaks about how people can be described as the sons of God. Irenaeus states that one can be a son in one of two ways, either biologically and/or by adoption. The reason he highlights this distinction is that all humanity and even angels are technically God's "sons" in the sense that they are all created beings. However, some angels chose to follow the fallen angel Satan and become his "sons" or angels. Humanity also chose the same plight through Adam who repeated Satan's antics by rebelling against God. They became the devil's progeny too.[29] Irenaeus concludes that even though all people remain God's children by nature, they forfeit their rank of sonship because of their sin. They lose their privilege as legal heirs unless they repent and are converted.[30]

26. Irenaeus, *Against Heresies*, 4.27.2.
27. Irenaeus, *Against Heresies*, 4.27.2.
28. Irenaeus, *Against Heresies*, 4.27.4.
29. Irenaeus, *Against Heresies*, 4.41.1–2.
30. Irenaeus, *Against Heresies*, 4.41.3.

The lingering question that remains at this point is whether one can be disinherited again once they become redeemed heirs in Christ. Irenaeus does observe that when some "believe and are subject to God, and go on and keep his doctrine, they are sons of God; but when they have apostatized and fallen into transgression, they are ascribed to their chief, the devil and to do his works."[31] Here it appears that here Irenaeus may be addressing the matter of perseverance but the interpretive dilemma is deciphering how exactly. Most likely he is either referring to gnostic false teachers who may have been false professors from the outset or former fallen "sons" who repented and later apostatized only to be disinherited once more.

Another area where Irenaeus speaks about apostasy is in his treatment of the eschatological beast described in the book of Revelation.[32] The figure, otherwise known as the antichrist, will unleash havoc upon the earth, including the instigation of a great apostasy. This kind of travesty is the very purpose of his existence. He will arrive to deceive and destroy. It is also why John ascribes the number 666 to him. Irenaeus postulates that this title is a conflation of 600 years of wickedness caused by apostate angels before Noah's flood and 6,000 years of apostasy that has transpired throughout human history.[33] But in the face of this final onslaught against humanity, Irenaeus says that the faith of the saints will endure. The chaff of the apostates will burn while the wheat of the faithful will be gathered into the barn.[34] At the same time, only those who overcome in the contest of righteousness against the deceptive ploys of the beast will be crowned with incorruption.[35] So in the end, while a case can be made that Irenaeus may or may not have explicitly affirmed that a true believer could apostatize (and possibly be restored if they repented), there is no question that he viewed perseverance as a necessary act to reach the goal of final eschatological salvation.

2.3 Tertullian

The fiery rhetorician from Carthage, North Africa, also had much to say about the idea of perseverance. One reason he did was because he was greatly troubled about the influence that false teachers could have on impressionable believers. He clearly expresses this concern in his classic work, *On Prescription Against Heretics*, where he uses Saul, David, and Solomon

---

31. Irenaeus, *Against Heresies*, 4.41.3.
32. Irenaeus, *Against Heresies*, 5.28–29.
33. Cf. Irenaeus, *Against Heresies*, 5.28–29; Oropeza, *Paul and Apostasy*, 6.
34. Irenaeus, *Against Heresies*, 5.28.
35. Irenaeus, *Against Heresies*, 5.29.

as test cases. Each of these kings started off well but eventually fell into serious sin. Similarly, some believers who start on the path of righteousness later become misguided by heretics and fall into ruin.[36] While they may have received the seal of salvation at their baptism, they tragically soil their wedding garments of sainthood, thereby becoming lost once again.[37] Or like the earth which was purged by Noah's flood and is now doomed to the judgment of fire, so too is the end of anyone who is cleansed in baptism only to renew their life of sin.[38]

Such hazards persuaded Tertullian that a healthy dose of trepidation could serve as a good preventative against apostasy. The possibility of falling from grace might motivate some to cling to Christ even more fervently. This is why Tertullian cautioned his readers that their confidence in God's sustaining grace, if left unchecked, could actually lead to presumption or taking salvation for granted. This could only end in ruin because if one drops their spiritual guard, then unbelief could eventually take root and give birth to apostasy. Thus, Tertullian argues that "no one is a Christian but he who perseveres even to the end.[39] So believers should possess a healthy dose of fear because it keeps one honest in their walk with the Lord.[40]

2.4 Clement and Origen of Alexandria

The two eminent theologians of Alexandria showed general agreement with the concerns that previous fathers emphasized about perseverance. For instance, Clement warned those who had received the gospel that they should not to be allured by the lusts of their previous ways of life or any potential heresies. To do so would put them in the same plight as Lot's wife who in

---

36. Tertullian, *On Prescription Against Heretics*, ch. 3. Tertullian's point is not necessarily that the first three kings of Israel ended up being unbelievers. He is using them as an analogical point of reference to argue that just as they fell into sin and were judged, those who apostatize will be judged as well.

37. Tertullian, *Scorpiace*, ch. 6.

38. Tertullian, *On Baptism*, ch. 8.

39. Tertullian, *On Prescription Against Heretics*, ch. 3.

40. See Tertullian's discussion of this point in Tertullian, *On the Apparel of Women*, 1.2. Tertullian makes this point in the context of temptation to sexual immorality. Having a healthy dose of fear can give people incentive to avoid temptation. However, before making this point, Tertullian states the overall purpose of this treatise is to discuss the important of modesty. He describes modesty as the caretaker, or priestess, of believers' bodies, which are the temples of the Spirit. Then he states that modesty "suffers nothing unclean or profane to be introduced (into it), for fear that the God who inhabits it should be offended, and quite forsake the polluted abode." See Tertullian, *On the Apparel of Women*, 1.1.

the midst of her very deliverance from Sodom and Gomorrah's destruction chose to look back to her own peril.[41] Origen concedes that such admonitions should be heeded because "a man may possess an acquired righteousness, from which it is possible for him to fall away."[42] It is therefore possible for a believer who at some point chooses not to deny himself and deny Christ, the fact is that Christ will deny him.[43] Likewise, they both reflect a commitment to the idea that sins committed after one's baptism must be addressed via repentance and other forms of penance. Clement states that "forgiveness of past sins, then, God gives; but of future, each one gives to himself. And this is to repent, to condemn the past deeds, and beg oblivion of them from the Father."[44] Origen goes as far as to call baptism the "laver of regeneration" because of its capacity to bring remission of sins.[45] Still, the benefits of this gift can be revoked in light of future sinful conduct or unbelief. That is partly why Origen actually deems some in error who teach that one can be saved in such a way that they can never be lost.[46] The reason being that such a notion mitigates against one's free will to either obey or renounce Christ.[47]

---

41. Clement of Alexandria, *Stromata*, 7.16.

42. Origen, *On First Principles*, 1.8.3. Here Origen's main topic of discussion is the nature of angels. Though created good, angels, including Satan himself before his fall, had the capacity to obey God, but this ability did not prevent them from have the capacity to rebel. Even so, people can have a similar status and choose to forfeit it. The interpretive issue is whether Origen is merely referring to Adam's fall or whether he would classify apostate believers in this category as well.

43. Origen, *Commentary on Matthew*, 11.24. The quotation applies to anyone who never professes Christ or those who maybe do for a time.

44. Clement, *Who Is the Rich Man*, ch. 40.

45. Cf. Origen, *Commentary on John*, 6.17; Origen, *Commentary on Matthew*, 13.27. Also see Ferguson's treatment of Origen's view of baptism in Ferguson, *Baptism in the Early Church*, 410–17. Here the point related to perseverance is that one can experience the preliminary salvific grace of salvation via baptism but later turn from that grace later in life through disobedience and/or apostasy.

46. Origen, *On First Principles*, 3.8. In context, this statement entails a possible implication that believers can apostatize. Origen's original point was that salvation is not determined by whether a person's nature is good or bad. God does not harden those who are already evil and save those whose natures are virtuous. Origen's argument is that natures can change as the human will encounters divine action. So a bad nature can be changed for the better. But the question remaining is whether a changed nature for the good can possibly revert back to corruption.

47. What is ironic is that if Origen did explicitly affirm that believers could apostatize, even such an act could potentially be redeemed depending on how one interprets his famous concept of the *apokatastasis*, or the restoration of all creation. Cf. Origen *On First Principles*, 1.6.3; 3.6.6.

2.5 Victorinus

One final source worthy of mention because it highlights an important wrinkle in early Christian perceptions of perseverance is a commentary on the book of Revelation provided by a late third-century bishop in Syria named Victorinus. The most pertinent section for our study occurs in the latter part of this work when he is providing input on the events surrounding the early part of Rev 20. He interprets the binding of Satan and being subsequently cast into an abyss with a seal being placed upon it as a cryptic allusion to his incapacity to deceive believers. The devil is shut up in this abyss, which Victorinus identifies as the collective hearts of the wicked, so he is restrained and unable to seduce those who identify with Christ.[48] Victorinus deduces that the reason a seal is placed over the abyss is because the true identity of those who belong to the devil or Christ is to remain a secret until the last day. He observes, "For we know not of those who seem to stand whether they shall not fall, and of those who are down it is uncertain whether they may rise."[49] His argument then is that while Satan is bound to those who reject Christ, we cannot conclusively identify someone as part of his regime or Christ's until the eschaton.[50]

3. EARLY CHRISTIAN DELIBERATIONS ON APOSTASY: THE NOVATIAN SCHISM

We see from this selection of sources that apostasy was an urgent concern in the minds of early Christian thinkers. Unfortunately, their constant appeals to remain in the faith did not prevent all professing believers from recanting. Some did—and often, as time wore on, the primary reason was imperial oppression. Many feared the threats of losing loved ones or being tortured and executed by Roman rulers who were hostile toward Christianity. So as the number of apostates sometimes increased in regions of the Roman Empire where persecution was the most intense, there was always a looming question that constantly had to be answered. What were Christian communities supposed to do when people, who had renounced their faith during a severe period of persecution, later repented and wanted to be restored after the time of affliction ended. This ordeal caused quite a bit of controversy in the early church because any proposed answer entailed a litany of complications. For instance, if these former apostates, otherwise

---

48. Victorinus, *Commentary on the Apocalypse*, 20.1–3.
49. Victorinus, *Commentary on the Apocalypse*, 20.1–3.
50. Victorinus, *Commentary on the Apocalypse*, 20.1–3.

known as the lapsed, were simply allowed to return, then there was concern that some might exploit the process and apostatize again because they knew they could always come back later.[51] Also, how would the restoration of the lapsed be perceived by believers who remained faithful during hard times. Or if a church chose to avoid these troubles by not permitting apostates back into the fold, then there were questions as to who could make such a determination and what would this kind of exclusion say about the gospel message of forgiveness.

One can quickly see that there were no easy answers to this issue. That is why it engendered significant disagreement. Many Christians just could not iron out an air-tight consensus on what the proper criteria should be for identifying who was truly part of the church. Some, who can be labeled as *rigorists*, argued that the church was to be made up of those who lived in strict piety and resisted all external pressures to apostatize. The Lord could possibly grant the lapsed absolution on the day of judgment, but the church could not risk reinstating them back into the fellowship.[52] Others, who could be seen as *laxists* because they feared the rigorist ideology as potentially legalistic, defined the church more in terms of a community who offered mercy and deliverance for sinners who struggled with sin.[53] Invariably, this difference of opinion led to an impasse among some Christian leaders. The robust dialogue sparked by the debate helped many churches develop approaches for receiving any lapsed converts. And it appears that by the end of the second century, there were some general steps which many followed to allow them back into restored communion.[54]

This process of reflection eventually reached a boiling point by the middle of the third century because of further concerns about church officers. The question pertained to the proper role that bishops were to have in helping restore the lapsed. This obscured matters quite a bit because by the third century, bishops had adopted a sort of gatekeeper status wherein their responsibilities went beyond just the pastoral care of one congregation. Periodically certain bishops took on more administrative duties that required them to oversee numerous churches in various territories. One of their tasks was supervising the guidance of any lapsed members who had expressed penitence for their actions, and it is here where complexities began to emerge.

---

51. To be fair, some believed that a lapsed convert could only be restored once.
52. Schaff, *History of the Christian Church*, 2.196; Ferguson, *Church History*, 145.
53. Ferguson, *Church History*, 145–46.
54. Ferguson, *Church History*, 146.

What if a bishop fell into heresy or a sinful vice? Or what if a political coup arose between rival candidates for a vacant position in a church that gave people reason to be suspicious of the selection process?[55] These kinds of scenarios caused many to reevaluate the ecclesiastical pull of church leaders and look for alternative sources of authority. One that gained some traction was paying special homage to believers who had faithfully withstood persecution without recanting their faith. Some saw these *confessors* as spiritual heroes who were worthy of honor and could be entrusted with the task of acknowledging whether a lapsed member could be readmitted. Others, however, who still wanted to revere the office of the bishop as having a bit more pull than confessors, thought a better strategy was to clean house among the clergy.

In various regions, many began renouncing any church officers who were guilty of lapsing themselves. They deemed such actions as automatically invalidating the integrity of a bishop's clerical duties, whether it be baptisms, ordinations, the leading of the Lord's Supper, or rendering verdicts over lapsed converts. Despite these various proposals, the fact of the matter was that a toxic divide was surfacing. It had begun with questions about restoring lapsed converts. Then it morphed into a larger debate about the unity of the church and ecclesiastical authority. It was now threatening the life of the church, especially in Rome and Northern Africa. And in our examination of how the idea of perseverance was perceived in early Christianity, some of the most significant details emerged during this crisis, especially during a dispute known as the Novatian schism.

3.1 A Synopsis of the Novatian Schism

The ancient Christians were accustomed to dealing with consistent waves of persecution. Random oppressions were sanctioned but were usually restricted to specific regions of the Roman Empire. So most of the severe suffering often fell upon those who were unable to flee from the hot-spots where oppression was being enforced. The violence fluctuated depending on the levels of rancor that new Roman Emperors expressed toward Christianity. Sometimes there were even lulls where aggression abated because new rulers were indifferent toward opposing religions. One significantly long remission occurred in the early third century where believers experienced a thirty-eight-year window of relative peace (AD 212 to 250).

But by the mid-third century, it all came to a screeching halt when the new emperor Decius came into power. Whatever his motives may have

---

55. Olson, *Story of Christian Theology*, 114–15.

been, he demanded that Roman leaders either eliminate Christians or "compel" them to pay homage to the gods through prescribed sacrifices or offering incense. The sources that are accessible to us indicate that the level of severity was executed at the discretion of the local authorities in each Roman region rather than by Decius directly.[56] This meant some received worse treatment than others. Still, this persecution stretched over the entire empire with many losing their lives and the number of lapsed converts reaching an all-time high. There were even bishops and priests who relinquished their duties when they merely heard about the impending edict that Decius had passed.[57] By the time it was over, the Decian persecution had reached such a tragic level of intensity that it would only be rivaled by the infamous Diocletian suppression some thirty-four years later.

The repercussions of such a devastating turn of events like this were massive to say the least. Two of the main ones were trying to arbitrate the vast number of lapsed converts who now wanted readmittance into the church and resolving the political turmoil that was surging because of the need to replace bishops who had been martyred. The areas that were hit the hardest with these problems were Rome, North Africa, and Egypt. But our discussion will focus on the initial ordeal in Carthage, North Africa, and a subsequent controversy in Rome because they are the ones that are most pertinent to the Novatian faction.[58]

The story begins with the one figure who carried the biggest burden in adjudicating much of the turmoil caused by these matters, namely Cyprian of Carthage. Thascius Cyprian was born sometime at the turn of the third century to pagan parents. He received a quality education and climbed the ladder of the North African Roman pecking order during his young adult years. Some speculate that he was a lawyer and professor of rhetoric.[59] What we do know was that around 246 he became a believer under the tutelage of a presbyter named Caecilius. Then within two years of his conversion, his unique rate of maturity and acclimation toward serving the poor convinced the Christian masses in Carthage that he should be ordained as a priest. He

56. Von Mosheim, *Historical Commentaries on the State of Christianity*, 2:31.

57. Von Mosheim, *Historical Commentaries on the State of Christianity*, 2:31.

58. An earlier schism possibly occurred in Rome that included the Christian leader Hippolytus (historical details on this matter are complex; see Dunbar, "Problem of Hippolytus of Rome," 63–74) and a later skirmish transpired in Egypt between a bishop named Meletius of Lycopolis and his superior, Peter of Alexandria. See overview in Telfer, "Meletius of Lycopolis," 227–37.

59. One can consult his biography written by a deacon named Pontius; an account of his martyrdom entitled *Acts of Cyprian*, his own corpus of letters and treatises, and other secondary sources by Jerome and a few others. See Ferguson, *Church History*, 163; Arnold, *Cyprian of Carthage*; and Benson, *Cyprian*.

reluctantly accepted the responsibility, shortly thereafter becoming bishop of the whole region. Yet some were not happy because they thought this series of events was unjustified.

Resistance initially came from five presbyters with the most vocal being a man named Novatus.[60] One of his colleagues, who was a deacon he had ordained named Felicissimus, also became a strong critic of Cyprian. The faction did not gain much momentum until the Decian persecution broke out a year later. Upon its inception, Cyprian thought it would be prudent to provide leadership from afar. So he fled to the desert for refuge. This decision was criticized initially because many feared that if he was killed, it would leave Carthage in dire straits. Thus, Cyprian remained in constant contact with church officers via a reliable stream of messengers.[61]

At the same time, though, his absence still allowed his opponents to enact practices with which Cyprian disapproved. The main one pertained to the restoring of lapsed converts without following the protocol that Cyprian had established through his network of bishops in Carthage. Thinking his approach was too strict, his antagonists relied more on the testimony of confessors to grant reinstitution in lieu of Cyprian's absence. Felicissimus also gathered support from others who were dissatisfied with Cyprian's treatment of the lapsed to mount a full-scale revolt. However, before it could gain much headway, Decius' oppression began to settle down which led to Cyprian's return in 251. He immediately summoned a synod to excommunicate Felicissimus and reaffirm the established rules for restoring the lapsed. The sentence was appealed the next year with Felicissimus trying to gain support from a similar schism in Rome, but to no avail. This faction eventually dissolved and Felicissimus was no more. Yet Novatus still had another role to fill in this story.

On the tail end of this feud was another altercation that was brewing in Rome and ironically, it too started over a disagreement on a newly elected bishop. One of the saddest losses during the Decian persecution was the martyrdom of the beloved Fabian who was the bishop of Rome at the time. After his death, the filling of his office was delayed for over a year until Decius' reign of terror finally ended. Once it did, there were many lapsed members knocking on the doors of churches wanting restoration. And to make matters even more complicated, their reasons for recanting were numerous. Some had renounced their faith by offering sacrifices in honor of Roman deities while others conceded an offering of incense to the emperor. Others tried a form of bribery to escape any potential civil pressure by purchasing

---

60. There is some debate as to whether Novatus was one of the five or not.

61. Olson, *Story of Christian Theology*, 116.

certificates from regional authorities that claimed they had paid their dues to the Roman gods. Altogether then, this was quite a predicament and now a new bishop had been elected named Cornelius.

His election was supported by Cyprian even though they differed on how strict the rules should be for restoring apostates. The real problem was an undercurrent of tension that had already been brewing because there were some who thought the standards should be even stricter than what Cyprian recommended. One who felt this way was Novatian, a presbyter in Rome who had gained some ecclesiastical clout during the hiatus between Fabian's death and Cornelius' appointment. During the dark times of Decius, he had consulted with Cyprian through several letters on the question of the lapsed and argued that letting them return would compromise the moral fiber of the church. In addition, before Cyprian returned to Carthage after his brief time of exile, his former opponent Novatus had become an associate of Novatian.[62]

Nevertheless, with his support along with several other presbyters, Novatian refused to cooperate with Cornelius' proposals. He even mounted the support of three other bishops in Italy who joined his entire faction to elect him as alternative bishop of Rome. This potential divide resulted in both Cornelius and Novatian sending messengers to surrounding churches as a means of mounting support for their respective stances. Their appeals eventually made their way to Cyprian who then persuaded his fellow North African bishops to back Cornelius. This sealed the deal in a sense because Cornelius now had the reinforcements he needed for convening a council to excommunicate Novatian. Yet the two parties continued to exist for quite some time with the Novatians declaring a perpetual rival Roman bishop to the traditional one.

3.2 Cyprian's Theological Assessments of Restoring the Lapsed

Cyprian's interaction with the Novatian faction is a critical moment in the development of early Christian views of perseverance for two reasons. One was that he combined his own beliefs with many of the conclusions that previous Christian thinkers had expressed on the matter and applied them to an extremely complicated situation. This is not to say that figures like Irenaeus, Ignatius, Clement, or Tertullian were not addressing practical matters during their lifetimes. Indeed they were. But the Novatian schism created an unprecedented crisis with the ministries of bishops and the lives

---

62. Note that confusion should be avoided and not mistake Novatus and Novatian as the same person. See Pose, "Novatus of Carthage," 938.

of penitent apostates hanging in the balance. Its complexity would only be rivaled by the later Donatist controversy that caused Augustine of Hippo so many problems. So, regardless of the accuracy of his conclusions, Cyprian's arguments acted as a rallying cry for many believers living in Northern Africa and Rome during the third century.

Second, his views on perseverance are significant because he had to express them in connection with several other key theological issues, including baptism, the episcopate, and the church. One could say that Cyprian integrated his convictions on perseverance into a larger systematic framework because it was intertwined with what he believed about so many other topics. Thus, the only way he could untie the one knot of perseverance was if he was willing to unravel a larger ball of ecclesiological yarn.

Cyprian met this challenge head on and if we want understand how he did so, the place to begin is with his view of the role that bishops had in the church. His classic work, *On the Unity of the Church*, encapsulates his entire case against the Novatians wherein he argues that the grounding source of the church's functional solidarity is not the purity of its members. Rather it is the collection of bishops known as the episcopate. This point required further clarification because the Novatians believed that they had a viable alternative group of bishops who had not apostatized nor were they willing to compromise the purity of the church by permitting apostates back into the fold. That is why Cyprian countered with the charge that they were false bishops because true ones must be placed within an episcopal position by the accepted ecclesiastical authorities.[63] This indicted the Novatians because they had installed a rival bishop to oppose Cyprian and Novatian had strong-armed a contested office in Rome contra Cornelius. Cyprian's point then was that the office of bishop, which is perpetuated through an exclusive line preserved all the way back to the Apostle Peter, is what is sacred, not any particular bishop.[64] Consequently, while the acceptance or denial of the lapsed was a concern that could impact the health of the church, it was not the glue that could make or break the church's identity altogether. The ingredient serving that role was the episcopate because where there was no true bishop, (i.e., true in accordance with the proper authority), there is no church.

Now it is in light of these polemics that Cyprian articulated his beliefs about perseverance. This makes perfect sense because his answers to questions about the church's unity were directly related to his concern about the lapsed having the capacity to reenter congregations. One could say that

---

63. McKim, *Theological Turning Points*, 53.
64. Cf. Cyprian, *On the Unity of the Church*, 1.4–5; Cyprian, *To Florentius*, 68.8–10.

his ecclesiology and soteriology were necessarily interconnected. When we read his treatments on apostasy and restoration, it is clear that he shared many of the same sentiments that earlier Christians had expressed on the matter. For starters, we discover that he saw many apostates as bona fide converts who had recanted a genuine faith. Any view to the contrary would have made his entire interchange with the Novatians nonsensical. They differed on whether to readmit apostates, not on whether they were formerly believers. We also see that Cyprian stood in line with how many previous Christian thinkers understood baptism and the real potential that any believer could turn away from Christ. He affirmed, for example, that the act of baptism extinguishes the fires of *gehenna* and grants remission of one's sins.[65] Likewise, it is the means whereby the new birth in the Spirit takes place.[66] Cyprian even goes a step further by arguing that baptism can erase the guilt of original sin that infants inherit from Adam. He reasons that

> if even to the greatest sinners, and to those who had sinned much against God, when they subsequently believed, remission of sins is granted—and nobody is hindered from baptism and from grace—how much rather ought we to shrink from hindering an infant, who, being lately born, has not sinned except in that, being born after the flesh according to Adam, he has contracted the contagion of the ancient death at its earliest birth who approaches the more easily on this very account to the reception of the forgiveness of sins—that to him are remitted, not his own sins, but the sins of another.[67]

At the same time, he is quick to point out that the salvific benefits of baptism do not ensure that believers will inevitably persevere. On the contrary sometimes the devil who was driven out in baptism is able to return if one's faith should ever fail.[68]

It is clear then that Cyprian believed apostasy was a dire reality to avoid at all costs. This is why discussions about abandoning the faith are sprinkled all throughout his writings. There are times where he echoes leaders such as Irenaeus in presenting characters like Saul and Solomon as perfect examples of those who started well in God's grace but tragically fell into idolatry and judgment.[69] He charges believers to learn from these stories that abandoning Christ will result in him forsaking them in judgment. At other times he

---

65. Cyprian, *On Works and Alms*, 8.2; Cyprian, *Exhortation to Martyrdom*, 11.4.
66. Cyprian, *To Pompey*, 73.7.
67. Cyprian, *To Fidus, On the Baptism of Infants*, 58.5.
68. Cyprian, *To Magnus*, 75.16.
69. Cf. Cyprian, *To Rogatianus*, 6.2–3; Cyprian, *On the Unity of the Church*, 1.20–21.

admonishes his readers to fight daily for their faith because the greatest part of salvation is successfully attaining its ultimate goal, not just experiencing a mere foretaste only to fall short of the prize.[70] He agrees with Tertullian that confidence in one's status as a believer can inadvertently erode into presumption, thereby becoming a hazardous step toward sin. This is why he advises believers to be confident in Christ's ability to sustain them while at the same time never praising anyone before their death because it is only those who endure to the end who will be rewarded and thereby saved.[71] Finally, he gives periodic instruction on how apostates can be permitted back to the church under certain stipulations that are enforced by the bishops. Here his basic argument against the Novatians' stringency was that the only real option for penitent apostates was to let them return because there is no forgiveness or salvation outside the church.[72] Cyprian asks, where else can they go? Or to quote his famous quip, "Can he have God as his Father, before he has had the church for his mother?"[73]

4. CONCLUSIONS ON THE EARLY CHURCH'S VIEW OF PERSEVERANCE

Looking back on what many of the early church fathers said about the role of perseverance in salvation is quite a sobering matter. Because these Christian thinkers were part of the immediate generations following the apostolic era, they saw their experiences as directly corresponding to what the congregations of the first century had faced, even arguably to greater lengths. Though the cultural climate of the Roman empire was changing and Christianity was expanding, believers still struggled with temptations to sin, the luring deception of false teachers, and the heavy burden of persecution. Moreover, as we have already observed, it is clear that many early Christian writers thought that the life of the church sometimes replicated the experiences of the old covenant people of Israel.[74] One reason for this was because they thought it was adopted by Christ and his new-covenant people, including

---

70. Cyprian, *To Rogatianus*, 6.2.

71. Cyprian, *To the Presbyters and Deacons*, 5.2; Cyprian, *On the Advantage of Patience*, 9.24.

72. Cyprian, *To Jubaianus*, 72.20–21.

73. Cyprian, *To Pompey*, 73.7.

74. This is not to say that they viewed the redemptive historical life of both entities as completely coterminous. They did see significant variances because of the covenantal transitions inaugurated by the work of Christ. But they were sensitive to how NT writers often used OT narratives to motivate NT believers to remain steadfast in their faith both individually as well as communally.

the portions that spoke of the possibility of being potentially cut off from the community and experiencing divine judgment. Just as Jews in the Mosaic economy could receive the blessings of grace and still fall short of it because of later rebellion, so could believers in the new messianic economy fall into unbelief and be cut off.

Another way of illustrating this point is to think of a baby at conception. Once fertilization occurs, a new human life begins to form. Similarly, at baptism the initial experience of spiritual life commences. Then just as a baby must develop properly in the womb to reach the final culmination of physical birth, a believer must follow the road of discipleship to reach the destination of eternal life in the age to come. If anyone commits apostasy instead, without subsequent repentance, they can potentially become a spiritual stillborn who will fall under judgment along with the rest of unbelieving humanity.

In either case, whether it be Israel's story or a baby's journey to being born, the point to see is that early Christian thought was in general agreement on the necessity of perseverance. Granted, there was some diversity of opinion regarding the role of baptism in the conversion experience or whether true believers could actually apostatize. But there was relative consensus that any professing believer who failed to persevere would not participate in the resurrection unto eternal life even if they may have received preliminary remission of sins or encountered the early stages of the new birth through the in-working of the Holy Spirit.[75] Admittedly, some church fathers are clearer than others on whether they thought apostates were initially genuine believers. Some did, whereas a case could be made that others may have spoken to believers about the realities of apostasy in the same way the NT writers did without explicitly claiming that believers really would apostatize. In any case, the emphasis upon the importance of perseverance that emerged among early Christian thinkers helped set the stage for much of what the fifth-century theologian Augustine of Hippo would say about the subject, barring his strong emphasis on determinism and modified treatment on the nature of the human will. This is why we now need to turn to his view of perseverance. As we shall see, his proposals on the subject would prove to be extremely influential on a host of Christian traditions in subsequent centuries.

---

75. It is key to clarify that many church fathers thought apostasy could be forgiven if repentance occurred before death. The real disagreement, as we have seen, was about whether one should be allowed back into the church.

Chapter 6

Augustine, Pelagianism, and Perseverance

WE SAW IN THE previous chapter that the Novatian schism of the mid-third century created a complicated situation where Christian leaders in the Roman west, such as Cyprian the bishop of Carthage, were forced to solidify some preliminary theological commitments that could address pressing questions about apostasy. Over a century and a half later, in the early fifth century, questions about the nature of grace and human nature intensified so much that even stronger doctrinal categories were created which would, in turn, impact how future generations of Christians would approach the subject of perseverance. During this period Christians were facing the social and economic pressures of war because the Roman Empire was being dismantled by invading Gothic tribes.

At the same time, Christian leaders in Rome and Northern Africa found themselves in the midst of a heated theological dispute known as the Pelagian controversy. Multiple theologians, bishops, and monks were involved in pertinent synods, councils, and debates, but the primary thinker who stood above them all was Augustine, the bishop of Hippo. This ordeal, along with the related skirmish of Semi-Pelagianism, acted as the last and most well-known theological conflict in which Augustine participated as a church official. He wrote various letters and treatises to deal with the assorted entanglements of this dispute. He even died while writing a piece against a Pelagian bishop named Julian of Eclanum.[1]

Today when we observe the corpus of literature that he bequeathed known as his Anti-Pelagian writings, several issues emerge as primary, with one definitely being the doctrine of perseverance. Yet before one can understand how he interpreted Scripture to shape his thoughts on this matter, we must first set the backdrop of the controversy. Then we can examine the issues that were being disputed, properly engage Augustine's own proposals, and finally reflect on how his views impacted future generations of theologians.

1. THE PELAGIAN CONTROVERSY

Pelagius, the individual at the center of the controversy which now bears his name, was a roaming ascetic about whom little biographical information exists. We are uncertain about the details of his life but we do know it ended in exile. It is possible he was born in Britain but scholars differ even on the details, proposing that he was maybe a Scot or perhaps an Irishman born in Britain.[2] He was also a monk or at least a believer heavily inclined toward asceticism who never held any type of clerical office. At some time nearing the end of the fourth century he journeyed to Rome where he gradually began spreading his teachings discreetly with no real problems arising at the outset.[3] Over time he gained pockets of followers who embraced his convictions, including one important figure, a former lawyer named Caelestius, who joined him around 390.

1.1 Pelagius and Caelestius Cause Initial Doctrinal Concern

When the fifth century came on the horizon, a debate emerged regarding death, sin, and the baptism which would set the initial backdrop for Pelagius to begin articulating his views in more public venues.[4] When tensions rose because of competing opinions, Pelagius joined the discussion by criticizing Augustine's views of sin, the will, and predestination that he had expressed

---

1. Because it was incomplete, it became known as *Unfinished Work*. See Warfield, "Introductory Essay on Augustine," lxv; and Markus, "Life of Augustine," 504.

2. Stortz, "Pelagius Revisited," 134. There are some disputes today as to whether Church historians have misconstrued his teachings and created a false narrative about his theology, e.g., Bonner, *Myth of Pelagianism*.

3. His first work dating around AD 405 in the early fifth century.

4. TeSelle, "Pelagius, Pelagianism," 633.

in a piece written to Simplicianus, Ambrose's successor as bishop of Milan.[5] Amid the conflict, Pelagius had an unfortunate episode with a bishop because of his disagreement with Augustine's famous line in his *Confessions* where he said prayerfully, "Give what you command and command what you will."[6] Augustine's point here was that during his spiritual pilgrimage, he had learned that the only way sinners could have the ability to obey any expectation that God revealed was if he provided the volitional capacity to do so by his empowering grace.

Pelagius was scandalized by such an idea. Not only did it seem to contradict what Augustine had written years earlier in his work *On Free Will*.[7] It nullified any grounds for Christian piety because it compromised a proper understanding of human nature and freedom. For Pelagius, obedience was only meaningful if one had the capacity to follow whatever demands were known. This is why he contended that humanity does not inherit any guilt or corruption from Adam as a result of his fall. Rather all people are born in innocence with the capacity to obey the Lord just as Adam could before his fall. Moreover, Pelagius defined sin in terms of action only as opposed to any state of being or condition. People could freely choose to achieve righteousness if they wanted to or rebel against God just as Adam did.[8]

Now up to this point, Pelagius had not encountered any significant opposition while in Rome. However, when Gothic regimes began to make their way toward the heart of the Empire in 409, both Pelagius and Caelestius made their way south to Northern Africa by 411. They visited the region of Hippo but Augustine was not there to meet them at the time. Afterward they arrived in Carthage and eventually Pelagius traveled further east to Palestine while Caelestius stayed behind. In doing so, the stage began to be set for the first wave of ecclesiastical entanglements. Trouble

---

5. *To Simplicianus* was written approximately in 396.

6. Augustine, *Thirteen Books of the Confessions*, 10.31.45.

7. *On Free Will* was written between 388–395. Pelagius was somewhat correct to point out the difference of opinion that Augustine originally expressed. This is partly why Augustine later wrote *On Grace and Free Will* in 426–427 to clarify matters relating to free will and God's sovereignty in providing grace for sinners.

8. Much of Pelagius' views were based on his interpretations of the writings of Paul, which was a common source of inquiry during Pelagius' lifetime. See Stortz, "Pelagius Revisited," 135; Brown, *Augustine of Hippo*, 151. An initial work of Pelagius where the elemental components of his theology is entitled *On Nature* which was given to two of his students, Timasius and Jacobus. They eventually sent a copy to Augustine to which he provided a response in his *On Nature and Grace*. Though Pelagius' work as a whole is lost to history along with other pieces, one can consult some of his letters in Pelagius, *Pelagius: His Life and Letters*. He also wrote his commentaries on Paul's epistles during this time (405–409) in which he carefully articulated many of his views on sin and grace. See Pelagius, *Pelagius' Expositions of Thirteen Epistles of Paul*.

ensued when Caelestius requested to be ordained into the priesthood. He was turned down because of accusations that were made by a deacon from Milan named Paulinus. He came forward at a synod in Carthage in 411 with charges of heresy against him, and the matter was brought before a bishop named Aurelius. The case included seven specific points that Caelestius (as possibly taught by Pelagius) was accused of teaching, including:

1. Adam, being created mortal, would have died even if he had not sinned.
2. Adam's sin harmed only himself, and not the entire human race.
3. Newborn children in a similar state in which Adam was before the fall.
4. The whole human race neither dies because of Adam's sin, nor rises because of Christ's resurrection.
5. Infants enjoy the status of Adam before the fall and hence may attain eternal life irrespective of baptism.
6. Both the law and the gospel are means of salvation.
7. There lived some sinless men prior to Christ.[9]

When the synod's exchange ended, Caelestius refused to recant of these charges except for the one concerning the destiny of unbaptized infants. He conceded that leaders in the church were equivocal at best regarding an answer to this question. So because he stood by the other points, he was excommunicated. But instead of accepting defeat, he revealed his intention to appeal to Rome in person but journeyed to Ephesus instead where he did receive ordination in 415.

While all of these events were transpiring, Pelagius was still in Palestine. Things became tense when a presbyter named Paulus Orosius came with letters from Augustine for Jerome. Augustine, by this time, had begun contributing to the debate in response to letters from Carthage that he had received. He had written *On the Merits and Forgiveness of Sins and on Infant Baptism* (411–412), *On the Spirit and the Letter* (412), and preached a sermon in which he appealed to Cyprian's view of baptism in a possible attempt to counter some in the Roman church who were sympathetic to Caelestius' views.[10] Later Orosius was invited to another synod that was led by John of Jerusalem where he informed the participants about Augustine's interaction with Pelagian, or at least Caelestian, viewpoints as well as the

---

9. See summaries in Warfield, "Introductory Essay on Augustine," xviii; Sell, "Augustine versus Pelagius," 120–21.

10. TeSelle, "Pelagius, Pelagianism," 636.

recent ousting of Caelestius in Carthage. This debriefing resulted in Pelagius being summoned so he could vouch for what his teachings actually were with the primary matter being about whether people could theoretically live without sin.

Surprisingly when he arrived, Pelagius evaded excommunication by appealing to Rome. But not too long after this impasse, two exiled bishops from Gaul, Heros of Arles and Lazarus of Aix, brought another charge against Pelagius which led the ecclesiastical authority, Eulogius of Caesarea, to form a synod in Diospolis in hopes of sorting out the matter. One would think that someone could not withstand these kind of critiques in back to back synods, yet Pelagius did. Apparently, the protocol of the synod was poorly followed, which allowed Pelagius to take advantage of the situation by disavowing some of the views held by Caelestius and deny some of the other beliefs he was charged with teaching. After the synod disbanded, though, many, including Augustine, argued that Pelagius had simply used flowery rhetoric to manipulate his audience, thereby dodging the substance of the charges made against him.

1.2 Political Conflict Arises regarding the Nature of Pelagian Teaching

Things began to reach a political boiling point because some began to wonder if Rome and/or Northern Africa would agree on the heretical nature of Pelagian teaching. After the fiasco in Diospolis, Pelagius produced his *In Defense of Free-Will* and announced his clear record, doctrinally speaking. Likewise, word spread to the western regions, including Rome and Northern Africa, that Pelagius had avoided excommunication. When the troubling news reached Northern Africa, leaders convened two additional synods so they could openly condemn Pelagius' teachings, one in Carthage and the other in Milevis in 416. This resulted in a divide between Palestine and North Africa thereby setting up a scenario where the bishop of Rome, Innocent I, would be contacted for support from both sides.

The synods of Carthage and Milevis first sent letters to Innocent informing him of their decisions. Additionally, five bishops, including Augustine, composed a third letter in hopes of persuading him to agree with their views of Pelagian teaching. And in 417 their efforts were well received by Innocent who agreed with the North African decision to excommunicate Pelagius and Caelestius. Yet things suddenly took a turn in Pelagius' favor because within six weeks of his concession, Innocent died. His successor was Zosimus, a Greek who apparently had no loyalty to the North African theological commitment to original sin.¹¹ Shortly after Zosimus was made the new bishop of Rome, Caelestius came to Rome to appeal for ecclesiastical clearance and coupled with this was another letter from Pelagius asking for the same verdict. It carried some weight because it came with an endorsement from Praylus, the new bishop of Jerusalem.

Zosimus evaluated the situation and determined that Caelestius should be cleared of all heretical charges. Then after receiving some documents from Pelagius, Zosimus declared him to be viewed as orthodox as well. Subsequently, there was a bitter interchange wherein a series of appeals were made between Rome and Northern Africa making an impasse seem inevitable. But two events suddenly sent the pendulum of momentum back in Africa's direction. One was amid the deliberations with Zosimus, the Emperor Honorius, who was in Ravenna, issued an imperial Roman decree that officially condemned Pelagius, Caelestius, and anyone who embraced their views within any cities of Italy. The other factor was that the day after the Ravenna edict, a council in Carthage was held that compiled nine canons refuting all the key teachings of Pelagius. Ultimately, this combination of civil power with the North African commitment to anti-Pelagian dogma proved to be too much for Zosimus to withstand. He submitted to this mandate by supporting the canons issued by Carthage as well as decreeing a tractate that condemned Pelagius and his supporters.

This turn of events led to one other transition in the Pelagian schism that would mark the last phase of which Augustine would be a part. When Zosimus' decisions were circulated, church officials recognized that along with the political rejection of Pelagianism and affirmation of African views of sin, grace, and baptism was also the demand that all bishops subscribe to the tenets. This caused a bit of unrest because some objected to how the demands were being enforced. So much so that eventually some eighteen Italian bishops, including one named Julian of Eclanum, refused to cooperate. Zosimus had no choice but to enforce his policy and so the bishops who chose to stand their ground were deposed from their positions, going into ecclesiastical exile. Julian, who now became the new defender of Pelagianism, and these other bishops initially found sanctuary with Theodore of Mopsuestia but then traveled to Constantinople in 429 where they stayed with Nestorius.¹² At this time, Pelagius had been expelled from Jerusalem and Antioch only to vanish off the pages of history somewhere in Egypt.¹³

---

11. TeSelle, "Pelagius, Pelagianism," 637.

12. Even in 431 at the Council of Ephesus, we read of the Caelestians being there with Nestorius. See Warfield, "Introductory Essay on Augustine," xxi.

13. TeSelle, "Pelagius, Pelagianism," 637.

Likewise, Julian engaged Augustine in a series of debates through an assortment of letters and treatises in which the primary topics of discussion were original sin, marriage, and the nature of saving grace.

1.3 The Rise of Semi-Pelagianism

While the influence of Pelagianism was continuing to fluctuate and Augustine was still engaged in polemics with Julian, another set of related concerns arose that he had to address. The cause was an inquiry that came from a monk named Florus in 427 who had recently read a letter that Augustine had written to a priest in Rome named Sixtus during the Pelagian dispute.[14] Florus was troubled with some of Augustine's comments regarding his beliefs about grace—in particular the idea that because it is a gift, all human merit or one's independent volitional capacity to receive it is to be excluded. He later sent the treatise to his colleagues at a monastery in Hadrumetum and they expressed similar concerns. However, their perplexity with Augustine's comments had nothing to do with any theological sympathies for Pelagius. They all affirmed the necessity of grace to enable sinners to live in obedience to Christ. Their objection was to Augustine's strong emphasis on predestination because they viewed it as a form of Christianized fatalism that essentially nullified the need for any sacrificial efforts to maintain spiritual piety.[15]

A colleague of Augustine named Evodius of Uzalis offered some initial replies.[16] When these efforts were met with further resistance from leaders of the abbey, Augustine drafted a new piece on grace entitled, *On Grace and Free Will* in 426 where he discussed the relationship between free will and divine grace. He argued that a person's will in and of itself is unable to initiate, perpetuate, or bring one's faith to perseverance and eternal life. Upon receiving this work, it simply elicited more questions from the inquiring monks because some misconstrued his claims. They wrongfully deduced that since salvation (and perseverance in particular) was a divine gift, one should not try to correct fellow believers when they fall into sin. This subsequent dilemma troubled Augustine. In an attempt to dissolve the confusion,

---

14. Sixtus became pope in 432. See details here by Babcock, "Grace, Freedom, and Justice," 2–5.

15. Hence the eventual labeling of this trajectory against Augustine known as "semi-Pelagianism." Adherents along with Cassian denied Pelagius' idea that grace was unnecessary for salvation. But they also rejected Augustine's idea that grace had to be effectual to address the will before it could respond to grace. For a full historical treatment of this idea, see Weaver, *Divine Grace and Human Agency*.

16. Leyser, "Semi-Pelagianism," 762.

he wrote *On Admonition and Grace* in 427 where he strongly supported acts of lovingly confronting fallen believers for the sake of restoration.

Along with this interchange, a final cluster of issues that motivated Augustine to write more on these issues occurred when he later received letters from two supporters in Gaul named Prosper and Hilary. Apparently after Zosimus outlawed Pelagianism, there were pockets of believers who agreed that Pelagius' views of grace were troubling. But they also thought that Augustine's strong views of predestination were equally unacceptable. One group who expressed such concern was a group of monks at the monastery of Saint Victor in Marseilles which was led by the abbot John Cassian. As opposed to Pelagians who believed people could achieve salvation without any internal work of divine grace, Henry Knapp rightly summarizes that

> these Semi-pelagians admitted the necessity of grace for some works and that salvation apart from the merit of Christ is impossible. With Augustine, they accepted the doctrines of original sin, the necessity of baptism, and the importance of the internal work of the Holy Spirit. Nevertheless, they maintained that the beginning of salvation *(initiwnfidei)* and the believer's perseverance in faith *(perseverantis fidei)* to the end depend upon the man himself. They taught that, through one's own natural powers, a person must make a necessary, positive preparation for the reception of God's grace. By piously seeking it, the person attains the necessary gift of grace to live in faith. Similarly, the grace of final perseverance is received when one, without any special assistance from God, perseveres in the initial grace received.[17]

Augustine saw the importance (and potential danger) of these nuanced positions because even though they clearly avoided the extremes of Pelagianism, they still advocated a synergistic approach to divine grace that did not take a robust view of sin into full account. While they denied the Pelagian notion that the human will could embrace salvation without any aid of divine grace whatsoever, they did affirm that the human will could somehow cooperate with divine grace so as to experience salvation. Some argued that the very exercising of faith could initially derive from the human heart before receiving divine grace. Therefore, Augustine felt compelled to clarify his views through two works. The first treatise, *On the Predestination of the Saints* was completed in 428–429 and shortly following was his second piece, *On the Gift of Perseverance*, which was probably intended to be the concluding segment of the work on predestination. In the long run, these

---

17. Knapp, "Augustine and Owen on Perseverance," 68.

works acted as Augustine's final thoughts in treatise form on issues related to the Pelagian (and Semi-Pelagian) debates.[18]

2. AUGUSTINE'S UNDERSTANDING OF SIN, SALVATION, AND ELECTION

It was during this flurry of theological clashes that Augustine fleshed out his full convictions on the nature of salvation. Throughout the years during the Pelagian controversy, he engaged all kinds of questions related to sin, regeneration, justification, predestination, and perseverance. And like any good theologian, how he synthesized Scripture to piece together his understanding of one particular subject helped set the trajectory for the direction he would take regarding another. So his view of sin led to his view of grace which in turn converged to help guide the way he understood election, justification, and so forth. Consequently, at the end of the day, Augustine's soteriology stood as one of the most cohesive perspectives up to that point in Christian history because of its thoroughness and internal coherency.

This means that if we want to know what Augustine thought about how believers could persevere in their faith and why they should, we must first briefly survey what he thought about how one becomes a believer in the first place. The best way to accomplish this task is to provide some summaries of what Augustine believed about three basic topics; those being sin, election, and justification. Then we can observe how these subjects interconnected in Augustine's thinking, thereby leading him to construct his view of perseverance.

2.1 Augustine's View of Original Sin

Augustine's understanding of salvation initially derives from his thoughts about creation and the fall. Augustine claims that when God made Adam and Eve, he placed them in a kind of probationary period wherein they were tested to see if they would obey his prohibition concerning the tree of the knowledge of good and evil. In their unfallen state, they had the volitional freedom to love God and obey him or ironically choose to love something less. Once they chose to love something more than God, they forfeited their

---

18. The Semi-Pelagian controversy continued for quite some time. Beginning with Prosper of Aquitaine, who again was a supporter of Augustine, and John Cassian, who disagreed with Augustine's strong predestinarian leanings, supporters on both sides grew with the result being assorted debates and councils. The most famous one to adjudicate the matter was the Synod of Orange which convened in 529.

unfallen environment, the potential for immortality, and brought divine curses upon themselves as well as the very earth over which they had originally been given dominion.[19] Likewise, they incurred a deep-seated corruption to their very nature, or inner disposition, which poisoned their will so they could no longer freely choose to love God. Apart from an initial work of grace, they would only love things in accordance with their fallen desires, which were now bound to pride and idolatry.

Moreover, all of these consequences are directly transferred to Adam's progeny. Otherwise known as original sin, this concept is the linchpin in Augustine's view of the doctrine of sin. He refers to this idea in his first anti-Pelagian work entitled *On the Merits and Remission of Sins* (412) where he is refuting the Pelagian belief that infants do not require baptism because they are not tainted with the sin of Adam.[20] Augustine retorts that the Pelagian notion that people only imitate Adam's rebellion is shortsighted. Why? Because we mimic Adam's actions by virtue of the fact that we are replicas of his fallen nature. We are "little Adams" at birth, not when we consciously choose to sin at some point in life.

So in essence, Augustine's interpretation of original sin entails two components. One is the actual act of sin that Adam initially committed. His transgression incurred guilt upon himself as well as his descendants because Adam is the prototype to which all humanity is ontologically and genetically linked. Therefore, all human beings are born (or conceived if you will) in a legal state of condemnation because what Adam did is what every human would have done and indeed did do. The other feature related to Augustine's emphasis on original sin is that along with the fact that all people are legally condemned *with* Adam, they have also become practically corrupt *like* Adam. This means that people are under the double burden of Adam's sin (i.e., original sin) as well as their own individual sins (i.e., actual sin).[21]

2.2 Augustine's View of Election

Hand in hand with Augustine's view of fallen humanity, or as he labeled it the mass of the damned (*massa damnata*), is his perspective on divine election.[22] Because humanity is now only free to follow tainted inclinations, no one on their own will ever pursue God or seek his mercy. If anyone is then

---

19. See Augustine, *City of God*, 14.16–19; and Mann, "Augustine on Evil," 47.
20. Augustine, *On the Merits and Remission of Sins and On the Baptism of Infants, Anti-Pelagian Writings*, 1.9.
21. Cf. Green, "Augustine," 251; Augustine, *Against Julian*, 3.57.
22. Augustine, *To Simplicianus*, 2.16.

to be delivered from their current plight, the Lord must make a sovereign choice to enact the power of his grace. And when he does so, his choice to provide salvation extends to specific recipients who will experience it. This idea, which later becomes known as unconditional election in the Reformed tradition, is at the heart of what caused such friction between Augustine and his opponents, especially the Semi-Pelagians.

Early on in Augustine's life, he considered an alternative possibility that God elected certain sinners unto salvation on the basis of foreknown faith. He deduced, for instance, that Jacob was chosen over Esau because the Lord knew he would eventually express faith in his promises.[23] Augustine gradually deduced that this approach was problematic because it based God's distribution of grace on human works (or response), which contradicts Paul's rhetorical question in 1 Cor 4:7 where he asks, "What do you have that you did not receive? And if you received it, why do you boast as though you did not receive it?" The obvious answer to the first question is nothing and therefore the second question should lead to humble repentance. This deduction led Augustine to change his mind. He concluded that even faith in Christ is from the Lord, not the will of man. Thus, he defined predestination as God's act of preparing to give grace as a gift and saw faith as the actual gift.[24]

Also, as a counterbalance, Augustine made sure to defend God's integrity in the act of election. For instance, consistent objections arose regarding the basis upon which God determines who will be part of the elect. Augustine's consistent response was simply that this kind of question hits against the bulwark of God's sovereignty. If election is based solely upon God's purposes to the exclusion of human activity, then such inquiries will always meet a dead end because the answers are not revealed to us.[25] Or in more emphatic terms, an unjust sinner cannot interrogate a just judge regarding his judgments. Such polemics led some to argue that Augustine's view of predestination depicted God as unjust and arbitrary. His response was that since there is no injustice if God chose to show rebellious humanity no mercy at all, then there is no injustice if he does choose to have mercy on some.[26]

---

23. Augustine, *On the Predestination of the Saints*, 5. Also see discussion in Wetzel, "Predestination, Pelagianism, and Foreknowledge," 53.

24. Augustine, *On the Gift of Perseverance*, chs. 41, 54. Lamberigts, "Predestination," 678.

25. Augustine, *On the Gift of Perseverance*, chs. 35–40.

26. Cf. Augustine, *To Simplicianus*, 2.16; Green, "Augustine," 258.

2.3 Augustine's View of Faith and Its Relationship to Regeneration and Justification

Moving to the topic of how sinners begin to experience God's grace, we quickly notice that Augustine's convictions about sin and predestination converge with a strong sacramental view of regeneration and justification. Such a combination begins with Augustine's understanding of baptism because for him, it is the means of addressing the immediate problem of original sin. He follows earlier church fathers in referring to baptism as the "laver of regeneration" and means of receiving "remission for sin." The reason for this is because he contended that its key function is to heal the wound of inherited sin that infants bring into this world when they are born.[27] While this went against the grain of Augustine's Pelagian opponents, it coincided well with Cyprian's theology of baptism and the majority opinion in the Christian west that baptism provided forgiveness for one's sins before becoming a Christian.[28]

From here, Augustine conflates the conception of regeneration at baptism with the event of justification. He does so by arguing that once the new birth commences, a sinner "merits" eternal life apart from works and thus receives God's righteousness. This is why baptized infants who die experience salvation because it is merited by virtue of the grace they received even though they have performed no works. Their new identity in Christ imparted at baptism eliminates their culpability in Adam.[29] At the same time, though, regeneration and justification begin with or lead to a faith that expresses itself in love and works. Once this takes place, believers now walk in obedience to God's law by the power of the Spirit so the event of justification can culminate in glorification. This means that for Augustine, justification is in one sense punctiliar because it takes place alongside the moment that regeneration commences. Yet in another sense, it seems to be progressive in nature because it continues to transform believers as they engage in consistent holiness.[30] Matthew Heckel summarizes this point well by stating that

---

27. See Augustine, *On the Merits and Remission of Sins*, I.40.24–30; Augustine, *City of God*, 1.27, 13.4.

28. McCure, "*Simul iustus et peccator* in Augustine, Aquinas and Luther," 84.

29. This argument is fleshed out in detail by Hiestand, "Augustine and the Justification Debates," 115–39.

30. The details of Augustine's view of justification can be difficult to discern because it is one subject that he did not explicitly address in any particular treatise. One has to observe periodic occasions where he touches upon the topic and try to piece together a feasible synthesis. Two excellent attempts at this are by Wright, "Justification

in the pre-conversion state the works of the law justify no one. But as soon as one passes over to Christ, grace relieves the tension between faith and works (by making justifying works the result of faith), and faith not only believes in God's grace to work love but also becomes active in love in order to bring about justification. In sum, grace pours in the love for God so that faith is produced that then turns love into action. In this way, God gives the righteous eternal life "in accord with their works." What we see is that Augustine's doctrine of justification is not "by faith" in the Reformation sense, but by the works of love produced by faith.[31]

Furthermore, the crux to our discussion is found in Augustine's additional contention that the experiences of regeneration and justification were not given to the elect only. The reason being that there are many saints who receive the new birth of the spirit and receive a right standing before God, yet still apostatize. When they do, they reject the grace they received at the outset and are therefore condemned as unbelievers. However, believers who do persevere prove to be the true elect, which means Augustine advocated what we could the perseverance of all the elect, but not all the saints. One might ask at this juncture how he defended such a concept? And such a question is what leads us to discuss the specifics of his view of perseverance.

3. AUGUSTINE ON PERSEVERANCE

Though we can look at segments of Augustine's anti-Pelagian writings to piece together some of his thoughts, the best place to look is his treatise that was solely devoted to the subject, which again was entitled *On the Gift of Perseverance*.[32] This work is made up of some sixty-eight chapters wherein Augustine weaves through the basic parameters of what perseverance is, how it is to be experienced, and why it is essential to the life of the believer. He begins the introduction by defining perseverance as "a divine gift by which an individual perseveres in Christ to the end of this life."[33] He fleshes out this thesis by showing how it coincides with NT warnings against apostasy, the

---

in Augustine," 55–72; and Bammel, "Justification by Faith," 223–35.

31. Cf. Augustine argument in *On Faith and Good Works*, 14.21; and Heckle's assessment in "Is R. C. Sproul Wrong about Martin Luther?," 96.

32. Cf. *On Admonition and Grace*, where Augustine gives some of his earlier thoughts with *On the Gift of Perseverance*.

33. Augustine, *On the Gift of Perseverance*, ch. 1.

teachings of earlier church fathers (e.g., Cyprian and Ambrose), the doctrine of predestination, and biblical examples of prayers for endurance.[34]

Throughout his discussion, the question that requires the most attention is why do some believers persevere while others do not? Augustine's response is that the true elect who are chosen by God to persevere indeed do so while those who are not fall away. This leads to the further deduction that no one knows for certain whether they are among the elect and will therefore persevere. So no one should presume that perseverance is given to anyone until they reach the end of their lives.[35] The apparent dilemma here is that because the human will still exists in a transitional state between the contexts of regenerating/justifying grace on the one hand and the flesh on the other, Augustine refrains from offering full assurance of perseverance because it would be presumptuous to do so. In his own words from his earlier work, *Treatise on Rebuke and Grace*, he writes,

> For who of the multitude of believers can presume, so long as he is living in this mortal state, that he is in the number of the predestinated? Because it is necessary that in this condition that should be kept hidden; since here we have to beware so much of pride, that even so great an apostle was buffeted by a messenger of Satan, lest he should be lifted up (2 Cor 12:7) . . . And many similar things are said. For on account of the usefulness of this secrecy, lest, perchance, any one should be lifted up, but that all, even although they are running well, should fear, in that it is not known who may attain—on account of the usefulness of this secrecy, it must be believed that some of the children of perdition, who have not received the gift of perseverance to the end, begin to live in the faith which works by love, and live for some time faithfully and righteously, and afterwards fall away, and are not taken away from this life before this happens to them.[36]

At the same time, as a pastor Augustine does assure his readers that perseverance is a divine gift which cannot be lost. The catch is that God does not provide the gift simply so it can be enjoyed. It is given so we are enabled to pursue Christ with passion and devotion. One could say that one reaches the goal of perseverance by striving after it and that struggle is the means whereby the elect (not all saints) experience it. This is partly why Augustine

---

34. Augustine alludes to Cyprian's discussion about how the Lord's Prayer includes several petitions for endurance and grace to persevere as well as Ambrose's teaching that apostasy should be sobering to believers who are still in the faith. See Augustine, *On the Gift of Perseverance*, chs. 4–7, 20, 48–49.

35. Augustine, *On the Gift of Perseverance*, chs. 1, 33.

36. Augustine, *Treatise on Rebuke and Grace*, ch. 39.

stresses the importance of prayer for perseverance. It is only given to those who in faith ask for it and seek it.[37] Additionally, because perseverance is a gift that is certain in God's decree but uncertain for believers practically, it should be preached to all so that the listeners will be admonished to look to the Lord for strength.[38] And if one should ask why God would decree that some saints lapse before the end of their lives without repenting, Augustine answers that such tragedies act as severe warnings to other believers against complacency in their own faith.[39]

In summary then, Augustine's view of perseverance essentially derives from his adaptation of sacramentalism (i.e., baptismal regeneration and the progressive work of divine grace) with strong determinism. It contains elements of determinism because God is the one who elects certain sinners unto salvation and enables them to persevere in their faith. If one attempts to interrogate God's justice in such an act, again Augustine's reminds readers that God's will is inscrutable and unchallengeable because he is pure whereas humanity is not. Also, God's mercy is exonerated by his willingness to save some in reality, not his willingness to save everyone potentially. Nevertheless, since salvation is not fully obtained until the sacramental processes of regeneration and justification reach their telic end in perseverance and resurrection, a saint can potentially prove to be defective. Thus, Augustine, for all practical purposes, allows for three categories of people; those being unbelievers who remain in unbelief, believers who later return to unbelief, and believers who persevere (the elect).

4. CONCLUSIONS ABOUT AUGUSTINE'S VIEW OF PERSEVERANCE

A final concern regarding Augustine's view of perseverance that deserves a bit of attention is the influence that it had on later Christian traditions that emerged in the church's history. This is a bit complicated because, as we have seen, his conclusions on this subject are tied to so many other beliefs. What we chronicle in subsequent chapters is that various facets of his theology were warmly embraced by assorted groups while other parts were adamantly rejected. That being said, the closest tradition to Augustine's theology *as a whole* is Roman Catholicism. The sacramental components of his views of regeneration and justification, which again supported his belief in a saint's capacity to apostatize, helped set the parameters for the later

---

37. Augustine, *On the Gift of Perseverance*, chs. 10–11, 39.
38. Augustine, *On the Gift of Perseverance*, chs. 25, 34, 51, 57–60.
39. Augustine, *On the Gift of Perseverance*, ch. 19.

theological systems of Thomas Aquinas, the Council of Trent and the subsequent Roman Catholic tradition.[40] But even here one should not assume that Catholic thinkers embraced all of the other components that Augustine formulated. While his links between original sin, baptism, and the new birth were upheld, most did not embrace his hard views of predestination and clusters of Catholic theologians often evaded his stringent application of original sin to the nature of the human will.[41]

A prime example of this is Thomas Aquinas himself. He affirmed a similar view of election, yet his explanation of perseverance was nuanced differently from Augustine's because he advocated a more synergistic interplay between divine grace and the human will.[42] He applied concepts, which he derived primarily from Aristotle, to construct a model that could delineate how believers exercise their intellect, will, and passions in the hopes of reaching final perseverance. In doing this, he conceded to Augustine's final conclusions even though he did not take the theological route of hard determinism to get there. Thus, whether it be in Augustinian, semi-Augustinian, or Thomistic form, the belief that not all saints persevere in their faith became the official position of the Catholic tradition as history moved forward to Trent and beyond.

In contrast, the Protestant Reformation was much more diverse in how it parsed out the viability of Augustine's view. Various traditions proposed all sorts of beliefs on the possible distinction between saints who persevere and apostates who do not. Nevertheless, the reason such a diversity of views was advocated was not because there was significant disagreement on whether apostasy could occur. Most Protestants affirmed such a possibility and still do. Rather the dilemma was identifying what apostates are before they recant. For Augustine, saints who eventually apostatize are those who genuinely experience the grace of regeneration and justification but choose to renounce those gifts in exchange for the love of the world; and in doing so, they prove not to be part of the elect. Protestants chose to couch their understanding of perseverance in different ways—and it is to those assorted proposals that we now turn.

---

40. Davis, "Perseverance of the Saints," 214.

41. For instance, at the Synod of Orange, it was argued counter Augustine that no one is specifically predestined to persevere or not to persevere. Instead, anyone who receives the grace of baptism can cooperate with the work of the Spirit and continue in the faith to the end. Fairbairn and Reeves, *Story of Creeds and Confessions*, 173.

42. Aquinas addresses the matter of perseverance in his *Summa Theologica* in the sections "Necessity of Grace," question 109.1–10, and "Of Perseverance," question 137.1–4. Also see treatments in Henžel, "When Conversion Is Joy," 128–30; and Meinert, "St. Thomas Aquinas," 823–42.

Chapter 7

The Reformation, Early Protestants, and Perseverance

WE HAVE SURVEYED MAJOR features in the constellation of views that some early patristic writers advocated on the idea of perseverance. We also saw how some of those ideas were replicated in Cyprian's theology as expressed in his pastoral recommendations on how to deal with apostates. We then examined how Augustine streamlined some of these factors into his own view of perseverance which largely derived from his conflation of theological determinism with a deeply sacramental understanding of grace and justification. Christian thought on the matter continued to diverge into various strands throughout the subsequent centuries of medieval Christianity; many not aligning with Augustine's emphasis on the moral impotency of the human will or strong predestination while some did.[1] But his version of baptismal regeneration, the progressive nature of justification, and how the church serves as the vehicle of divine grace became major parts of the theological evolution of Roman Catholic sacramentalism.[2]

---

1. One famous instance where someone echoed many of Augustine's theological convictions was the Saxon monk named Gottschalk of Orbais. His teachings marked one of the first times that Augustine's views of grace and predestination were explicitly advocated since the decisions at the Synod of Orange (AD 529). See assessments of Gottschalk's views in Gumerlock, "Predestination in the Century before Gottschalk: Part 1," 195–209; Gumerlock, "Predestination in the Century before Gottschalk: Part 2," 319–37; Genke and Gumerlock, *Gottschalk & a Medieval Predestination Controversy*; and Gillis, *Heresy and Dissent in the Carolingian Empire*.

2. See Oropeza's brief but helpful survey of views here in Oropeza, *Paul and*

Moreover, the ramifications of such ideas left significant marks on how the doctrine of perseverance was conceptualized. So much so that by the time the church reached the era of the Reformation, many Protestants believed that the subject deserved reconsideration and serious revisions.

One of the primary issues with which Protestants would wrestle was whether there was any valid theological basis for distinguishing between persevering and non-persevering believers, and if there was, what was it exactly. We have seen in earlier chapters that sometimes the NT clearly warns believers to endure in their faith under warning of divine judgment if they do not. However, layers of Christian thought had come to interpret this biblical language in ways that often fostered a high level of personal uncertainty among the masses because they often had been programmed to always question the authenticity of their faith. Many had embraced Gregory the Great's adage that "we are aware only of our call but unsure of our election."[3] This kind of perplexing doubt created quite a dilemma pastorally speaking because people naturally became prone to doubt their devotion because they were unsure whether they would persevere or not. Such a climate is partly why the larger sacramental system of the Roman Catholic tradition became so crucial. It created a way in which the church could be the leading authority on assuring people that their salvation was secure.[4] But in time, the Protestants deemed this situation to be disastrous because one's assurance of salvation had become based on works via sacramental activity as opposed to faithful trust in the person and work of Christ.

Relatedly, the Reformers expressed consternation over an apparent disconnect between the new birth, justification, and the final resurrection. By the sixteenth century, the Catholic tradition followed the Aquinas/Augustinian trail in viewing grace as something that is initially experienced in baptism and nurtured through other sacramental means.[5] Yet at the end of the day, any amount of grace could be repudiated by apostate actions. This

---

Apostasy, 10–13.

3. Mentioned by Calvin, *Institutes of the Christian Religion*, 3.14.9.

4. Another factor that drove the medieval sacramental model was the distinction between venial and mortal sins. Venial sins are transgression that can be addressed by certain sacraments and/or purgatory while mortal sins must be remedied before death by other sacraments such as penance. See summation of these points in Demarest, *Cross and Salvation*, 432–33.

5. The predominant ethos of Christian thought in medieval history adopted Augustine's repudiation of Pelagianism, his sacramental views of grace, and the general tenets of his ecclesiological commitments as displayed in his anti-Donatist writings. However, the strong determinist bent of Augustine's theology was largely abandoned in exchange for a view of the human will that saw salvation as being attained by sinners as they chose to partake of grace via the sacraments and gradually become righteous.

proved to be problematic because it raised questions about the nature of justification as well as the relationship between faith and grace. The issue of election also became skewed because how could one be sovereignly chosen to experience divine grace but freely choose to short-change its full results. This, again, is what left the door open to distinguish between elect persevering saints and non-elect apostates who were former saints. This kind of formula was unacceptable for many Reformers. However, as we shall see, their conclusions remained diverse because agreement could only be found in individual Protestant traditions. One could say that after the Reformation, differences over the nature of perseverance were not resolved. Instead, the diversity of views simply multiplied.[6]

1. LUTHER, LUTHERANISM, AND PERSEVERANCE

Martin Luther and the Lutheran wing of the Reformation represented a unique view of perseverance because even though they agreed that believers could potentially apostatize, their reasoning for affirming such a tragedy differed from what the mainstay Catholic tradition advocated. Luther's view of perseverance was similar to Augustine's in that it was an outflow of his convictions about predestination, sin, justification, and the rite of baptism.[7] But what marked his view as distinct were his arguments on how one receives a right legal standing before God and experiences the import of grace through the sacraments.

To begin, Luther viewed predestination in light of his Augustinian understanding of the human will.[8] This was an important part of Luther's thinking because even though Pelagianism had been officially condemned at church councils centuries earlier, many theologians still defended models of election that gave priority to the human capacity for responding to divine grace instead of God sovereignly choosing some sinners unconditionally.[9] Luther sided with Augustine by concluding that the capacity for people to make free choices regarding their salvation was an illusory notion. One cannot and will not freely choose to embrace God's salvific grace in any form.

---

6. Oropeza, *Paul and Apostasy*, 13; Pinson, introduction to *Four Views*, 7–8.

7. Some concise discussions about the theological capital that Luther used in the development of his beliefs can be found in Cary, "Lutheran Codicil," 5–9; Pereira, *Augustine of Hippo and Martin Luther*; Maxwell, "Justification in the Early Church," 26–28; Wilson-Kastner, "On Partaking of the Divine Nature," 113–24; and Ramos, "In Between St. Augustine and Luther," 34–39.

8. Luther thought the issue of the will was central to the whole debate about justification. See his famous *Bondage of the Will*.

9. George, *Theology of the Reformers*, 74.

The only way one could be freed from such spiritual shackles was if God decided to initiate a type of preemptive act of grace, which is exactly what happens in his decree to save some sinners.[10]

This leads to a second concern which is how does God grant the elect a right standing before his divine tribunal. How does he justify sinners? Luther's answer to this question is what initially sparked a firestorm of controversy because it fueled his adamant disagreement with the Catholic use of indulgences. By the sixteenth century, this rite had become a subset practice of penance which was a means of repentance in the larger sacramental system.[11] The main problem that triggered Luther's outcry was that they were being distributed to people in exchange for financial donations so that they would allegedly receive lesser punishment for sin in the afterlife. Luther opposed this abuse along with several others that he believed the church was practicing which then spawned his famous ninety-five theses and subsequent debates with his former Catholic colleagues. Eventually, these events resulted in a growing number of sympathizers who either joined his cause as allies or splintered off into their own individual Protestant directions.

Luther responded the way he did, in part, because these abuses were indicative of previous struggles that he had gone through already in his own personal life. For years, Luther had been vexed over the concept of the righteousness of God. But in time, he realized that God's righteousness was not only his holy standard whereby he judged all humanity.[12] It was also a gift that he provided in the redemptive work of Christ. Therefore, by faith, and faith alone, sinners are able to gain a legal standing before God because of what Christ has done on their behalf. More specifically, sinners who believe the gospel receive forgiveness of sin and Christ's righteousness is fully imputed to them.[13] They are now acquitted of their guilt as a transgressor of God's law. So even while sinners who believe are still practically corrupt

---

10. Some argue that Luther affirmed the idea of double predestination, see George, *Theology of the Reformers*, 77. It is clear that he affirmed unconditional election. See Luther's comments in *Bondage of the Will*, 168–70; Luther, *What Luther Says*, 1:461; and Luther, *Commentary on Romans*, 122–28. However, by the time that the Lutheran Formula of Concord was drafted, many of Luther's followers had come to affirm the idea of single predestination. See *Formula of Concord*, in Schaff, art. 11; and Campbell's assessment in *Christian Confessions*, 157.

11. McKim, *Theological Turning Points*, 121; cf. treatments of the subject by Barrois, "What Are Indulgences," 266–68; Mattiox, "Indulgences," 89–90.

12. Luther, *Preface to the Epistle of Saint Paul to the Romans*, 98–107; and McGrath, *Iustitia Dei*, 218–35.

13. See Luther's distinction between alien (i.e., a righteousness that is given to believers) vs. proper actual righteousness (i.e., a righteousness that believers express because of Christ's redemptive work) in Luther, *Two Kinds of Righteousness*, 135–40.

and in need of transformation, they are now saints (or righteous) legally before God.[14] Thus, this tension helps set the stage for what Luther says about apostasy.

Before that can be addressed, however, Luther's view of baptism must be briefly mentioned because of how it converged with his understanding of salvation in general. Luther conceded with his medieval forebears that a sacrament is a means of conveying grace to a participant. What he rejected was the notion of *ex opere operato* which postulated that grace was extended through a sacrament regardless of the bishop who administered it or the active faith of the participant.[15] Luther contended that what made baptism actually significant was that Christ commanded it as a rite of obedience. The fact that the word of God demanded sinners to be baptized was what made the act sacramental when it was embraced in faith. This raises a question then—how did the concept of faith alone coincide with the practice of infant baptism, which Luther did support. His argument was that when believing parents bring their infants to be baptized in faith, Christ, in a sense, imputes faith unto them.[16] This does not mean they must not exercise their own faith in due time. They must if justification is to be maintained. Nevertheless, baptism was a means of extending a type of proto-regenerative act, a mysterious transfer where the grace of justification was received prior to one's personal declaration of faith and repentance. So for Luther and the later Lutheran tradition, the act of regeneration can commence in preliminary form at baptism in the life of an infant or adult.[17]

14. This dynamic is summarized in Luther's famous dictum *simul justus et peccator*—at the same time righteous and a sinner. One can find a selective compilation of Luther's works where he discusses this concept in Althaus, *Theology of Martin Luther*, 242–45.

15. There is still debate today on whether the idea of *ex opere operato* necessitated any function of faith in a participant for a sacrament to be effectual. However, it is clear that Luther viewed this concept as locating the power of grace in the act itself through the church. And his response to this proposal was that faith alone in Christ alone was what made sacraments effective, not the church or the rite itself.

16. Cf. Luther, "Of Infant Baptism," *Larger Catechism*, 86–90; Luther, *Concerning Rebaptism*, 247; Luther, *Luther's Works*, 40:245–46; cf. George, *Theology of the Reformers*, 94. There is also debate as to whether Luther affirmed some type of unconscious faith in the baptized infant.

17. Luther even concedes that an infant being baptized can be more promising because an adult candidate can be more prone to deceit or be a false convert like Judas, see Luther, *Luther's Works*, 40:244. Also, Luther did on occasion state that there could be rare cases in which a believer received eternal life without baptism. See short assessment of this point in Allison, *Historical Theology*, 625n81. Finally, there is still significant disagreement on how Luther's view of baptism fit with his understanding of justification alone. See contrasting views in Trigg, *Baptism in the Theology of Martin Luther*; and Ramsey, "Sola Fide Compromised?," 179–93.

Collectively, these points about election, justification, and baptism created a grid through which Luther understood the nature of perseverance. His stoutly Augustinian understanding of election and his modified view of sacramental grace in baptism enabled him to remain in step with the idea that believers could apostatize. Those who were elect could avoid such a plight but this did not necessitate that all professing saints do. The key difference in Luther's view was that justification was not something that progressively became a reality over time. Rather it was a gift believers received that could subsequently be abandoned through an act of unbelief. We see these kinds of deductions in comments like the one Luther makes on 2 Pet 2:22. Here, he states that the sacrament of baptism is the means whereby some have their unclean life washed away in exchange for a pure one. Yet these same people can return to their previous way of life and fall into unbelief once more.[18] Some simply dismiss this quote as a reference to false teachers alone. In his commentary in Galatians, however, he states that Paul's idea of "falling from grace" refers to "losing the atonement, the forgiveness of sins, the righteousness, liberty, and life which Jesus has merited for us by his death and resurrection."[19] What these comments show is that Luther did think believers may abandon the grace that begins in baptism. While he concedes that all the elect do persevere, some saints defect through sin and unbelief. So Luther and his tradition tried to maintain a balance between the assurance of grace to persevere and the moral impetus to avoid taking salvation for granted because apostasy was possible. This tension remained consistent in Luther's thought and was perpetuated by future Lutheran confessions like the *Augsburg Confession* and the *Formula of Concord*.[20]

Now some might deduce at this point that Luther was still mired in the same quagmire as the medieval Catholic tradition. This would be a bit shortsighted, though, because his acceptance of apostasy did not lead him to overemphasize the uncertainty of one's eternal destiny. He believed the topic of perseverance should primarily be addressed pastorally in a nurturing way. Luther thought that when the church spoke to believers about their eternal destiny, the primary focus should be on what they have in Christ by faith, not what they could potentially lose through future unbelief. The reason being that focusing on the former can enable believers to avoid the latter. He was convinced that the preacher's task was to extend comfort and assurance to believers, not provoke despair or morbid introspection. This

---

18. Luther, *Luther's Works*, 30:190.

19. Luther, *Commentary on Galatians*, 108.

20. Cf. *Augsburg Confession*, in Schaff, art. 12; *Formula of Concord*, in Schaff, art. 11.7–8; Luther, *What Luther Says*, 1:280.

was a crucial point for Luther because he consistently accused the Catholic church of going too far in the other direction by stressing the dangers of apostasy at the expense of assuring believers of their position in Christ. He lamented the fact that many church leaders were better at instilling paralyzing doubt in the minds their hearers instead of confidence and faith.[21] This is why he argued vehemently that a preacher should point a person to Christ's provision, not leave them in a deficit of fear that could only be appeased by a sacramental economy. His contention was that the church must balance its message in a way that concedes to the genuine possibility of apostasy while maintaining a pastoral shepherd's heart that builds up one's faith, not tear it down.[22] So what we see in Luther is an attempt to maintain a robust theology of personal assurance while still conceding that apostasy was a true possibility (and reality for some).

2. CALVIN, THE REFORMED TRADITION, AND PERSEVERANCE

The Reformed tradition contributed a distinct voice to the Protestant discussion about apostasy and the nature of perseverance. Its theological groundwork was laid by the French-Swiss scholar John Calvin and then carried on by numerous believers who studied under him at Geneva, such as John Knox and Theodore Beza, as well as other clusters of Reformed advocates abroad, including the French Huguenots and the later English Puritans.[23] In some areas, Reformed thinkers held much in common with Luther because they mutually affirmed select segments of Augustinian theology. They agreed on the concepts of original sin, unconditional election, and the need for grace to function monergistically in the hearts of unbelievers so that they could be enabled to believe the gospel.[24] They, likewise, resonated with

---

21. Luther expressed some stern words for those that he thought were fostering fear among God's people instead of assurance. Cf. Luther, *Luther's Works*, 24:218; Luther, *What Luther Says*, 1:457.

22. Cf. his comments in Luther, *What Luther Says*, 3:11–16; Luther, *Luther's Works*, 24:218.

23. Many other thinkers could be mentioned and examined here as well, including Zacharias Ursinus, Jerome Zanchi, and William Perkins. See treatments in Muller, *Christ and Decree*, 97–128; 149–70.

24. Monergistic in the sense that grace must initially change the human disposition of corruption first before a person can or will respond to the gospel in faith and repentance. This corresponds with Augustine's view of election and sin but stood in contrast to the later dominant synergistic approach of sacramentalism which emphasized the cooperative interplay between grace and the human will.

Luther's emphasis on *sola fide* as it pertained to justification. Nevertheless, these similarities did not negate the fact that Reformed theology offered an alternative view of perseverance.

The reasons for its distinctiveness were primarily grounded in the Reformed understanding of regeneration as well as God's providence in election and reprobation.[25] Reformed perspectives on these matters postulated that any person truly born of the Spirit could never lapse back into an unconverted state. The reason being that all believers are sovereignly elected by God. Therefore, if all believers are chosen to become part of God's people, they are necessarily enabled to endure in their faith unto death. This would also mean that anyone professing to be a believer who eventually apostatizes is simply revealing that their faith was spurious rather than from the Lord. Such logic means the Reformed tradition eliminated any distinction between believers and the elect. They are one in the same, meaning all true believers are part of the elect and will thereby be saved.[26] What remains in question, however, is how did Reformed thinkers justify their view that apostates were never regenerate when NT warnings of apostasy appear to have been given to true believers.

The place to begin finding an answer is with Calvin's understanding of election. Notwithstanding current debates among scholars about the level of centrality that divine providence had in Calvin's theology as a whole, there is little doubt that his view of perseverance (along with all subsequent Reformed thinkers and confessions) was inherently linked to his convictions about predestination unto salvation.[27] He believed that Scripture described God's rule over creation as being meticulous, inscrutable, and ultimately irresistible. Because the scope of his sovereignty is exhaustive, it necessarily includes his plans to oversee the saving of a remnant of fallen of humanity through the redemptive work of Christ. Every facet of this plan is a by-product of divine activity, exercised according to God's good pleasure. The act of the new birth by the Spirit, the expressions of faith in Christ and repentance

---

25. There is actually significant debate among Reformed scholars on the exact loci that drove Calvin's theology. See discussion of this issue in Muller, *Christ and Decree*, 1–16.

26. What must be kept in mind here is that for the Reformed view, perseverance of the saints should not be equated with the popularized idea of eternal security. While the Reformed perspective affirms that no true believer can lose their salvation, it pushes forward to make the argument that all true believers endure in their faith. One could say that God sovereignly preserves the elect in Christ and evidence of this divine action is that all believers persevere.

27. See discussion about the question of whether God's sovereignty or the nature of God himself was the central focus of Calvin's theology in Partee, *Theology of John Calvin*, 240–50.

from sin, the process of sanctification in the life of a believer, and the spiritual incorporation into Christ's death and resurrection are all gifts that are initiated as well as perpetuated by divine power. And they are bestowed to those whom God chooses.[28] So for Calvin, the kind of faith which leads to justification and final salvation can only be exercised by those who God supernaturally enables to do so. If saving faith is a divine gift, then one's endurance in that faith must necessarily come from the Lord as well. This requires perseverance to be an essential result of God's sovereignty just as much as every other dynamic involved in the salvation experience.

Notably this thesis made Reformed thought stand apart from both Roman Catholic and Lutheran traditions. It critiqued the synergistic interplay between the human will and the divine grace infused by the sacraments as advocated by medieval sacramentalism. This process may or may not result in final justification, depending on whether a sinner receives enough grace to become righteous. Calvin, in contrast, argued that a person's assurance of salvation should be grounded solely in God's faithfulness to save all of the elect, not just some.[29] This was a significant move because it retained the Augustinian emphasis on human depravity that much of Roman Catholic thought had either repudiated or revised. Calvin and Augustine would agree that only if God sovereignly chose to initiate his grace in a sinner's heart could anyone believe and receive the benefits of the gospel. But Calvin's ideas moved away from Augustine's belief that not all believers persevere. As we saw earlier, Augustine contended that election only applied to saints who reached final justification via the grace of the sacraments. Calvin argued, instead, that justification is not a reality that unfolds over time as sinners are gradually transformed by grace. It is a punctiliar event that becomes realized in the declaration of saving faith in Christ.[30]

Calvin's proposals diverged from Lutheranism as well because, again, Luther agreed that not all saints necessarily endure in their faith. And a major reason he did so was because of his nuanced link between regeneration and baptism. One may receive the seed of regeneration via the act of baptism, yet later repudiate the salvific grace they had received. Calvin proposed that baptism did not initiate the grace of regeneration in ways that

---

28. At the same time, Calvin balanced his stress on God's sovereign actions in bestowing the salvific experience upon sinners with the belief that people are still responsible to obey the gospel and continue in godly living. Cf. Calvin, *Institutes of the Christian Religion*, 2.3.11–12; and Allison's overview of this point in *Historical Theology*, 550–51.

29. See Calvin's discussion about assurance in *Institutes*, 3.2.7; 3.2.16; 3.2.41–42; cf. treatment of Calvin in Beeke, *Quest for Full Assurance*, 39–54.

30. See Calvin on justification in *Institutes*, 3.11.1–16.

Lutherans or Roman Catholics proposed.[31] While he did agree that infants should be baptized, he defended the practice by arguing that the sacrament allowed participants to become part of the corporate group that receives grace, namely the church.[32] Infants were considered part of the covenant community until they possibly exhibited unregenerate lifestyles or apostate attitudes in adulthood. He contended that just as Israel gave the physical sign of the old covenant to the male infants so they could have solidarity with God's people, now all infants of believers in the church were to receive the new-covenant sign of baptism.[33] In the former case, sometimes baptized males would not grow up expressing full obedient faith to the Lord or his law. Similarly, many who receive the seal of baptism tragically renounce their identity with the new-covenant community. This logic is what compelled Calvin and future Reformed thinkers to concede that there are some people within the church who experience the grace of Christ via baptism and communal identity that are not truly regenerate.[34] They are incorporated into the community of faith temporarily until they reveal that they do not possess the faith of the community.

This last point is what sets the stage for how Calvin and the Reformed tradition address the reality of apostates in the church. Again, unlike Augustine and Luther who believed some saints do not persevere, Calvin contended that all saints must, and will, do so. Nonetheless, when it comes to those who receive the grace of baptism only to later rebel against the faith, the Reformed answer was that not only does God sovereignly choose who the elect will be. He determines who will remain hardened in their corrupt state as condemned sinners, or what is more commonly known as reprobation. The difference between the two is that the elect are recipients of salvific grace by the Spirit whereas some of the non-elect can experience assorted non-salvific promptings of the Spirit. In Calvin's own words, God "sometimes causes those who he illumines only for a time to partake of it"

---

31. Calvin's treatment on baptism can be found in *Institutes*, 4.15–16.

32. Cf. Calvin, *Institutes*, 4.15–16; Grislis, "Calvin's Doctrine of Baptism," 46–65; and McGaughey, "Baptism in the Protestant Reformation," 104–7.

33. Calvin, *Institutes*, 4.16.5–6.

34. Horton, "Classical Calvinist View," 37. This distinction creates a question regarding the details of Calvin's idea of baptism. Some argue that he viewed it as a promissory act, meaning baptism was a sign of the promise of salvation that could be received fully when one was converted. Others contend that his view saw baptism as presumptive meaning that baptism marked a person as potentially regenerate unless they were to later show signs that proved otherwise. Bruce Demarest provides a helpful discussion of this difference and how it exists on the spectrum of Reformed thought in Demarest, *Cross and Salvation*, 285–87.

(i.e., an operation of the Spirit); "then he justly forsakes them on account of their ungratefulness and strikes them with even greater blindness."[35]

The point is that the Lord sometimes offers some sort of general work of grace to unbelievers that provides further warrant for their condemnation because sooner or later, they will reject it. Such scenarios are the key moments for identifying apostates. Those who externally seem to be abandoning the faith are actually those who only experienced an initial work of the Spirit that does not entail grace leading to salvation.[36] One could say that for Calvin and the Reformed tradition, God not only saves all of the elect by effectual grace that results in the new birth of the Spirit, repentance, and saving faith in Christ. He also justifiably condemns the non-elect by sometimes offering a foretaste of grace that they eventually choose to abandon. Thus, for Calvin and his Reformed successors, apostates are not defective saints because that would mean God's grace in Christ can be thwarted. Rather they are unbelievers who receive a token work of the Spirit which they inevitably reject because it falls short of actual regeneration.[37]

Moreover, it was this line of thought that came to undergird the Reformed belief that all of the elect necessarily persevere, thereby establishing what became known as the "perseverance of (all) the saints." All subsequent strands of Reformed traditions adhered to this idea, which helped distinguish this segment of Christianity from the broader spectrum of Protestant views of apostasy that came out of the Reformation. In contrast to Catholic, Lutheran, some Anabaptist, and later Arminian approaches, the Reformed tradition abrogated the distinction between the elect and the saints. They are viewed as one in the same. One can trace this belief consistently throughout the documented trail of major Reformed creeds and catechisms all the way from the French, Helvetic, and Belgic Confessions to the Heidelberg Catechism, the Synod of Dort, and the Westminster Confession.[38] Each of them, as well as the long line of other Reformed declarations of faith, consistently

---

35. Calvin, *Institutes*, 3.24.8. An excellent treatment of this part of Calvin's theology can be found in McMahon, *Calvin's View of God's Love*.

36. Such a thesis is a primary strategy for Calvin and later the later Reformed interpretation of Hebrews 6.

37. See Calvin, *Institutes*, 2.2.6–7; McMahon, *Calvin's View of God's Love*, 53n65. Also, a clear syllogism that illustrates this is provided by the Puritan John Owen. He contended that: (1) The elect cannot fall away; (2) Some professors fall away; and (3) Hence, those professors are not elect believers. This is found originally in Owen, *Doctrine of the Saint's Perseverance*. And a treatment of the overall argumentation of Owen's point can be found in Beeke, *Quest for Full Assurance*, 165–73.

38. Cf. *French Confession*, art. 21; *First Helvetic Confession*, chs. 10, 14; *Belgic Confession*, art. 16; *Heidelberg Catechism*, question 1; *Synod of Dort*, 5:1–15; *Westminster Confession*, ch. 17 (all in Schaff).

upheld this belief. So much so that the Reformed belief in perseverance became an essential theological fiber in the larger framework of Reformed covenantal theology and eventually received a place in the famous TULIP acronym of Calvinism.[39]

3. ANGLICANISM AND PERSEVERANCE

Discerning views of perseverance and apostasy in the Anglican tradition can be somewhat daunting because the Reformation's impact on England was complex and noticeably distinct from other parts of Europe. The main reason for this was that the country's move toward Protestantism was in constant flux because of a series of dramatic reversals in religious policies that were instigated by rulers who were sometimes sympathetic to the movement while others were not.[40] Initially, Henry VIII instilled a form of neo-Catholicism where the king was in charge of the church instead of the pope. Some practical and theological differences also emerged during his reign as early discussions were held regarding the development of a confessional document that could represent the beliefs of the newly born Anglican Church. After Henry's death, his Edward VI became king when he was just a boy. This meant his regents and advisors actually ruled the country, most of them having Reformed leanings theologically. This allowed England to foster a more explicitly Protestant climate. But unfortunately, problems arose after Edward's premature death when his half-sister, Mary Tudor, became queen. She was an avid Catholic who led a severe persecution of Protestants in England which only came to an end after her death when her half-sister Elizabeth took the throne. She, along with her advisors, saw Reformed thought and Catholicism as two traditions that could go in potentially harmful directions politically.[41] So she pursued a kind of middle ground (i.e., *via media*) where believers from both traditions could coexist along with the larger Church of England. This attempt was successful to a degree. Yet over time, strife ensued because Anglican and Reformed constituents (i.e., the Puritans) both pressed England to align their political identity to their rivaling theological views of the church. Consequently,

---

39. Otherwise known after Dort as the five points of "Calvinism," the TULIP acronym fit nicely because it was the famous Dutch flower and this codification of Reformed thought resembled a similar attempt that Puritans had spearheaded in England to install their view of predestination to creedal status. See Thuesen, *Predestination*, 39–40.

40. Campbell, *Christian Confessions*, 124–25. Also see Marshall, *Heretics and Believers*; Duffy, *Reformation Divided*; and Bernard, *King's Reformation*.

41. Campbell, *Christian Confessions*, 127.

the constant change of political climate forced the doctrinal leanings of the Anglican Church to vary from period to period depending upon which tradition(s) had the most pull at the time. And, again, this creates a bit of a murky paper trail when it comes to ascertaining an official Anglican "view" of perseverance.

That being said, the first place one can go to for ascertaining some point of reference is the famous *39 Articles*. This confessional document of the Anglican tradition was originally drafted in 1563 as an edited version of a previous *42 Articles* (1553) that had been compiled by Archbishop Thomas Cranmer some ten years earlier. The subject of perseverance is addressed, at least implicitly, in article 17 under the heading "Of Predestination and Election." The statement appears to adopt language that reflects Lutheran and Reformed leanings regarding the concept of election unto salvation while avoiding the Augustinian-Reformed idea of predestination unto reprobation. The article claims that the Lord "hath constantly decreed by his counsel secret to us, to deliver from curse and damnation those whom he hath chosen in Christ out of mankind, and bring them by Christ to everlasting salvation, as vessels made to honor,"[42] with no further assertion about any vessels made unto dishonor. Subsequently, there is a point where the idea of perseverance is alluded to in the statement that believers "walk religiously in good works, and at length, by God's mercy, they attain to everlasting felicity."[43] The language at face value seems to imply that believers endure unto eternal life. However, the document had to balance a theological tightrope between Anglican *and* Reformed ranks, which necessitated an evasion of more explicit language about perseverance that other Reformed confessions used.

In time, other confessional documents were proposed in various regions that were a bit more emphatic on the concept of perseverance. *The Lambeth Articles* (1595), for instance, offered some added expansions to *The 39 Articles* that revealed more Reformed leanings. One includes article 5, which offers input on perseverance when it states that "a true, living, and justifying faith, and the Spirit of God justifying [sanctifying], is not extinguished, falleth not away; it vanisheth not away in the elect, either finally or totally."[44] Then, later in the early seventeenth century (1615), this idea was incorporated into *The Irish Articles of Religion*, another confessional

---

42. *39 Articles*, in Schaff, art. 17.

43. *39 Articles*, in Schaff, art. 17.

44. *Lambeth Articles*, in Schaff, art. 5. Article 6 also states that "such a one who is endued with justifying faith, is certain, with full assurance of faith, of the remission of his sins and of his everlasting salvation in Christ." *Lambeth Articles*, in Schaff, art. 6. See history of these developments in Shuger, "Mysteries of the Lambeth Articles," 306–25.

document that revealed a more explicit commitment to Reformed convictions. One can consult article 15 where it states that all those predestinated unto eternal life will attain to everlasting felicity. Article 38 also echoes the Lambeth language when it claims that "a true, lively, justifying faith and the sanctifying Spirit of God is not extinguished nor vanished away in the regenerate, either finally or totally."[45] The importance of these confessional clarifications should not be underestimated because they created certain doctrinal fibers that would eventually help many who affirmed *The 39 Articles* to lock arms with others who would later abide by the tenets of *The Westminster Confession*.[46] At the same time, to be fair, it is true that other segments of the Anglican tradition would eventually embrace more of an Arminian understanding of election and perseverance which, as we shall see in the next chapter, allowed for the possibility of apostasy.[47] So in the end, the Anglican tradition made room for both those who wanted to advocate a Reformed understanding of perseverance as well as those who did not.

4. ANABAPTISTS AND PERSEVERANCE

Another important subset of Protestants who offered input on the idea of perseverance were those that make up the Free Church traditions of the Reformation beginning with the Anabaptists. Known today as "Radical Reformers," the Anabaptists were distinct from those who church historians label as the "Magisterial" Reformers like Luther, Zwingli, and Calvin, primarily because of their distinct views on baptism, the importance of human freedom to Christian discipleship, and the relationship between the church and the state.[48] These subjects were important matters not only because they pertained to theological disputes about ecclesiology, the sacraments, and conversionism. They were also intertwined with civil issues of the state because at that time being a citizen of a European region was linked to being a member of the "church." The issue that initially caused serious conflict was the Anabaptist conviction that only professing believers should receive baptism, not infants. This meant that churches were to be made up

---

45. Cf. *Irish Articles of Religion*, in Schaff, arts. 15 and 38.

46. Davis, "Perseverance of the Saints," 220. Also consult discussion of Reformed thought in the Anglican Church in Collier, *Uneasy Reception of a Reformed Distinctive*.

47. Campbell, *Christian Confessions*, 157–58.

48. One interesting feature that has been pointed out is that the Anabaptists were "radical" to Catholics because of their antipathy for sacramentalism but were radical to Protestants because they often emphasized the importance of human freedom in ways that many reformers repudiated. See discussion in Steenbuch, "Anabaptists and the Magisterial Reformation," 16–31.

of a regenerate membership only. But such a belief was antithetical to other Protestant and Catholic perspectives because it went against the grain of all forms of paedobaptism as well as any interaction between the church with the state. This is why antagonists came to label these rebels as Anabaptists, meaning rebaptizers, or those who baptized people again.[49]

The seedbed of the movement was in Zurich, Switzerland, during the time when a former sympathizer of Luther named Ulrich Zwingli had sway of the city council because of his influence as the town pastor. Certain students and supporters, including Conrad Grebel and Felix Manz, opposed his views on several matters, among them being his beliefs about paedobaptism and the nature of the church. Eventually Grebel and Manz amassed a small following that Zwingli felt he had to confront. This resulted in the perceived faction being banished from Zurich. Afterward, followers of this new movement continued to grow even in the face of increasing persecution.[50] Roman Catholic areas of Switzerland began to condemn all Anabaptist sects. At the Diet of Speyer in 1529, Charles V declared them as heretical, demanding that every city council condemn them to death. Such opposition all but eradicated Anabaptist groups in Zurich. Many scattered over the Alps into Germany and Austria while others fled to find refuge in Moravia. Yet the surges of persecution did not prevent these believers from spreading their convictions. The Anabaptist faith eventually became one of the most significant Christian grassroots movements in the sixteenth century with some of its most well-known leaders being Grebel, Manz, George Blaurock, Michael Sattler, Pilgram Marpeck, Melchior Hoffman, Jacob Hutter, Balthasar Hummaier, and Meno Simons. Through their efforts, the Anabaptists sprouted into a larger cluster of traditions, including the Mennonites, Amish Christians, and some scholars dispute their influence on the later English Separatists who spearheaded the early stages of the Baptist tradition.[51]

Because the movement was so broad and provided such a diverse trail of confessional documents, it can be challenging to identify all of the nuances that the spectrum of Anabaptist thought has regarding the subject of perseverance.[52] However, there were several basic components that emerged.

---

49. The term "anabaptist" was actually ascribed to all kinds of religious dissenters during the sixteenth century. Durnbaugh, "Membership in the Body of Christ," 52.

50. See Estep's concise summary of this events in *Anabaptist Story*, 29–55.

51. Full commentary in Finger, *Contemporary Anabaptist Theology*, 17–45.

52. One of the most well-known Anabaptist confession was drafted in a village in Schaffhausen called Schleitheim. In 1527, seven articles were recorded and unanimously adopted by all the attenders, thereby becoming known as *The Seven Articles of Schleitheim*. They included believer's baptism, self-examination before communion, communion is for baptized believers only, believers are to live in holiness, churches are

One is that the Anabaptist perceptions of conversion and regeneration are were not tied to the rite of baptism. While numerous thinkers did affirm the concept of original sin in a qualified sense, none saw baptism as a means of remedying its effects for infants. Only those who exercised personal faith in Christ could receive forgiveness of sin whether it be the corruption incurred from Adam or one's own sinful actions. Another feature was that Anabaptist thinkers generally denied the strong predestinarian leanings that Lutherans and Reformed thinkers advocated.[53] Originally several Anabaptist thinkers were former followers of Luther. In time, some of them eventually concluded that any theological merger between the notion of autocratic sovereign election and the legal imputation of Christ's righteousness could potentially negate the New Testament emphasis on moral conversion and discipleship. Consequently, much of Anabaptist polemics focused upon the theological interplay between justification and the ethics of discipleship.[54] One could not speak of experiencing the former unless it was coupled with the praxis of the latter.

Thus, it is not unfair to categorize the spectrum of Anabaptist thought as synergistic in nature not because the will was seen as cooperating with divine grace via the partaking of the sacraments.[55] Rather it is because the human will is able to submit or freely come under the leadership of the Spirit, thereby receiving divine grace by faith. Some have argued that even though such an idea escapes the problems of medieval sacramentalism, it still borders on the danger of Pelagianism. Kenneth Ronald Davis offers a helpful corrective to such a charge when he observes that there are "many variations and complexities, to discover and unravel the exact nature of the principle of free, human cooperation with grace for the 'attainment' of salvation which permeates the Anabaptists' soteriological formula is vital to any attempt to isolate its intellectual antecedents."[56] In other words, synergistic models of soteriology should not all be automatically lumped into the category of Pelagianism because views of the human will, in particular Anabaptist ones, are parsed in carefully nuanced and diverse ways. So to

---

to have biblically qualified pastors, pacifism, and believers are not swear any kind of oath. See discussion of this document in Snyder, "Influence of the Schleitheim Articles," 323–44. And treatments of various strands of Anabaptist confessions can be found in Koop, *Anabaptist-Mennonite Confessions*; and Koop, *Confessions of Faith*.

53. See discussion of various thinkers such as Casper Schwenckfeld, Andreas Karlstadt, Hans Denck, Thomas Münster, and several others who rejected the concept later known as unconditional election in Snyder, *Anabaptist History*, 35, 44, 160, 305–6.

54. Cf. Snyder, *Anabaptist History*, 384–85; Krahn, *Dutch Anabaptism*, 261–62.

55. Keefer, "Arminian Motifs in Anabaptist Heritage," 312.

56. Davis, *Anabaptism and Asceticism*, 149.

discard them with the theological ghosts of the past is simply reductionistic. In any case, the constellation of Anabaptist views of soteriology strongly denied the predestinarian emphases of Lutheran and Reformed communities.

Likewise, for many in the vast Anabaptist theological stream, regeneration as well as conversion were seen as experiences that initially placed one on the path to salvation. One must then nurture their faith through ongoing personal discipleship and communal solidarity with other believers in the church if they desired to remain undeterred on their spiritual pilgrimage to the kingdom of heaven. If one were to neglect these features and not grow in their devotion to Christ, one could possibly turn away, eventually being tempted to apostatize. When such instances did happen, Anabaptists sometimes considered them unregenerate.[57] Perhaps in some cases, they were actually unbelievers from the outset or in other instances, they were genuine disciples who needed to be expelled temporarily via church discipline. In some cases, though, apostates were usually just that, believers who began the trail of discipleship only to turn away later because they did not walk worthy of the calling they had originally embraced.[58] One could deduce then that many Anabaptists viewed salvation as a conditional process because it was inseparably linked to the journey of Christian discipleship, not just the initial event of justification (or conversion). A believer could turn aside from the path of salvation, possibly failing to reach the ultimate goal of eternal life.[59]

Furthermore, this conception of perseverance found a theological haven in the later Arminian tradition of the early seventeenth century as we shall see.[60] And scholars continue to dispute the amount of influence that Anabaptist traditions exerted on later English Separatists from which Baptist traditions emerged. What can be said is that unlike the Anabaptists who remained predominately non-Reformed, the subsequent streams of Baptist thought went in various directions when it pertained to perseverance. Some held a Calvinistic view (i.e., Particular Baptists), others followed the later Ariminian perspective (General and Freewill Baptists), and even

---

57. Snyder, *Anabaptist History and Theology*, 385. It is also interesting to note that Anabaptists differed somewhat on the details of apostasy because we find in the Lutheran Augsburg Confession that there is a statement of condemnation against the "Anabaptists who deny that men once justified can lose the Spirit of God, and do contend that some men may attain to such a perfection in this life that they cannot sin." See *Augsburg Confession*, in Schaff, art. 12.

58. See fuller discussion in Keefer, "Arminian Motifs," 314–18.

59. Keefer, "Arminian Motifs," 316–17.

60. What is interesting, though, is that when the Arminian dispute became an issue with Calvinists, many Anabaptists did not fully support the Arminian proposals.

others embraced a modified version of perseverance known as eternal security wherein believers' identity is secure regardless of their behavior after conversion.[61]

5. ROMAN CATHOLICISM, THE COUNCIL OF TRENT, AND PERSEVERANCE

Amid the evolution of Protestant beliefs about Christian doctrines, including the topic of perseverance, periodically some refutations of Protestant ideas began to be administered through various papal decrees and imperial declarations during the early parts of the sixteenth century. For instance, Pope Leo X issued the papal bull *Exsurge Domine* in 1520 that included a command for Luther to recant. However, such efforts did not deter Protestants nor did they serve as any official assessment of all the major theological impasses that were on the rise. Tensions continued to surge but many Catholic authorities were reluctant to summon any sort of council for interacting with Protestants because they feared such a platform might birth a new conciliarist movement. The papacy had already been through the French debacle with a rival pope as well as the Great Schism. This is why Pope Pius II issued a bull in the fifteenth century asserting papal authority over any future council (1460) and Clement VII in the throngs of the Reformation feared a possible Protestant coup.[62] Nevertheless, the expansion of Protestantism throughout Europe and the opposition that had been fueled by the growing number of outspoken Reformers showed that certain doctrinal breaches had become virtually unbridgeable. An official and detailed response was needed that could both clarify Catholic beliefs on the major tenets of the faith as well as confront the perceived error of Protestant teachings. And in doing so, such an endeavor would have to address the issues of perseverance and apostasy.

Following numerous consultations, Clement was succeeded by Paul III with the agreement among some that he would call a council to address these matters. Ironically, he met some resistance at the outset from his cardinals who rejected the proposal. He still continued to press forward with plans for the council only to be forced to postpone deliberations because a

---

61. Cf. statements on perseverance in the *London Baptist Confession of Faith of 1689*, ch. 17, (Calvinistic); *New Hampshire Confession*, art. 11 (nominally Calvinistic because it affirms that all true believers persevere but does not explicitly affirm unconditional election, see art. 9); and the *Confession of the Free Will Baptists*, art. 13 (classical Arminian); all in Schaff.

62. Woodbridge and James, *Church History*, 208–9; Minnich, *Councils of the Catholic Reformation*, 1–37.

war erupted between Francis I and Charles V. The council was finally able to convene in the Italian city of Trent in 1545 just two months before Luther died. But it would not be able to complete its sessions uninterrupted. The Council of Trent would span the reign of three popes (Paul III, Julius III, Pius IV) and take almost twenty-three years to complete its meetings because it kept being interrupted by conflicts in the surrounding regions. It would go through three major phases, beginning in 1545 and finally ending in 1563.

Among the decisions, the sixth session in the first phase of Trent's meetings addressed several key matters of soteriology, including the nature of perseverance. Chapter 1 begins by highlighting the effects of sin upon humanity with the brief qualification that "although free will, attenuated as it was in its powers, and bent down, was by no means extinguished in them."[63] The point here being that although original sin has infected the human race with moral corruption and everyone has inherited the legal guilt of Adam, the human will still retains the capacity to respond to grace as it is offered in the gospel and the sacraments.

From here, the articles begin to address the topic of justification, highlighting the major rift with Protestant thought. The question was whether justification strictly pertains to sinners receiving a legal change of status before God (i.e., they are declared righteous instead of guilty) or does it also encompass a required moral change that transforms the actual disposition of sinners (i.e., they become righteous practically). Chapter 7 addresses this matter, stating that "justification itself, which is not remission of sins merely, but also the sanctification and renewal of the inward man, through voluntary reception of the grace, and of the gifts, whereby man of unjust becomes just and of an enemy a friend, that so he may be an heir according to the hope of life everlasting."[64] Trent's point is that being justified not only concerns the act of being rendered to be righteous legally before God. It also entails the moral renewal (i.e., sanctification) of sinners. Thus, at this point Trent is building a case. The capacity of the will to cooperate with the sacramental infusion of grace works in tandem with the progressive nature of justification to bring salvation to its culmination. By use of the will, one can choose by faith to partake of Christ through the sacraments and gradually become righteous, thereby experiencing justification before God once the sanctifying process is completed.[65]

---

63. *Council of Trent*, session 6, ch. 1, in Minnich, *Councils of the Catholic Reformation*.

64. *Council of Trent*, session 6, ch. 7, in Minnich, *Councils of the Catholic Reformation*.

65. This is why Trent offers several canons condemning the belief that justification

Moving forward, these ideas helped set the trajectory for later observations about predestination and perseverance, which begin in chapters 12 and 13. It is interesting to note that while the council aligned more with Aquinas' view of the will, it leaned more toward Augustine when it came to assurance of salvation. Trent admonishes readers to never presume any knowledge of one's own assured election because it is bound up in the secret mystery of God's will. Such an act is the height of foolishness because only a special revelation from God himself could give warrant to such a belief.[66] Trent states that while perseverance was indeed a gift given by God to believers, it does not mitigate against the numerous warnings that the NT gives to live according to the Spirit and put to death the works of the flesh so that one might live. In other words, one can have the assurance that there are saints who persevere. But to be convinced that one is among that assembly before death is to adopt a belief that could compel one not to persevere. This is why Trent adds a remedial claim in chapter 14 for those who do fall into certain kinds of sin that could lead one to apostasy. If one falls from the grace received in justification, one may be restored by partaking of the sacrament of penance.[67]

So what we see is that a major part of the disagreement over perseverance between Protestants and Catholics was driven by differing opinions on the nature and grounds of personal assurance of salvation. Even though Lutherans and Anglicans did allow for the possibility of apostasy, they along with Reformed thinkers believed that perseverance was a part of the overall gift of salvation that one received in Christ by faith, not some added remedial sacrament. Likewise, one's confidence in their present salvation did not lead to presumption against the importance of perseverance. Just the opposite was the case. It instilled a passionate abandonment of all worldly things for the sake of Christ because one could rest assured that their eternal destiny was settled.[68] Tridentine Catholics, however, did not see it that way. They thought such a perspective undermined the fear that the NT says believers should have because of the danger of apostasy. They believed that perseverance was a by-product of the synergistic interplay between human effort (qualified by faith) and divine sacramental grace. This is why Trent proceeded in the further "Canons on Justification" to condemn anyone who

can be received by faith "alone." *Council of Trent*, session 6, ch. 11–14, in Minnich, *Councils of the Catholic Reformation*.

66. *Council of Trent*, session 6, ch. 12 and canons 15–16, in Minnich, *Councils of the Catholic Reformation*.

67. *Council of Trent*, session 6, ch. 14, in Minnich, *Councils of the Catholic Reformation*.

68. See Allison's comments here, *Historical Theology*, 553–54.

(1) views the human will as not being able to respond to divine grace,[69] (2) sees justification as something that cannot be lost by post-conversion sins except for apostasy,[70] and (3) believes that salvation cannot be lost once someone has claimed to know they were part of the predestined (canon fifteen) or say that they have the gift of perseverance apart from a special revelation (canon sixteen).[71] Essentially, like Augustine, Trent affirmed that a believer could only be certain of their perseverance until the point of death, not before.

6. CONCLUSIONS

We clearly see that the Reformers' adamant rejection of previous Roman Catholic views of perseverance fostered a climate in which a host of alternative proposals could develop. Lutherans, Anglicans, numerous Anabaptists, and the post-Tridentine Roman Catholic tradition continued to affirm that not all saints persevere. They just thought the theological underpinnings for such a reality were different. The Council of Trent followed Augustine in denying the idea that all believers persevere because many could later deny the grace of baptismal regeneration or fall into certain sinful patterns from which there was no forgiveness. Again, it was because of these dangers that Catholic leaders thought Protestant views of perseverance could engender an attitude of presumption regarding one's claim to be part of the elect. Or even worse, it might even nullify the moral urgency to stay in union with the sacramental conduits of the church. In contrast, Lutherans and many Anglicans affirmed that God promises to preserve his people so that they do not have to live under a looming cloud of doubt and fear. But these traditions still conceded that apostasy was a potential hazard for saints if one did abandon their faith in Christ, thereby maintaining some continuity with Augustine's elect/saint dichotomy, just to a lesser degree than Trent. Many Anabaptists agreed with these groups that apostasy was a possible pitfall into which followers of Christ could fall. If such an event were to occur, though, it had nothing to do with the loss of any grace that was incurred in baptism as an infant or any other sacramental activity. It had to do with one choosing to leave the path of discipleship for the love of the world. Finally,

---

69. *Council of Trent*, session 6, canons 4–5, in Minnich, *Councils of the Catholic Reformation*.

70. *Council of Trent*, session 6, canons 9, 11–12, in Minnich, *Councils of the Catholic Reformation*.

71. *Council of Trent*, session 6, canons 27–28, 30, in Minnich, *Councils of the Catholic Reformation*.

Reformed believers argued that no true believer fails to persevere because saving faith is a divine gift that God gives to all the elect, not just some. A saving faith is by its very definition a persevering faith.

What we discover from this analysis is that among the many issues that were being hammered out during the Reformation, perseverance was unquestionably high on the list. Like many debates at this time, Protestant agreement that the Roman Catholic sacramental matrix was a defective tool for deciphering a biblical answer to this issue did not result in a unified alternative response. And some of the underlying reasons for diverging proposals were because Protestants disagreed on how regeneration relates to baptism as well as how God elects believers unto salvation and passes over unbelievers in reprobation. The fact that Lutherans, Anabaptists, Reformed believers, and Anabaptists differed significantly on these matters made it inevitable that they would have a hard time finding a complete consensus on defining the nature of apostasy and the role of perseverance in salvation.

Chapter 8

Perseverance in the Classical Arminian and Wesleyan Traditions

ANOTHER SEGMENT OF PROTESTANT thought that must be given serious consideration when charting the development of Christian perspectives of perseverance and apostasy is the Arminian tradition. Today this approach is known primarily as the classic theological antithesis to the Reformed view of predestination and undoubtedly, this is justified.[1] But

---

1. While Arminian and Reformed thought are indeed at odds with each other on predestination, one must be careful because sometimes classic Arminianism is caricatured as a set of beliefs that are completely antithetical to every facet of Reformed thought. But this is simply not the case. While both approaches do diverge significantly on how to define the elements most pertinent to God's sovereignty in salvation such as the nature of human freedom, election, and the extent of the atonement, there are many basic beliefs that these traditions held in common. This is why scholars like F. Leroy Forlines helped spearhead a strand of Arminian scholarship that has become known as "Reformed Arminianism." Originally dubbed by Arminian scholar Robert Picirilli, this phrase is used to describe commitments to penal substitution, the imputation of Christ's righteousness, and several other key doctrinal tenets that the Reformed tradition mutually upholds. Cf. discussions in Pinson, "Introduction to *Classical Arminianism*," iv–ix; Picirilli, *Grace, Faith, Free Will*, i–iv; Ashby, "Reformed Arminianism," 137–87; and Forlines, *Classical Arminianism*. Also, for discussions on how studies on Arminius and his engagement with Reformed thought continues to develop, cf. Pinson, "Will the Real Arminius Please Stand Up?," 121–39; Muller, "Arminius and the Reformed Tradition," 19–48; Bangs, *Arminius*, 21–22; 332–49; and Olson, *Arminian Theology*, 51–58. When consulting Bang's original definitive work and Muller's more recent analysis, one can see that studies on Arminius are experiencing significant shifts because more attention is being given to the historical nuances of his time instead of initially fixating on the details of his theological convictions. See Stanglin and McCall, *Jacob Arminius*, 14–15.

despite this famous impasse, Arminianism has significantly impacted the ways in which vast numbers of Protestants conceptualize their beliefs concerning the question of whether believers can lose their salvation. So a proper assessment of what makes this viewpoint unique is crucial to our discussion.

We will begin by assessing the initial context in which Arminian thought was born, that being a late sixteenth- to early seventeenth-century dispute in Holland and other provinces in the Netherlands concerning the biblical viability of Reformed views of election and lapsarianism.[2] It was during these polemical fires that Arminianism's progenitor, Jacob Arminius forged his views on salvation, election, and for our concerns, perseverance. Then after his death, his followers promoted, and arguably expanded, his ideas to the point where another clash ensued with the religious authorities in the Netherlands who were predominately Reformed. This resulted in the well-known proposal of the five Remonstrance, which articulated five Arminian convictions regarding the doctrine of salvation, and a subsequent rebuttal at the Synod of Dort.[3]

This conflict caused quite a bit of turmoil among churches on both sides of the debate. It eventually served as a theological fork-in-the-road that allowed both Reformed and Arminian perspectives to follow their own paths. Arminian treatments on perseverance went through further developments as seen in the later works of the famous First Great Awakening preacher John Wesley and his many sympathizers in the subsequent Wesleyan traditions. Arminian views on perseverance developed to the point where a noticeably diverse spectrum of ideas emerged. This is why various traditions such as Methodism, the later Holiness movement, Pentecostalism, and General Baptist / Free Will Baptist churches, who historically have embraced major components of Arminian theology, actually advocate their own distinct (though sometimes similar) positions on apostasy and perseverance. They serve as heirs of different strains of Arminian thought as we will see.

---

2. *Lapsum* derives from the Latin, meaning "to fall." As will be discussed later, lapsarianism refers to views that attempt to explain how God's decrees to permit man to sin, save sinners, and condemn the reprobate interrelate logically. Cf. overviews of this matter in Beeke, *Debated Issues in Sovereign Predestination*, 71–82, 135–52, 165–74; Boughton, "Supralapsarianism and the Role of Metaphysics," 63–96; Fesko, *Diversity within the Reformed Tradition*; and especially Stanglin and McCall, *Arminius*, 106–29, 140.

3. There is a bounty of studies that can be consulted on the history of Arminianism and its development in relationship to Dort. Two excellent works that cover many of the intricacies of both are provided Brill's series on church history. Cf. Van Leeuwen, Stanglin, and Tolsma, *Arminius, Arminianism, and Europe*; Goudriaan and Lieburg, *Revisiting the Synod of Dort*.

1. SETTING THE STAGE FOR THE ARMINIAN VIEW(S) OF PERSEVERANCE

The main historical factor that led to the earliest developments of Arminian thought was the sheer amount of influence that Reformed theology had on Dutch Christianity in the sixteenth and seventeenth centuries. Europe had become a divided continent because various nation-state territories were selective in their sympathies toward the ideologies of various Reformers. Lutherans found major support in regions of Germany, Anglicans clearly had a home in England, and Anabaptists were tolerated in Bohemia and Moravia. Likewise, the primary locations where Calvin's followers were able to advocate their ideas freely were Geneva as well as some areas in France, England, and the Netherlands.

The Dutch territories are most pertinent to the original Reformed-Arminian divide because midway through the sixteenth century, the regions fell on turbulent times. The country was beginning to reject its Roman Catholic heritage by pulling away from political subservience to Spain. This struggle continued to escalate until it eventually reached a lull in 1559 which allowed an influx of Reformed Christians primarily from France to make their way into the Netherlands. Then by 1566, the political hiatus gave the Dutch time to establish their own Protestant identity via the Reformed Church of Amsterdam.[4] At the outset, this entity was broadly Protestant in the sense of being non-Catholic. In its early years, it avoided favoritism toward any particular form of Protestant thought, whether it be Lutheran or Reformed.[5] Yet these accomplishments did not prevent national conflict from reemerging. The first phase of the Eighty Years War broke out the very same year that the Amsterdam church was founded. And it lasted until 1609 when a twelve-year truce was signed to end the conflict temporarily.

It was amid these national pressures that Reformed thought began to gain serious strides in the Netherlands. One main reason for this was because by the late sixteenth century, many aspiring Dutch ministers were studying in Geneva so they could be under the tutelage of Reformed leaders like Theodore Beza. Then they returned home to begin their ministries, which meant the number of Reformed preachers in pulpits and professors in universities grew exponentially. What is also important to note is that the version of Reformed theology that they often defended was a systematized

---

4. Cf. Olson, *Story of Christian Theology*, 460; Woodbridge and James, *Church History*, 255–56; and Lake, "Jacob Arminius' Contribution," 228. This political climate also affected some of the decisions that Arminius made during his early years as well, see Stanglin and McCall, *Arminius*, 26–27.

5. Olson, *Story of Christian Theology*, 460–61; Bangs, *Arminius*, 96.

formulation of Calvin's theology which Beza and his colleagues promoted. Specifically, Beza helped lay some of the foundational work that would set the stage for the later development of Reformed Scholasticism, a systematization of Reformed theology that built upon and even expanded Calvin's theology.[6] One component that was of particular interest to Beza as well as other Reformed scholars pertained to the question of how God expresses his sovereignty through his "decrees."

The concern was how God's choice to save the elect logically corresponds with his predetermination to create Adam and allow the fall. The term that eventually came to be used for describing their answer was supralapsarianism.[7] The word combined the term lapse, or a fall (of Adam) with the Latin prefix supra meaning before, or preceding. Together, the label was adopted to describe the argument that God's decree to save the elect and condemn the reprobate (i.e., the non-elect) must logically precede, or come before (supra), his decree to create the world and permit the fall. Put another way, God decreed Adam's sin because it set the stage for a prior objective which was to save a select group from a fallen humanity. This proposal served as an apologetic for two Reformed beliefs; one being that God's purpose in saving a people was to bring unmitigated glory to himself and the other being the idea of double predestination, which sees God as actively choosing who he will save as well as hardening those who he will damn.[8]

Supralapsarianism circulated throughout different Reformed-friendly regions with many communities finding its polemical structure appealing while others were uncertain of its biblical validity. Some thinkers proposed that the primary intent of God's decrees was to bring glory to himself in

---

6. There are ongoing disputes on the relationship between Calvin's original theological method and the later approaches of Reformed theologians in the scholastic tradition. See, e.g., Vos, "Systematic Place of Reformed Scholasticism," 29–42; Van Asselt and Dekker, *Reformation and Scholasticism*; Van Asselt, *Introduction to Reformed Scholasticism*; McGraw, *Reformed Scholasticsm*, 95–120, 129–38.

7. The actual term supralapsarian did not come into use in Beza's or Arminius' day, but the idea certainly was. The famous English translation of Arminius' *Declaration of Sentiments* includes the term to clarify this was the idea that Arminius was denying. Cf. Arminius, *Works of Arminius*, 1:614; Stanglin and McCall, *Arminius*, 108.

8. One must be careful here because some tend to argue that this proposal was indicative of a transition in Reformed thought that moved away from a biblical-theological approach, as represented by Calvin, to a method that was more reliant on logical deduction and classical argumentation. Such an objection has received significant responses showing that Beza and his colleagues strove to base their beliefs on a cumulative reading of Scripture and then show how key doctrinal themes emerge as well as intersect (e.g., Scripture, God, salvation). See important clarifications here by Muller, "Calvin and the 'Calvinists': Part 1," 345–75; Muller, "Calvin and the 'Calvinists': Part 2," 125–60; and Bray, *Theodore Beza's Doctrine of Predestination*.

creation, of which the plan of redemption was an essential part, but not necessarily central. These proponents argued for infra (after) lapsarianism meaning that the divine decree to save the elect and condemn the reprobate follows the decrees to create the world and permit the fall. In many ways, such revision was not altogether earth shattering because the difference between the two views was still an in-house discussion. Both supra and infralapsarians agreed on God's sovereignty in salvation and that the fall was a necessary part of the divine plan. Where they differed was on the decretal priority of election over creation.[9] In either case, though, the cultural, ecclesiastical, and academic climate of many Dutch territories was filled with Reformed Christians who affirmed one of these ideas. And this climate created the threshold for controversy once Jacob Arminius came on the scene.

2. KEY FACETS IN JACOB ARMINIUS' SOTERIOLOGY

Jacobus Arminius (1559[1560]–1609) was born in Oudewater, Holland as Jacob Harmenszoon.[10] It was only later when he applied to the University of Leiden in 1576 that he followed the standard academic custom of latinizing his name where he chose Arminius, the name of a German leader who conquered Varus' armies in the early first century.[11] He endured a difficult childhood because his father died most likely before he was born, which left his mother widowed and burdened with the responsibility of raising him along with his other siblings. Fortunately, Arminius was able to receive an education because of external support and the local priest, Theodore Aemillius, taking him under his wing.[12] He lived with Aemillius in Utrecht during his early teen years until he died in 1575. A professor at the University of Marburg later that year was so impressed with Arminius after meeting him that he invited him to enroll as a student. Tragically, it was during this time away from his homeland that he was informed of a retaliatory invasion by

9. Some maintain a distinction between supralapsarians and infralapsarians regarding their views on the nature of divine activity in reprobation. Whereas supralapsarians are typically labeled as advocates of what is called *double predestination* (i.e., God actively determines those who will be saved and providentially hardens the non-elect who have freely chosen to remain in their sinful state), infralapsarians often support *single predestination* (i.e., God actively determines those who will be saved but "passes over" or turns away from the non-elect). See further clarifications of this divergence in Thuesen, *Predestination*, 36n97.

10. Originally, his name was Jacob Harmenszoon (meaning Harmen's son). Arminius is a Latin rendition of his last name and James is just an English translation of Jacobus. See Picirilli, *Grace, Faith, Free Will*, 3–4.

11. Stanglin and McCall, *Arminius*, 3.

12. Picirilli, *Grace, Faith, Free Will*, 3.

Spain upon Oudewater because of its decision to join other Dutch regions who were seeking independence from Spaniard rule.[13] He made a visit back home only to discover that his loved ones had been killed in the attack.

Heartbroken, Arminius made his way back to Marburg to continue his academic endeavors for a few more months. He eventually decided to return home in 1526 where he then enrolled at the new and upstanding University of Leiden. He immersed himself in the liberal arts so he could study a plethora of subjects, including theology, which proved to be a wise choice since he was able to study under the Reformed scholar Lambert Daneau.[14] Arminius finished his studies at Leiden in 1582 with nothing but potential. So much so that Amsterdam clergy recognized his talents, offering to underwrite him for further preparation. And this is what opened the door of opportunity for him to make his way to Calvin's prestigious academy in Geneva, where he was able to study under Calvin's successor, Theodore Beza himself. Scholars quibble at this point on whether Arminius embraced Beza's high Calvinism while he was there. What we do know was that the only controversy with which Arminius did become involved during his initial stay at Geneva had nothing to do with disagreements over divine sovereignty or election. Unfortunately, however, the tensions caused by this ordeal compelled Arminius to leave. He then traveled to Basel where he stayed for almost a year and after having a promising time there academically, he finally returned to Geneva in 1586 to complete his studies.

2.1 Arminius' Controversies as a Pastor

Now with all of his preparation behind him, Arminius was able to go through the final stages for pastoral ministry. He came to Amsterdam in 1587, with a personal recommendation by Beza, so he could take the necessary examinations. He was ordained a year later into the Dutch Reformed Church a year later and began to gain popularity as a leader. Crowds enjoyed listening to his preaching and he was able to marry Lijsbet Reael in 1590. She was the daughter of a member of the city council, which allowed him to rub shoulders with the higher ranks of society. It was during these pastoral years that disputes about predestination and election began to emerge. The first major wave of controversy ensued when he was asked to intervene in a debate about the viability of unconditional election and predestination. Apparently a humanist named Dirck Coornhert was a critic of Reformed theology who

---

13. Picirilli, *Grace, Faith, Free Will*, 3.
14. Stanglin and McCall, *Arminius*, 27.

offered a concept of conditional election as an alternative proposal.[15] Two pastors attempted to respond to Coornhert's arguments by offering some modifications to Beza's system of supralapsarianism. Amid this banter, it was requested that Arminius either publicly correct these changes or just go to the heart of the matter and refute Coornhert's polemics. The problem was that Arminius did not agree with Beza nor the two pastors who tried to revise his system. Arminius believed all versions of lapsarian determinism were wrongheaded.[16]

The tensions just increased when Arminius began preaching through Romans chs. 7 and 9 at his church. In his sermon on Romans 7, Arminius challenged the popular Reformed interpretation that Paul was speaking of his own struggles to do good and resist evil as a believer. He claimed instead that Paul was speaking of an unregenerate person under the law. And later in his exposition of Romans 9, which must be understood in light of his later writings on the matter, Arminius claimed that the gist of Paul's discussion pertains to God's free mercy that he freely determines to save believers but not to choose those who will believe.[17] Arminius faced opposition in both of these instances, typically facing charges of espousing Pelagianism. Yet he was always acquitted. By 1593, the tensions created by his ideas subsided and would not become a problem again until he accepted a teaching position at the University of Leiden in 1603.

2.2 Arminius' Controversies as a Professor

At the turn of the seventeenth century, Arminius was given the opportunity to become a faculty member of Staten (Theological) College, a school that had been established by Leiden in 1592 for the training of clergy in the Dutch Reformed tradition. The school had three teaching faculty members and two of them had lost their lives to the plague as it made its way through the country in 1602. Afterward, the university sought out Arminius thinking he was the best potential candidate to fill one of the faculty vacancies. Arminius was initially reluctant to accept the position because of his humble demeanor but leaders and friends supported the school's choice. There

---

15. Stanglin and McCall, *Arminius*, 28–29.

16. Arminius would eventually propose a fourfold alternative wherein (1) God appoints Christ to be the savior, (2) determines to save all those who believe, (3) efficiently provides all the means whereby anyone can exercise repentance and faith, and (4) elects to salvation all those that he knows will believe. Cf. Arminius, *Works of Arminius*, 1:653–54; Bangs, *Arminius*, 350–55; and Thuelen, *Predestination*, 38.

17. Arminius, *Works of Arminius*, 3:554–59.

were some who opposed his nomination, including some vocal Reformed pastors, former colleagues of Arminius who knew his theological leanings, and most importantly, the remaining faculty member at Leiden, Franciscus Gomarus. To his credit, Arminius overcame these obstacles after passing all the academic interviews, which included an examination by Gomarus himself. Gomarus approved of Arminius' nomination, the school granted him a doctoral degree, and he began teaching in 1603. Once his academic career started, Arminius was in constant conflict with various colleagues, especially Gomarus who was an avid supralapsarian. There were two main reasons for this. One was that Arminius rejected the idea that God decreed Adam's fall in light of his prior choice to save a select number of humanity and condemn the remaining masses. He questioned this strong view of predestination, which in the minds of many, put him at odds with the Belgic Confession, the confessional standard of the Dutch Reformed Church.[18] This charge also caused great concern among many of his antagonists because it made them suspect that Arminius was possibly sympathetic to Catholic views of grace since he did not view election as an act that was based solely on God's choice apart from action that man could perform. The other factor that complicated matters were the tensions between the Netherlands and Spain that had reached a breaking point.

The ongoing disputes between Arminius and the opposition led by Gomarus overlapped with questions about national loyalty to the Dutch homeland. There were those who wanted the Netherlands to be free from the rule of Catholic Spain and often, supporters of this perspective were Reformed. Yet there were others who conceded that perhaps a better option was to find some sort of compromise between the civil and ecclesiastical authorities of Spain. Arminius, along with his sympathizers, thought this was a safer option. The problem, then, was that his views were not only controversial because they challenged certain axioms in Reformed theology. They were likewise perceived by Reformed loyalists as an ideology that sought a political compromise with the Catholic church.[19] Together these factors led to all kinds of confrontations between Arminius and critics, especially his colleague Gomarus. After back-and-forth arguments between the two, deliberations were made with a session finally meeting in 1608 for Arminius to clarify his views. Gomarus reacted vehemently because he was not allowed to attend, which fueled his desire to attack Arminius' beliefs all the more. Ultimately, they were expected by the civil authorities to meet

---

18. Woodbridge and James, *Church History*, 256. Also see Gootjes, *Belgic Confession*, in Schaff, 13–32.

19. Picirilli, *Grace, Faith, Free Will*, 10–11.

the next year so they could publicly debate their theological differences but when the conference finally met, Arminius had to leave early because of health problems that had been increasing over the years. He traveled home to Leiden where he died October 19, 1609.

2.3 Arminius' Beliefs about Election, Apostasy, and Perseverance

It was amid these many controversies about God's sovereignty in salvation that Arminius did express his thoughts on the related topics of apostasy and perseverance. This is only natural since views about how one is elect go hand in hand with views on how one remains as such. When comparing his works, we discover that Arminius clearly rejected all forms of Reformed lapsarianism. But he did construct his own version of divine decrees. They simply excluded any notion of God decreeing the fall as a necessary event or God determining to save anyone apart from faith, Arminius objected that God does not elect unbelievers to believe. God, instead, elects those who believe to be saved. This is why God provides a kind of pre-regenerate grace (a.k.a., prevenient grace) that can enable someone potentially to respond to the gospel.[20] Those who do are the ones that are elect. At the same time, this grace is resistible because obviously not everyone receives it in faith.[21]

So, if sinners, by virtue of a kind of prevenient grace, are free to exercise faith in Christ and thereby become part of the elect, then it would follow, at least in theory, that they could later freely choose to renounce that faith as well. What is ironic is that while Arminius clearly articulated his critiques of Reformed views of unconditional election as postulated in the related frameworks of supra- and infralapsarianism, scholars actually differ on his thoughts about apostasy. A major reason for this is because some find it difficult to discern Arminius' convictions when he discusses the differences between the *possibility* as opposed to the *actuality* of apostasy. Sometimes he speaks about the capacity that believers have to resist the process of remaining incorporated into Christ and cease to be a member of his people.[22] He juxtaposes examples like David and Peter, who did fall

---

20. Arminius affirmed this idea partly because he wanted to maintain a clear distance from Pelagianism. See his comments in Arminius, "Examination of Predestination and Grace," pt. 2, 5.

21. See Picirilli's full discussion about prevenient grace at this point in *Faith, Free Will*, 53–55. Cf. Arminius' comments in *Works of Arminius*, 1:383; 3:334.

22. Arminius, *Works of Arminius*, 1:667; 3:455, 458. Arminius concedes elsewhere that it is "possible" for believers to fall away and that there is no final certitude that a believer "may" not fall away (*Works of Arminius*, 2:725–26). Those who faithfully work out their salvation need not fear that they are in jeopardy (*Works of Arminius*,

away through disobedience and apostasy but were later restored, with others, like Judas, who betrayed Christ and was rejected.[23] He goes as far to say that even though one may have assurance of salvation when their faith is directed at Christ, such confidence should never foster a presumptuous kind of certainty.[24] But in other instances, he claims that he could not be accused of teaching explicitly that some true believers do fall away while he admits there are some biblical texts that appear to teach that they can.[25]

Combined with these comments, two further issues arise from Arminius work that bear on this topic. One is the question as to whether a believer could be part of the elect and apostatize. Arminius alludes to Augustine so he can distinguish between the elect, or believers who endure in their faith, and believers who are not elect because they do not endure to obtain final salvation.[26] Like Augustine, Arminius on occasion affirms the idea of the perseverance of the elect, not the saints, even though he strongly disagrees with the bishop of hippo as to why some saints fail to endure. They fail in Augustine's line of reasoning because God did not grant them persevering grace while for Arminius, some freely reject such grace. The other concern is whether he believed apostasy, in whatever form it is committed, can be forgiven. Arminius answers that if a believer apostatizes out of contempt for God's law, or the moral expectations that are placed on them, then they can indeed be forgiven and restored. Yet if they turn away from the faith because they are denying Christ outright, then reconciliation is unattainable.[27] So in light of all this, the safest deduction to make is that Arminius wrestled with the very real possibility of apostasy throughout his theological pilgrimage and whether it could be forgiven seems to still be open for debate.[28]

2:725–26). Also Stanley's discussion in *Did Jesus Teach Salvation by Works?*, 51–55.

23. Arminius, *Works of Arminius*, 2:725, 740–43; 3:463–64. At the same time, though, Arminius does say that "if David had died in the very moment in which he had sinned against Uriah by adultery and murder, he would have been condemned unto eternal death." Cf. Arminius, *Works of Arminius*, 2:725; and Vesko's assessment in, "Union with Christ," 446–47.

24. Arminius, *Works of Arminius*, 1:255.

25. Arminius, *Works of Arminius*, 1:254. He also denied teaching explicitly that apostasy in fact "does" happen in his *Declarations of Sentiments*. Cf. Arminius, *Works of Arminius*, 1:667; Bangs, *Arminius*, 312–13; and Oropeza, *Paul and Apostasy*, 16.

26. Arminius, *Works of Arminius*, 2:68; Stanglin and McCall, *Arminius*, 173.

27. Cf. Arminius, *Works of Arminius*, 2:743–50; Stanglin and McCall, *Arminius*, 174–75. An interesting note is that Arminians would later come to disagree on whether Arminius thought apostasy could be forgiven. Some think the correct interpretation of Arminius, and the NT, is that apostasy cannot be forgiven. See, e.g., Picirilli, *Grace, Faith, Free Will*, 198; and Ashby, "Reformed Arminianism," 149–54.

28. Another factor that deserves consideration in determining what Arminius

3. THE CLASH BETWEEN THE REMONSTRANTS AND THE SYNOD OF DORT

Even though Arminius was subject to all kinds of accusations during his career, he did not shy away from theological debates about Reformed theology both in person or in print. Because of this, his gifted abilities to express his views helped him garnish a significant audience of sympathizers who came to agree with many of his proposals. But this also created a scenario for a theological firestorm because shortly before his death, some ecclesiastical authorities wanted their clergy to officially declare what their views were on the Reformed confessions so they could weed out any potential Arminius supporters. This fanned the flames of controversy because when Arminius did die, he bequeathed a passionate group of successors who wanted to see the Netherlands become officially tolerant of his views. Such zeal alarmed the States General because it was viewed as potentially subversive to their authority. This is why state authorities proposed that local synods issue their grievance to their representatives so a solution could be deliberated.[29]

This declaration proverbially broke the camel's back because it was at this point in 1610 that some forty-six supporters of Arminius' views made up of scholars, clergy, statesman, and laity issued a petition expressing their desire to be allowed to promote their views and choose church leaders who espoused them. They followed the leadership of a scholar named Simon Episcopius in drafting five declarations that they believed clarified their theological convictions. The document countered five specific Reformed beliefs concerning election and salvation. They were called the Remonstrance, which led to supporters being called Remonstrants.[30] Many were initially tolerated in positions of leadership. But problems arose because there was a lingering suspicion that they may have been supporters of Spain. This rumor convinced some to publish fiery rhetoric charging them with heresy and even start riots in certain cities. The tensions reached such a level

---

affirmed is his view of justification. While maintaining continuity with other Reformers regarding its forensic nature, he did see justification as being incomplete until the final judgment. Its completion will "be near the close of life, when God will grant, to those who end their days in the faith of Christ, to find his mercy absolving them from all the sins which had been perpetrated through the whole of their lives. The declaration and manifestation of justification will be in the future general judgment." Cf. Arminius, *Works of Arminius*, 2:407; Vesko "Union with Christ," 446–47; Hampson, *Christian Contradictions*, 9–55; and Stanglin, *Arminius on the Assurance of Salvation*, 236–44.

29. Picirilli, *Grace, Faith, Free Will*, 12–13. In a true sense, the Reformation's identity in Holland was at stake because of this impasse. See Thuesen, *Predestination*, 39.

30. Episcopius was most likely the primary author of the document. Olson, *Arminian Theology*, 23.

that the Prince Maurice of Nassau felt compelled to intervene. He bought into the charge that the term Remonstrant was code for national traitor and so he imprisoned various supporters and replaced political vacancies with Reformed leaders.[31]

Leadership in the Netherlands by this time knew a synod was needed to settle this controversy. Eventually one met in Dordrecht in November of 1618 and it took over six months to issue its final decisions. Now known as the Synod of Dort, in May of 1619 the joint members convened and even though the group represented the Reformed churches of the Netherlands, it actually included twenty-six delegates from eight foreign countries.[32] The synod made the final charge that the Remonstrants affirmed heretical beliefs and declared that both the Belgic confession and Heidelberg catechism were to be adopted as the doctrinal safeguards of the Reformed church. In addition, five canons in opposition to the Remonstrance were adopted, which became known as the five points of Calvinism.[33] The aftermath of the synod was tragic for Arminian pastors because many were ejected from their churches, some had to leave the country because they refused to not voice their beliefs, and some were once again imprisoned.[34] Yet after Maurice died in 1625, Arminians were allowed to live in the country without persecution as long as they made no attempts to unite themselves to the Reformed church. However, the question with which we are concerned is the view of perseverance that the Remonstrants advocated and Dort opposed.

3.1 The Claims of the Remonstrants

The five articles of Remonstrance deal with issues pertaining to election, regeneration, the nature of grace, the extent of the atonement, and the possibility of apostasy. Each of these tenets are well-known, especially because of how later Christian traditions adopted and expanded the ideas in various ways. Nonetheless, the last article, which covers the issue of apostasy, opened a door of inquiry that Protestants could pursue for the purpose of possibly conceiving a way in which apostasy could be theologically tenable. And they could do so to the exclusion of any stringent view of sacramentalism or

---

31. Olson, *Story of Christian Theology*, 463–64.

32. Venema, *But for the Grace of God*, 13. Also for much more details, see DeJong, *Crisis in the Reformed Churches*.

33. This is where the link was eventually made to create an acronym with the word tulip, since it was one of the most famous Dutch flowers. See Thuesen, *Predestination*, 39–40.

34. See Picirilli, *Grace, Faith, Free Will*, 16–17.

notion of Pelagianism. The fifth section begins with a statement that is not controversial because it emphasizes a believer's security in Christ. It states,

> That those who are incorporated into Christ by a true faith, and have thereby become partakers of his life-giving Spirit, have thereby full power to strive against Satan, sin, the world, and their own flesh, and to win the victory; it being well understood that it is ever through the assisting grace of the Holy Ghost; and that Jesus Christ assists them through his Spirit in all temptations, extends to them his hand, and if only they are ready for the conflict, and desire his help, and are not inactive, keeps them from falling, so that they, by no craft or power of Satan, can be misled nor plucked out of Christ's hands, according to the Word of Christ, Jn 1:28 "Neither shall any man pluck them out of my hand."[35]

Note that these initial claims coincided well with what Reformed believers affirmed. All agreed that by virtue of believers being identified with Christ and recipients of the Spirit, they were assured that divine grace would protect them in all their temptations and struggles. It is the article's conclusion that caused such a stir.

> But whether they are capable through negligence, of forsaking again the first beginnings of their life in Christ, of again returning to this present evil world, of turning away from the holy doctrine which was delivered them, of losing a good conscience of becoming devoid of grace, that must be more particularly determined out of the Holy Scripture, before we ourselves can teach it with full persuasion of our minds.[36]

Here we see that while Arminians were certain that God's grace was more than able to preserve all believers from any external pressures mounted by Satan or temptations, the possibility that believers could choose of their own accord to forsake his grace was another matter entirely. Like Arminius, the jury was still out in the minds of his followers as to whether parts of Scripture taught that this could happen. In time, Arminians did conclude that apostasy could (and did) happen. But the friction caused by the article at the outset was that it denied the assurance of perseverance, which all Dutch Reformed churches affirmed.

---

35. "Five Arminian Articles, Article 5," in Schaff, 3:548.
36. "Five Arminian Articles, Article 5," in Schaff, 3:548–49.

3.2 The Responses of Dort

Years later, when the Synod of Dort finally convened to issue their responses to the doctrinal proposals of the Remonstrance, the series of statements on perseverance affirmed that its reality in the lives of believers is based on God's previous choice to elect them to salvation. Put bluntly, Arminians thought a believer's freedom to choose salvation must necessarily entail their ability to potentially reject it later. The Reformed leaders of Dort countered that election is based on unconditional grace that God bestows according to his own good pleasure. Therefore, anyone who is chosen to become a recipient of his grace will also reach the ultimate end for which they were chosen, which is perseverance and glorification. We see this argument develop in the fifth section of the canons of Dort where the first five articles speak about the fact that believers may struggle with sin and even fail at times. But then for the rest of the section from articles 6–14, the composers argue that

> God who is rich in mercy, according to his unchangeable purpose of election, does not wholly withdraw the Holy Spirit from his own people, even in their melancholy falls; nor suffer them to proceed so far as to lose the grace of adoption, and forfeit the state of justiciation, or to commit the sin unto death; nor does he permit them to be totally deserted, and to plunge themselves into everlasting destruction.[37]

This link to unconditional election was the polemical key that Dort used to defend its view of perseverance, namely if all saints are elect, then none of them can fall away. Otherwise, God's sovereignty in election could be thwarted. We see this emphasis on the theological necessity of perseverance continue to unfold in subsequent articles where Dort contends that regeneration births an incorruptible seed that always results in spiritual fruit and salvation (art. VII); that God always provides sufficient grace for everyone he chooses so they can persevere and glory in his provision (arts. VIII–IX); and that believers can overcome all of their doubts and struggles by relying on the grace that God provides through the Spirit, the preaching of the word, and the sacraments (arts. X–XIV).[38] One could say Dort's contention was that since grace was always effectual in bringing the elect to the threshold of salvation, it must likewise continue to be effectual in bringing the elect to its culmination. Finally, what made these declarations so controversial was not simply that they conflicted with the Remonstrance. That was to be expected. The source of conflict arose out of article XVI which claimed

---

37. "Canons of the Synod of Dort," in Schaff, 3:593.
38. "Canons of the Synod of Dort," in Schaff, 3:593–95.

that the perseverance of the saints was hated by the devil, mocked by the world, abused by the foolish, and opposed by heretics.[39] This statement did not simply object to the Remonstrance. It declared that its supporters were outside the bounds of orthodoxy. This is why such a severe rift was forged between Arminians and Dortians at that time. Their disagreement did not pertain simply to the theological details of apostasy and perseverance. For the Arminians, it was about the right to propagate their views in the Netherlands and for Dort, their concerns were tethered to larger concerns about who could be considered orthodox.

4. ARMINIAN THEOLOGY TRANSITIONS: WESLEYAN VIEWS ON PERSEVERANCE

Although the budding Arminian tradition fell on hard times in the Netherlands after Dort's decisions, it did flourish in other regions. It gained traction in England because of its impact on segments of the Anglican Church and as we saw in the previous chapter, many Anabaptist thinkers resonated with Arminian ideals as well.[40] Yet a true revival in Arminian thought emerged a century later due to the contributions of John Wesley and the Methodist movement.[41] Wesley's religious context began in the Anglican tradition since his father, Samuel, was a former priest and his mother, Susanna, was avidly devoted to the faith of the Church of England. In his early adult years, Wesley attended Oxford for two degrees and eventually became ordained into the Anglican clergy. It was during his time at Oxford that he became a part of a campus society of believers, which his brother Charles helped start, who were committed to spiritual disciplines like prayer and Bible study; so much so that their patrons scoffed at their activities by labeling them as a "holy club."

Wesley's spiritual pilgrimage later reached a turning point after he traveled to Savannah, Georgia to minister to colonists. He returned from

---

39. "Canons of the Synod of Dort," in Schaff, 3:595.

40. This was covered in the previous chapter. But again, an excellent source to consult here is by Keefer, "Arminian Motifs in the Anabaptist Heritage," 293–323.

41. There were unfortunate turns that Arminianism did take. For instance, a Remonstrant named Philip Limborch developed an approach that was more conducive to semi-Pelagianism than the original followers of Arminius. A large segment of later eighteenth-century self-acclaimed Arminians followed Limborch's approach and conflated their theological commitments with naturalized versions of religion popularized by the Enlightenment. Cf. Olson, *Arminian Theology*, 23; Harper, "Wesleyan Arminian View," 213–17; Oropeza, *Paul and Apostasy*, 19; and Chamberlain, "New Look at the Rise of Arminianism," 335–56.

this disappointing visit with serious doubts about his own faith and calling.[42] It was at this time that he visited the now famous Moravian church on Aldersgate Street where he possibly experienced his actual conversion or at least encountered a turning point in his commitment to the Lord. It was after this event that his ministry exploded. He began preaching with his efforts quickly making inroads with a former member of the Oxford group, George Whitefield. And it was here where his thoughts on apostasy began to emerge because in interactions with Whitefield, who was a lay Calvinist, Wesley expressed antipathy toward much of Reformed theology, especially its ideas on predestination and perseverance.

4.1 Theological Influences on Wesley's Thought

Today Wesleyan scholars debate the sources that contributed to the doctrinal ideas that Wesley proposed in his lifetime. All agree that he rejected Dort's Calvinism in exchange for the general tenor of classical Arminian theology that had not been contaminated by Enlightenment skepticism as seen in the thoughts he expressed in the *Arminian Magazine* that he started in 1778.[43] But some of the beliefs that he advocated did not correspond to traditional Arminianism at every level.[44] A major reason for this was because the majority of influences that helped shape his theological convictions were different from those that were instrumental in the lives of Arminius or his successors. Arminius was heavily influenced by thinkers like Augustine (from his earlier writings); medieval thinkers like Bernard of Clairvaux, John Duns Scotus, and Aquinas; Catholic scholars such as Erasmus, Biel, and Molina; and Reformed thinkers such as Calvin, Beza, Junius, and Bullinger.[45] Wesley, on the other hand, interpreted Arminian thought more likely through the lenses of its Anglican revisions and seventeenth-century English anti-Calvinism.[46] This can be seen in sources that show Wesley's indebtedness to thinkers such as Hugo Grotius, Anglican scholar Jeremy Taylor, and the Arminian-minded Puritan, John Goodwin,

---

42. On the perplexity that Wesley went through here, see his thoughts in "Troubles in Georgia," 38–58; and Tomkins, *John Wesley*, 43–55; Collins, *John Wesley*, 54–76.

43. See Shetler, "John Wesley," 85–100; Rogal, "John Wesley's Arminian Magazine," 231–47.

44. One helpful work highlights this fact by arguing that Wesley drew more from segments of Anglican theology more than that of the Remonstrants. See McGonigle, *Sufficient Saving Grace*.

45. Stranglin and McCall, *Arminius*, 41–45.

46. Pinson, introduction to *Four Views*, 16–17.

who supported the Arminian view of apostasy.[47] Therefore, it is only natural that Wesley's version of Arminianism would diverge from its original form a century earlier.

This is not to minimize points of similarity, because Wesley did affirm concepts like conditional election and prevenient grace. However, he views on apostasy exceeded the bounds of what Arminius and his immediate followers were willing to concede with utter certainty. Arminius and the Remonstrants focused mainly on the possibility that believers could deny the Lord, thereby becoming apostates who reach a point of no return.[48] But, as we discussed, there was a bit of equivocation on whether one could fall into an egregious pattern of sinfulness that led to a loss of salvation, claiming that the biblical data required more attention before any conclusive arguments could be made.[49] Wesley and his followers thought otherwise.[50]

4.2 Wesley's Views of Apostasy

Wesley and his theological sympathizers agreed with the Arminian tradition that the grace of salvation was amissible, meaning it could be lost under certain circumstances. What distinguished Wesleyan versions of Arminianism from its more classical forms, however, was the belief that such amissibility could become a reality in one of two ways. First of all, believers could commit outright apostasy by repudiating their faith in Christ altogether. One work where Wesley addresses this matter is in his treatise *Serious Thoughts upon the Perseverance of the Saints*. He begins by claiming that the question about apostasy only makes sense if one is speaking about true believers, those who are saints that have endured with faith, received purified hearts, been sanctified by the blood of the covenant, and so on.[51] Wesley says that

---

47. Pinson, introduction to *Four Views*, 17. Scholars debate other influences on Wesley such as Pietism and even Eastern Orthodoxy. Cf. O'Malley, "Pietistic Influence," 48–70; Collins, "Influence of Early German Pietism," 23–42; and Merritt, "Wesley and Eastern Orthodoxy," 23–163. Pinson asserts that four major schools of thought exist regarding Wesley's placement in Christian thought—those being Catholic, Calvinist in a strict "Reformation" tone, Anglican, and eclectic, Pinson, "Atonement, Justification, and Apostasy," 75.

48. Again, the idea is that believers must continually express faith in Christ because if one defects from the faith via apostasy, their condition is irreparable. See summary of this point in Ashby, "Reformed Arminian View," 180–86.

49. Some think the Remonstrants affirmed the idea that unrepentant sin could lead to apostasy. We would argue that while Arminius wrestled with the possibility, the Remonstrants were closer to accepting it as a potential reality.

50. Cf. Pinson, introduction to *Four Views*, 18–19.

51. Wesley, *Serious Thoughts upon the Perseverance of the Saints*, 1153.

"falling away" refers to the idea of a saint forsaking the Lord so as to perish everlastingly.[52] He openly admits that based on his understanding of "the oracles of God," he believes that a saint can fall away, citing Ezek 18:24 as his initial proof text.[53] He then works his way through other biblical texts that he thinks support this belief and responds to some objections that advocates of perseverance typically raise.[54] He concludes that anyone who does suffer eternal judgment does so as an unbeliever. Therefore, while it is true that no child of God can perish, one who renounces their identity as one of God's children indeed can and will. In his own words, "God is the Father of them that believe, so long as they believe. But the devil is the father of them that believe not, whether they did once believe or no."[55]

What is interesting about these claims is that he makes them both as a keen theologian as well as a compassionate pastor. One can see his role as the former when looking at instances where he wrestles with passages, which at face value, could be interpreted to mean apostasy is unforgivable. Two examples are 1 Tim 1:19–20, which speaks of believers "shipwrecking their faith," and the famous text Heb 6:4–6, which speaks about the impossibility of some being renewed to repentance if they choose to hold Christ in contempt. He deduces that texts such as these extend no hope of restoration. Apostasy is an act, for all practical purposes, that appears to be a point of no return.[56]

Yet in other works, like his famous sermon *A Call to Backsliders*, Wesley reveals a more pastoral tone when considering whether there can be possible restitution. Toward the end of his discussion, he acknowledges that the question of whether apostates can find mercy and be renewed to repentance is a serious one. He reflects on his experience as a minister saying he has seen "several thousands. In every place where the arm of the Lord has been revealed, and many sinners converted to God, there are several found who

---

52. Wesley, *Serious Thoughts upon the Perseverance of the Saints*, 1153–54.

53. Wesley, *Serious Thoughts upon the Perseverance of the Saints*, 1154.

54. He works through eight major theses that he believes highlight the NT emphasis on the possibility of apostasy. One can potentially be condemned eternally even if one (1) begins in righteousness because the Lord promises to judge anyone who falls into unrepentant rebellion, (2) has exercised faith and had their heart purified, (3) has been grafted into the invisible church, (4) has become a branch connected to the vine, which is Christ, (5) escaped the pollutions of the world by effectually knowing Christ, (6) has seen the glory of Christ and become a partake of the Holy Spirit, (7) currently lives by faith, or (8) has been sanctified by the covenant. In each of these cases, Wesley argues that Scripture never assures a believer that they are beyond condemnation if they fall into unbelief subsequent to receiving these blessings. See Wesley, *Serious Thoughts*, 1154–64.

55. Wesley, *Serious Thoughts*, 1165.

56. Cf. See Wesley, *Serious Thoughts*, 1138–39, 1141–42.

'turn back from the holy commandment that delivered to them.'"[57] Wesley concludes that the severe warnings of Scripture are there to sober obstinate apostates about impending doom while at the same time admonishing fallen saints to be restored while there is time. He ends this plea by stating that "it is not for these desperate children of perdition that the preceding considerations are designed; but for those who feel the remembrance of their sins is grievous unto them, the burden of them intolerable."[58] Thus, Wesley held out hope that penitent prodigals could be restored because of the practical perplexities that it raised to think apostasy was completely unforgiveable. He believed in its severity, its finality, and the impending judgment that it incurred while having great confidence that God's grace could reach even the vilest apostate who returned home for forgiveness.

Along with these concerns, the other way in which Wesley believed saints could jeopardize their salvation was through patterns of unrepentant sin. Notably Wesley's line of thought on this matter is a bit more complex than his reflections on explicit apostasy. This is why scholars differ on the details of what Wesley actually believed. Most accept the idea that his view of apostasy was based on his belief that grace was resistible both before and after conversion.[59] While Wesley thought prevenient grace could potentially enable someone to freely receive salvation, it could not safeguard one's ability to freely reject it later through unbelief or sinful conduct. Likewise, some contend that his thoughts on how unconfessed sin can threaten one's salvation are based on his views on justification and the atonement.[60] Some argue, for example, that Wesley believed Christ's death provided atonement

---

57. Wesley, *Call to Backsliders*, 529.

58. Wesley, *Call to Backsliders*, 530.

59. One can see this idea, for example, in one particular treatise (*Predestination Calmly Considered*, 1147–51) where Wesley argues that Scripture does not describe election as being unconditional. What is ironic at this point is that he refuses to be put in the logical corner of necessarily affirming conditional election. He contends for what could be called "provisional" election in that he thinks Scripture presents the simple idea that anyone can come to faith in Christ but just as they can freely accept it because of prevenient grace, they can later abandon it through sin. Also, in a sermon (*On Predestination*, 700), Wesley contends that the famous golden chain of Romans 8:28–29 is not describing a series of definitive cause and effects. Rather it is describing the method God uses to save all believers. What one sees then is that since Wesley rejected unconditional election and believed it was ultimately contingent on a believers' response to divine grace, final perseverance was similarly contingent on a believer's continued reliance on God's justifying and sanctifying grace. See Davis, "Perseverance of the Saints," 224.

60. E.g., Pinson, "Atonement, Justification, and Apostasy," 73–92; Pinson, introduction to *Four Views*, 16–19. Also see these articles and additional insights in Pinson, *Arminian and Baptist*.

initially for the sins which people commit before they are converted. But its benefits are only applied to believers' sins after conversion as they continually confess and repent.[61] Similarly, the act of justification, which is based on the work of Christ, only remedies believers' fallen condition. Subsequent to the choice to follow Christ, their experience of his righteousness is inherently linked to their willingness to walk in the Spirit and be continually cleansed of unrighteousness through prayer and repentance.[62] So the argument here is that Wesley viewed unresolved post-conversion sin as something that can indeed lead one to condemnation.[63]

Here scholars do differ as to whether Wesley did affirm the full imputation of Christ's righteousness to believers and if his death atoned for every sin that believers commit, both before and after their conversion. Some propose that the reason he thought unrepentant sin would lead to the loss of salvation was because the application of Christ's righteousness (via justification), and his atoning death (via penal substitution), were always conditioned on faith.[64] So salvation from all sin both before and after one's conversion is solely grounded in the work of Christ. Nonetheless, its experience is only maintained through one's faith. In Wesley's mind then, if faith becomes deadened by harboring sinful conduct, a believer can enter a downward spiral of rebellion and if left unchecked, revert back to the same kind of life that they exhibited before conversion, which, in turn, can end in apostasy.[65]

In any case, regardless of which reading of Wesley's works is correct, a consensus still remains among Wesleyan scholars that he believed the application of salvation was not grounded in election like the Calvinists, but

---

61. See, e.g., Wesley's comments in *On Sin in Believers*, 349–50. At the same time, there appear to be some unresolved tensions in his overall view of sin. See Olson's in-depth analysis in "Wesley's Doctrine of Sin Revisited," 53–71. This idea also has massive implications for how Wesley develops his theology of assurance. Collins (*Theology of John Wesley*, 140–42) surveys Wesley's works and shows that he spoke of assurance as growing incrementally in stages throughout the sanctification process. Also see Noll on the matter in "Wesley and the Doctrine of Assurance," 161–77.

62. Such a reading is based on an understanding of Wesley that sees him as rejecting the strict concept of imputation that other Reformers used in their defense of forensic justification. Cf. Wesley, *Thoughts on the Imputed Righteousness of Christ*, 1183–86; Wesley, *Justification by Faith*, 286; and Pinson, "Atonement, Justification, and Apostasy," 86–88.

63. A prime example can be seen in Harper, "Wesleyan Arminianism," 232–42.

64. Harper, "Wesleyan Arminianism," 232–38; Also see Olson in *Arminian Theology*, 231–33.

65. Cf. Wesley's comments in "Great Privilege," 331–40; Harper, "Wesleyan Arminianism," 241.

rather in an abiding faith in Christ.⁶⁶ If someone were to renounce their faith outright or let it gradually erode through constant unrepentant disobedience, the result would be a loss of salvation. Moreover, this development marked a significant shift in Arminian thought because it linked the amissibility of salvation to apostasy as well as sinful conduct. In turn, the latter connection fit hand-in-hand with Wesley's views of justification, sanctification, and his gradual expression of Christian perfectionism.⁶⁷

5. CONCLUSION: ARMINIANISM IN SUBSEQUENT PROTESTANT TRADITIONS

We can see in retrospect that the Arminian tradition proved to be a significant theological force in the development of Christian thought on the subject of perseverance for several reasons. Three will suffice here. One is that it provided a matrix of biblical interpretations which supported the idea of apostasy in ways that were robustly Protestant. As opposed to previous conceptions of apostasy that were linked to sacramental views of regeneration and justification, Arminianism, both in its classical and Wesleyan forms, mounted a defense for the belief that saints could fall from grace which could, in theory, align with Reformation ideals such as imputation, forensic justification, and penal substitution (although in different ways depending on which Arminian thinker one studies).⁶⁸

Second, Arminian views on perseverance and apostasy served as an alternative to the strong deterministic tradition of Calvinism. Whereas both traditions affirmed that apostasy did happen, Reformed thinkers conceded that such instances revealed that apostates were never genuine believers. Such a deduction was necessary because, again, in the Reformed approach, perseverance as well as regeneration and conversion are all grounded in election (and ultimately divine sovereignty). Anyone who is elect inevitably becomes regenerate, converted by faith, and that faith necessarily perseveres because God can lose none of those whom he chooses to be saved.

---

66. At the same time, the disagreement about the mechanics of Wesley's theology on perseverance can be significant. E.g., see the critique that Ashby poses against Harper's reading of Wesley in "Reformed Arminian Response to Steve Harper," 273–77.

67. Pinson, "Atonement, Justification, and Apostasy," 92. One could say his view of election supported his view of apostasy and perseverance as well.

68. Granted, other strands of Arminian thought went in other directions that rejected these ideals as seen in its post-Enlightenment forms as well as the aberrant version promoted by Charles Finney. But neither traditional or Wesleyan Arminians affirm the revisions that these sources advocated. See summary in Olson, *Arminian Theology*, 23–24, 27–28.

Arminian thinkers countered that perseverance is grounded in faith, not election. Election is conditioned on one's belief, which, in turn, is only possible because of the preliminary working of the Spirit in prevenient grace. So if a believer's election is conditioned on their initial act of faith, then the ongoing spiritual benefits of salvation are necessarily linked to the continued expression of that faith. This is why all Arminians contend that apostasy in the NT makes no sense as a term if those who commit it were never believers at the outset. It is meaningless to say that unbelievers apostatize.

Third, the Arminian tradition served as the theological foundation for numerous other Protestant denominations that would emerge long after the Reformation was over. The thoughts of Arminius were expanded by the Remonstrants and their core commitments about apostasy became instrumental in the views espoused by an assortment of later traditions. One example can be seen in certain strands of the Baptist tradition. Specifically, in the early sixteenth century, there were two English separatist groups who forged different theological paths apart from both Anglican and Puritan traditions. Some followed Reformed trajectories and became known as Particular Baptists, while others who embraced classical (non-Wesleyan) Arminian theology gradually emerged as General Baptists.[69] Another tradition, which advocated Arminian ideals primarily because it exhibited a strong anti-Calvinist bent, surfaced in the second great awakening through the ministries of Barton Stone and the father-son preacher duo of Thomas and Alexander Campbell who spearheaded the Stone-Campbell, or Restorationist, movement.[70] Finally, the modified Arminianism advocated by Wesley was streamlined in the subsequent Methodist traditions and became part of the later Holiness and Pentecostal denominations as well.[71] So what can be deduced from the history of these traditions is that the influence of Arminian views on perseverance is substantial among Protestants to say the least.

---

69. There are numerous works on the early history of Particular Baptists but a good concise introduction can be seen in Belyea, "Origins of the Particular Baptists," 40–67; and an excellent examination of Arminian theology in the General Baptist tradition is provided by Pinson, *Arminian and Baptist*.

70. For an excellent resource on the groups that came from this movement, including the Churches of Christ, Disciples of Christ, and the Christian Church, see Foster et al., *Encyclopedia of the Stone-Campbell Movement*.

71. During the first great awakening, it is well known that Wesley had significant disagreements with his good friend George Whitefield over the matters of election, human freedom, and perseverance. See Harrington, "Friendship Under Fire," 167–81. Yet the impact of their ministries was felt throughout Protestantism both in America and Britain. Cf. surveys by Noll, *Age of Edwards, Whitefield, and the Wesleys*; Schwenk, *Wesley, Whitefield, and the Quest for Evangelical Unity*.

Chapter 9

Perseverance and the Modern Lordship Salvation Debate

Up to this point, we have summarized a number of proposals that select Christian thinkers over the centuries have offered in their attempts to express what they believe the Scriptures teach on the matters of apostasy and perseverance. We have outlined views that arose in early Christian history, the influential perspective of Augustine of Hippo, and several others promoted by mainstay Protestant traditions. Now our historical survey comes to a close with a leap forward to the twentieth century. In this chapter, we want to provide one last survey covering an in-house dispute among American evangelicals and fundamentalists popularly known as the Lordship Salvation controversy, which reached a fever pitch in the 1980s and '90s. The basic gist of this rift pertained to how one should reconcile Christ's demanding summons to discipleship with his consistent invitation to believe the gospel and receive salvation.[1] The looming question among disputing parties was famously worded like this—must someone receive Christ as "Lord" in order to believe upon him as "Savior," or are these affirmations two separate actions? Or put in more Protestant-specific terminology, must a faith that leads to justification necessarily result in subsequent obedience and spiritual endurance? And if so, what does that look like?

---

1. See a further synopsis in Olson, "Lordship Controversy," 317–19.

The reason we are choosing to engage this debate as opposed to other treatments on perseverance in modern critical scholarship is because this particular altercation unveils a deep-seated difference in how many within evangelical and fundamentalist circles understand the meaning of perseverance even to this day.[2] As we have seen historically, the concept has been couched in terms of believers enduring in their personal faith so they can enter the age to come. The vast majority of Christian traditions mutually concede to this minimalist definition. What causes differences of opinion is whether a true believer can fail to do so.

Many, arguably even most, have conceded for different theological reasons that believers can apostatize and forfeit the grace they may have previously received in Christ. We have shown how such conclusions sometimes follow certain components of the Augustinian paradigm which again makes a distinction between God's elect saints who always persevere and saints who, for one reason or another, choose to apostatize. Likewise, we saw that the Reformed tradition argued against such a distinction. No true believer can renounce their faith because it is a divine gift that is linked to their very election as a part of God's people. All believers must therefore persevere in their faith because it is indicative of God's promise to preserve them in Christ. But despite these differences, the one common denominator among non-Reformed and Reformed venues alike has been that perseverance is a necessary component of final salvation. The irony, though, is that the quarrel over the Lordship issue revealed another form of thought had developed which saw perseverance as having nothing to do with salvation whatsoever.

1. THEOLOGICAL FACTORS INVOLVED IN THE DEBATE

This debate hit quite a high number on the theological Richter scale among numerous Christian conservatives because it awakened a significant source of contention that had been bubbling under the surface for quite some time. It was fueled by thinkers and authors within Fundamentalism and evangelicalism, two significant Protestant movements in early to mid-twentieth-century American culture. Because they were trans-denominational by nature, this meant pastors, leaders, and church laity who were connected to these guilds held an assortment of ideas that were intrinsic to their own doctrinal traditions. Yet this diversity did not prevent these groups from being unified by certain Protestant axioms that had stood the test of time

---

2. Oropeza provides a helpful assessment of works on perseverance over the last few decades in *Paul and Apostasy*, 22–53.

from the Reformation all the way through the great awakenings down to the denominational context of the modern era.

One belief, in particular, that was (and still is) cherished by both fundamentalists and evangelicals was justification by faith alone. These conservatives mutually agreed that people initially experienced salvation by exercising personal faith in Christ and his atoning work on their behalf. However, this general point of consensus did not pacify a host of other concerns where agreement was not always as common. Two such issues were: (1) What relationship does saving faith have with repentance? And (2) how does perseverance relate to justification and final judgment? These questions elicited a variety of answers, which in turn created the theological breeding ground for the Lordship impasse. Consequently, before we begin our tour of the debate itself, it would be helpful to see how these issues contributed to this debate.

1.1 The Meaning of Conversionism

One major reason this controversy exploded on the scene was because of an underlying tension on the meaning of conversion. Both fundamentalists and evangelicals used this term to describe the initial change people exhibit when they embrace the gospel message. Such an emphasis highlighted the transition people exhibit outwardly once they experience an inward transformation otherwise known as the "new birth." One might say it is the initial rite of passage into individual salvation.

The idea of conversion was also a hallmark belief because it served as the objective of the evangelistic mission of conservatives. One need only to think of the mid-twentieth-century image of evangelist Billy Graham making a mass appeal in a crusade for attendants to "get saved." Following his plea, thousands would then stream forward to "receive Christ as Savior," or become new converts.[3] While conservatives knew that walking an aisle did not necessarily mean any transformation occurred, and some were even uncomfortable with such revivalist methods, all generally agreed that such acts could at least serve as a visual aid that illustrated a change of identity which occurred when a person who was once an unbeliever now truly became a follower of Christ.

At the same time, even though there was a broad consensus on the importance of conversion, there were still some well-known differences among fundamentalists and evangelicals on the details of how it was experienced. This was the case because, again, there were so many traditions that

3. Olson, "Conversion," 160–61.

were part of these larger conservative coalitions. For instance, there were ongoing quibbles over the Reformed/Arminian wedge as to whether conversion preceded regeneration and many still perpetuated the well-known debate on whether there was any link between baptism and regeneration. Still, these disagreements did not mitigate against a majority consensus that conversion was an experience that entailed the external acts of faith and repentance—faith being understood as an act of trust or placing one's confidence in Christ for their salvation and repentance being seen as the expression of a penitent heart that someone has when they renounce their former way of living in exchange for a new life in Christ. The problem was that these perceptions came under scrutiny when the Lordship debate emerged. As we shall see, a renewed emphasis upon the role of repentance in the conversion experience triggered a response from an assortment of authors who thought faith and repentance are synonymous terms. Faith was seen as trust in Christ and repentance was couched in terms of merely changing one's mind about Christ's true identity.

1.2 Eternal Security vs. Perseverance of the Saints

A second factor that fed the tension of this debate was a redefining of the meaning of perseverance. Before the Lordship ordeal commenced, fundamentalists and evangelicals had been well accustomed to the age-old dividing line between Reformed and Arminian views on this matter. Many had Calvinistic leanings and affirmed that all true believers persevere in their faith because they are divinely appointed to do so as God's elect while others who gravitated toward Arminian thought argued that just as people are free to believe the gospel (via the work of prevenient grace), they are likewise able to later turn away and become apostate.

These were common mainstay disagreements that had been delineated over the centuries. But what helped set the stage for this new wedge on Lordship was a shift in thinking about this Reformed/Arminian standoff. Some conservatives rejected the Arminian allowance for apostasy as well as the Reformed focus on saints persevering to show they were truly converted. Both of these approaches were perceived as destroying any hope of having real assurance of salvation because believers were either doomed to live in constant fear of losing their salvation or incessantly examining themselves because they could never be sure they were part of the elect.

These concerns led some to affirm a form of unconditional preservation. Here, a believer's identity in Christ is retained despite any potential patterns of sin or apostasy that they may commit after their conversion.

This proposal countered the Arminian belief that "saved" people could once again become "unsaved" as well as the Reformed idea that "saved" people would never become "unsaved" because they always persevere. Instead, perseverance was separated entirely from the question of whether some are "saved" or stay "saved." This idea of preservation came to be labeled as eternal security or the security of the believer, especially within many Baptist circles.[4] The overall point was that once a person became a believer, their salvific status could never be lost regardless of their future behavior. If any pattern of sinful conduct could potentially reveal that a person was really not a believer or lead to a person's spiritual demise, then one's salvation was necessarily linked to their works. This would then eliminate any possibility of personal assurance of salvation as well compromise the Protestant commitment to justification by faith alone.

Now, no doubt, such an idea was distinct from Arminian camps because it denied the very possibility of apostasy. But what made this idea tricky was that it overlapped with Reformed thought to a degree because advocates agreed with Calvinists that believers always remain as such. The key difference, however, was that proponents of eternal security did not view Christian conduct as a necessary result of conversion whereas Reformed thinkers did. Consequently, the idea of eternal security became difficult to categorize. Those who affirmed it could theoretically qualify themselves as "modified Calvinists" because they believed that true believers could never lose their salvation. Yet they could also deny the first four points of Calvinism or possibly even affirm four of the five Remonstrants. To complicate matters even more, no traditional Calvinist would ever consider such a seriously revised version of perseverance to be tenable.[5] Moreover, this variance on what perseverance meant was the key factor that surfaced as the Lordship debate unfolded.

2. PRECURSORS TO THE LORDSHIP SALVATION DEBATE

The rise of the Lordship controversy was like any other theological breach in that it was an outgrowth of an increasing set of fractures that preceded it. The disagreement on what the meaning of Christ's Lordship meant and its implications for how a believer experiences salvation had been surging slowly for quite some time. Evangelicals and fundamentalists within all kinds of conservative guilds were using terms like faith, repentance, discipleship,

---

4. Olson, "Perseverance," 238.
5. Such an example is Geisler. See his article "Moderate Calvinist View," 63–112.

lordship, justification, belief, and perseverance to describe the biblical dynamics of salvation as a whole. What made things potentially combative was their mutually shared glossary of terms was not always based on the same theological dictionary. Their definitions varied significantly at times, thereby setting the stage for conflict. Two examples illustrate the tensions that were developing prior to the first official rupture of the actual debate. The first was an interchange between Princeton theologian B. B. Warfield and classical dispensationalist Lewis Sperry Chafer. The second was a later engagement that included Everett Harrison and John R. W. Stott.

2.1 B. B. Warfield and Lewis Sperry Chafer

There is little doubt that some of the facets of Lewis Sperry Chafer's soteriology provided initial fodder for the Lordship firestorm. The backdrop of his work was during the early stages of dispensational thought at the turn of the twentieth century. Early on, he learned under the tutelage of numerous speakers and pastors such as James Orr, R. A. Torrey, G. Campbell Morgan, W. H. Griffith Thomas, and most importantly, the well-known expositor and pastor, C. I. Scofield.[6] These men helped equip Chafer so he could become a major contributor to the general structure of classical dispensationalism and eventually become the founder and first president of what became known as Dallas Theological Seminary, an institution that has been known as a bastion of dispensational theology.

Chafer also wrote several books on various Christian doctrines, including his own multivolume systematic theology and a short volume on spiritual maturity. This latter monograph, entitled *He That Is Spiritual*,[7] was written to clarify the criteria that he believed must be followed for believers to experience the work of the Spirit in their everyday lives. The main point in the book that instigated debate is found in Chafer's first chapter, where he elaborates on Paul's discussion in 1 Cor 2–3 about the nature of those who have the Spirit as opposed to those who do not. Chafer focuses on Paul's added indictment against some of the Corinthian believers who were behaving as though they were clueless infants, or of the flesh (i.e., carnal, 1 Cor 3:1). He concludes that Paul's comments give support to the idea that three different kinds of people exist, those being (1) unbelievers, or those without the Spirit, (2) believers who are indwelled and controlled by the Spirit, (3) and finally believers who are indwelled by the Spirit but are not

---

6. Cf. Gleason, "B. B. Warfield and Lewis S. Chafer," 244; Hannah, "Early Years of Lewis Sperry Chafer," 3–23.

7. Chafer, *He That Is Spiritual* (1918; repr., 1964).

following his guidance or will.[8] Such a set of categories clearly effects the idea of perseverance because the reality of "carnal Christians" serves as a reminder that some believers live as though they do not have the Spirit because if they did, according to Chafer, there would be no reason for Paul to correct the Corinthians.[9]

Furthermore, this paradigm fit with the prerequisites that Chafer thought one must meet to experience conversion. He argued that a person's expressions of faith and repentance were for all practical purposes the same act. Whereas faith is an act of trust that one commits because they "believe" who Christ is, repentance is a term that refers to the change of mind that one makes about Christ when they place their faith in him.[10] The end result of this kind of argument was that Chafer could affirm that repentance was an essential part of conversion while at the same time argue that no moral imposition was initially placed upon an unbeliever who wanted to become a convert. A person's experience of regeneration transitions them from one status to another but it does not guarantee that they will necessarily follow Christ the way that they should. That kind of commitment is only fostered by a continual yielding to the Spirit after one's conversion. Consequently, any moral impetus of repentance or significant transformation of behavior at conversion was all but jettisoned in Chafer's theology.

These ideas were eventually confronted by Princeton Reformed theologian B. B. Warfield who wrote a biting review of Chafer's book.[11] Warfield claimed that Chafer's arguments concerning "carnal Christianity" were indicative of a divided allegiance between his previous theological roots in Presbyterianism and his apparent affinity toward the higher life movement which was derivative of a Wesleyan view of sanctification.[12] According to Warfield, Chafer was trying to strike a balance with some sort of Reformed emphasis on the indissoluble nature of a believer's relationship to Christ that also avoided the wrongheaded views of Wesleyan perfectionism or any notions of a Second Blessing theology.

The problem, as Warfield argued, was that Chafer's acceptance of God's sovereignty stopped with regeneration. When it came to the progressive transformation of the moral character of believers, otherwise known as sanctification, Chafer conceded to a synergistic model in which believers

---

8. Chafer, *He That Is Spiritual*, 6–14.

9. Chafer, *He That Is Spiritual*, 12.

10. Chafer, *Systematic Theology*, 3:371–80.

11. Warfield, review of *He That Is Spiritual*, 322–27; reprinted in Horton, *Christ the Lord*, 211–18.

12. Warfield, review of *He That Is Spiritual*, 211.

may or may not grow in holiness. So Warfield thought Chafer's view still reflected some Wesleyan notions because he viewed the process of becoming Christ-like as a contingent reality that could only occur if believers chose to take a step beyond conversion to a higher plane of commitment. This proved to be a significant divergence on the interplay between justification and sanctification because future fundamentalists and evangelicals would eventually extend its implications to the matter of perseverance.

2.2 Everett Harrison and John R. W. Stott

These theological divides between Chafer and Warfield intensified among other thinkers as time progressed. One can see that the growing opinions began to polarize a bit more as seen in an interaction in the late 1950s and early 1960s between Everett F. Harrison and John R. W. Stott.[13] Harrison was a professor of New Testament at the newly established Fuller Theological Seminary and Stott was an Anglican rector of All Souls Church in London. Their main point of contention was how a person's initial act of faith in the gospel message relates to the kingdom-ethical mandates that Christ expects believers to follow. Harrison argued that one must be careful to delineate a person's confession of Jesus as Lord and Savior from the subsequent responsibilities of Christian living. One must see repentance as an ongoing practice that consistently takes place after one's conversion, not before.[14] Stott retorted that accepting Christ as Savior not only entailed an act of faith. In the NT, it was always coupled with an act of repentance from one's previous life of unbelief and sin.[15]

The rift here pertained to whether any kind of moral "submission" was required to affirm the gospel message. Some like Harrison, thought such language needed to be parsed carefully to stay faithful to the Reformation emphasis on *sola fide*. Others, such as Stott, saw a tighter relationship between saving faith and one's willingness to become a disciple. Both sides of this discussion continued to grow with a crescendo moment finally arriving in the late eighties.

---

13. Cf. Harrison, "Must Christ Be Lord," 14–18, 36–37, 48; Stott, "Must Christ Be Lord," 14–18, 36–37, 48.

14. Harrison, "Must Christ Be Lord," 18.

15. Stott, "Must Christ Be Lord," 18.

3. THE BEGINNING OF THE LORDSHIP CONTROVERSY

The official shot heard around the world regarding the Lordship controversy was fired by a well-known conservative evangelical named John MacArthur. At that time, he was the senior pastor of Grace Community Church in Los Angeles, California and had become nationally known for his syndicated radio program *Grace to You*.[16] His influence within many evangelical and even many fundamentalist circles was significant, which is largely why his thoughts on the matter of how Christ's lordship relates to conversion caused such a stir. Fellow scholars, pastors, and laypeople who were familiar with his ministries and publications paid close attention to what he had to say regardless of whether they always agreed.

The contention began when MacArthur wrote a book in 1988 entitled *The Gospel according to Jesus*.[17] He states in the introduction that it was the product of seven years of study in the gospels where he gave special attention to how Jesus interacted with people about their need for salvation.[18] He laments that the ways in which Jesus spoke about the gospel message often stand in stark contrast to assorted evangelistic approaches that many present-day preachers and evangelical laity use today.[19] MacArthur believes the primary reason for this disparity is that many in the American church define conversion strictly within terms of affirming certain truths about the identity of who Jesus is—that he is the divine Son of God who became incarnate, died an atoning death, and was raised from the dead so that anyone who places their trust in his redemptive work can receive forgiveness of their sins. The problem is not with these points as they stand. Indeed, MacArthur acknowledges that they are key components of what conversion is. The issue is that while they are essential, they are not sufficient.

The gist of his book is that embracing, or converting, to the gospel entails more than just affirming what Christ does or has done *for* those who believe. It also includes an acceptance of what Christ does *to* them. Or stated another way, MacArthur thinks that many have mistakenly separated

---

16. He still pastors this congregation and is the voice of this show to this day.

17. MacArthur, *Gospel according to Jesus*, 1988. When this book came on the scene, it rode smaller waves of momentum caused by a slow but consistent trickle of volumes that were beginning to instigate disagreement on how Christian discipleship related to conversion. Authors who echoed many points that MacArthur later heralded include Alderson, *No Holiness, No Heaven!*; Boice, *Christ's Call to Discipleship*; and Chantry, *Today's Gospel*. Other authors who were writing material that MacArthur would oppose included Hodges, *Gospel Under Siege*; Kendall, *Once Saved, Always Saved*; and Cocoris, *Lordship Salvation*.

18. MacArthur, *Gospel according to Jesus*, 15.

19. MacArthur, *Gospel according to Jesus*, 16–17.

conversion from discipleship, which has led many to accept the disastrous notion that the initial receiving of salvation includes no moral demands. Such expectations are linked to the process of discipleship that occurs after conversion, thus fueling what MacArthur labels "easy-believism."[20] This notion goes to the heart of what he wants to critique with his basic thesis being that becoming a Christian convert means becoming a disciple. In other words, conversion and discipleship are two sides of the same coin. One could say that the confession of Christ as one's king entails a willingness to follow the virtue of the kingdom that he represents.

3.1 MacArthur Critiques the Category of a "Carnal Christian"

After introducing these points, MacArthur's first chapter engages several thinkers who defended the idea that conversion and discipleship are completely separate components of the Christian experience. What is interesting is that the authors he critiques are thinkers within the guilds of dispensationalism of which he himself is a part. This creates an interesting venue of debate because dispensationalism as a theological system is not restricted to any sort of confessional tradition.[21] Consequently, dispensational thinkers can be part of a host of denominations—in fact today there are dispensationalists among Baptists, Methodists, Pentecostals, Charismatics, and many other groups.[22] This means that thinkers can simply conflate their dispensational leanings with the theological features within their own individual traditions. A prime example of such practices occurs within the Lordship debate because MacArthur is an avowed dispensationalist who

---

20. MacArthur, *Gospel according to Jesus*, 16.

21. The primary tenet of dispensationalism is the belief that the scope of biblical history transpires in successive temporal stages (i.e., dispensations) that culminate with God establishing his kingdom upon the earth. As they unfold, each dispensation marks a specific period of time where God relates to humanity in a unique way; e.g., God relating to Adam and Eve with certain expectations that changed significantly after their fall; God relating to believers like Noah, Abraham, Jacob, or Joseph in ways that differ once the nation of Israel is liberated and receives the Mosaic law. The overall point is that every passage of Scripture is written within the context of a given dispensational time frame and must therefore be interpreted primarily, if not exclusively, as applying to the audience that exists within that dispensation. When this approach is followed consistently, dispensationalists contend that a certain chronology surfaces requiring one to see Israel and the church as distinct peoples who have different, although related, roles to play in redemptive history.

22. The closest thing to an official dispensational "group" would be those who affiliate with the Bible-church movement because this phenomenon was an outgrowth forged predominately by dispensational leaders.

also affirms the soteriological tenets of Calvinism. This proves to be a key factor in the controversy because dispensational thinkers disagreed on the viability of Reformed views of predestination, the nature of saving faith, and especially the standard belief in perseverance. In fact, the situation remains that way today.

These differences sparked immediate tension between MacArthur and some of his peers. We see this early on when he initially engages the idea promoted by some that Christian conversion includes no moral obligations upon those who believe. He cites the works of former professors at Dallas Theological Seminary, Zane Hodges and Charles Ryrie, who argued that people are not saved by faith alone if they must place their faith in Christ and *necessarily* exhibit works to show that their faith is authentic.[23] MacArthur contends that such an idea is a misrepresentation of what the Reformers meant by *sola fide*. Even worse, it contradicts the ways in which the gospel is preached both by Jesus and the early church. Likewise, it clearly erodes the theological relationship between justification and sanctification.

MacArthur then traces this kind of argumentation back to Chafer's original interpretation of 1 Cor 2–3, which again supported the idea of carnal Christians. MacArthur rightly argues that the reason scholars like Hodges and Ryrie say that Christian converts may or may not become obedient disciples is because they have embraced Chafer's notion that many believers simply remain spiritually immature, or in a carnal post-conversion state.[24] Such a dichotomy between spiritual and carnal believers leads MacArthur to examine other problematic distinctions that some mainline dispensationalists make when interpreting the gospels, such as the relationship between the law and grace and the meaning of Christ as Savior versus Lord. MacArthur makes the point that while they are correct in some of their categorical readings of Scripture, the attempts to separate "salvation" texts from "discipleship" texts are unsupportable because there are too many instances where the NT treats these topics interchangeably.

3.2 MacArthur Interconnects Faith, Repentance, and Perseverance

From here, MacArthur spends the rest of his time fleshing out his understanding of how Jesus confronted both crowds and individuals with his kingdom-gospel message, with occasional appeals to some of the NT epistles. Among the numerous points that MacArthur makes, three in

---

23. Cf. MacArthur, *Gospel according to Jesus*, 22; Hodges, *Gospel Under Siege*, 14; and Ryrie, *Balancing the Christian Life*, 169–70.

24. MacArthur, *Gospel according to Jesus*, 24–27.

particular jump-started the debate about Lordship. One is the repudiation of the view, as originally proposed by Chafer and later taken up by Hodges, Ryrie, and others, that repentance is functionally equivalent to faith.[25] MacArthur ardently contends that while it is inextricably related to saving faith, it is a distinct element wherein a new believer abandons their previous way of life so they can embrace a new life in Christ.[26] He argues that the very act of believing in Christ entails a moral repudiation of how one previously lived without him. Relatedly, a second major factor that consistently flows throughout MacArthur's analysis is the nature of saving faith itself. He even devotes an entire chapter to it.[27] And this is sensible since he has to define faith carefully so it can clearly be distinguished from his view of repentance. He follows the general thrust of the Reformed tradition in arguing that the kind of faith which inherits eternal life is not only expressed out of a sense of desperate need. It also is an act of obedience. MacArthur contends that one's act of believing in Christ is indicative of their submission to follow him as a disciple.[28] Finally, a third factor that undergirds parts of MacArthur's argument for his Lordship position is his defense of the Reformed idea of perseverance. Sporadically throughout the book, MacArthur claims that anyone who becomes an apostate proves that they were never truly converted. Judas, for example, is seen as axiomatic of such a view. He was someone who looked as if he were a believer until his true colors were eventually exposed. So is the case with any professing believer who ultimately defects.[29] For MacArthur then, belief that later turns back to unbelief is not true belief at all.[30]

---

25. One interesting note is that Hodges did not see repentance and faith as being equivalent terms whereas Ryrie and other sympathizers did. Hodges conceded that repentance did pertain to a turning away from sin whereas Ryrie and other saw it as synonymous with faith. The key difference with MacArthur, though, was that Hodges thought repentance was an act performed by believers. It had nothing to do being converted or initially receiving eternal life. Only faith was required. See Hodges, *Absolutely Free*, 160–63.

26. MacArthur, *Gospel according to Jesus*, 162–63.

27. MacArthur, *Gospel according to Jesus*, 169–78.

28. MacArthur, *Gospel according to Jesus*, 178. MacArthur argues that saving faith reveals its authenticity through works.

29. MacArthur, *Gospel according to Jesus*, 98–105.

30. MacArthur, *Gospel according to Jesus*, 172.

4. THE LORDSHIP DEBATE ERUPTS: MACARTHUR, HIS CRITICS & HIS RESPONSES

The circulation of *The Gospel according to Jesus* immediately sparked lively interaction. MacArthur's polemics spread like a theological wildfire across the mainline conservative landscape, receiving a host of responses. Many pastors, leaders, and scholars who were long-standing defenders of Reformed thought strongly resonated with his arguments.[31] Others among Christian laity who were indecisive or even ambivalent on how conversion and discipleship interrelated found his book to be a tour de force that helped them settle the matter in their own minds. And some evangelical scholars who agreed with MacArthur's case overall offered words of caution and clarification. These readers conceded that while his main thesis was essentially correct, some of his arguments needed more nuancing because the theological balance between conversion and discipleship was a bit more complex than what MacArthur sometimes conveyed.[32] But the real heart of the debate was obviously in the large amount of pushback. There were opponents who thought MacArthur's proposals convoluted any basis for personal assurance of salvation. Some went a step further in arguing that he was inadvertently supplanting the simple gospel mandate that one must only believe to receive eternal life. Two initial books that offered these kinds of concerns were again from Zane Hodges and Charles Ryrie.[33] These volumes acted as a springboard for bringing the conversation full circle so readers could see the differences between MacArthur's "Lordship" position and the opposing "no-Lordship" view.[34]

---

31. Many traditional Reformed thinkers (who were not in any way dispensationalists) supported MacArthur's stance against his no-Lordship opponents even though they often honed their views a bite more stringently. The reason for this was because MacArthur's Lordship view was not an outflow of Reformed theology as a whole. It was more of an eclectic perspective that drew from soteriological features in Calvin, the Puritans, and other Reformed thinkers. Consequently, many Reformed scholars who tipped their hats to MacArthur's book made sure to couch their support in terms that defined the Lordship position within the larger scope of Covenant Theology and the broader Reformed tradition. Cf. Gentry, *Lord of the Saved*; and Horton, *Christ Is Lord*.

32. Several balanced reviews that show this kind of judicious treatment include Bock, review of *Gospel according to Jesus*, 21–40; Erickson, "Lordship Theology," 5–15; Gleason, "Lordship Salvation Debate," 55–72; and a reprint from an original 1989 article by Johnson, "How Faith Works," 21–25. Also, Belcher provided a basic overview of MacArthur's arguments in contrast to mainly Hodges in *Layman's Guide to the Lordship Controversy*.

33. Hodges, *Absolutely Free*; Ryrie, *So Great a Salvation*.

34. Here "no-Lordship" meaning that a conscience act of submitting to the moral demands of Christian discipleship is not a prerequisite to Christian conversion. That is

Alongside the efforts of Hodges and Ryrie also came the strongest source of resistance that was spearheaded by a larger conglomerate of thinkers who united to vocalize their objections to the growing Lordship camp. The upsurge of this group actually began to take form just two years before MacArthur's book even came out. In 1986 a former staff worker of Campus Crusade for Christ and Dallas Theological Seminary graduate, Robert Wilkin, had grown concerned over the diverse spectrum of views that evangelicals held regarding the relationship between salvation by grace through faith and Christian discipleship. He was convinced that various evangelical circles were skewing the gospel with assorted versions that mixed faith and works, thereby compromising Paul's emphasis on justification and the gospel accounts' focus on believing in Christ to receive eternal life. He began networking with pastors and scholars who were sympathetic to his concerns with the result being the start of parachurch coalition named the Grace Evangelical Society (GES). Then in 1988 when MacArthur's book was published, GES also started its own journal, the *Journal of the Grace Evangelical Society*, with a colleague of Wilkin, Arthur L. Farstad being the first editor. This organization became the champion defender for what is known as the Free-Grace position in the Lordship debate, which is somewhat helpful because the title "no-Lordship" is a bit deceiving. Free-Grace advocates do not deny that the Lordship of Christ is an essential component of everyday discipleship. Their contention is that this dynamic of discipleship should not be seen as a prerequisite to conversion. The grace of salvation is offered "freely" to all who believe in Christ as Lord in the sense that he is the divine Son of God. But the willingness to submit to Christ as Lord in the sense that he is the moral arbiter of one's everyday life is an ongoing experience which takes place gradually after one believes, not before. The question arises then as to what are some of the arguments that Free-Grace advocates and no-Lordship thinkers propose. Three will suffice in our treatment here.

4.1 Repentance and Its Relationship to Faith & Discipleship

Differences on the meaning of repentance and its relationship to saving faith became one of the most volatile debates in the Lordship ordeal. The reason was a fundamental divide between MacArthur and his opponents on whether any type of moral demands are a necessary part of conversion. MacArthur thinks repentance entails a turning to God in faith that can only occur if there is a concurrent turn from one's previous way of life. Embracing

---

something believers learn to do after conversion.

the righteousness of Christ by faith is inseparable from forsaking one's own unrighteousness.[35]

Opponents like Ryrie and Hodges countered that such an understanding of repentance does not square with Scripture. Ryrie, for instance, appeals to the fact that repentance has different shades of meaning which must be kept in mind when interpreting its usage in the context of conversion. He agrees with MacArthur that repentance can mean a moral repudiation from sinful conduct. But no such decision, no matter how strong one's willpower, brings forth salvation. Only when one recognizes their need for forgiveness and turns to Christ in faith can eternal life be received. Ryrie concedes that the Spirit may indeed convict someone to a point of repentance, but only for the purpose of leading them to faith, not any moral resolution that must necessarily be combined with faith.[36] Ryrie echoes the thought of Chafer here in arguing that repentance as a term can be seen as being essential to salvation if one means by it that people must change their mind about who Christ is in order to believe.[37] Furthermore, Hodges and other Free-Grace thinkers contend that the kind of repentance MacArthur thinks is essential to conversion is actually required for fellowship with Christ after conversion. One must cast themselves on the mercies of Christ to receive salvation first and only then can they possibly change their ways of living if they subsequently submit to the power of the Holy Spirit in everyday life.[38] Therefore, the Lordship impasse on repentance was no small matter. MacArthur and his supporters see a moral turning from sin as a counterpart to faith that is required for conversion to occur, while Ryrie, Hodges and other Free-Grace thinkers view this kind of repentance as something that has no bearing on salvation whatsoever. It is a component of practical holiness that believers only experience after conversion as they grow in spiritual maturity.

4.2 The Relationship between Justification & Sanctification

Another major concern expressed by MacArthur's opponents was that they believed his view of Lordship undermines any real assurance which believers can have of their future salvation. The basis for this charge was their opposing views the relationship between justification (i.e., receiving a right standing for God) and sanctification (i.e., the process of becoming Christ-like in everyday life). Both MacArthur and Free-Grace advocates

---

35. MacArthur, *Gospel according to Jesus*, 162–63.
36. Ryrie, *So Great a Salvation*, 98–99.
37. Ryrie, *So Great a Salvation*, 94–95.
38. Hodges, *Absolutely Free*, 146–47.

were united in their belief that sinners are only justified through an act of faith in Christ as their redeemer and mediator. But they strongly disagreed on what kind of faith actually justifies. For MacArthur, a major way to determine if faith is saving is if it produces the fruit of personal holiness. Here he believes that sanctification is an inevitable reality that every believer experiences because it is an outflow of the spiritual transformation beginning at conversion.[39] No one can be initially born of the Spirit and then not grow in the Spirit. This connection aligns perfectly with MacArthur's Reformed reading of the NT because just as regeneration is a sovereign act of God, so is the ongoing moral transformation of everyone who is born again. This means one can find assurance of salvation both in Christ (via justification) and the practical transformation one receives from the work of the indwelling Spirit (via sanctification).[40]

The objection posed by Free-Grace thinkers on this point is that viewing sanctification as a *necessary* result of justification inadvertently opens the door to works being a source for assurance of salvation.[41] And if one has to look inwardly at their own character in hopes of verifying the authenticity of their faith, then assurance will always be in flux depending on one's level behavior at a given time. The counter argument is that while justification is based on faith in Christ as Savior, the process of sanctification is grounded in subsequent obedience to Christ as Lord which varies from person to person. This means a person's justification before God and their experience of personal sanctifying grace are not symmetrical realities. While justification must occur before sanctification may commence, the reality of the former does not ensure the full experience of the latter. This is because not all those who initially believe in Christ as their Savior necessarily walk in obedience to him as their Lord. As Hodges puts it, one must distinguish between being a recipient of eternal life and being a pupil of Christ.[42] His point is that while discipleship is a desired outcome of conversion, it is not automatic. Otherwise, how does one make sense of the numerous rebukes, warnings, and correctives that NT writers issue to believers who are living in rebellion. The only way to make sense of these passages is if one recognizes the contingencies that exist in how believers experience sanctification in different ways. To argue otherwise, for Free-Grace thinkers, is to dilute the gospel because if a believer must do something to prove their faith is saving, then saying one is saved by faith alone is really just double-talk.

39. MacArthur, *Gospel according to Jesus*, 23, 187–88.
40. MacArthur, *Gospel according to Jesus*, 126–27.
41. Olson, "Lordship Controversy," 318.
42. Hodges, *Absolutely Free*, 68.

4.3 Perseverance Pertains to Rewards That Converts Receive

A third significant argument that many Free-Grace advocates and other no-Lordship thinkers began to promote in response to Lordship apologists was that NT texts which admonish believers to persevere in their faith have nothing to do with any potential loss of salvation or means of weeding out those who may not have genuine faith. Rather they pertain to potential loss of rewards that believers will incur if they choose to live in sin. This approach is seen as the proper way of harmonizing Scripture's emphasis on salvation by grace through faith alone and the constant warnings of potential judgment against believers if they live in disobedience. Arminians interpret these texts to mean that believers will suffer God's wrath if they apostatize. Calvinists, including those in the MacArthur's Lordship camp, understand them as a means of exposing those who are not truly believers at all. In either case, what is at stake is one's salvation. And it is this very point that Free-Grace thinkers find unacceptable. If salvation is obtained by belief apart from works, then warnings against potentially losing it contradict such an idea. Therefore, what these various passages must be addressing is a loss of something else, to which their answer is heavenly rewards. Some articulate this idea by focusing on the concept of eternal inheritance. Authors like Michael Eaton argue that one enters Christ's kingdom through faith in the grace provided by his death and resurrection. Yet receiving the full bounty of one's heavenly inheritance or in some instances experiencing the present-day power of the Spirit is contingent upon one's subsequent obedience to the moral demands of that kingdom[43] Other Free-Grace thinkers who embrace dispensational premillennialism often think the warning passages are speaking about heavenly rewards that one will experience during the intermediate kingdom.[44] Here the idea is that the NT cautions believers to avoid falling into unbelief and rebellion so that they can face the bema seat of Christ with confidence instead of shame. Those who heed such warnings will be heralded as faithful servants who will ultimately become co-rulers during the period of Christ's millennial kingdom.[45] Moreover, perseverance

---

43. Eaton, *No Condemnation*, 111–13. He even goes as far as to propose that some NT passages that speak of gehenna may be referring to a purifying fire that temporarily judges believers for their unfaithfulness (*No Condemnation*, 206–7). To be fair, this proposal is unique to Eaton. Free-Grace thinkers do not go this far in their ways of interpreting warning passages.

44. The most concise treatment of this view can be seen in Wilkin, "Christians Will Be Judged," 25–50.

45. One volume that uses the concept of inheriting the kingdom through obedience (as opposed to entering it by faith) as a sort of hermeneutical grid for sifting through the vast majority of warning texts in the NT is by Dillow, *Reign of the Servant Kings*.

is viewed not as a necessary fruit of saving faith as MacArthur argues. It is a contingent act that believers may or may not express. If they do, they are rewarded and if they do not, they will suffer loss. Nevertheless, their identity in Christ remains secure regardless of their actions.[46]

5. CONCLUSIONS ON HOW THE LORDSHIP DEBATE IMPACTS EVANGELICAL VIEWS OF PERSEVERANCE

This in-house debate continued to rumble with further publications on both sides, especially as the Free-Grace movement grew in opposition to Lordship advocates. In 1993, MacArthur produced another volume, entitled *Faith Works: The Gospel according to the Apostles*. The main purpose of the book was to clarify his own views, respond to various criticisms, and provide his own assessment of what the debate was really about. Interestingly enough, MacArthur stated that he disapproved of the phrase "Lordship salvation" to describe his view because for all practical purposes, it was a redundant title.[47] Yet he concedes to its usage for practical purposes, responds to critics, and then discusses more ramifications of his view that he did not cover in his previous work. The debate continued on from here with lively interchanges and ongoing publications from evangelicals on both sides of the issue.

But as the discussion has continued over the years, one topic that has been strongly affected by the conversation is the idea of perseverance. Today, there are those on the Lordship side who unify around certain tenets of Reformed theology, wholeheartedly supporting this position. In fact, evangelical scholars in the debate knew that MacArthur really was not saying anything new. He just struck a chord at the right time that exposed an unaddressed set of issues within certain North American conservative guilds. On the other side, though, are other conservatives who embrace some form of Free-Grace thought and do not speak about perseverance in the traditional way. Appeal is now often made to phrases like eternal security or the "preservation of the saints" so one can avoid the perceived theological baggage that comes with the term perseverance. Free-Grace advocates believe the historical meaning of this word distorts the real meaning of grace that the gospel provides, rendering the message of salvation unintelligible. For these thinkers, perseverance pertains to something other than salvation if the Bible is to make any sense theologically. In Robert Wilkin's own words, "If

---

46. This is why some Free-Grace advocates are comfortable speaking of the preservation of the saints as opposed to perseverance; e.g., Ryrie, *So Great a Salvation*, 137.

47. John MacArthur, *Faith Works*, 23.

we do not recognize the difference between the free gift of eternal life, which is received by faith apart from works, and the rewards that are earned by persevering in faithful works, the Bible will seem needlessly paradoxical and self-contradictory."[48] Hence, in today's context of North American Christian conservativism, not only is there theological debate about whether perseverance is required to remain saved or prove one is a true convert. Now there are many who think perseverance has virtually no bearing on whether someone is a true believer or not.

---

48. Wilkin, "Christians Will Be Judged," 50.

Chapter 10

Final Thoughts on the Doctrine of Perseverance

Can Anything New Be Said?

THE PURPOSE OF THIS primer has been to navigate many of the contours in Christian thought that exist on the matters of apostasy and perseverance. We strove to achieve this goal by first probing the bulk of relevant biblical data and then surveying a spectrum of positions that major Christian traditions advocate. Now we want to close our study with some reflections on three final areas of concern. First, we want to offer some remarks about the approach one should take when trying to conceptualize a theological understanding of any given doctrine, whether it be perseverance or otherwise. While it is in no way a groundbreaking observation, the point needing attention is that one's interpretive assumptions help set the course for the direction that one's theological viewpoints will go. Second, we will then discuss several key ideas that we believe encapsulate what the NT emphasizes about the doctrine of perseverance. Some of them are highly contestable among certain theological camps. But, be that as it may, it will still be argued that they should be integrated into a biblical-theological synthesis of this subject. Third, we will finally address the pressing question that emerges in discussions about perseverance concerning the grounds one can have to find any personal assurance of salvation.

Our ultimate hope in these endeavors is to foster future dialogues about this doctrine that perhaps can move the discussion forward, even if it be minimal. By doing so, we do not think we can overcome centuries of debate on these matters. As much as we would like to think we could accomplish such a feat, we do not want to be blinded by naïve optimism or hubris. Much greater minds have wrestled with these matters and come up with significantly different viewpoints. These disagreements are long-standing and will not go away completely until the eschaton, most likely. Nevertheless, that does not mean that at least some evangelicals who often are so polarized on this topic cannot hopefully come together at certain points as our understanding of Scripture continues to expand.

1. PUTTING TOGETHER A THEOLOGY OF PERSEVERANCE

To begin, although we have already alluded to these points earlier, some comments about the nature of biblical theology and doctrinal language bear repeating here. When we say we want to express a "theology" of a given topic, like perseverance, for example, our objective is to understand the meaning of all the pertinent texts of Scripture as best we can and then show *how they fit together* as a whole. Note the two commitments in this description. One is that everything Scripture says about a specific subject must be given an equal hearing, not simply the parts that are convenient to a cherished system or tradition. We should listen to every biblical author, hearing all their concerns no matter how perplexing their points may be or how diverse they may seem. As one theology professor taught me in seminary, "when compelled by Scripture, we must be willing to let goods and systems go." But this is only half of the task. We cannot stop there because we must show how the biblical witness coalesces. The net result of what all of Scripture says about perseverance and apostasy is not a set of random voices that express rival claims. They are not a mere collection of individual solos. They are a choir that resounds with a distinct harmony and we must strive to tune into it.[1]

---

1. One added qualification that should be mentioned here is the nature of progressive revelation. While we do want to decipher how all of Scripture addresses a given matter, such as perseverance, we always have to be mindful that no particular passage encapsulates everything that should be said about any doctrine. So we must be careful in how we balance our theological understanding of individual texts with the subsequent task of synthesizing them together. If we are not careful, we can inadvertently

Admittedly, these convictions are nothing new for evangelicals. They have always been nonnegotiable beliefs that flow from a robust commitment to the Bible's inspiration and theological unity. However, if we are honest with ourselves, we should acknowledge that these affirmations must be balanced carefully because overemphasizing either one can lead to trouble. On the one hand, solely championing the unity of Scripture cannot be an airtight safeguard against all potential interpretive mishaps because if embraced uncritically, it can blind us to the Bible's diversity. Ironically the belief that Scripture never contradicts itself can inadvertently lead to arbitrary proof-texting. The reason being that one can sometimes make texts say things that fit preconceived constructs all in the name of biblical authority. On the other hand, the opposite trend of downplaying or even abandoning any commitment to Scripture's veracity is dangerous as well. This mistake breeds an unhealthy skepticism that treats the Bible as a mosaic of contradictions made up of competing and possibly even mutually exclusive theologies.[2]

This interplay between attempts to discern legitimate ways of harmonizing biblical texts and views that see them as offering countering ideas is what often fuels the divergence of opinions in this long-standing debate about perseverance (or any other doctrine for that matter). Biblical scholars and theologians differ on what they think texts mean in their own individual contexts and/or they cannot come to a consensus on how the meaning of various texts should be reconciled. And then added to the mix are numerous others in mainline biblical scholarship, not necessarily on the evangelical radar, who are suspicious of attempts to synthesize what all the texts say about these issues because they are convinced such an enterprise precludes the possibility of understanding the original authors on their own terms. So it is amid these differences on how a doctrine should be put together that the perfect breeding ground for theological disagreements is produced.

What must be recognized then is this—differences on the meaning of major doctrines is partly driven by how interpreters think they should be construed. Or said another way, what one thinks about how doctrines should be formulated impacts what one thinks about the doctrines

---

apply anachronistic interpretations to texts that make them say more (or less) than what the biblical authors intended, ironically in the attempt to uphold Scripture's unity.

2. As an example, many approach Scripture, or the NT in particular, in the way that Dunn proposes wherein the unity of Scripture is to be found in its witness to the historical Jesus as the exalted Messiah. But this does not mean that Scripture provides a harmonized theological portrayal of this reality. See Dunn, *Unity and Diversity*, 1–7, 369–88. Cf. similar perspectives that emphasize diversity over unity in other ways in Sparks, *God's Word in Human Words*, 329–56; Enns, "Inerrancy," 83–116.

themselves. This is true because no approach to understanding biblical texts precedes beliefs about their divine authority (or the lack thereof).[3] One is an outflow of the other, and looking at a few examples of contemporary thinkers who have engaged the doctrine of perseverance can illustrate this point quite effectively.

1.1 The Challenge in Harmonizing Pertinent Biblical Texts

Evangelicals (including myself) are known for affirming that all the teachings of Scripture on a given subject are in accord with one another. No matter how complex their claims may be, we have not understood them properly until we see how they complement each other. Any construction of a Christian doctrine that denies this commitment always has elements that are suspect. As we have said, though, devotion to Scripture's unity is a two-edged sword. Our desire to uphold Scripture's coherency by showing how texts connect together can go awry when we try to make every passage fit unjustifiably into a system that is overtly rigid or confining. Offering a systematic reading of Scripture that is consistent constructively does not necessarily mean one is interpreting Scripture accurately. One author who illustrates this tension is Reformed scholar Michael Horton. In dealing with the issue of perseverance, Horton contends that we should approach all the pertinent biblical texts in a way similar to how we address questions about science. Horton points out that scientists attempt to examine a given field of inquiry and subsequently develop theories that account for all the data. However, the success of a proposed theory is determined by its ability to account for all of the empirical information, including the portions that are clearly understandable as well as any odd anomalies that seem to go against the norms of nature.[4] Comparably, Horton argues that synthesizing a doctrine entails the ability to provide an interpretive lens that can address all the points that Scripture makes, regardless of how difficult they may be to fit together theologically.[5]

With this in mind, Horton believes the best paradigm for reconciling the interpretive dilemma between eternal security passages versus warning

---

3. In other words, biblical interpretation in many ways is postdogmatic, not predogmatic. See Lints, *Fabric of Theology*, 12–19, 279–81.

4. Horton, "Classical Calvinist View," 29. By no means is this an unworthy goal in biblical interpretation. The question is whether one theme, taxonomy, or theological rubric can make every text fit as well as we would like. In Horton's case, is covenant theology a sufficient (or accurate) paradigm for tying together all of the ways in which Scripture speaks about perseverance and apostasy?

5. Horton, "Classical Calvinist View," 30.

texts is his unique application of covenant theology. Typically, Horton argues, the standard distinction between people who are "saved" and "unsaved" is what normally causes exegetical consternation about apostasy.[6] Restricting people to these two categories forces one either to conclude that the NT warnings against it are merely hypothetical or that genuine believers can lose their salvation. Horton thinks the former deduction empties the warnings of their true severity while the latter idea contradicts numerous passages that emphasize God's sovereignty in the culmination of salvation.

This is why Horton thinks that adding a legitimate third class of people avoids these errors, thereby saving the exegetical day. One only needs to acknowledge another group of people who are part of the new-covenant community that have experienced God's grace only in external ways. These people have received the outward rites of the covenantal community such as baptism and communion, but they have not experienced the internal work of the Spirit that leads to regeneration. It is to this group within the church that the numerous NT warnings of apostasy are directed.[7] Thus, the new-covenant people is a mixed consortium made up of people who are all benefactors of qualified covenantal blessings but are not all true converts. The elect community is made up of saints who prove to be true believers via their perseverance and other members who evidence their lack of true conversion via their acts of apostasy.

One can see that Horton is trying to provide an interpretive grid that can retain God's preservation of those who have genuinely experienced salvation while at the same time take the warning passages in a way that describes people who are somehow unbelievers within the believing community. This is commendable and, as we will argue shortly, a justifiable approach overall. Horton is also correct that identifying this "third" category of people goes to the very heart of the question about perseverance. Nevertheless, the lingering problem is whether all the relevant texts about perseverance fit within his paradigm or more specifically, whether his theological categories of Reformed covenantalism align with the original perceptions that the biblical writers expressed to audiences about the realities of apostasy. For example, would the AOH think he was talking to adults who had been baptized as infants yet were still not converted and only their perseverance would prove whether they indeed part of the invisible church. This has to be assumed. It cannot be sustained explicitly from what the author claims.

6. Horton, "Classical Calvinist View," 37.

7. To a degree, as we shall argue momentarily, Horton is on to something here. The question is whether first-century churches viewed their faith communities in ways the correspond with the Reformed covenantal lenses that he is using to read the NT.

Another example of how to reconcile texts about perseverance from a modern Reformed perspective is Sam Storms. At the end of his recent book on the security of the believer, Storms concludes that Scripture can sometimes appear to teach conflicting ideas about apostasy and perseverance.[8] He even confesses that he sometimes struggles to explain every NT text with equal clarity and harmonize all of them perfectly.[9] Still, he believes that this challenge is actually an encouragement to a degree because it forces him always to go back to Scripture so he can reexamine its teachings about perseverance and discover how its various ideas intersect. The key for Storms, though, is he is convinced that "the hermeneutical scales of balance weigh heavily in favor of affirming that those whom God elected and brought to faith ... will never fail to reach heaven's gates."[10] This means that for Storms, when he engages NT warning passages about apostasy, his go-to theological assumption is that they must be interpreted in light of other NT texts that "clearly teach" believers cannot possibly lose their salvation. One corpus of texts that Storms believes teaches one idea should be used as a grid for interpreting another set of passages even if at face value they appear to teach otherwise.

Notice that while Storms and Horton take different routes to make their case for a Reformed view of perseverance, their commitment to the unity of Scripture remains the same. All of the NT, no matter diverse their claims, must be exegetically synced somehow. But an unsettling question lurks amid their proposals—that being who is to say that "eternal security passages" should trump apostasy-warning passages (Storms' deduction) or that warning passages apply to non-elect members within the believing community who have received the sign of the covenant as infants (Horton). What is interesting is that evangelical Arminians of all stripes are quick to argue for the exact opposite conclusion while using the same methodological commitment. They affirm the harmony of biblical teaching. The only difference is that they think apostasy passages are clear references to lapsed believers. Therefore, the Arminian counter is that these texts should be the primary point of reference when dealing with any potential reference to eternal security or perseverance. When one does this, the typical deduction is that passages used to defend the security of the believer are actually being mishandled because they are not being read in light of the many instances where the NT teaches that believers can potentially defect.

---

8. Storms, *Kept for Jesus*, 173.
9. Storms, *Kept for Jesus*, 173.
10. Storms, *Kept for Jesus*, 173.

In a similar methodological vein, Free-Grace advocates also concede to the consistency of Scripture's teachings. And similar to Horton's proposal, they argue for three classes of people as opposed to two. The only difference is that they believe the warning passages do not apply to believers in danger of forfeiting their salvation or church members who are not elect, but to carnal Christians on the cusp of losing their eschatological inheritance. Consequently, the threats against apostasy are not really the issue at all. The concern is about abandoning one's full commitment to discipleship and the potential loss of heavenly rewards.

What should be seen in all these comparisons is that commitments to biblical inspiration, inerrancy, and the analogy of faith in no way ensure that interpretive harmony will be attained. Actually, one's efforts to preserve the unity of Scripture's teaching can lead to conflicting proposals because readers sometimes differ on how passages should conform to one another, which then compels readers to choose sides. This means there is no easy solution to this dilemma because developing a sound theological synthesis of a biblical doctrine is by necessity an intertextual enterprise, not just textual. A doctrinal construct summarizes what "all" of Scripture says about a given subject, not just certain texts. So the great tension with which evangelical interpreters wrestle is how to understand textual meanings and discover legitimate and textually natural ways in which they correspond to each other. The question is whether can this be done, and if so, how?

1.2 Questions on Letting Texts about Perseverance Stand on Their Own

Some scholars view such approaches as inherently flawed because they are searching for something that does not exist. One need only to note the observation of B. J. Oropeza, for example, who contends that discussions about apostasy often reach an impasse because many theologians and exegetes assume a unilateral conception of what various NT authors thought about the subject, whether it be Calvinist in orientation, Arminian, or something else.[11] Oropeza thinks this is highly problematic, especially in light of the fact that the authors, who came from various cultural, ethnic, and educational backgrounds, addressed a host of different circumstances and problems.[12] Instead, he thinks that the NT reflects a variety of opinions

---

11. Oropeza, *Paul and Apostasy*, 33.

12. Oropeza, *Paul and Apostasy*, 33–34. Here Oropeza appeals to scholars such as Dunn to argue that NT believers, including the actual biblical writers themselves, differed on numerous topics, including those they wrote about. It makes sense for

on these matters just as later traditions in Christian history would. Oropeza expresses this same argument in his important three-volume work on apostasy in the NT where he states that

> we should not be reinterpreting every relevant verse in the NT in light of the apostates in Hebrews 6:4–9, or the defectors in 1 John 2:19, or the mitigated punishment in 1 Corinthians 3:10–15. Nor should we assume that because the false prophets in Matthew 7:15–23 never belonged to Christ, this means that the false teachers in 2 Peter 2:1–22 also never belonged to Christ.[13]

Oropeza's point is that the way a given author describes an apostate or false teacher in one text does not have to coincide with how other writers refer to the other defectors in their own contexts. Authors in different venues can make assessments of apostasy that may or may not agree with each other because they may be describing different kinds of apostates. Consequently, he proposes that the best option for covering all the possible theological bases that the NT writers mention is to say certain authors speak about genuine believers who persevere; at other times some describe nominal converts who are not genuine and defect; and in other instances, others speak of real believers who fall away.[14]

To a degree, Oropeza's promotion of the NT's diversity is important to hear. We should always let the individual voices of the biblical writers be heard first before we begin looking for intertextual connections and theological synthesis (at least as best as we can). We should heed Oropeza's caution when he says that "if we already aim to defend a theological position when interpreting a text, our outcomes will be very predictable, sometimes to the point of getting the New Testament authors to say what we want them to say even if they are saying something else quite different."[15] What is disconcerting, though, is that Oropeza's solution opens the door to thinking texts could advocate competing, maybe even antithetical, views of apostasy. While there might be some areas of overlap, there can be significant variations or dare we say, contradicting perspectives. Such a charge is difficult to avoid when reading Oropeza's critique that "we should not make grand statements about New Testament apostates as is typically done by certain theologians who claim that all apostates have lost their salvation and cannot be restored, or they will all be restored at a future time, or they all were never

---

Oropeza to advocate this notion because of the impact that Dunn had on his approach. See analysis here by Peterson, review of *Paul and Apostasy*, 116–17.

13. Oropeza, *Churches under Siege*, 247.
14. Oropeza, *Paul and Apostasy*, 34.
15. Oropeza, *Churches under Siege*, 246.

truly saved in the first place, or they will lose all heavenly rewards rather than their salvation."¹⁶ Instead, we should admit that the author of Hebrews teaches that apostates cannot be restored while James thinks they can or that Peter may believe apostates were genuine believers whereas John believes they never truly were.¹⁷

We must confess that such an approach is prominent within a significant amount of biblical scholarship. This methodological wedge between biblical and theological studies is par for the course in recent decades. Yet our willingness to concede that Scripture presents diverse angles and teachings on perseverance does not necessitate the notion that it provides contrary perspectives. Such an attitude that portrays NT authors as vouching for discordant proposals on a given issue reveals quite a troublesome perspective on inspiration. Oropeza openly acknowledges that his work challenges traditional views of this topic. His solution is simply to say that perhaps NT authority rests on God's authority.¹⁸ In other words, the authority does not rest in Scripture's consistency as much as its heavenly source of endorsement.

Such a proposal strikes me as something similar to how doctors work in the medical field today. There are all kinds of specialists who devote their attention to certain parts of the body—there are ENT's, cardiologists, podiatrists, brain surgeons, and so forth. But all of these professionals agree that they are treating various parts of the "one" human body. Some spend their careers mending limbs, organs, or addressing other important bodily maladies. Still, no matter how distinct the physical features are for the areas that they treat, doctors in all fields acknowledge that they treating parts of one unified anatomy. Every body part works together as an organic whole. Unfortunately, all too often some scholars do not treat the NT writings with

---

16. Oropeza, *Churches under Siege*, 246.

17. Oropeza, *Paul and Apostasy*, 34. He knows that such a claim rubs against the grain of how many evangelicals view biblical authority and inspiration. But he counters that perhaps the "divine" intent of Scripture includes the reality of diversity as well as unity. In response, though, the issue is not that commitment to verbal inspiration mitigates against diversity of claims about a given topic or doctrinal idea. The issue is that ideas can be complimentary without being contradictory. This is the actual rub of the issue here. I have no doubt that men like Paul, Peter, John, James, and Jude may have had differences of opinions on all sorts of matters. If one were to put them into a room to have a NT author colloquium, I am sure we would hear them speak on many matters, sometimes in agreement and at other times in disagreement. Yet this does not mean that what they were "inspired" to write in Scripture necessitates a conflict of viewpoints that clash against each other. Our contention is that this way of speaking about Scripture's "diversity" is partly driven by a phobia for the analogy of faith, which is the result of post-Enlightenment historical-critical approaches to biblical interpretation.

18. Oropeza, *Churches under Siege*, 247–48.

the same assumption. Instead of seeing the biblical authors as providing a unified corpus of ideas, including some that overlap easily while other times having complex nuances, their writings are sometimes seen only as distinct parts that do not connect to form a canonical body. We can understand the parts, but if we try to see how they fit together organically, then we are somehow compromising the original ideas of the authors.

1.3 Putting Method into Practice

What this impasse shows us is that a hermeneutical (dare we say even theological) choice has to be made. Does one believe that the biblical authors wrote what we call God-breathed "words" that collectively form a corpus of texts ultimately given by one divine author. Or did they merely bequeath a complex set of written artifacts that sometimes retain some ideological continuity and at other times significantly conflicting proposals. We would argue that Scripture is indeed a set of historical documents, but it is so much more than that. Furthermore, to deny that a full theological symmetry can be found in the apostolic witness inevitably leads to all kinds of interpretive problems that can prevent us from conceptualizing any Christian doctrine, perseverance or otherwise.[19]

So a careful summation of the doctrine of perseverance must take these commitments and potential hazards into account. Our endeavors must be tempered with the fact that sometimes a biblically faithful expression of doctrine must highlight tensions that exist within Scripture that do not necessarily have easy, air-tight solutions. At the same time, we cannot be satisfied with any notion that praises diversity while expelling synthesis. Though they can be messy at times, biblical and systematic theology are necessary enterprises even though they will not always fit hand-in-glove the way we would like.

---

19. It is this struggle between exegetes and theologians to maintain a balance between the unique voices of biblical writers and the overall unity of Scripture that has resulted in various trends such as a rekindled interest in the early church's views of biblical interpretation and the recent emergence of literature on what is known as TIS (Theological Interpretation of Scripture). Emphases on the former can be seen in O'Keefe and Reno, *Sancitifed Vision*; Boersma, *Scripture as Real Presence*; and Carter, *Interpreting Scripture with the Great Tradition*. For works on the latter, cf. Treier, *Introducing Theological Interpretation of Scripture*; Bartholomew and Thomas, *Manifesto for Theological Interpretation*; and Green, *Practicing Theological Interpretation*.

2. DEVELOPING A BIBLICAL-THEOLOGICAL UNDERSTANDING OF PERSEVERANCE

That being said, we now want to put our method into practice by tying together some of the most significant features about perseverance that emerge consistently from the pages of Scripture. Again, these points will not resolve all the exegetical or theological conundrums that fuel debates among Christian traditions. The nuances that the NT uses to describe the dynamics of persevering faith are too rich to address fully in a few axioms. Yet there are some predominant themes that warrant the lion's share of attention. The first pertains to the specific roles that perseverance has in the minds of the NT writers. The second concerns the exact nature of apostasy and how the NT identifies apostates. And, finally, the third element, which is derivative from the second point, is that the biblical writers often shared the assumption that their audiences could be mixed communities because they were sometimes uncertain as to whether all the recipients would endure in their faith.

2.1 Is It That Believers Will, Must, or Should Persevere?

The first observation to make about Scripture's teaching on the doctrine of perseverance is simply this—*all new-covenant believers are expected to endure in their faith in Christ and not be lured away by the enticements of worldly lusts, deceived by false doctrines, or buckle to the pressures of persecution.*[20] Whether it be Jesus in the gospel accounts, or Paul, Peter, James, Jude, John, or the AOH, we have seen how all of them encourage, even command, believers to remain steadfast in their faith. And the importance of this point can be seen in light of three important dynamics that consistently emerge in the New Testament.

First, the necessity of perseverance can be seen in the fact that the NT authors include themselves in their admonitions to persevere and warnings against apostasy. Paul, for example, admonishes the Corinthians to learn from the mistakes of the wilderness generation of Israelites (1 Cor 10). He says that God's judgment upon those who rebelled at that time should serve as a sobering teaching moment for *both* he and his readers (1 Cor 10:6, 11).[21] The demise of the unfaithful Israelites served as a reminder that Paul

---

20. This is not to imply that believers under the old-covenant economy did not need to persevere. Indeed they did as we have discussed in chapter 1. But our primary concern here is whether believers who have experienced the full blessings of the Spirit and the new birth in Christ can fail to persevere, thereby losing their salvation.

21. Notice that Paul is telling Israel's story about God's judgment, provision, and deliverance during the nation's time in the wilderness. What the ancestors did then is

and the Corinthian believers alike should not crave evil vices such as idolatry and immorality. If they did, Paul says that divine judgment could fall on any of them.[22]

He does the same thing in his Letter to the Galatians. As we discussed earlier, this audience was most likely made up of Gentile converts who were being compelled by Judaizers to submit to circumcision so they could truly be considered part of God's covenant people. Paul indicts them for considering such a notion, claiming that they would be "falling from grace" if they tried to revert back to the remnants of Judaism (cf. Gal 4:11; 5:4). In other words, they would be denying the grace they claimed to have found in Christ. This is why Paul implores them to remember how important it is for the Galatians to listen only to those who proclaim the gospel that he was commissioned to preach. He tells them that if anyone, or an angel, *or even himself* were to come preaching a different gospel, they should be deemed accursed (Gal 1:8–10).[23] His point is that if he were to advocate a different message than what Christ had commissioned him to share, he would be judged as well. So the warnings for the Galatians are also applicable to Paul, the very one who wrote them.

Similarly, the AOH at times says "we" or "us" (not just they, the audience, e.g., Heb 4:1) in making his points about faithfully enduring. Again, like the wilderness generation who failed to enter the promised land because of unbelief, the author says that his audience would not enter the eschatological kingdom-rest if they turned away from the confession they had made to Christ—and his inclusion of himself implies the same would be true in his life. This kind of collective language is used elsewhere by other writers who encourage believers to endure faithfully. The point to see then is that the writers themselves believed they were just as responsible as their audiences to remain loyal to Christ and his kingdom.[24] Thus, many of the NT writers along with their related audiences of professing believers were

---

indicative of what could potentially happen to the Corinthian believers if they proved to be unfaithful. Just as old-covenant provisions were rejected by a generation of Israelites who came out of the exodus event and were subsequently judged, now new-covenant provisions have been granted to Corinthian Gentile believers who have experienced a new exodus and Paul was admonishing them to avoid incurring similar consequences. Israel's story was their story because the God they served as now the one the followers of Christ worshipped. Cf. comments by Gardner, *Gifts of God*, 116, 133; Ciampa and Rosner, *First Letter to the Corinthians*, 433–38; Fee, *1 Corinthians*, 441–43.

22. Cf. assessments by Fee *1 Corinthians*, 459; Hays, *1 Corinthians*, 165–66.

23. The term carries the idea of handing something over to divine destruction. See discussion of the lexical background of the word in Longenecker, *Galatians*, 17.

24. At the same time, they were also confident that the Lord would keep them as well as all of those who were truly his.

expected to persevere in the *present* so eschatological salvation could be experienced in the *future*.

Second, these warnings to persevere are often treated by NT writers as pertaining to final judgment if they are not obeyed. Contra the Free-Grace polemics that see these warnings as being given so believers do not potentially lose rewards, such proposals simply do not do justice to the severe language that many warnings employ. Instances where Jesus describes the nature of apostasy, Paul warns believers not to emulate the failures of Israel, the AOH's warnings to not miss the eschatological-Sabbath rest by straying away from the faith, John's claims that those who leave communities of faith were never truly part of them, Peter's claims that false teachers who were originally part of certain congregations would perish, and various others simply cannot be explained away with such a notion.[25] They cannot be convincingly relegated to some kind of theological construct that distinguishes middle-of-the-road believers who will serve as "privates" in the eschatological kingdom from "spiritual" believers who become ruling "generals."[26] Instead, just as ancient Israelites under the Mosaic economy could miss out on the covenantal blessings of the land of promise through various acts of unbelief, NT writers teach that *professing* believers could also fall short of inheriting the eschatological new creation if their faith did not endure.[27]

This leads to a third point, which usually stirs up the most exegetical and theological controversy. No NT author views their beliefs about the necessity of perseverance as somehow contravening a believer's assurance of their position in Christ. Said another way, they see no theological contradiction in maintaining a balance between a believer's present possession of salvation and its necessary outworking in the act of perseverance. All the NT voices collectively display a delicate balance between a believer's identity as a spirit-regenerated citizen of the kingdom of heaven and their Spirit-enabled loyalty to that kingdom.[28] Now admittedly for many, this sounds

---

25. This is not to say that the NT does not speak of heavenly rewards that believers can receive or potentially lose, depending on their faithfulness. There are passages that arguably allow for this idea (e.g., Mark 10:29–30; 1 Cor 3:10–15).

26. E.g., Dillow, *Reign of the Servant Kings*, 515–32; Wilkin, "Christians Will Be Judged," 41–47.

27. To assert that a believer's faith must necessarily endure is the major theological rub that exists between Arminians and Calvinists over against Free-Grace advocates.

28. Though the idea of compatibilism as it relates to election and volitional responsibility entails several complexities and concerns, we cannot enter that debate here. However, NT authors do speak about the divine dynamics of grace that preserve believers while at the same time expecting believers to persevere. And in doing so, Carson is correct is observing that there is no "qualitative, absolute disjunction between genuine believers who display obedience to Jesus in their lives, and genuine believers who do

like an all-out assault on the concept of *sola fide*. And to be fair, there is nothing wrong with expressing some caution here. The concern that is normally raised is that if a believer is expected or "required" to persevere, then how can justification by faith be honestly maintained. Any attempt to join faith to faithfulness is perceived by many as opening the door to all kinds of theological chaos because salvation becomes somewhat based on what a believer does instead of what Christ has done. As the old saying goes, if Christ is supplemented, then he is supplanted.

What must be conceded in response to this objection is that all Protestant traditions, which historically have affirmed justification by faith alone, believe that saints must persevere, albeit for different reasons. We have already surveyed how Lutherans, Anglicans, Anabaptists, and Arminians of both classical and Wesleyan brands are convinced that believers can choose to apostatize and thereby fail to persevere while others such as Reformed Christians contend that all genuine converts are divinely enabled to do so. So viewing perseverance as a "necessary" dynamic in the experience of salvation does not automatically compromise one's commitment to *sola fide*. If it did, then one would have to deduce that no Protestant tradition has consistently affirmed justification by faith alone, which would be quite a stretch.

The fact is that none of the Reformers originally interpreted faith alone in terms that excluded the necessity of perseverance. They all affirmed the reality of apostasy and wrestled with how it applies to believers because they saw a particular tension in Scripture. Granted, they did not agree on how to resolve it. Yet they did believe it exists. They all agreed (obviously with carefully nuances regarding the details) that Scripture teaches faith is the means whereby a sinner experiences salvation in Christ. Protestants also conceded to the fact that NT always describes final judgment in terms that address a person's works, not merely their professions of faith. Consequently, what we discover is a hermeneutical struggle that Christian interpreters face on how to reconcile the theological implications of people being initially converted in the present with the fact that they will not receive eschatological vindication before the Lord until the future day of resurrection.[29]

---

not." Carson, "Reflections on Assurance," 390.

29. As we have seen, today treatments of this point are also complicated by debates about the millennial reign of Christ as portrayed in Revelation 20 and whether there will be two distinct judgments, one being for believers only and the other for unbelievers. Regardless of one's position here, the one point that must be conceded in this interpretive quagmire is that the NT emphasizes a final eschatological judgment by works. The question is whether believers are judged to vindicate their faith or to determine their level or rewards, or both. See further discussion of the relationship between works and judgment in Stanley, *Did Jesus Teach Salvation by Works*, 294–314; Schreiner, "Justification Apart From and By Works," 71–98; and Schreiner, *Faith Alone*, 191–206.

Our contention is that we must strive to find a theological equilibrium that preserves the importance of both these points. Undoubtedly the NT provides believers with hope amid their trials and hardships. They can always be confident in their identity in Christ. At the same time, believers are admonished to never fall into any pattern of sin that could foster a presumptuous attitude. Early Christians are assured of their identity in Christ while simultaneously being warned to endure in their faith so they can reach the final eschatological prize. When we hold ourselves accountable to these twins truths, we discover that the idea of perseverance touches upon an important nerve in the NT, namely that believers are sometimes addressed in light of what they possess while at other times in view of what they have not received.

They can be described as converts who are current heirs to the riches of the new covenant in Christ or as those who still await the culmination of their faith in resurrection and the inheritance of the new creation. We would join a host of voices here in saying that the well-established concept of the already/not yet applies to salvation, not just eschatology.[30] In fact, we

30. The phrase "already/not yet" is normally used as theological shorthand for what is called inaugurated eschatology. This concept highlights a theological tension in the New Testament between the temporary coexistence of two mutually exclusive realms. There is the present age, which is marked by all the consequences of sin upon the world, including the divine curse as well as satanic oppression. While this era continues to wreak havoc upon humanity, it does so with one crucial difference. It exists on borrowed time because of the beginning of another age established by the finished work of Jesus Christ. His act of redemption defeated death, made atonement for sin, thwarted the works of the devil, and provided a means whereby the kingdom of heaven might eventually become a full reality on earth. Consequently, the completion of his Father's mission marked the dawning of a new eschatological era which would bring salvation and restoration from sin. The key, though, is that the full realization of this *telos* is not instantaneous. The resurrection and ascension of Christ set in motion, or inaugurated, the gradual ushering of the age to come into the present. Now the present age commences on a divinely-set stopwatch ticking down the last days until the impending kingdom of God arrives when the glorified Christ returns to save his people and judge his enemies. Furthermore, this future is certain not only because of promises regarding Christ's second advent. It is experienced now, in part, because Christ is currently executing the power of the future kingdom amid the very time of spiritual darkness in which his people still live. Many of the blessings of the eschatological age, including the forgiveness of sins, the indwelling of the Spirit, and the gift of eternal life are experienced presently. And they are foretastes of future realities not yet received such as resurrection from the dead, the absence of sin's carnal influence, and a new creation. Cf. Cullman, *Christ and Time*, 139–74; Ladd, *Presence of the Future*, 105–21; Hoekema, *Bible and the Future*, 68–75. As this concept applies to salvation, a believer's enablement to persevere by the power of the Spirit is a proleptic (already) expression of their vindication that is to come at the final judgment (not yet). Essentially, justification, sanctification, and perseverance are all present-day evidences of a future eschatological reception.

contend that any attempt to accept only part of this tension or explain it away altogether leads to a deficient view of how the NT talks about perseverance. Or in Jesus' own words to the church at Smyrna, which contained people who would endure in their faith and others who might not, the Lord said to all of them that those who remain faithful would receive the crown of life (or that which is life) and that those who conquered would escape the second death (Rev 2:10–11).[31] Their *already* present status would become a future *not yet* reality partly through their expression of faithful endurance.[32]

Finally, we would be remiss if we did not mention that the expectation for believers to persevere does not mitigate against situations where the Lord may providentially choose to intervene in believers' lives to enact significant discipline if they possibly become morally obstinate in certain situations. We have seen that the NT does include some instances where believers fall into patterns of sin and the Lord uses various means to address the problem, whether it be church excommunication to confront them publicly or even death when a believer refuses to repent (e.g., Ananias and Sapphira, the situations in Corinth). So while believers are expected to endure in their faith, this does not automatically mean there are not instances where rebellious children (who do not apostatize) may experience severe life consequences or premature death if they refuse to submit to the Lord's kingdom mandates upon their lives. This means it is a mistake to equate one's perseverance in faith with some sort of uninterrupted obedience to Christ. Sometimes the life of a believer is complicated, which means we cannot put everyone on a theological assembly line to stamp or categorize every situation in the same way.

2.2 Identifying Three Types of People in the NT—Unbelievers, Believers, and Apostates

Moving past our attempts to highlight the theological importance of perseverance in Scripture, we need to press on now and approach the knottiest issue that is the most formidable to untie. That would be identifying those who, for whatever reason, fail to persevere in their faith, or apostatize. Thus far, we have seen throughout our survey that all Christian traditions

---

31. The second death is reserved for those outside of Christ, whether they reject him altogether or eventually forsake him and choose not to be overcomers (as portrayed in Revelation). See Fee, *Revelation*, 32. So if these believers are faithful even if it means physical death, they will never be touched by the eternal second death. Osborne, *Revelation*, 136.

32. Or as Blount observes, in Revelation, the ones who are judged as well as those who are praised are both tested on the same basis, namely their witness (*Revelation*, 55).

concede that the NT speaks about believers who remain in the faith and unbelievers who maintain their rejection of the gospel throughout their lifetimes. The question for the ages when it comes to the issue of perseverance, however, is how Scripture speaks about a third category of people who seem to be converted for a time, but ultimately fall away. We have examined how some traditions see these people as bona fide saints who turn away from Christ for a host of reasons. Others see them as people who reveal that they never truly converted to Christ. And still others, who see these two options as unacceptable think most biblical texts that are normally ascribed to apostasy are not about that at all. Rather, virtually all the warning passages about the dangers of turning from the faith are addressing the potential of losing eschatological reward.

Looking back on these views, it is clear that they reach an impasse with each other for at least two reasons. One is they differ significantly on how to understand the interplay between promises throughout the NT about salvation, perseverance, and final judgment. How can one reconcile promises, which at face value, assure believers that their identity in Christ cannot be forfeited, with other claims that pronounce judgment on those who do not endure in their faith? Coupled with this ordeal is the related perplexity of personal assurance. Some believe that if one concludes that salvation can be lost, then there is no way to be certain that one can avoid such a plight. Others counter that if the opposite is true that all true believers always persevere, then how can one know whether they truly are converted before death since there is always the possibility of apostatizing up until that point. These are the concerns that really fuel the debate. We see that one's definition of apostasy really helps set the stage for how one thinks the NT speaks about perseverance and the "security" of the believer. So what should be said here?

Well, first, the NT clearly speaks of occasions where some people within early Christian communities defected. Some fell prey to false teachers or worse, became false teachers themselves; others chose to follow a path of sinful rebellion with no concern to ever repent; and even some just flatly denied the Lord to whom they originally pledged their allegiance. At a more personal level, many of us today know people who initially expressed all the external signs of conversion only to later renounce their faith entirely and/or fall into patterns of sin with no intent of turning from them. Such unfortunate realities settle any debate on whether defections from Christ occur. Where the land mines begin to go off is when we move forward to figure out how the NT identifies apostates before they eventually defected.

This matter is perplexing not only because interpreters differ on whether believers can lose their salvation. There is also serious disagreement as to whether all the NT authors see apostates through one uniform lens or in different ways depending on the situation. All agree, for example, that the NT clearly alludes to instances of bogus conversions. Sometimes people claimed to have had some sort of experience where they expressed faith in Christ only to be tested by suffering, persecution, or unforeseen expectations of sacrifice. We typically think of the famous passage in 1 John 2:19 where again, John says that some false teachers, as well as those who followed them, left their communities as evidence that their solidarity with Christ was suspect. Or we are reminded of those that John records in his gospel who initially believed in Jesus because of his miracle-performing abilities. But when he later confronted them with the demands of discipleship, they turned away never to follow him again (John 2:23–24).

Such a tragedy harkens to the parable Jesus told about the sower where some receive the word of the kingdom initially but in time defected because it did not take full root in their heart (Matt 13:21). In these cases, people are described as appearing to be believers for a time until their true colors are revealed when pressure is applied. The question, however, is whether these instances are axiomatic for every other occurrence of apostasy in the NT. When someone loses their faith because they are abandoning sound doctrine or indulging in unrepentant sin, is the proper prognosis always that they were never true believers from the outset? Put another way, does the "never really was a believer" paradigm always work when we are reading everything that Peter, Paul, James, Jude, or even Jesus himself said about apostasy.

In many cases, this proposal does clearly hold. Paul speaks of faithless deceivers who intentionally enter the church for the purpose of undermining the faith of many (Acts 20:29–30). Jude describes certain false teachers as being corrupt from the start as well (Jude 4). Jesus predicts that many will turn away from the faith as the present age comes to an end but tempers his prophecy with the promise that the elect will not be deceived (Matt 24:24). Yet these deductions are not as easy to substantiate in many other cases as we have seen. What can one do with the host of texts that have a long history of interpretive difficulty like certain warning passages in Hebrews, Paul's warning to believing Gentiles that they could be cut off from the blessings of the covenant if they revert to unbelief (Rom 11:22), or Peter's discussion about false teachers who were originally part of the community of faith only later to apostatize (2 Pet 2:1–2). Here, the difficulties are a bit more challenging because there are legitimate concerns as to whether these audiences are merely posing believers. Thus, the bottom-line question emerges—does the NT ever describe genuine converts who become apostates?

We would argue that although some texts are often read this way, it is exegetically sustainable to argue that *all NT writers saw apostates as people who evidenced a lack of spiritual transformation.* It should be noted that this conclusion is not being offered simply because it is theologically convenient or merely part of a larger soteriological reading of the NT with Reformed leanings. Indeed many scholars dismiss such a proposal on these grounds. Often such charges are couched in terms that accuse interpreters of conflating the insights of different biblical authors so they can create some sort of exegetical hegemony that ensures they are all saying the same thing about a given topic.[33] Our point here is not that NT writers do not address matters from different angles. Of course they do. Our argument is that their diverse ways of addressing apostasy create layers of insight that form a complimentary understanding of the subject, not competitive or contradictory perspectives.

We contend that NT warning passages and the assorted descriptions of apostates fit quite well with other texts that explicitly describe them as never being truly regenerate. For instance, Jesus' parable of the sower effectively compliments the well-known passage in Hebrews 6. Jesus, again, speaks of some who hear the word of the kingdom and believe "for a while" only to defect in time as opposed to bearing spiritual fruit. Similarly, the AOH claims that some can be exposed to certain spiritual realities and even join new-covenant communities so as to claim the blessings of salvation but still fail to endure and bear fruit (hearkening back to the sower imagery), thereby not being spiritually salvageable nor able to inherit the eschatological rest of the age to come.[34] None of his audience had reached the full in-

---

33. Two illustrations of this concern can be seen in some interactions in biblical studies. One is in Streett's review of Schreiner's commentary on 1, 2 Peter and Jude. Toward the end, Streett contends that instead of developing a distinct theology of Peter or Jude, Schreiner describes their thoughts in wholly Pauline terms and categories, Streett, "Review of *1, 2 Peter, Jude*," 250. Another example is found in Dunn's interaction with Wilkin, a Free-Grace advocate. Dunn responds to Wilkin's understanding of perseverance as pertaining to rewards only and states that his dispensational interpretation of Scripture "is a classic case of a solution to various problem texts drawn from an unequivocal reading of one or two texts and imposed on the problem texts with the sole justification that they resolve the problem." See Dunn, "Response to Wilkin," 57. In both of these cases, the concern is with squeezing the thoughts of certain authors into the mold of others, with the result being a lack of sensitivity to the diverse ideas promoted in the New Testament as a whole.

34. Or as Fanning states, the AOH portrays an apostate in distinct Christian terms to emphasize how close they have been to the faith and what they are rejecting if they depart. See "Classical Reformed View," 217–18. Also, among the plethora of approaches to reading the warning passages in Hebrews, some such as Ellingworth argue that the rhetorical impetus of these texts (in particular, ch. 6) is to nurture the faith of the audience rather than pronounce final judgment upon them, see *Hebrews*, 317–18. In any case, though, Hagner is correct when he states that for the AOH, only perseverance can ultimately demonstrate the reality of Christian faith (*Hebrews*, 92).

heritance and the main thrust of the treatise is that only those who endure are the ones who receive the salvation of their souls.

Likewise, Paul speaks to his audiences in similar fashion as we have seen in that he encourages believers with theological realities while at the same time warning them to persevere so they may be vindicated in resurrection just as Christ was. The book of Revelation echoes the same thing by proclaiming to Christian communities that only those who listen to the words of Christ and do not worship the beast will escape the second death and reign in the new creation. Furthermore, Peter uses grim images to describe any who become part of Christian communities and identify with those for whom Christ died only to renounce their faith, embrace false doctrines, and even worse, lead others into such lies. They are like dogs returning to their vomit or pigs to their slop. They illustrate the true nature of unclean things because sooner or later, they go back to their former ways. They had been part of believing communities, which are the groups for whom Christ gave his life, and they chose to abandon these ancient families of faith because their desire to lapse back into their sinful ways forced them to play their spiritual hand as mere unclean professors.

So in retrospect, we would argue that closer scrutiny shows that the NT writers actually describe apostasy in ways which coincide theologically. No doubt, they add their own unique input at times. Nevertheless, their observations connect at the point of recognizing that one who professes belief has no hope of salvation unless that profession sets out on a trajectory of endurance. Therefore, this troubling "third" category of people known as apostates are those who in Jesus' words, believe for a while, but do not bear fruit. They grasp on to the gospel with certain motives other than the divine enablement of grace. That is why they eventually fall away because their faith is self-originating, not a by-product of the new birth. Paul, Peter, Jude, John, and the AOH all would agree, but they would approach matters from an assortment of angles because they spoke of the dangers of apostasy in different circumstances. If all of this is the case then, another question begins to emerge which is how to make sense of the soterically-inclusive language that Scripture often uses to describe both believers and mere professors.

2.3 The Dilemma of New-Covenant "Mixed" Communities

The last component that we would argue is a critical part of a theology of perseverance is *often NT authors address believing communities with the recognition that they are comprised of believers who will persevere and other members who possibly will not (and sometimes do not).*[35] It is difficult to avoid such a conclusion because of so many instances where groups of professing followers almost always include both groups. Jesus himself claimed that among the disciples that he himself chose, he prayed for Peter so his upcoming failure would not be the last word for his life whereas he knew that Judas was "a devil" from the outset. This is why he warned that any branch "in him" that did not bear fruit would be cut off and thrown away to be burned. Paul appeals to similar imagery in Romans 11 when he speaks to believing Gentiles who have been incorporated into the vine, or covenantal bond in Christ. If they choose to fall into unbelief the way many unbelieving Jews did when the Messiah arrived, they too would be "cut off" in judgment. We could mention numerous other examples where salvific language is applied to people who do not persevere in faith (which we have in previous chapters). We are reminded of the descriptions in Hebrews of those who have partaken of the heavenly gift, tasted God's word, and been sanctified by the blood of the covenant or Peter who refers to false teachers as those who denied the Lord "who bought them."

These sorts of texts illicit a question, namely whether they can justifiably be interpreted to refer to people who are not believers or must it be conceded that they in fact were. In many ways, this is the million-dollar question in the perseverance debate. How do we account for biblical texts that describe apostates as people who were formerly part of believing communities? We have seen that Arminians affirm that churches are made up of some believers who persevere and others who do not. Calvinists counter that instead churches are comprised of genuine believers who are divinely enabled to persevere and others who claim to be converted but reveal otherwise by their failure to endure. Then in the mix are the Free-Grace advocates who contend that churches are made up of several groups, those being false believers who do not, believers who do, and carnal, immature believers who do not. We have shown our hand by opting for the alternative that leans in a more Reformed direction.

But there is still one more feature that complicates this issue of mixed communities. There is the dilemma regarding the nature of the new covenant. We argued earlier that the covenant framework of the Mosaic economy

---

35. Because there are defections (both in the first century as well as today), our argument here is not that warnings are given primarily as a divine means of enabling the elect to persevere. See Schreiner and Caneday, *Race Set Before Us*, 38–45. This may be a by-product of NT warnings but our contention is that their primary purpose is to warn all believers that final judgment awaits those who do not persevere. And the reason for this is because there are many within communities of faith who do apostatize. See Thomas, *Case for Mixed-Audience*, 95–96, 237–74.

functioned in such a way that the people of God were identified as a nation of Israelites which included a remnant of Jews who were true believers who coexisted within the larger conglomerate of people who often were not. The later promissory expectation of the new covenant was that this dichotomy would be removed. All of God's people, including every believing Jew and Gentile, would receive the Spirit, be forgiven of their sins, and have the law written on their hearts. Whereas the people of God were formerly made up of a nation in which a remnant resided, the new covenant would transform the group so that there would be no distinction. Again, the remnant and the "nation" would be identical.[36]

Under the old covenant, there were both *theological* and *practical* reasons why the people of God were a mixed community. Theologically speaking, as descendants of Abraham, Isaac, and Jacob, Israel was collectively considered God's "elect" because the nation as a whole was given the promises of the covenants. Every Jew was considered a part of the "chosen" people regardless of whether they were a genuine believer, hence a mixed community. And practically speaking, only a remnant of Jews throughout Old Testament history remained loyal to the covenants. Again, this meant the whole group carried the mantle of being God's people, but in practice only the remnant embraced this identity in their hearts. Or as Paul would later say, there was an Israel (i.e., a remnant) within Israel (i.e., the nation as a whole).

With regard to the new covenant, however, at the theological level everyone becomes an equal benefactor because the community is only made up of those who have the Spirit. There is no longer a distinction between those who receive new-covenant blessings and those who do not. Everyone who receives them is a part of the new remnant. Where the irony emerges is that while Christ's redemptive work ensures all within the community are recipients of spiritual transformation, it does not eliminate the possibility that some could still become part of the group at an external level. *While it is theologically prohibited for the church to be a mixed community, that does not prevent it from being one practically.*

This is to say that everyone who becomes a recipient of new-covenant blessings is truly part of the people of God (or the church). Nevertheless, the unfortunate reality is that none of these promises prohibit some from joining Christian communities without necessarily experiencing a true spiritual transformation. In some cases, they may think they have believed, or as Jesus said, they "believe for a while." They may have professed faith

---

36. See treatment of this theme in Gentry and Wellum, *Kingdom through Covenant*, 644–52.

and experienced the rite of baptism as a profession of faith, partaken of the Lord's Supper with God's people, or even prayed. Yet the NT is clear that discernment of one's conversion often comes with time. If one is a true believer indwelled by the Spirit, then they will bear fruit that lasts. And part of the way of seeing if fruit of conversion is legitimate is by whether it endures. One's apostasy or permanent turning away from Christ shows that one's self-acclaimed faith is temporal. It is not born of the Spirit by its very nature. Only Spirit-induced transformation can enable a believer to face the many obstacles that the present age hurls at God's people. As Calvin and many Reformers have argued, "saving faith is an enduring faith."[37] Consequently, we contend that apostates are viewed by NT writers as false professors who can only be identified by whether they heed all the warnings to persevere. One could say then that *NT authors express their various warnings against apostasy so that the theological reality of a fully regenerate church can be practically maintained by individual congregations.*

Finally, it should be noted that aside from the obvious clashes that this point has with Arminian views, it faces a bit of a theological rub in some current discussions about perseverance within Reformed circles as well. One example can be seen in the interest among some Calvinistic evangelicals concerning a nuanced proposal that revisits the theological purpose of the warning passages in the NT. The contention, which in recent years has been made by Tom Schreiner and Ardel Caneday, is that biblical warnings against apostasy are primarily given because they are the divine means of enabling true believers to persevere.[38] Believers endure in their faith, in part, because they are supernaturally motivated to do so by heeding warnings to the contrary. Since this is the case, it would make no sense for NT admonitions to be offered to some who might not be believers. Such passages would lose their rhetorical force.[39] Why would one encourage an unbeliever to persevere? This is a formidable point and to an extent, one can see the reasoning here. The problem is that the warnings are given in some contexts where people *within* Christian communities had already apostatized or were possibly on the verge of doing so. Consequently, the warnings are issued not only to benefit believers. They are given because there is the possibility that

---

37. E.g., Calvin, *Institutes*, 3.2.1–24; 3.11.19.

38. Two key works that defend this position are Schreiner and Caneday, *Race Set Before Us*; and Schreiner, *Run to Win the Prize*. The position that they defend in the former volume is not entirely new. There are numerous authors who have offered earlier versions, including Bavinck, Berkhof, Dabney, and Hodge. See comparison of sources in Cowan, "Warning Passages of Hebrews," 211–12.

39. A thorough discussion of this same approach can be seen in a treatment of the warnings in Hebrews in Cowan, "Warning Passages of Hebrews," 189–213.

anyone who *claims* to be a believer could defect (and sometimes do). We would say, then, that there is a dual purpose for the warnings. One indeed is to encourage believers to be vigilant in their faith. But this does not mitigate against another intent. NT authors equally assumed that there may be others who were listening that may only have a temporal faith. This means that warnings against apostasy carry weight in large part because they were directed at communities made up of true believers and others who would not endure in their faith.[40]

Another venue that our thesis resists is a heated controversy in Presbyterian and other historically Reformed traditions caused by what is often called Federal Vision Theology (FV).[41] The relevance this theological development has to perseverance and apostasy emerges in how FV advocates define the church as a covenant community. Though thinkers in this strand diverge on various details, the gist of FV on this matter is that there are some who are genuine members of new-covenant communities because of their baptism into Christ and/or an initial act of faith. However, their membership within the visible church does not mean they are part of the elect people of God. This is still contrary to Arminianism because this approach views apostates as a part of all the reprobate who God does not elect to be saved. Yet it moves away from traditional Reformed views of ecclesiology which maintain a distinction between the elect, who receive the full benefits of salvation, including perseverance, and those who only receive the external rites of the new covenant but have no saving faith. Some FV supporters contend that saving new-covenant grace is given both to the elect who persevere and those who only believe for a time. This means the new covenant is virtually symmetrical with the old covenant wherein the elect

---

40. See more technical discussion of this point against Schreiner and Caneday specifically in Thomas, *Case for Mixed-Audience*, 79–84. Schreiner tries to illustrate his point about biblical warnings being the means of enabling believers to persevere by recounting a story. One time his son said "watch out" while Schreiner was driving in reverse because he was about to back into a parked car. Schreiner observes that his son's warning caused him to respond in time and avoid a potential collision. See Schreiner, *Run to Win*, 94. Our response would be that there are other fathers who do not respond to sudden warnings like this for whatever reason, therefore experiencing wrecks. So the reason the illustration is powerful is not only because Schreiner experienced a positive outcome. It is impactful because we know there are many others who have not avoided inadvertent fender benders. Comparatively speaking, warnings against apostasy may enable the elect to persevere. But they are also given to believing communities that had some who either were about to apostatize or already had.

41. It is known by other titles such as Auburn Avenue Theology, Shepherdism, monocovenantalism, and neonomism. For treatments on these terms as well as the history of FVT, see Waters, *Federal Vision*, 1–29; and Beisner, *Auburn Avenue Theology*.

people of God are mixed community by theological necessity.[42] However, we have argued that those who turn away from the faith are described as being part of God's people only at the external level. While some within the elect covenant-nation of Israel were individual (elect) believers and others were not under the Mosaic economy, that distinction is abrogated under the new covenant. There is no longer a distinction between the corporate-elect identity of God's people versus the personal elect identity of individual believers. Being a true believer necessitates that one is a full benefactor of new-covenant blessings, not just a partial recipient. True faith that leads to forgiveness of sin and union with Christ culminates in perseverance, not apostasy. In other words, the terms of the new covenant mitigate against the notion of an elect remnant within the elect community.

3. WHAT ARE THE GROUNDS AND MEANS OF HAVING PERSONAL ASSURANCE OF SALVATION?

Now that we have traveled through much of the theological forest on the matters of perseverance and offered our final analysis of how Scripture addresses the subject, we want to close our discussion with what I like to call a "so what" issue. Every major belief in the Christian faith has significant practical implications for what believers should think and do—the doctrine of perseverance being no exception. Deciphering whether or not Scripture teaches that believers can lose their salvation is as "practical" a concern as one can imagine. But a closely related question that always emerges once disputes about the possibility of apostasy are deliberated is how a person can be assured that they are a true believer. How can someone find rest for their souls and know they belong to Christ if (1) it is possible that they could apostatize and lose their salvation, or, as we have argued, (2) they must persevere in their belief in Christ because this is the only kind of faith that leads to salvation. Said another way, if the NT teaches that endurance is part of what it means to express true faith in Christ, then how can one be assured that they will do so before the fact. How can one know they are converted by the grace of the gospel *now* if one must persevere to the *end* to prove it?

This is an enormous question that should not be treated lightly. I recall being in a doctoral seminar once and during a lively discussion about perseverance between two students, one asked the other how he could be assured

---

42. This is part of the real disagreement between FV thinkers and traditional Presbyterians. The FV project is perceived by many opponents as distorting the overall structure of covenant theology, which is at the theological heart of Reformed theology. See discussion in Waters, *Federal Vision*, 30–58.

of his own salvation. The student responded that all we can be certain of is that God will save some. The inquiring student then followed up by asking whether this other student wanted to be a pastor, to which he responded "no." The discussion ended with the inquiring student replying "good." The reason I mention this interchange is because it really goes to the heart of the matter. The subject of assurance does not merely concern whether someone else will persevere and be saved. The crux issue is how does one know that they personally will be saved on the last day. The concern is not simply how I know someone else is a believer. It is how can "I" know if I am.

Undoubtedly, how such a question is answered has a significant impact on Christian praxis at numerous levels. For example, it affects how individual believers evaluate their own Christian conversion as being genuine. How do I know that my self-acclaimed faith is authentic or not? One's views on personal assurance also help shape interpretations of other pertinent doctrines such as election, justification, and sanctification. Asking how one can know if they are in Christ entails related questions about how one can know they are in a right standing before God or that the Spirit is truly working in their lives to conform them to the image of Christ. Likewise, how pastors believe someone should be confident of their salvation helps guide the ways they disciple their congregations or how they counsel individual believers when they struggle with doubts in their walk with the Lord.

We recognize in every case, then, that the stakes are indeed high. Therefore, we propose that the best way to develop a theology of assurance is to be reminded once more about the most common pressures that the NT says can tempt people to abandon their faith—again, those being the dangers of false teaching, the sinful pull of temptations, and the pressures of persecution. Our contention is that the NT offers some theological provisions which specifically address these moral pitfalls. And believers can use them to develop a healthy assurance of their relationship with Christ.

3.1 Believing in Christ

We begin by mentioning the most important factor that is needed when constructing a biblical/theological understanding of assurance, namely a steadfast belief in who Christ is and what he has accomplished in his death and resurrection. Here the role of what we can call faith, trust, or confessional allegiance cannot be underestimated because NT writers often view it as the best defense against the deceptive antics of false teachers.[43] This is

---

43. Although the idea of allegiance as a means of recalibrating one's understanding of imputation and forensic justification is causing some debate, some find it to be a

why we see believers being constantly reminded of what they have come to affirm in the gospel message. They believed that Jesus was the Christ, the Son of God. And now all the spiritual benefits that Christ has been authorized to share by virtue of being the glorified resurrected Messiah are their inheritance. Because of their faith in the Lord, they are identified as God's people; they are deemed righteous in God's sight; they have received the Spirit as a down payment of their coming salvation; and they are heirs of a redeemed creation that will arrive in the age to come.[44]

Likewise, it must be kept in mind that one's act of faith in Christ is treated in Scripture as a specifically defined event. What we mean here is that people who come to the Lord for forgiveness are not embracing the mercies of an undefined, generic deity who has no specific identity or theological shape. Rather, Christ is the Son of God who became incarnate in the person of Jesus of Nazareth. He is the redeemer of the nations who was proclaimed by the apostolic witness. So a person's faith is placed in a specifically defined Savior. This does not mean a comprehensive understanding of Christology is a prerequisite to conversion. Nonetheless, new believers in the early church were required to affirm a minimal, though specified, amount of content about who Christ is. And they were expected to affirm more truths as they grew in their faith.[45]

---

helpful concept, e.g., Bates, *Salvation by Allegiance Alone*; Bates, *Gospel Allegiance*.

44. Evangelicals are often careful to describe justification (i.e., being declared to be righteous in Christ) as a facet of the salvation experience that is a distinct act which is separate, though related, to the work of the Spirit in the process of sanctification (i.e., becoming transformed to be like Christ). This clarification has its roots in the historical debate of the Reformation concerning the means whereby sinners receive the saving power of divine grace. The Catholic tradition was accused of conflating justification with sanctification by arguing that sinners are *infused* (or endowed) with grace as they partake of the sacraments by faith and are gradually made righteous in the process. The end result being that God justifies those who become just. Protestants objected, maintaining that sinners are granted the status of being righteous *legally* when they exercise faith in Christ and then subsequently experiencing the work of the Spirit to be changed *morally*. Cf. treatments by Bray, "Late-Medieval Theology," 85–93; Maas, "Justification by Faith Alone," 511–45; Horton, *Justification*, 1:221–80; and McGrath, *Iustitia Dei*, 186–248. Amid the many debates today as to whether these two options are the only viable ones (this is especially an issue because of alternative proposals such as the New Perspective[s] on Paul or the "apocalyptic" Paul in broader NT scholarship), some offer a third option. It attempts to uphold the importance of *sola fide* while at the same time emphasizing the interplay between the forensic and participatory dynamics of salvation. To avoid the sacramental overtones of infusion while also wanting to shore up some of the nuances of coming into union with Christ by faith, some like Michael Bird choose to use the word "incorporate" because it highlights what they become, not just what they receive. Cf. Bird, *Saving Righteousness of God*, 60–87; Bates, *Salvation by Allegiance Alone*, 182–91.

45. This is largely why the catechumens became prominent because eventually

We could say that the NT treats one's conversion as a kind of "first step" that is to be followed by subsequent steps whereby believers gradually embrace a larger corpus of doctrinal content. In fact, the NT has such high expectations that it equates denials of any fundamental Christian belief (whether it be a future resurrection of believers, the deity or humanity of Christ, the gospel message of salvation by faith and not of works, etc.) as potentially being equivalent to repudiating the very faith that one claims to have initially expressed in Christ.[46] Consequently, a believer's childlike faith, which is indicative of the new birth, is something that gradually develops to affirm the full matrix of apostolic teaching.[47]

We see this kind of trajectory all throughout Scripture. John, for example, assures his early communities of believers that if they believe in Jesus as the Son of God, they can be assured that they have eternal life. They have fellowship with him. They can know that they are his people and will be like him at his return. At the same time, John rebukes some in the communities who had come to deny that Christ was the Son of God. Despite whatever claims to faith they may have made in their alleged conversion experiences, John says they were never truly part of the church. He apparently assumed that right belief about Christ is not only correct in what it affirms at a given moment. It must endure as well.

Similarly, Paul in his First Letter to Timothy is confident of how he has grown in his own walk with the Lord. However, as he was later ministering in the church of Ephesus on Paul's behalf, Timothy is commissioned to remain committed to the truths that he had learned. If he did so, his endurance would lead to his own salvation because he himself would not be deceived by the impending false teachings that were evidently infiltrating parts of the Ephesian church. Furthermore, those who listened to Timothy as he taught sound doctrine would be saved too. In the end, then, we see that doctrinal fidelity to Christ is interwoven with the nature of the kind of

---

more and more gentiles came into the church with minimal understanding of Judaism or early Christianity. See Hall, *Doctrine and Practice in the Early Church*, 15–22; Sittser, "Catechumenate," 340–41; and Johnson, *Rites of Christian Initiation*, 1–40.

46. As we have seen in the NT, in all these cases, people were treated as if they had abandoned Christ, left the faith, and separated themselves from believing communities (or worse, they were remaining within them to spread their defective beliefs).

47. This does not mean that there was not significant diversity of theological convictions on many details throughout the world of early Christianity. Indeed, there was. Yet there were attempts within strands of early Christian thought to demarcate certain doctrinal convictions that communities of faith were expected to affirm and that served as boundaries which must be followed by anyone who wanted to interpret biblical texts. An example was the development of the *regula fidei*, or the rule of faith. See treatment here by Ferguson, *Rule of Faith*, esp. 67–82.

faith that clings to Christ, thereby nurturing a believer's personal assurance of salvation.

3.2 Following Christ

Even though right belief in the Christ of Scripture is a reliable source for one's assurance, the NT connects it with other truths as well. We would be remiss to say that theological accuracy on its own is sufficient to grant someone robust confidence that they are a true believer. Although a right understanding about who Jesus is and what it means to follow him is essential to this, it is insufficient by itself. The reason why is because the NT connects one's abiding faith with other spiritual dynamics. While believers are encouraged to rest in the sure work of Christ on their behalf, the NT also combines trust in biblical truth with faithful attempts to obey its moral mandates. So right belief in Jesus is inseparably linked to right actions that strive to follow his commands. As the Lord himself said, "Why call me Lord if you do not do what I say."

Such a point does require caution, however, because if taken uncritically, it can be dangerous, even emotionally paralyzing. If believers try to be assured of their salvation by simply looking at their feeble attempts to obey Christ in everyday life, they can easily be overcome by their failures and shortcomings. Our contention here is not that personal assurance is partly based on one's ability to be effectively introspective. Looking to ourselves strictly speaking can foster a merit-based notion for assurance that is theologically disastrous. Still, it cannot be denied that NT writers do view a believer's conversion whereupon they confess Christ as Lord to be an act of obedience that is followed by a life of discipleship.[48]

Paul, for instance, reminds his readers on many occasions of what they used to be before they met Christ and contrasts it with the new creatures they have become since their conversions. We see this when he tells the believing Thessalonians that they had turned from worshipping idols to serve the living and the true God and wait for the coming of the Son. Notice that Paul connects their initial change (i.e., turning away from what they were and believing in the true God) with their present-day actions, which were encapsulated in waiting for Christ's return. The Thessalonians could be assured that their salvation would come not only because they could trust in God's promises. Their experience of abandoning idols and living in light of the hope of the *parousia* were also means of assurance as well. The Savior

---

48. It is only in select modern venues of evangelicalism where one sees attempts to distinguish between being a believer vs. a follower of Jesus.

who was going to return in the future was the same one who had changed them and was still in the process of doing so.[49]

Another way we could flesh this point out would be to say that the Spirit who works in a person to lead them to faith and repentance is the same source who gradually produces spiritual character in that person's life. We see a balance between these ideas numerous times in the theology of many NT writers. We can read of Paul admonishing believers to avoid the works of the flesh and yield to the fruit of the Spirit. He argues in several of his letters (e.g., Galatians, Romans, Ephesians) that the same Spirit who brought sinners to faith can now enable them to walk by faith. James also speaks about the fact that faith that leads to salvation always has works to show it is alive. Relatedly, John teaches that those who can be confident that they have eternal life because they are born of God must also resist the temptation to stay in unrepentant patterns of sin. If they do not, they are liars and the truth is not in them. And even in the visions of Revelation, those who have their names written in the Lamb's book of life are those who refuse to worship the satanic powers.[50] Consequently, in connecting this kinds of passages together, the point is not that believers must look to themselves and create some sort of "works" barometer to determine whether they are measuring up. Rather it is that believers who wrestle with sin, confess it, and engage in a battle to defeat it are the ones who can have assurance while those who claim to be believers and simply remain resigned to sinful conduct should be concerned, not confident.

3.3 Serving Christ Communally

Finally, a third provision that the NT stresses for nurturing a believer's confidence in their own salvation is solidarity with a local community of faith (or church). The previous two safeguards for assurance, which again are a believer's ongoing trust in Christ and the pursuit of personal holiness, are always connected with the reality that the Christian faith is to be lived out in concert with ecclesiology, not simply personal individual piety.[51] Such a

---

49. If Paul thought they were on the verge of turning back to the idols that they had abandoned, he would have warned them of impending judgment just as he did in similar contexts (e.g., Galatians, Colossians, 1 Timothy, etc.).

50. Note that both certainty and responsibility are intertwined together. Their names are already recorded but they are still admonished to persevere and not follow the lies of the beast or succumb to the ordeals of persecution. It is a both/and scenario, not either/or. See Resseguie, *Revelation of John*, 249–50.

51. While conversion is experienced individually, it is never for the purpose of only being experienced privately. Becoming a part of Christ and coming into union with his

point can be easily misconstrued. The point here is not that one's assurance is partly based on the spiritual consistency of any given congregation. We are well aware that sometimes local churches fail to accomplish their God-given tasks. The idea that the NT promotes is that trusting in the Lord's saving grace and following him in discipleship are to be done with God's people, not without them.

This seems somewhat obvious since at face value it addresses each of the major apostasy pitfalls quite well. Believers can endure the pressures of persecution with more boldness when they lock arms with a church family who is suffering and praying together with them. They can wrestle against the temptations of the flesh more forthrightly when they know others are confessing their shortcomings as well. And it is much more difficult to woo someone with false doctrines if they are deeply grounded not in only in their own faith but also in relationships with doctrinally like-minded believers.

Yet alongside these basic points, when we probe the NT a bit more carefully, we discover a few more features that show how the doctrine of the church helps undergird one's assurance of personal salvation. One is that a believer's love for Christ matures insofar as it learns to cherish his people. We see this correlation all throughout Scripture. Jesus himself tells his disciples that others will know they are his followers not just by their love for him but for one another. Paul instructs believing spouses to function as couples who reflect the same kind of love that Christ has for the church. John is also insistent with his audience that they cannot say they love God who they cannot see but express hatred toward their spiritual family who they can see. What can be said, then, is that the church is a sort of litmus test for one's claim to love Christ. If a professing believer cannot exhibit love toward those for whom Christ died, then how can they have assurance that they love Christ himself.

Closely related to this idea are occasions in the NT where eschatological judgment is described in terms of determining who has served the Lord by loving his people. One of the clearest examples of this can be found in Jesus' own teachings about his return to judge humanity. In Matt 25 (which is part of larger discussion about the coming of the Son of Man in the Olivet Discourse), Jesus discusses in parabolic form how some will be ready for the eschatological age while others will not. Some will be faithful in waiting for the end of the present age just as five faithful virgins are always ready for

---

death and resurrection necessarily entails solidarity with his people. Thus, becoming a participant in a local covenant community of believers entails a present manifestation of being a citizen of heaven, which means one is part of a conglomerate of tribes and tongues who will inherit the new creation. See Harper and Metzger, *Exploring Ecclesiology*, 60–77.

the imminent return of a bridegroom for a wedding (Matt 25:1–13). Said another way, Jesus makes the same point by describing faithful servants who are given talents by their master. They prove to be good stewards because they know they will be audited when their master returns and so they always remain prepared (Matt 25:14–32).

Similarly, Jesus makes the same point again by describing the Son of Man's coming in the glory of his kingdom to judge the nations (Matt 25:33–46). Here the heavenly shepherd/judge symbolically separates the sheep, or his people, from the goats, or those who are not. The way their identity is discerned is by whether they were gracious to Christ's "brothers and sisters," or those who are considered by the world to be the least. Those who were not considerate to his own are marked as the goats who are judged. Evidently how one treats fellow believers of Christ's flock can be indicative of whether one is part of the flock.

This idea is echoed in the moment where the resurrected glorified Christ confronts Saul/Paul on the road to Damascus as he was going to have believers incarcerated. Paul was on his way to arrest believers when Christ unexpectedly and supernaturally confronts him. Note that he does not ask Paul why he is persecuting believers. Instead, he inquires "Why are you persecuting Me?" The assumption here is that wrongful opposition against God's people is equivalent to resisting Christ himself. Even the author of Hebrews implies that the gradual abandoning of consistent involvement with a Christian assembly can lead to the dangers of apostasy. That is why he urges his readers not to forsake their presence with the group because they know the "day" (i.e., time of judgment) is soon to come. What we see in these instances is that one's love for Christ cannot be authentic in the present age or vindicated at the final judgment unless it is expressed in love for his people now.

Lastly, another reason a believer's relationship to a congregation serves as an important ingredient to their personal assurance of salvation is that certain elements of Christian praxis are commanded to take place strictly within the context of the church. Numerous examples could be discussed here. We could mention the act of baptism wherein new converts visually replicate the gift of salvation that they have received and identify with others who have done the same. Subsequently, all baptized believers are then to partake of the Lord's Supper regularly. They are to remember Christ's sacrifice, look forward to his return, and celebrate their union with his people. We could highlight the enactment of spiritual gifts, which are not given only so believers can be benefited personally. They are to be used for the edification of the church. Or we could discuss the importance of church discipline. Periodically throughout the NT, believers, or at least those who profess to be, are held accountable by individual congregations—sometimes even to the extent of excommunication in hopes that they will repent.

In any of these cases (of which many more could be mentioned), the overall point is clear. The NT teaches that many of the ways in which believers express their faith must take place in cooperation with local churches. Thus, when the first two factors we discussed—again those being a believer's steadfast trust in Christ and their slow but steady journey in discipleship—are combined with their faith being developed in the life of the church, one's personal assurance of salvation can extend to the heavens.

4. FINAL CONCLUSION

As we bring this study to a close, we again want to mention the fact that the reason the subject of perseverance is so perplexing is primarily because of the struggle to find a theological balance between what is certain and what is contingent. We have argued that in many instances, Scripture emphasizes certain dynamics about the nature of salvation that are fixed, irreversible, and settled by God's divine initiative. We recognize that some competing Christian traditions differ on how this point is parsed out in detail whereas others deny this claim altogether. But be that as it may, every tradition must wrestle with the question of what is contingent. What parts of the experience of salvation, if any, are dependent upon something that is still yet to happen in the future. Some evangelicals may quickly respond by saying "nothing," Jesus has accomplished it all. And as it pertains to the basis of salvation, they would be correct. Nevertheless, the heart of the matter is that while the basis of a believer's salvation is settled, whether they will persevere in their own faith is not. That is what is contingent, practically speaking.[52] That is what makes this issue thorny. That is what gives it its teeth.

We have argued that the NT writers are certain that all of those in Christ are secure in their salvation. Yet this certainty does not eradicate their concerns that some may not persevere in their faith. That is why these dual truths leave us with a bequeathed corpus that includes all kinds of encouraging promises about what is ours in Christ on the one hand and strong warnings about the eternal consequences of apostasy on the other. What is certain is that believers will be saved but what is not certain is whether everyone claiming to be a believer will endure as such. The NT does not shy away from this tension and we would argue that all attempts to domesticate

---

52. And even if one wants to argue that it has already been divinely ordained whether one will persevere or not, the question still remains as to how one can know if they will do so.

or play down this dynamic are not facing the full weight of the issue at hand. Indeed, all of those who are true believers belong to Christ and will persevere. At the same time, though, the theological rub emerges when we recognize the fact that the NT not only teaches the grace of preservation, or that all the saved will endure. It equally teaches the grace of perseverance, which means that only those who endure to the end will be saved.

Bibliography

Alderson, Richard. *No Holiness, No Heaven! Antinomianism Today*. Carlisle, PA: Banner of Truth, 1986.
Aldrich, Willard M. "Perseverance." *Bibliotheca Sacra* 115 (1958) 9–19.
Alexander, T. Desmond. *From Eden to the New Jerusalem: An Introduction to Biblical Theology*. Downers Grove: InterVarsity, 2008.
Alford, Henry. *The Greek New Testament*. 4 vols. Revisions by Everett F. Harrison. 1958. Reprint, Chicago: Moody Press, 1968.
Allen, David L. *Hebrews: An Exegetical and Theological Exposition of Holy Scripture*. New American Commentary. Nashville: B & H, 2010.
Allison, Dale C., Jr. *The End of the Ages Has Come: An Early Interpretation of the Passion and Resurrection of Jesus*. Minneapolis: Fortress, 1985.
Allison, Gregg R. *Historical Theology: Introduction to Christian Doctrine*. Grand Rapids: Zondervan, 2011.
Althaus, Paul. *The Theology of Martin Luther*. Minneapolis: Fortress, 1966.
Aquinas, Thomas. *Summa Theologica*. 5 vols. English ed. Translated by Fathers of the English Dominican Province. Library of Christian Classics. Reprint. Notre Dame: Christian Classics, 1981.
Arand, Charles P. *That I May Be His Own: An Overview of Luther's Catechisms*. St. Louis: Concordia, 2000.
Arminius, James. *The Works of James Arminius*. 3 vols. Translated by James Nichols. Reprint. Grand Rapids: Baker, 1999.
Arnold, Brian. *Cyprian of Carthage: His Life and Impact*. Early Church Fathers. Rev. ed. Fearn, Scotland: Christian Focus, 2017.
Ashby, Stephen M. "A Reformed Arminian View." In *Four Views on Eternal Security*, edited by J. Matthew Pinson, 137–200. Grand Rapids: Zondervan, 2002.
Augustine, Aurelius. *Against Julian*. Translated by Matthew A. Schumacher. Fathers of the Early Church Series. New York: Catholic University Press of America, 1957.
———. *The City of God*. In Nicene and Post-Nicene Fathers, vol. 2, translated by Marcus Dods, edited by Philip Schaff, 1–511. Christian Literature, 1887. Reprint, Peabody: Hendrickson, 1999.
———. *On Faith and Good Works*. Edited by Gregory J. Lombardo. Mahwah, NJ: Newman, 1988.
———. *On the Gift of Perseverance*. In Nicene and Post-Nicene Fathers, vol. 5, translated by Peter Holmes and Robert E. Wallis, edited by Philip Schaff, 525–52. Christian Literature, 1887. Reprint, Peabody: Hendrickson, 1999.

———. *On the Merits and Remission of Sins and On the Baptism of Infants*. In Nicene and Post-Nicene Fathers, vol. 5, translated by Peter Holmes and Robert E. Wallis, edited by Philip Schaff, 15–78. Christian Literature, 1887. Reprint, Peabody: Hendrickson, 1999.

———. *On the Predestination of the Saints*. In Nicene and Post-Nicene Fathers, vol. 5, translated by Peter Holmes and Robert E. Wallis, edited by Philip Schaff, 493–519. Christian Literature, 1887. Reprint, Peabody: Hendrickson, 1999.

———. *The Thirteen Books of the Confessions of Augustine*. In Nicene and Post-Nicene Fathers, vol. 1, translated by J. G. Pilkington, edited by Philip Schaff, 45–207. Christian Literature, 1887. Reprint, Peabody: Hendrickson, 1999.

———. *To Simplicianus*. In *The Works of Saint Augustine: A Translation for the 21st Century*, vol. 1, translated by Boniface Ramsey, edited by J. E. Rotelle and Boniface Ramsey. New York: New City, 2008.

———. *Treatise on Rebuke and Grace*. In Nicene and Post-Nicene Fathers, vol. 5, translated by Peter Holmes and Robert E. Wallis, edited by Philip Schaff, 471–91. Christian Literature, 1887. Reprint, Peabody: Hendrickson, 1999.

Aune, David E. *Apocalypticism, Prophecy, and Magic in Early Christianity*. Grand Rapids: Baker, 2008.

———. *Revelation 1–5*. Word Biblical Commentary 52A. Nashville: Nelson, 1997.

Averbeck, Richard E. "Clean and Unclean." In the *New International Dictionary of Old Testament Theology & Exegesis*, edited by Willem A. VanGemeren, 4:477–86. 5 vols. Grand Rapids: Zondervan, 1997.

Babcock, William S. "Grace, Freedom, and Justice: Augustine and the Christian Tradition." *Perkins Journal* 26 (1973) 1–15.

Baker, William R. "Endurance, Perseverance." In *Dictionary of the Later New Testament and Its Developments*, edited by Ralph P. Martin and Peter H. Davids, 326–30. Downers Grove: InterVarsity, 1997.

Bammel, Caroline P. "Justification by Faith in Augustine and Origen." *Journal of Ecclesiastical History* 47 (1996) 223–35.

Bangs, Carl. *Arminius: A Study in the Dutch Reformation*. Nashville: Abingdon, 1971.

———. "Arminius as a Reformed Theologian." *Church History* 30 (1961) 155–70.

———. "Recent Studies in Arminianism." *Religion in Life* 32 (1963) 421–28.

Barbour, John D. *Versions of Deconversion: Autobiography and the Loss of Faith*. Charlottesville: University of Virginia Press, 1994.

Barclay, John M. G. "Deviance and Apostasy: Some Applications of Deviance Theory to First-Century Judaism and Christianity." In *Modelling Early Christianity: Social-Scientific Studies of the New Testament in Its Context*, edited by Philip F. Esler, 114–27. New York: Routledge, 1995.

———. *Obeying the Truth: Paul's Ethics in Galatians*. Minneapolis: Fortress, 1991.

———. "Paul among Diaspora Jews: Anomaly or Apostate?" *Journal for the Study of the New Testament* 60 (1995) 89–120.

———. *Paul and the Gift*. Grand Rapids: Eerdmans, 2015.

Barnabas. "The Epistle of Barnabas." In *The Apostolic Fathers*, edited and translated by Michael W. Holmes, 11–31. 3rd ed. Grand Rapids: Baker, 2007.

Barnett, Paul W. "Apostasy." In the *Dictionary of the Later New Testament and Its Developments*, edited by Ralph P. Martin and Peter H. Davids, 73–76. Downers Grove: InterVarsity, 1997.

Barrois, Georges Augustin. "What Are Indulgences?" *Christian Century* 67 (1950) 266–68.
Bartholomew, Craig G. and Heath A. Thomas, eds. *A Manifesto for Theological Interpretation.* Grand Rapids: Baker, 2016.
Bass, Christopher D. *That You May Know: Assurance of Salvation in 1 John.* New American Commentary Studies in Bible and Theology. Nashville: B & H, 2008.
Bassett, Paul Merritt, ed. "Wesley and Eastern Orthodoxy: Theological Influences, Convergences, Implications." *Wesleyan Theological Journal* 26 (1991) 23–163.
Bassler, Jouette M. "'He Remains Faithful' (2 Timothy 2:13a)." In *Theology and Ethics in Paul and His Interpreters: Essays in Honor of Victor Paul Furnish*, edited by Eugene H. Lovering Jr., 173–83. Nashville: Abingdon, 1996.
Bateman, Herbert W., IV. "Introducing the Warning Passages in Hebrews: A Contextual Orientation." In *Four Views on the Warning Passages in Hebrews*, edited by Herbert W. Bateman IV, 23–85. Grand Rapids: Kregel, 2007.
Bates, Matthew W. *Gospel Allegiance: What Faith in Jesus Misses for Salvation in Christ.* Grand Rapids: Brazos, 2019.
———. *Salvation by Allegiance Alone: Rethinking Faith, Works, and the Gospel of Jesus the King.* Grand Rapids: Baker, 2017.
Bauckham, Richard. *The Bible in Politics: How to Read the Bible Politically.* 2nd ed. Louisville: Westminster John Knox, 2011.
———. *Jude–2 Peter.* Word Biblical Commentary 50. Nashville: Nelson, 1983.
———. "Judgment in the Book of Revelation." *Ex Auditu* 20 (2004) 1–24.
———. "The Parable of the Royal Wedding Feast (Matthew 22:1–14) and the Parable of the Lame Man and the Blind Man (*Apocryphon of Ezekiel*)." *Journal of Biblical Literature* 115 (1996) 471–88.
Baugh, S. M. "The Meaning of Foreknowledge." In *The Grace of God, The Bondage of the Will: Historical and Theological Perspectives on Calvinism*, vol. 1, edited by Thomas R. Schreiner and Bruce A. Ware, 183–200. Grand Rapids: Baker, 1995.
Beagley, Alan J. "Babylon." In *The Dictionary of the Later New Testament*, edited by Ralph P. Martin and Peter H. Davids, 111–12. Downers Grove: InterVarsity, 1997.
Beale, G. K. *The Book of Revelation.* New International Greek Testament Commentary. Grand Rapids: Eerdmans, 1999.
———. *The Temple and the Church's Mission: A Biblical Theology of the Dwelling Place of God.* New Studies in Biblical Theology. Downers Grove: InterVarsity, 2004.
———. *The Use of Daniel in Jewish Apocalyptic Literature and in the Revelation of St. John.* Reprint. Eugene, OR: Wipf and Stock, 2010.
Beasley-Murray, George R. *John.* Rev. ed. Word Biblical Commentary. Grand Rapids: Zondervan, 2015.
Beeke, Joel R. *Assurance of Faith: Calvin, English Puritanism, and the Dutch Second Reformation.* Rev. ed. American University Studies. New York: Lang, 1991.
———. *Debated Issues in Sovereign Predestination: Early Lutheran Predestination, Calvinian Reprobation, and Variations in Genevan Lapsarianism.* Reformed Historical Theology. Göttingen: Vandenhoeck & Ruprecht, 2017.
———. *The Quest for Full Assurance: The Legacy of Calvin and His Successors.* Carlisle, PA: Banner of Truth, 1999.
Begg, Christopher T. "Solomon's Apostasy (1 Kgs 11,1–13) according to Josephus." *Journal for the Study of Judaism* 28 (1997) 294–313.

Beisner, E. Calvin, ed. *The Auburn Avenue Theology: Pros & Cons, Debating the Federal Vision.* Fort Lauderdale, FL: Knox Theological Seminary, 2004.

Beker, J. Christiaan. *Paul the Apostle: The Triumph of God in Life and Thought.* Philadelphia: Fortress, 1980.

Bekken, Per Jarle. *The Word Is Near You: A Study of Deuteronomy 30:12-14 in Paul's Letter to the Romans in a Jewish Context.* Beihefte Zur Zeitschrift Fur Die Neutestamentliche Wissenschaft. Berlin: de Gruyter, 2007.

Belcher, Richard. *A Layman's Guide to the Lordship Controversy.* Southbridge, MA: Crowne, 1990.

Belyea, Gordon L. "Origins of the Particular Baptists." *Themelios* 32 (2007) 40-67.

Benson, Edward White. *Cyprian: His Life, His Times, His Work.* New York: Macmillan, 1897. Reprint, London: Wentworth, 2019.

Bercot, David W., ed. *A Dictionary of Early Christian Beliefs.* Peabody: Hendrickson, 1998.

Berkouwer, G. C. *Faith and Perseverance.* Studies in Dogmatics. Grand Rapids: Eerdmans, 1958.

Bernard, G. W. *The King's Reformation: Henry VIII and the Remaking of the English Church.* New Haven, CT: Yale University Press, 2007.

Berry, C. Everett. "How Can the Theological Construct of Inaugurated Eschatology Help Us in Forming a Biblical Understanding of Christian Sanctification?" *SBJT* Forum: "The Kingdom of God." *Southern Baptist Journal of Theology* 12 (2008) 109-11.

Berthelot, Katell. "The Notion of Anathema in Ancient Jewish Literature Written in Greek." In *The Reception of Septuagint Words in Jewish-Hellenistic and Christian Literature,* edited by Eberhard Boss et al., 35-52. Wissenschaftliche Untersuchungen Zum Neuen Testament, Reihe, 367. Tübingen: Mohr Siebeck, 2014.

Biguzzi, Giancarlo. "Is the Babylon of Revelation Rome or Jerusalem?" *Biblica* 87 (2006) 371-86.

Bird, Michael F. *The Gospel of the Lord: How the Early Church Wrote the Story of Jesus.* Grand Rapids: Eerdmans, 2014.

———. *Romans.* Story of God Bible Commentary. Grand Rapids: Zondervan, 2016.

———. *The Saving Righteousness of God: Studies on Paul, Justification, and the New Perspective.* Biblical Monographs. Reprint. Eugene, OR: Wipf and Stock, 2007.

Blackwell, Ben C. *Christosis: Engaging Paul's Soteriology with His Patristic Interpreters.* Grand Rapids: Eerdmans, 2016.

Blauvelt, Livingston, Jr. "Does the Bible Teach Lordship Salvation?" *Bibliotheca Sacra* 143 (1986) 37-45.

Block, Daniel L. *The Book of Ezekiel: Chapters 1-24.* New International Commentary on the Old Testament. Grand Rapids: Eerdmans, 1997.

———. *The Book of Ezekiel: Chapters 25-48.* New International Commentary on the Old Testament. Grand Rapids: Eerdmans, 1998.

Blomberg, Craig L. "Degrees of Reward in the Kingdom of Heaven." *Journal of the Evangelical Theological Society* 35 (1992) 159-72.

Blomberg, Craig L. and Mariam J. Kamell. *James.* Zondervan Exegetical Commentary on the New Testament. Grand Rapids: Zondervan, 2008.

Blount, Brian K. *Revelation: A Commentary.* New Testament Library. Louisville: Westminster John Knox, 2013.

Bock, Darrell L. *Luke 1:1–9:50*. Baker Exegetical Commentary on the New Testament. Grand Rapids: Baker, 1994.

———. *Luke 9:51–24:53*. Baker Exegetical Commentary on the New Testament. Grand Rapids: Baker, 1994.

———. "A Review of *The Gospel according to Jesus*." *Bibliotheca Sacra* 146 (1989) 21–40.

Boersma, Hans. *Scripture as Real Presence: Sacramental Exegesis in the Early Church*. Grand Rapids: Baker, 2017.

Boice, James Montgomery. *Christ's Call to Discipleship*. Chicago: Moody, 1986.

Bolster, George R. "Wesley's Doctrine of Justification." *Evangelical Quarterly* 24 (1952) 144–55.

Bolt, Peter. "What Fruit Does the Vine Bear: Some Pastoral Implications of John 15:1–8." *Reformed Theological Review* 51 (1992) 11–19.

Bonner, Ali. *The Myth of Pelagianism*. British Academy Monographs. Oxford: Oxford University Press, 2018.

Boughton, Lynne Courter. "Supralapsarianism and the Role of Metaphysics in 16th Century Reformed Theology." *Westminster Theological Journal* 48 (1986) 63–96.

Bray, Gerald. "Late-Medieval Theology." In *Reformation Theology: A Systematic Summary*, edited by Matthew Barrett, 67–110. Wheaton, IL: Crossway, 2017.

Bray, John S. *Theodore Beza's Doctrine of Predestination*. Bibliotheca Humanistica & Reformatorica. Leiden: Brill, 1975.

Bromley, David G. *Falling from the Faith: Causes and Consequences of Religious Apostasy*. Newbury Park, CA: SAGE Focus, 1988.

Brown, Basil S. "The Great Apostasy in the Teaching of Jesus." *Australian Biblical Review* 10 (1962) 14–20.

Brown, Peter. *Augustine of Hippo*. Berkeley: University of California Press, 1969.

Brown, Raymond E. *The Epistles of John*. Anchor Yale Bible Commentaries. New York: Doubleday, 1982.

Brown, Schuyler. *Apostasy and Perseverance in the Theology of Luke*. Analecta Biblica, 36. Rome: Pontifical Bible Institute, 1969.

———. "The Hour of Trial (Rev 3:10)." *Journal of Biblical Literature* 85 (1966) 308–14.

Bruce, F. F. *1 and 2 Thessalonians*. Word Biblical Commentary. Nashville: Nelson, 1984.

Bryan, Steven M. *Jesus and Israel's Traditions of Judgment and Restoration*. Society for New Testament Studies Monograph Series 117. Cambridge: Cambridge University Press, 2002.

Bumgardner, Charles. "Paul's Letters to Timothy and Titus: A Literature Review." *Southeastern Theological Review* 7 (2016) 77–116.

Busenitz, Irvin A. "The Sin unto Death." *Master's Seminary Journal* 1 (1990) 17–31.

Calvin, John. *The Institutes of the Christian Religion*. Edited by J. T. McNeill. Translated by Ford Lewis Battles. 2 vols. Library of Christian Classics. Philadelphia: Westminster, 1960.

Campbell, Douglas A. *The Deliverance of God: An Apocalyptic Reading of Justification in Paul*. Grand Rapids: Eerdmans, 2013.

Campbell, Ted A. *Christian Confessions: A Historical Introduction*. Louisville: Westminster John Knox, 1996.

Caragounis, Chrys C. "Vine, Vineyard, Israel, and Jesus." *Svensk exegetisk arsbok* 65 (2000) 201–14.

Carson, Don A. *Basics for Believers: An Exposition of Philippians*. Grand Rapids: Baker, 1996.

———. *The Gospel according to John*. Pillar New Testament Commentary. Grand Rapids: Eerdmans, 1990.

———. "Reflections on Assurance." In *The Grace of God, The Bondage of the Will: Historical and Theological Perspectives on Calvinism*, vol. 2, edited by Thomas R. Schreiner and Bruce A. Ware, 383–412. Grand Rapids: Baker, 1995.

———. "When Is Spirituality Spiritual? Reflections on Some Problems of Definition." *Journal of the Evangelical Society* 37 (1994) 381–94.

Carter, Craig A. *Interpreting Scripture with the Great Tradition: Recovering the Genius of Premodern Exegesis*. Grand Rapids: Baker, 2018.

Cary, Phillip. "The Lutheran Codicil: From Augustine's Grace to Luther's Gospel." *Logia* 20 (2011) 5–9.

Cavallin, Hans Clemens C. "The False Teachers of 2 Peter as Pseudo-Prophets." *Novum Testamentum* 21 (1979) 263–70.

Chafer, Lewis S. *He That Is Spiritual*. Dunham, OH: Dunham, 1918.

———. *Systematic Theology*. 8 vols. Dallas: Dallas Seminary Press, 1948.

Chamberlain, Ava. "The Theology of Cruelty: A New Look at the Rise of Arminianism in Eighteenth-Century New England." *Harvard Theological Review* 85 (1992) 335–56.

Chantry, Walter J. *Today's Gospel: Authentic or Synthetic?* Carlisle, PA: Banner of Truth, 1970.

Chapman, David W. *Ancient Jewish and Christian Perceptions of Crucifixion*. Grand Rapids: Baker, 2010.

Charmé, Stuart L. "Heretics, Infidels, and Apostates: Menace, Problem, or Symptom?" *Judaism* 36 (1987) 17–33.

Chisholm, Robert B., Jr. "'For this Reason': Etiology and Its Implications for the Historicity of Adam." *Criswell Theological Review* 10 (2013) 27–51.

Choi, P. Richard. "I Am the Vine: An Investigation of the Relations between John 15:1–6 and Some Parables of the Synoptic Gospels." *Biblical Research* 45 (2000) 51–75.

Ciampa, Roy E., and Brian S. Rosner. *The First Letter to the Corinthians*. Pillar New Testament Commentary. Grand Rapids: Eerdmans, 2010.

Ciocchi, David M. "Understanding Our Ability to Endure Temptation: A Theological Watershed." *Journal of the Evangelical Theological Society* 35 (1992) 463–79.

Claybrook, Frederick W., Jr. *Once Saved, Always Saved? A New Testament Study of Apostasy*. Lanham, MD: University Press of America, 2003.

Clement (of Alexandria). *The Stromata: Book VII*. In Ante-Nicene Fathers, vol. 2, translated and edited by Alexander Roberts and James Donaldson, 523–56. Christian Literature, 1885. Reprint, Peabody: Hendrickson, 1999.

———. *Who Is the Rich Man That Shall Be Saved?* In Ante-Nicene Fathers, vol. 2, translated by William Wilson, edited by Alexander Roberts and James Donaldson, 591–604. Christian Literature, 1885. Reprint, Peabody: Hendrickson, 1999.

Clement (of Rome). "1 Clement." In *The Apostolic Fathers*, edited and translated by Michael W. Holmes, 98–116. 3rd ed. Grand Rapids: Baker, 2007.

Clement. "2 Clement." In *The Apostolic Fathers*, edited and translated by Michael W. Holmes, 117–33. 3rd ed. Grand Rapids: Baker, 2007.

Clements, Ronald E. "'A Remnant Chosen by Grace' (Romans 11:5): The Old Testament Background and Origin of the Remnant Concept." In *Pauline Studies: Essays Presented to Professor F. F. Bruce on His 70th Birthday*, edited by Donald A. Hagner and Murray J. Harris, 106–21. Grand Rapids: Eerdmans, 1980.

Cocoris, G. Michael. *Lordship Salvation: Is It Biblical?* Denton, TX: Redencion Viva, 1983.

Collier, Jay T. *Debating Perseverance: The Augustinian Heritage in Post-Reformation England*. Oxford Studies in Historical Theology. Oxford: Oxford University Press, 2018.

Collins, Adela Yarbro. "The Function of 'Excommunication' in Paul." *Harvard Theological Review* 73 (1980) 251–63.

Collins, Kenneth J. "The Influence of Early German Pietism on John Wesley." *Covenant Quarterly* 48 (1990) 23–42.

———. *John Wesley: A Theological Journey*. Nashville: Abingdon, 2003.

———. *The Theology of John Wesley: Holy Love and the Shape of Grace*. Nashville: Abingdon, 2007.

———. *Wesley on Salvation: A Study in the Standard Sermons*. Grand Rapids: Zondervan, 1989.

Compton, R. Bruce. "Persevering and Falling Away: A Reexamination of Hebrews 6:4–6." *Detroit Baptist Seminary Journal* 1 (1996) 135–67.

Cook, Robert R. "Apostasy: Some Logical Reflections." *Evangelical Quarterly* 65 (1993) 147–53.

Cowan, Christopher W. "The Warning Passages of Hebrews and the New Covenant Community." In *Progressive Covenantalism: Charting a Course between Dispensational and Covenant Theologies*, edited by Stephen J. Wellum and Brent E Parker, 189–213. Nashville: B & H Academic, 2016.

Cox, Leo G. "The 'Straw' in the Believer: 1 Corinthians 3:12." *Wesleyan Theological Journal* 12 (1977) 34–38.

Coxhead, Steven R. "Deuteronomy 30:11–14 as a Prophecy of the New Covenant." *Westminster Theological Journal* 68 (2006) 305–20.

Craig, William Lane. "'Lest Anyone Should Fall': A Middle Knowledge Perspective on Perseverance and Apostolic Warnings." *International Journal for Philosophy of Religion* 29 (1991) 65–74.

Crisp, Oliver D. "The Election of Jesus Christ." *Journal of Reformed Theology* 2 (2008) 131–50.

Crouteau, David. "Repentance Found? The Concept of Repentance in the Fourth Gospel." *Master's Seminary Journal* 24 (2013) 97–123.

Crowe, Brandon D. *The Last Adam: A Theology of the Obedient Life of Jesus in the Gospels*. Grand Rapids: Baker, 2017.

Cullman, Oscar. *Christ and Time: The Primitive Christian Conception of Time and History*. Rev. ed. Louisville: Westminster John Knox, 1964.

Cyprian (of Carthage). *Exhortation to Martyrdom, Addressed to Fortunatus*. In Ante-Nicene Fathers, vol. 5, translated by Earnest Wallis, edited by Alexander Roberts and James Donaldson, 496–507. Christian Literature, 1886. Reprint, Peabody: Hendrickson, 1999.

———. *On the Advantage of Patience*. In Ante-Nicene Fathers, vol. 5, translated by Earnest Wallis, edited by Alexander Roberts and James Donaldson, 484–91. Christian Literature, 1886. Reprint, Peabody: Hendrickson, 1999.

———. *On the Unity of the Church*. In Ante-Nicene Fathers, vol. 5, translated by Earnest Wallis, edited by Alexander Roberts and James Donaldson, 421–29. Christian Literature, 1886. Reprint, Peabody: Hendrickson, 1999.

———. *On Works and Alms*. In Ante-Nicene Fathers, vol. 5, translated by Earnest Wallis, edited by Alexander Roberts and James Donaldson, 476–84. Christian Literature, 1886. Reprint, Peabody: Hendrickson, 1999.

———. *To Fidus, On the Baptism of Infants*. In Ante-Nicene Fathers, vol. 5, translated by Earnest Wallis, edited by Alexander Roberts and James Donaldson, 353–54. Christian Literature, 1886. Reprint, Peabody: Hendrickson, 1999.

———. *To Florentius Pupianus on Calumniators*. In Ante-Nicene Fathers, vol. 5, translated by Earnest Wallis, edited by Alexander Roberts and James Donaldson, 421–29. Christian Literature, 1886. Reprint, Peabody: Hendrickson, 1999.

———. *To Jubaianus, Concerning the Baptism of Heretics*. In Ante-Nicene Fathers, vol. 5, translated by Earnest Wallis, edited by Alexander Roberts and James Donaldson, 379–86. Christian Literature, 1886. Reprint, Peabody: Hendrickson, 1999.

———. *To Magnus, On Baptizing the Novatians and Those Who Obtain Grace on the Sick-Bed*. In Ante-Nicene Fathers, vol. 5, translated by Earnest Wallis, edited by Alexander Roberts and James Donaldson, 397–402. Christian Literature, 1886. Reprint, Peabody: Hendrickson, 1999.

———. *To Pompey, Against the Epistle of Stephen about the Baptism of Heretics*. In Ante-Nicene Fathers, vol. 5, translated by Earnest Wallis, edited by Alexander Roberts and James Donaldson, 386–90. Christian Literature, 1886. Reprint, Peabody: Hendrickson, 1999.

———. *To Rogatianus the Presbyter, and the Other Confessors*. In Ante-Nicene Fathers, vol. 5, translated by Earnest Wallis, edited by Alexander Roberts and James Donaldson, 283–85. Christian Literature, 1886. Reprint, Peabody: Hendrickson, 1999.

———. *To the Presbyters and Deacons*. In Ante-Nicene Fathers, vol. 5, translated by Earnest Wallis, edited by Alexander Roberts and James Donaldson, 282–83. Christian Literature, 1886. Reprint, Peabody: Hendrickson, 1999.

Davids, Peter H. *The Epistle of James*. New International Greek Testament Commentary. Grand Rapids: Eerdmans, 2013.

Davies, W. D., and D. C. Allison. *Matthew 8–18*. International Critical Commentary 2. Paperback ed. New York: T. & T. Clark, 2004.

Davis, George, Jr. "Sin unto Death: Some Observations on 1 John 5:16." In *The Church at the Dawn of the 21st Century*, edited by John Pretlove et al., 251–65. Dallas: Criswell, 1989.

Davis, John Jefferson. "The Perseverance of the Saints: A History of the Doctrine." *Journal of the Evangelical Theological Society* 34 (1991) 213–28.

Davis, Kenneth Ronald. *Anabaptism and Asceticism*. Studies in Anabaptist and Mennonite History. Harrisonburg, VA: Herald, 1974.

Day, Alan. "The Lordship Salvation Controversy." *Theological Educator* 45 (1992) 23–29.

Deenick, Karl. *Righteous by Promise: A Biblical Theology of Circumcision*. New Studies in Biblical Theology. Downers Grove: InterVarsity, 2018.

DeJong, Peter Y. *Crisis in the Reformed Churches: Essays in Commemoration of the Great Synod of Dort*. Grand Rapids: Reformed Fellowship, 2008.

Demarest, Bruce. *The Cross and Salvation: The Doctrine of Salvation*. Foundations of Evangelical Theology. Wheaton, IL: Crossway, 2006.

Dempsey, Carol J. "Revelation 21:1–8." *Interpretation* 65 (2011) 400–402.

Dempster, Stephen G. *Dominion and Dynasty: A Theology of the Hebrew Bible*. New Studies in Biblical Theology. Downers Grove: InterVarsity, 2003.

Denton, D. R. "Hop and Perseverance." *Scottish Theological Journal* 34 (1981) 313–20.
Derrett, J. Duncan M. "Simon Magus (Acts 8:9–24)." *Zeitschrift für die neutestamentliche Wissenschaft und die Kunde der älteren Kirche* 73 (1982) 52–68.
DeSilva, David A. "Exchanging Favor for Wrath: Apostasy in Hebrews and Patron-Client Relationships." *Journal of Biblical Literature* 115 (1996) 91–116.
———. *Perseverance in Gratitude: A Socio-Rhetorical Commentary on the Epistle to the Hebrews*. Grand Rapids; Eerdmans, 2000.
Dickens, A. G. *The English Reformation*. 2nd ed. Reprint. University Park: Pennsylvania State University Press, 1993.
Dillow, Joseph. "Abiding Is Remaining in Fellowship: Another Look at John 15:1–6." *Bibliotheca Sacra* 147 (1990) 44–53.
———. *The Reign of the Servant Kings: A Study of Eternal Security and the Final Significance of Man*. 3rd ed. Haysville, NC: Schoettle, 2002.
Docherty, Susan E. *The Use of the Old Testament in Hebrews: A Case Study in Early Jewish Bible Interpretation*. Wissenschaftliche Untersuchungen zum Neuen Testament 2, Reihe. Tübingen: Mohr Siebeck, 2009.
Donfried, Karl P. "Justification and Last Judgment in Paul." *Interpretation* 30 (1976) 140–52.
Duffy, Eamon. *Reformation Divided: Catholics, Protestants, and the Conversion of England*. New York: Bloomsbury Continuum, 2017.
Dulk, Matthijs den. "The Promises to the Conquerors in the Book of Revelation." *Biblica* 87 (2006) 516–22.
Dunbar, David. "The Problem of Hippolytus of Rome: A Study in Historical-Critical Reconstruction." *Journal of the Evangelical Theological Society* 25 (1982) 63–74.
Dunn, James D. G. *Neither Jew Nor Greek: A Contested Identity*. Christianity in the Making 3. Grand Rapids: Eerdmans, 2015.
———. "Response to Robert N. Wilkin." In *The Role of Works at the Final Judgment*, edited by Alan P. Stanley, 57–62. Grand Rapids: Zondervan, 2013.
———. *Romans 1–8*. World Biblical Commentary. Nashville: Nelson, 1988.
———. *Romans 9–16*. World Biblical Commentary. Nashville: Nelson, 1988.
———. *The Theology of Paul the Apostle*. Grand Rapids: Eerdmans, 1998.
———. *Unity and Diversity in the New Testament: An Inquiry into the Character of Earliest Christianity*. Philadelphia: Westminster, 1977.
Dunnett, Walter M. "The Hermeneutics of Jude and 2 Peter: The Use of Ancient Jewish Traditions." *Journal of the Evangelical Theological Society* 31 (1988) 287–92.
Durnbaugh, Donald F. "Membership in the Body of Christ as Interpreted by the Radical Reformation." *Brethren Life and Thought* 9 (1964) 50–62.
Dykstra, William. "1 Corinthians 15:20–28: An Essential Part of Paul's Argument Against Those Who Deny the Resurrection." *Calvin Theological Journal* 4 (1969) 195–211.
Eaton, Michael. *No Condemnation: A Theology of Assurance of Salvation*. Downers Grove: InterVarsity, 1997.
Edgar, Thomas R. "The Meaning of 'Sleep' in 1 Thessalonians 5:10." *Journal of the Evangelical Theological Society* 22 (1979) 345–49.
Ellingworth, Paul. *The Epistle to the Hebrews*. New International Greek Testament Commentary. Grand Rapids: Eerdmans, 1993.
Elliot, J. Keith. "Is Post-Baptismal Sin Forgivable?" *Bible Translator* 28 (1977) 330–32.

Enns, Peter. "Inerrancy, However Defined, Does Not Describe What the Bible Does." In *Five Views on Biblical Inerrancy*, edited by J. Merrick et al., 83–116. Counterpoints. Grand Rapids: Zondervan, 2013.

———. *Inspiration and Incarnation: Evangelicals and the Problem of the Old Testament*. 2nd ed. Grand Rapids: Baker, 2015.

Erickson, Millard J. "Lordship Theology: The Current Controversy." *Southwestern Journal of Theology* 33 (1991) 5–15.

Estep, William R. *The Anabaptist Story: An Introduction to Sixteenth-Century Anabaptism*. Grand Rapids: Eerdmans, 1996.

Evans, Craig A. "How Are the Apostles Judged: A Note on 1 Corinthians 3:10–15." *Journal of the Evangelical Theological Society* 27 (1984) 149–50.

Evans, Robert F. *Pelagius: Inquiries and Reappraisals*. Seabury, 1968. Reprint, Eugene, OR: Wipf and Stock, 2010.

Eybers, Ian H. "Aspects of the Background of the Letter of Jude." *Neotestamentica* 9 (1975) 113–23.

Fairbairn, Donald, and Ryan M. Reeves. *The Story of the Creeds and Confessions: Tracing the Development of the Christian Faith*. Grand Rapids: Baker, 2019.

Fanning, Buist M. "A Classical Reformed View." In *Four Views on the Warning Passages in Hebrews*, edited by Herbert W. Bateman IV, 172–219. Grand Rapids: Kregel, 2007.

Fee, Gordon D. *1 and 2 Timothy, Titus*. New International Biblical Commentary. Peabody: Hendrickson, 2000.

———. *Church History*. Vol. 1, *From Christ to Pre-Reformation*. Grand Rapids: Zondervan, 2005.

———. *The First and Second Letters to the Thessalonians*. The New International Commentary on the New Testament. Grand Rapids: Eerdmans, 2009.

———. *The First Epistle to the Corinthians*. The New International Commentary on the New Testament. Grand Rapids: Eerdmans, 1987.

———. *Revelation*. New Covenant Commentary Series. Eugene, OR: Cascade, 2011.

Ferguson, Everett. *Baptism in the Early Church: History, Theology, and Liturgy in the First Five Centuries*. Grand Rapids: Eerdmans, 2013.

———. *The Rule of Faith: A Guide*. Cascade Companions. Eugene, OR: Wipf and Stock, 2015.

Ferguson, John. *The Religions of the Roman Empire*. Ithaca, NY: Cornell University Press, 1970.

Ferreiro, Alberto. *Simon Magus in Patristic, Medieval and Early Modern Traditions*. Studies in the History of Christian Traditions. Leiden: Brill, 2005.

Fesko, J. V. *Death in Adam, Life in Christ: The Doctrine of Imputation*. Reformed Exegetical Doctrinal Studies Series. Great Britain: Mentor, 2016.

———. *Diversity within the Reformed Tradition: Supra- and Infralapsarianism in Calvin, Dort, and Westminster*. Greenville, SC: Reformed Academic, 2001.

———. "Union with Christ." In *Reformation Theology: A Systematic Summary*, edited by J. Matthew Barrett, 423–50. Wheaton, IL: Crossway, 2002.

Finger, Thomas N. *A Contemporary Anabaptist Theology: Biblical, Historical, Constructive*. Downers Grove: InterVarsity, 2004.

Fitzmyer, Joseph A. *The Letter to Philemon*. Anchor Yale Bible Commentaries. New Haven, CT: Yale University Press, 2000.

Forlines, F. Leroy. *Classical Arminianism: A Theology of Salvation*. Nashville: Randall House, 2011.
Foster, Douglas A., et al., eds. *The Encyclopedia of the Stone-Campbell Movement*. Grand Rapids: Eerdmans, 2004.
Foster, Paul. "Who Wrote 2 Thessalonians? A Fresh Look at an Old Problem." *Journal for the Study of the New Testament* 35 (2012) 150–75.
France, R. T. *The Gospel of Matthew*. New International Critical Commentary on the New Testament. Grand Rapids: Eerdmans, 2007.
Friesen, Steven J. *Imperial Cults and the Apocalypse of John: Reading Revelation in the Ruins*. New York: Oxford University Press, 2001.
Fung, Ronald Y. K. "Curse, Cursed, Anathema." In the *Dictionary of Paul and His Letters*, edited by Gerald F. Hawthorne et al., 199–200. Downers Grove: InterVarsity, 1993.
Gadenz, Pablo T. *Called from the Jews and from the Gentiles: Pauline Ecclesiology in Romans 9–11*. Wissenschaftliche Untersuchungen Zum Neuen Testament 2, Reihe, 267. Tübingen: Mohr Siebeck, 2009.
Gamble, Harry Y. *Books and Readers in the Early Church: A History of Early Christian Texts*. New Haven, CT: Yale University Press, 1995.
Gardner, Paul Douglas. *The Gifts of God and the Authentication of a Christian: An Exegetical Study of 1 Corinthians 8—11:1*. New York: University Press of America, 1994.
Garlington, Don. *Faith, Obedience, and Perseverance: Aspects of Paul's Letter to the Romans*. Tübingen: Mohr Siebeck, 1994. Reprint, Eugene, OR: Wipf and Stock, 2009.
Gaston, Lloyd. "Beelzebub." *Theologische Zeitschrift* 18 (1962) 247–55.
Geisler, Norman. "A Moderate Calvinist View." In *Four Views on Eternal Security*, edited by J. Matthew Pinson, 63–112. Grand Rapids: Zondervan, 2002.
Genke, Victor, and Francis X. Gumerlock, eds. and trans. *Gottschalk & a Medieval Predestination Controversy*. Medieval Philosophical Texts in Translation. Milwaukee: Marquette University Press, 2010.
Gentry, Kenneth L., Jr. *Lord of the Saved: Getting to the Heart of the Lordship Debate*. Philipsburg, NJ: P & R, 1992.
Gentry, Peter J., and Stephen J. Wellum. *Kingdom through Covenant: A Biblical-Theological Understanding of the Covenants*. 2nd ed. Wheaton, IL: Crossway, 2018.
George, Timothy. *Theology of the Reformers*. Rev. ed. Nashville: Broadman & Holman, 2013.
Gillis, Matthew Bryan. *Heresy and Dissent in the Carolingian Empire: The Case of Gottschallk of Orbais*. Oxford: Oxford University Press, 2017.
Glancy, Jennifer A., and Stephen D. Moore. "How Typical a Roman Prostitute Is Revelation's 'Great Whore'?" *Journal of Biblical Literature* 130 (2011) 551–69.
Gleason, Randall. "B. B. Warfield and Lewis S. Chafer on Sanctification." *Journal of the Evangelical Theological Society* 40 (1997) 241–56.
———. "The Lordship Salvation Debate." *Evangelical Review of Theology* 27 (2003) 55–72.
———. "The Old Testament Background of the Warning in Hebrews 6:4–8." *Bibliotheca Sacra* 155 (1998) 62–91.
Goldsworthy, Graeme L. "Regeneration." In the *New Dictionary of Biblical Theology*, edited by T. Desmond Alexander et al., 716–20. Downers Grove: InterVarsity, 2000.

Gootjes, Nicholas H. *The Belgic Confession: Its History and Sources*. Grand Rapids: Baker, 2007.

Gorman, Michael J. *Cruciformity: Paul's Narrative Spirituality of the Cross*. Grand Rapids: Eerdmans, 2001.

———. *Inhabiting the Cruciform God: Kenosis, Justification, and Theosis in Paul's Narrative Soteriology*. Grand Rapid: Eerdmans, 2009.

Goudriaan, Aza, and Fred Lieburg, eds. *Revisiting the Synod of Dort (1618–1619)*. Brill's Series in Church History 49. Leiden: Brill, 2010.

Green, Bradley G. "Augustine." In *Shapers of Christian Orthodoxy*, edited by Bradley G. Green, 235–92. Downers Grove: InterVarsity, 2010.

Green, Gene L. *The Letters to the Thessalonians*. Pillar New Testament Commentary. Grand Rapids; Eerdmans, 2002.

Green, Joel B. *Practicing Theological Interpretation: Engaging Biblical Texts for Faith and Formation*. Grand Rapids: Baker, 2012.

Greenman, Jeffrey P., and Timothy Larsen, eds. *Reading Romans through the Centuries: From the Early Church to Karl Barth*. Grand Rapids: Brazos, 2005.

Grisanti, Michael A. "The Davidic Covenant." *Masters Seminary Journal* 10 (1999) 233–50.

Grislis, Egil. "Calvin's Doctrine of Baptism." *Church History* 31 (1962) 46–65.

Gumerlock, Francis X. "Predestination in the Century before Gottschalk: Part 1." *Evangelical Quarterly* 81 (2009) 195–209.

———. "Predestination in the Century before Gottschalk: Part 2." *Evangelical Quarterly* 81 (2009) 319–37.

Gundry Volf, Judith M. "Apostasy, Falling Away, Perseverance." In *Dictionary of Paul and His Letters*, edited by Gerald F. Hawthorne et al., 39–45. Downers Grove: InterVarsity, 1993.

———. *Paul and Perseverance: Staying In and Falling Away*. Louisville: Westminster John Knox, 1991.

Gundry, Robert. "Grace, Works, and Staying Saved in Paul." *Biblica* 66 (1985) 1–38.

Guthrie, Donald. *New Testament Introduction*. Rev. ed. Master Reference Collection. Downers Grove: InterVarsity, 1990.

Hadaway, C. Kirk. "Five Types of Apostates." *Urban Mission* 9 (1992) 26–34.

Hagner, Donald A. *Hebrews*. New International Biblical Commentary. Peabody: Hendrickson, 1990.

———. *Matthew 1–13*. Rev. ed. Word Biblical Commentary. Grand Rapids: Zondervan, 2015.

Hahn, Scott W. *Romans*. Catholic Commentary on Sacred Scripture. Grand Rapids: Baker, 2017.

Hall, Stuart G. *Doctrine and Practice in the Early Church*. Grand Rapids: Eerdmans, 1992.

Hamilton, James M., Jr. *God's Indwelling Presence: The Holy Spirit in the Old and New Testaments*. NAC Studies in Bible and Theology. Nashville: B & H Academic, 2006.

Hannah, John D. "The Early Years of Lewis Sperry Chafer." *Bibliotheca Sacra* 144 (1987) 3–23.

———. "The Meaning of Saving Faith: Luther's Interpretation of Romans 3:28." *Bibliotheca Sacra* 140 (1983) 322–34.

Harper, J. Steven. "A Wesleyan Arminian View." In *Four Views on Eternal Security*, edited by J. Matthew Pinson, 209–55. Grand Rapids: Zondervan, 2002.

Harrington, Susan F. "Friendship Under Fire: George Whitefield and John Wesley, 1739–1741." *Andover Newton Quarterly* 15 (1975) 167–81.
Harris, Murray J. *Colossians and Philemon*. Exegetical Guide to the Greek New Testament. Grand Rapids: Eerdmans, 1991.
———. *The Second Epistle to the Corinthians*. New International Greek Testament Commentary. Grand Rapids: Eerdmans, 2013.
Harrison, Everett F. "Must Christ Be Lord to Be Savior? No!" *Eternity* 10 (1959) 14–18, 36–37, 48.
Harrison, R. K. "Vine." In *The International Standard Bible Encyclopedia*, edited by Geoffrey W. Bromiley et al., 986. Grand Rapid: Eerdmans, 1979–88.
Harper, Brad, and Paul Louis Metzger. *Exploring Ecclesiology: An Evangelical and Ecumenical Introduction*. Grand Rapids: Brazos, 2009.
Hart, D. G. *Calvinism: A History*. New Haven, CT: Yale University Press, 2013.
Harvey, John D. *Romans*. Exegetical Guide to the Greek New Testament. Nashville: B & H Academic, 2017.
Hasel, Gerhard F. *The Remnant: The History and Theology of the Remnant Idea from Genesis to Isaiah*. 3rd ed. Berrien Springs, MI: Andrews University Press, 1980.
Hawthorne, Gerald F. "Letter to the Philippians." In *The Dictionary of Paul and His Letters*, edited by Gerald F. Hawthorne et al., 707–13. Downers Grove: InterVarsity, 1993.
Hays, Richard B. *First Corinthians*. Interpretation. Louisville: Westminster John Knox, 2011.
Hays, Richard B., and Stefan Alkier, eds. *Revelation and the Politics of Apocalyptic Interpretation*. Waco, TX: Baylor University Press, 2012.
Heckle, Matthew C. "Is R. C. Sproul Wrong about Martin Luther? An Analysis of R. C. Sproul's *Faith Alone: The Evangelical Doctrine of Justification* with Respect to Augustine, Luther, Calvin, and Catholic Luther Scholarship." *Journal of the Evangelical Theological Society* 47 (2004) 89–120.
Hedrick, Pamela. "Fewer Answers and Further Questions: Jews and Gentiles in Acts." *Interpretation* 66 (2012) 294–305.
Heiser, Michael S. "Monotheism, Polytheism, Monoatry, or Henotheism? Toward an Assessment of Divine Plurality in the Hebrew Bible." *Bulletin for Biblical Research* 18 (2008) 1–30.
———. *The Unseen Realm: Recovering the Supernatural Worldview of the Bible*. Bellingham, WA: Lexham, 2015.
Helm, Paul. "Preserving Perseverance." *International Journal for Philosophy of Religion* 33 (1993) 103–9.
Henžel, Ján. "When Conversion Is Joy and Death Victory: Historical Foundations of the Doctrine of Perseverance." *Tyndale Bulletin* 54 (2003) 123–48.
Hermas. "The Shepherd of Hermas." In *The Apostolic Fathers*, edited and translated by Michael W. Holmes, 134–58. 3rd ed. Grand Rapids: Baker, 2007.
Herms, Ronald. "'Being Saved without Honor': A Conceptual Link Between 1 Corinthians 3 and 1 Enoch 50?" *Journal for the Study of the New Testament* 29 (2006) 187–210.
Hiebert, D. Edmond. "A Portrayal of False Teachers: An Exposition of 2 Peter 2:1–3." *Bibliotheca Sacra* 141 (1984) 255–65.
Hiestand, Gerald. "Augustine and the Justification Debates: Appropriating Augustine's Doctrine of Culpability." *Trinity Journal* 28 (2007) 115–39.

Hildebrandt, Wilf. *An Old Testament Theology of the Spirit of God*. Peabody: Hendrickson, 1995.
Hill, Craig Allen. "The Use of Perfection Language in Hebrews 5:14 and 6:1 and the Contextual Interpretation of 5:11–6:3." *Journal of the Evangelical Theological Society* 57 (2014) 727–42.
Hillyer, Norman. *1 and 2 Peter, Jude*. New International Biblical Commentary 16. Peabody: Hendrickson, 2002.
Hodges, Zane C. *Absolutely Free: A Biblical Reply to Lordship Salvation*. Grand Rapid: Zondervan, 1989.
———. *Grace in Eclipse: A Study on Eternal Rewards*. Denton, TX: Redencion Viva, 1985.
———. *The Gospel Under Siege: A Study on Faith and Works*. Dallas: Redencion Viva, 1981.
Hodges, Zane, and Robert N. Wilkin. *What Is the Outer Darkness?* Denton, TX: Grace Evangelical Society, 2016.
Hoehner, Harold W. *Ephesians: An Exegetical Commentary*. Grand Rapids: Baker, 2002.
Hoekema, Anthony A. *The Bible and the Future*. Grand Rapids: Eerdmans, 1979.
———. *Saved by Grace*. Grand Rapids: Eerdmans 1989.
Holmes, Michael W. Introduction to *The Apostolic Fathers*, edited and translated by Michael W. Holmes, 3–19. 3rd ed. Grand Rapids: Baker, 2007.
Horton, Michael. "A Classical Calvinist View." In *Four Views on Eternal Security*, edited by J. Matthew Pinson, 23–42. Grand Rapids: Zondervan, 2002.
Horton, Michael, ed. *Christ the Lord: The Reformation and Lordship Salvation*. Grand Rapids: Baker, 1992.
———. *Justification*. 2 vols. New Studies in Dogmatics. Grand Rapids: Zondervan, 2018.
Howard-Brook, Wes, and Anthony Gwyther. *Unveiling Empire: Reading Revelation Then and Now*. Bible & Liberation. Maryknoll: Orbis, 1999.
Hughes, Philip E. *A Commentary on the Epistle to the Hebrews*. Grand Rapids: Eerdmans, 1987.
———. "Hebrews 6:4–6 and the Peril of Apostasy." *Westminster Theological Journal* 35 (1973) 137–55.
Hurst, L. D. *The Epistle to the Hebrews: Its Background of Thought*. Society for New Testament Studies Monograph Series. Cambridge: Cambridge University Press, 1990.
Ignatius (of Antioch). "The Letters of Ignatius." In *The Apostolic Fathers*, edited and translated by Michael W. Holmes, 53–71. 3rd ed. Grand Rapids: Baker, 2007.
Irenaeus (of Lyons). *Against Heresies*. In Ante-Nicene Fathers, vol. 1, translated and edited by Alexander Roberts and James Donaldson, 315–567. Christian Literature, 1885. Reprint, Peabody: Hendrickson, 1999.
Jefford, Clayton N. *Reading the Apostolic Fathers: An Introduction*. Grand Rapids: Baker, 1996.
Jessop, Harry Edward. *That Burning Question of Final Perseverance*. Winona Lake, IN: Light and Life, 1942.
Jobes, Karen H. *1 Peter*. Baker Exegetical Commentary on the New Testament. Grand Rapids: Baker, 2005.
Johnson, Clinton A., Jr. "Paul's 'Anti-Christology' in 2 Thessalonians 2:3–12 in Canonical Context." *Journal of Theological Interpretation* 8 (2014) 125–43.

Johnson, Luke Timothy. *The Letter of James*. Anchor Yale Commentaries. New York: Doubleday, 1995.

Johnson, Maxwell E. *The Rites of Christian Initiation: Their Evolution and Interpretation*. Rev. ed. Collegeville, MN: Pueblo, 2007.

Johnson, S. Lewis. "How Faith Works." *Christianity Today* 33 (1989) 21–25.

Keathley, Ken. "Does Anyone Really Know If They Are Saved? A Survey of the Current Views on Assurance with a Modest Proposal." *Journal of the Grace Evangelical Society* (2002) 37–59.

Keefer, Luke L. "Arminian Motifs in Anabaptist Heritage." *Brethren in Christ: History and Life* 13 (1993) 292–323.

Keener, Craig S. *The Gospel of John: Commentary*. 2 vols. Grand Rapids: Baker, 2010.

Kendell, R. T. *Once Saved, Always Saved*. Chicago: Moody, 1985.

Kim, Johann D. *God, Israel, and the Gentiles: Rhetoric and Situation in Romans 9–11*. SBL Dissertation Series 176. Atlanta: Society of Biblical Literature, 2000.

King, Martha. *An Exegetical Summary of Colossians*. 2nd ed. Dallas: SIL International, 2008.

Kingsbury, Jack Dean. *The Parables of Jesus in Matthew 13: A Study in Redaction Criticism*. Louisville: Westminster John Knox, 1969.

Kirk, J. R. Daniel. *Unlocking Romans: Resurrection and the Justification of God*. Grand Rapids: Eerdmans, 2008.

Kitchens, Kenneth A., and Paul J. N. Lawrence, eds. *Treaty, Law, and Covenant in the Ancient Near East*. 3 vols. Wiesbaden, Germany: Harrassowitz Verlag, 2012.

Knapp, Henry. "Augustine and Owen on Perseverance." *Westminster Theological Journal* 62 (2000) 65–87.

Knight, George W., III. *The Faithful Sayings in the Pastoral Letters*. Baker Biblical Monograph. Grand Rapids: Baker, 1979.

———. *The Pastoral Epistles*. New International Greek Testament Commentary. Grand Rapids: Eerdmans, 1992.

Koop, Karl. *Anabaptist-Mennonite Confessions of Faith: The Development of a Tradition*. Anabaptist and Mennonite Studies 3. Kitchener, ON: Pandora, 2004.

———. *Confessions of Faith in the Anabaptist Tradition, 1527–1660*. Classics of the Radical Reformation 11. Kitchener, ON: Pandora, 2006.

Köstenberger, Andreas. "John." In the *Commentary on the New Testament Use of the Old Testament*, edited by G. K. Beale and D. A. Carson, 415–522. Grand Rapids: Baker, 2007.

Kovalishyn, Mariam Kamell. "Endurance unto Salvation: The Witness of First Peter and James." *Word & World* 35 (2015) 231–40.

Krahn, Cornelius. *Dutch Anabaptism: Origin, Spread, Life, and Thought*. 2nd ed. Harrisonburg, VA: Herald, 1981.

Kreitzer, Larry J. "Eschatology." In the *Dictionary of Paul and His Letters*, edited by Gerald F. Hawthorne et al., 253–69. Downers Grove: InterVarsity, 1993.

Kruse, Colin G. *The Letters of John*. Pillar New Testament Commentary. Grand Rapids: Eerdmans, 2000.

Kubo, Sakae. "1 John 3:9: Absolute or Habitual?" *Andrews University Seminary Studies* 7 (1969) 47–56.

Laato, Timo. "Justification according to James: A Comparison with Paul." *Trinity Journal* 18 (1997) 43–84.

Ladd, George E. *A Theology of the New Testament*. Rev. ed. Grand Rapids: Eerdmans, 1993.

———. *The Presence of the Future: The Eschatology of Biblical Realism*. Rev. ed. Reprint. Grand Rapids: Eerdmans, 2000.

Lake, Donald M. "Jacob Arminius' Contribution to a Theology of Grace." In *Grace Unlimited*, edited by Clark H. Pinnock, 223–42. Minneapolis: Bethany Fellowship, 1975.

Lamberigts, Mathijs. "Predestination." In *Augustine through the Ages: An Encyclopedia*, edited by Allan D. Fitzgerald, 707–13. Grand Rapids: Eerdmans, 1999.

Lambert, David A. *How Repentance Became Biblical: Judaism, Christianity, and the Interpretation of Scripture*. Oxford: Oxford University Press, 2017.

Larkin, William J., Jr. *Acts*. IVP New Testament Commentary. Downers Grove: InterVarsity, 2011.

Levenson, Jon D. *Resurrection and the Restoration of Israel: The Ultimate Victory of the God of Life*. New Haven, CT: Yale University Press, 2006.

Lewellen, Thomas G. "Has Lordship Salvation Been Taught throughout Church History?" *Bibliotheca Sacra* 145 (1990) 54–68.

Leyser, Conrad. "Semi-Pelagianism." In *Augustine through the Ages: An Encyclopedia*, edited by Allan D. Fitzgerald, 761–66. Grand Rapids: Eerdmans, 1999.

Lints, Richard. *The Fabric of Theology: A Prolegomenon to Evangelical Theology*. Grand Rapids: Eerdmans, 1993.

———. *Identity and Idolatry*. New Studies in Biblical Theology. Downers Grove: InterVarsity, 2015.

Litfin, A. Duane. "Revisiting the Unpardonable Sin: Insight from an Unexpected Source." *Journal of the Evangelical Theological Society* 60 (2017) 713–32.

Llewelyn, S. R. "The Prescript in James." *Novum Testamentum* 39 (1997) 385–93.

Longenecker, Bruce W. "Different Answers to Different Issues: Israel, the Gentiles, and Salvation History in Romans 9–11." *Journal for the Study of the New Testament* 11 (1989) 95–123.

Longenecker, Richard N. *The Epistle to the Romans*. New International Greek Testament Commentary. Grand Rapids: Eerdmans, 2016.

———. *Galatians*. Word Biblical Commentary. Reprint. Grand Rapids: Zondervan, 2015.

———. *Introducing Romans: Critical Issues in Paul's Most Famous Letter*. Grand Rapids: Eerdmans, 2011.

López, René. "Does the Vice List in 1 Corinthians 6:9–10 Describe Believers or Unbelievers?" *Bibliotheca Sacra* 164 (2007) 59–73.

Lumpkin, W. L. *Baptist Confessions of Faith*. Rev. ed. Valley Forge, PA: Judson, 1969.

Luomanen, Petri. *Entering the Kingdom of Heaven: A Study on the Structure of Matthew's View of Salvation*. Tübingen: Mohr, 1998.

Luther, Martin. *The Bondage of the Will*. Translated by J. I. Packer and O. R. Johnson. 1st ed. Reprint. Grand Rapids: Revell, 1990.

———. *Commentary on Galatians*. Modern English ed. Paperback ed. Reprint. Grand Rapids: Revell, 1998.

———. *Commentary on the Epistle to the Romans*. Translated by J. Theodore Mueller. Grand Rapids: Zondervan, 1954.

———. "Concerning Rebaptism." In *Martin Luther's Basic Theological Writings*, edited by Timothy F. Lull, 239–58. 2nd ed. Minneapolis: Fortress, 2005.

———. *Larger Catechism*. Translated by Robert H. Fischer. Philadelphia: Fortress, 1959.

———. "Preface to the Epistle of St. Paul to the Romans (1522, revised 1546)." In *Martin Luther's Basic Theological Writings*, edited by Timothy F. Lull, 98–107. 2nd ed. Minneapolis: Fortress, 2005.

———. "Two Kinds of Righteousness (1519)." In *Martin Luther's Basic Theological Writings*, edited by Timothy F. Lull, 134–40. 2nd ed. Minneapolis: Fortress, 2005.

———. *What Luther Says: An Anthology*. Edited by Ewald M. Plass. 3 vols. St. Louis: Concordia, 1959.

———. *The Works of Martin Luther*. Edited by Jaroslav Pelikan et al. 55 vols. St. Louis: Concordia, 1955–86.

MacArthur, John F., Jr. *Faith Works: The Gospel according to the Apostles*. Dallas: Word, 1993.

———. *The Gospel according to Jesus: What Is Authentic Faith?* Grand Rapids: Zondervan, 1988.

Maccoby, Hyam. *Ritual and Morality: The Ritual Purity System and Its Place in Judaism*. Cambridge: Cambridge University Press, 2009.

MacDonald, Deven K. "The Characterization of a False Disciple: Judas Iscariot in Mark's Gospel." *McMaster Journal of Theology and Ministry* 15 (2013–2014) 119–35.

MacLaurin, E. Colin B. "Beelzeboul." *Novum Testamentum* 20 (1978) 156–60.

Mann, William E. "Augustine on Evil and Original Sin." In *The Cambridge Companion to Augustine*, edited by Eleonore Stump and Norman Kretzmann, 40–48. Cambridge: Cambridge University Press, 2001.

Markus, Robert A. "Life of Augustine." In *Augustine through the Ages: An Encyclopedia*, edited by Allan D. Fitzgerald, 498–504. Grand Rapids: Eerdmans, 1999.

Marshall, I. Howard. *Kept by the Power of God: A Study of Perseverance and Falling Away*. London: Epworth, 1969. Reprint, Eugene, OR: Wipf and Stock, 2008.

———. *The Pastoral Epistles*. International Critical Commentary. Edinburgh: T. & T. Clark, 1999.

———. "The Problem of Apostasy in the New Testament." *Perspectives in Religious Studies* 14 (1987) 65–80.

———. "Recent Study of the Pastoral Epistles." *Themelios* 23 (1997) 3–29.

———. "Salvation, Grace, and Works in the Later Writings in the Pauline Corpus." *New Testament Studies* 42 (1996) 339–58.

Marshall, Peter. *Heretics and Believers: A History of the English Reformation*. New Haven, CT: Yale University Press, 2018.

Martin, Ralph P. *James*. Word Biblical Commentary. Grand Rapids: Zondervan, 2015.

———. *2 Corinthians*. 2nd ed. World Biblical Commentary. Grand Rapids: Zondervan, 2014.

Martin, Troy. "Apostasy to Paganism: The Rhetorical Stasis of the Galatian Controversy." *Journal of Biblical Literature* 114 (1995) 437–61.

Martyr, Justin. *Dialogue with Trypho*. In Ante-Nicene Fathers, vol. 1, translated and edited by Alexander Roberts and James Donaldson, 194–270. Christian Literature, 1885. Reprint, Peabody: Hendrickson, 1999.

Mass, Korey D. "Justification by Faith Alone." In *Reformation Theology: A Systematic Summary*, edited by Matthew Barrett, 511–47. Wheaton, IL: Crossway, 2017.

Mathewson, David. "Reading Hebrews 6:4–6 in Light of the Old Testament." *Westminster Theological Journal* 61 (1999) 209–25.

Mattill, A. J., Jr. "The Way of Tribulation." *Journal of Biblical Literature* 98 (1979) 531–46.

Mattiox, "Indulgences." In *The Westminster Handbook to Theologies of the Reformation*, edited by R. Ward Holder, 89–90. Louisville: Westminster John Knox, 2010.

Maxwell, David R. "Justification in the Early Church." *Concordia Journal* 44 (2016) 25–40.

McAffee, Matthew. "Covenant and the Warnings of Hebrews: The Blessing and the Curse." *Journal of the Evangelical Theological Society* 57 (2014) 537–53.

McCabe, David R. *How to Kill Things with Words: Ananias and Sapphira under Prophetic Speech-Act of Divine Judgment (Acts 4:32–5:11)*. Library of New Testament Studies. New York: T. & T. Clark, 2013.

McCall, Tom, and Keith D. Stanglin, "S. M. Baugh and the Meaning of Foreknowledge: Another Look." *Trinity Journal* 26 (2005) 19–31.

McCartney, Dan G. *James*. Baker Exegetical Commentary on the New Testament. Grand Rapids: Baker, 2009.

McComiskey, Thomas E. *The Covenants of Promise*. Grand Rapids: Baker, 1985.

McCue, James F. "*Simul iustus et peccator* in Augustine, Aquinas and Luther: Toward Putting the Debate in Context." *Journal of the American Academy of Religion* 48 (1980) 81–96.

McCure, James F. "*Simul iustus et peccator* in Augustine, Aquinas and Luther." *Journal of the American Academy of Religion* 48 (1980) 81–96.

McDermott, Gerald. *Israel Matters: Why Christians Must Think Differently about the People and the Land*. Grand Rapids: Brazos, 2017.

McGaughey, Don H. "Baptism in the Protestant Reformation." *Restoration Quarterly* 2 (1958) 99–114.

McGinn, Thomas A. J. *The Economy of Prostitution in the Roman World: A Study of Social History and the Brothel*. Ann Arbor: University of Michigan Press, 2004.

McGonigle, Herbert Boyd. *Sufficient Saving Grace: John Wesley's Evangelical Arminianism*. Studies in Evangelical History and Thought. Carlisle: Paternoster, 2001.

McGrath. Alister. *Iustitia Dei: A History of the Christian Doctrine of Justification*. 3rd ed. Cambridge: Cambridge University Press, 2005.

McGraw, Ryan. *Reformed Scholasticism: Recovering Tools of Reformed Theology*. New York: T. & T. Clark, 2019.

McKim, Donald K. *Theological Turning Points*. Atlanta: John Knox, 1988.

McKnight, Scot. "The Warning Passages of Hebrews: A Formal Analysis and Theological Conclusions." *Trinity Journal* 13 (1992) 21–59.

McMahon, C. Matthew. *John Calvin's View of God's Love and the Doctrine of Reprobation*. Crossville, TN: Puritan, 2015.

McNeill, John T. *The History and Character of Calvinism*. Oxford: Oxford University Press, 1954.

Meadors, Gary T., et al. *Four Views on Moving Beyond the Bible to Theology*. Counterpoint Series. Grand Rapids: Zondervan, 2009.

Meinert, John. "St. Thomas Aquinas, Perseverance, and the Nature/Grace Debate." *Angelicum* 93 (2016) 823–42.

Middleton, J. Richard. *The Liberating Image: The Imago Dei in Genesis 1*. Grand Rapids: Brazos, 2005.

Milgrom, Jacob. "Rational for Cultic Law: A Case of Impurity." *Semeia* 45 (1989) 103–9.

Minnich, Nelson H. *Councils of the Catholic Reformation: Pisa I (1409) to Trent (1545–63)*. Burlington, VT: Ashgate, 2008.

Mitchell, Margaret M. "'Diotrephes Does Not Receive Us': The Lexicographical and Social Context of 3 John 9–10." *Journal of Biblical Literature* 117 (1998) 299–320.

Moo, Douglas J. *The Epistle to the Romans*. New International Commentary on the New Testament. Grand Rapids: Eerdmans, 1996.

———. *The Letter of James*. Pillar New Testament Commentary Series. Grand Rapids: Eerdmans, 2000.

Moody, Dale. *Apostasy: A Study in the Epistle to the Hebrews and in Baptist History*. Greenville, SC: Smyth & Helwys, 1991.

———. *The Word of Truth: A Summary of Christian Doctrine Based on Biblical Revelation*. Grand Rapids: Eerdmans, 1981.

Morgan-Wynne, John E. "Attitudes towards Erring Brothers and Sisters in Early Christianity as Reflected in the New Testament." In *Ecumenism and History: Studies in Honor of John H. Y. Briggs*, edited by Anthony R. Cross, 225–53. Waynesboro, GA: Paternoster, 2002.

Morris, Leon. *The Gospel according to John*. Rev. ed. New International Commentary on the New Testament. Grand Rapids: Eerdmans, 1995.

———. "Man of Lawlessness and Restraining Power." In *Dictionary of Paul and His Letters*, edited by Gerald F. Hawthorne, et al., 592–94. Downers Grove: Intervarsity, 1993.

Morrow, William S. *An Introduction to Biblical Law*. Grand Rapids: Eerdmans, 2017.

Moses, Robert E. "Physical and/or Spiritual Exclusion? Ecclesial Discipline in 1 Corinthians 5." *New Testament Studies* 59 (2013) 172–91.

Mounce, William D. *Pastoral Epistles*. Word Biblical Commentary. Grand Rapids: Zondervan, 2016.

Muller, Richard A. "Arminius and the Reformed Tradition." *Westminster Theological Journal* 70 (2008) 19–48.

———. "Calvin and the 'Calvinists': Assessing Continuities and Discontinuities between the Reformation and Orthodoxy; Part 1." *Calvin Theological Journal* 30 (1995) 345–75.

———. "Calvin and the 'Calvinists': Assessing Continuities and Discontinuities between the Reformation and Orthodoxy; Part 2." *Calvin Theological Journal* 31 (1996) 125–60.

———. *Christ and the Decree: Christology and Predestination in Reformed Theology from Calvin to Perkins*. Studies in Historical Theology. Grand Rapids: Baker, 1986.

Newman, Carey C. "Election and Predestination in Ephesians 1:4–6a: An Exegetical-Theological Study of Historical, Christological Realization of God's Purpose." *Review & Expositor* 93 (1996) 237–47.

Noll, Mark A. "John Wesley and the Doctrine of Assurance." *Bibliotheca Sacra* 132 (1975) 161–77.

———. *The Rise of Evangelicalism: The Age of Edwards, Whitefield, and the Wesleys*. A History of Evangelicalism. Downers Grove: InterVarsity, 2018.

Oberholtzer, Thomas Kem. "The Warning Passages in Hebrews—Part 3: The Thorn-Infested Ground in Hebrews 6:4–12." *Bibliotheca Sacra* 145 (1988) 319–28.

O'Brien, Peter T. *Colossians-Philemon*. Word Biblical Commentary. Nashville: Nelson, 1982.

———. *The Letter to the Ephesians*. Pillar New Testament Commentary. Grand Rapids: Eerdmans, 1999.

O'Keefe, John J., and R. R. Reno. *Sanctified Vision: An Introduction to Early Christian Interpretation of the Bible*. Baltimore: Johns Hopkins University Press, 2005.

Olson, Mark K. "John Wesley's Doctrine of Sin Revisited." *Wesleyan Theological Journal* 47 (2012) 53–71.

Olson, Roger E. *Arminian Theology: Myths and Realities*. Downers Grove: InterVarsity, 2006.

———. "Conversion." In *The Westminster Handbook to Evangelical Theology*, Roger E. Olson, 160–62. Louisville: Westminster John Knox, 2002.

———. "Lordship Controversy." In *The Westminster Handbook to Evangelical Theology*, Roger E. Olson, 317–19. Louisville: Westminster John Knox, 2002.

———. "Perseverance." In *The Westminster Handbook to Evangelical Theology*, Roger E. Olson, 237–39. Louisville: Westminster John Knox, 2002.

———. *The Story of Christian Theology: Twenty Centuries of Tradition and Reform*. Downers Grove: InterVarsity, 1999.

O'Malley, J. Steven. "Pietistic Influence on John Wesley: Wesley and Gerhard Tersteegen." *Wesleyan Theological Journal* 31 (1996) 48–70.

Origen (of Alexandria). *Commentary on John: Sixth Book*. In Ante-Nicene Fathers, vol. 9, translated and edited by Allan Menzies, 349–80. Christian Literature, 1896. Reprint, Peabody: Hendrickson, 1999.

———. *Commentary on Matthew*. In Ante-Nicene Fathers, vol. 9, translated John Patrick, edited by Allan Menzies, 413–512. Christian Literature, 1896. Reprint, Peabody: Hendrickson, 1999.

———. *On First Principles: Book I*. In Ante-Nicene Fathers, vol. 4, translated and edited by Alexander Roberts and James Donaldson, 242–67. Christian Literature, 1885. Reprint, Peabody: Hendrickson, 1999.

———. *On First Principles: Book III*. In Ante-Nicene Fathers, vol. 4, translated and edited by Alexander Roberts and James Donaldson, 301–48. Christian Literature, 1885. Reprint, Peabody: Hendrickson, 1999.

Oropeza, B. J. "Apostasy in the Wilderness: Paul's Message to the Corinthians in a State of Eschatological Liminality." *Journal for the Study of the New Testament* 75 (1999) 69–86.

———. *Churches under Siege of Persecution and Assimilation*. Apostasy in the New Testament Communities. Eugene, OR: Cascade, 2012.

———. *In the Footsteps of Judas and Other Defectors*. Apostasy in the New Testament Communities. Eugene, OR: Cascade, 2011.

———. *Jews, Gentiles, and the Opponents of Paul*. Apostasy in the New Testament Communities. Eugene, OR: Cascade, 2012.

———. *Paul and Apostasy: Eschatology, Perseverance, and Falling Away in the Corinthian Congregation*. Reprint. Wipf & Stock, 2007.

———. "Paul and Theodicy: Intertextual Thoughts on God's Justice and Faithfulness to Israel in Romans 9–11." *New Testament Studies* 53 (2007) 57–80.

———. "The Warning Passages in Hebrews: Revised Theologies and New Methods of Interpretation." *Currents in Biblical Research* 10 (2011) 81–100.

Ortlund, Dane C. "Justified by Faith, Judged according to Works: Another Look at a Pauline Paradox." *Journal of the Evangelical Theological Society* 52 (2009) 323–39.

Ortlund, Raymond C., Jr. "Apostasy." In the *New Dictionary of Biblical Theology*, edited by T. Desmond Alexander et al., 383–86. Downers Grove: InterVarsity, 2000.

———. *God's Unfaithful Wife: A Biblical Theology of Spiritual Adultery*. New Studies in Biblical Theology. Downers Grove: InterVarsity, 2003.

———. *Whoredom: God's Unfaithful Wife in Biblical Theology*. New Studies in Biblical Theology. Grand Rapids: Eerdmans, 1996.

Osborne, Grant R. *Revelation*. Baker Exegetical Commentary on the New Testament. Grand Rapids: Baker, 2002.

Owen, John. *The Doctrine of the Saints' Perseverance Explained and Confirmed: The Certain Permanency of their Acceptation with God and Sanctification from God (1654)*. Reprint. Ann Arbor, MI: Proquest, 2011.

Page, Sydney H. T. "Satan: God's Servant." *Journal of the Evangelical Theological Society* 50 (2007) 449–65.

Palmer, Darryl W. "Mission to Jews and Gentiles in the Last Episode of Acts." *Reformed Theological Review* 52 (1993) 62–73.

Partee, Charles. *The Theology of John Calvin*. Louisville: Westminster John Knox, 2008.

Pelagius. *Pelagius' Expositions of Thirteen Epistles of Paul*. Edited by Alexander Souter and J. Armitage Robinson. 9 vols. Contributions to Biblical and Patristic Literature. Cambridge: Cambridge University Press, 1922–1931. Reprint, Eugene, OR: Wipf & Stock, 2004.

———. *Pelagius: His Life and Letters*. Edited by B. R. Rees. Suffolk, UK: Boydell, 2004.

Pereira, Jairzinho Lopes. *Augustine of Hippo and Martin Luther on Original Sin and Justification of the Sinner*. Refo500 Academic Studies. Göttingen: Vandenhoeck & Ruprecht, 2013.

Perkins, Robert L. "Two Notes on Apostasy." *Perspectives in Religious Studies* 15 (1988) 57–60.

Peterson, David. *Hebrews and Perfection: An Examination of the Concept of Perfection in the "Epistle to the Hebrews."* Society for New Testament Studies Monograph Series 47. Cambridge: Cambridge University Press, 2005.

Peterson, Robert A. "Apostasy." *Presbyterion* 19 (1993) 17–31.

———. "Apostasy in the Hebrews Warning Passages." *Presbyterion* 34 (2008) 27–44.

———. *Our Secure Salvation: Preservation and Apostasy*. Phillipsburg, NJ: P & R, 2009.

———. "Perseverance and Apostasy: A Bibliographic Essay." *Presbyterion* 16 (1990) 119–25.

———. "The Perseverance of the Saints: A Theological Exegesis of Four Key New Testament Passages." *Presbyterion* 17 (1991) 95–112.

———. "Preservation, Perseverance, Assurance, and Apostasy." *Presbyterion* 22 (1996) 31–41.

———. Review of *Paul and Apostasy: Eschatology, Perseverance, and Falling Away in the Corinthian Congregation*, by B. J. Oropeza. *Presbyterion* 29 (2003) 116–17.

Phillip, Mario. "Delivery into the Hands of Satan: A Church in Apostasy and Not Knowing It: An Exegetical Analysis of 1 Corinthians 5:5." *Evangelical Review of Theology* 39 (2015) 45–60.

Picirilli, Robert E. *Grace, Faith, Free Will: Contrasting Views of Salvation: Calvinism and Arminianism*. Nashville: Randall House, 2002.

Pinson, J. Matthew. *Arminian and Baptist: Explorations in a Theological Tradition*. Nashville: Randall House, 2015.

———. "Atonement, Justification, and Apostasy in the Thought of John Wesley." *Integrity* 4 (2008) 73–92.

———. "Introduction to *Classical Arminianism*." In *Classical Arminianism: A Theology of Salvation*, by Leroy Forlines, iv–xii. Nashville: Randall House, 2011.

———. Introduction to *Four Views on Eternal Security*, edited by J. Matthew Pinson, 7–19. Grand Rapids: Zondervan, 2002.

———. "Will the Real Arminius Please Stand Up? A Study of the Theology of Jacobus Arminius in Light of His Interpreters." *Integrity* 2 (2003) 121–39.

Pitre, Brant. *Jesus, the Tribulation, and the End of the Exile: Restoration, Eschatology, and the Origin of the Atonement*. Grand Rapids: Baker, 2006.

Polhill, John B. *Acts: An Exegetical and Theological Exposition of Holy Scripture*. New American Commentary. Nashville: Holman, 1992.

Popkes, Wiard. "Two Interpretations of 'Justification' in the New Testament: Reflections on Galatians 2:15–21 and James 2:21–25." *Studia Theologica* 59 (2005) 129–46.

Porter, Steven L. "On the Renewal of Interest in the Doctrine of Sanctification: A Methodological Reminder." *Journal of the Evangelical Theological Society* 45 (2002) 415–26.

Pose, E. Romero. "Novatus of Carthage." In *The Encyclopedia of Ancient Christianity*, edited by Angelo Di Berardino et al., 2:938. 3 vols. Downers Grove: InterVarsity, 2014.

Ramos, Michael M. "In between St. Augustine and Luther: Grace and Justification." *Asia Pacific Journal of Multidisciplinary Research* 2 (2014) 34–39.

Ramsey, D. Patrick. "Sola Fide Compromised? Martin Luther and the Doctrine of Baptism." *Themelios* 34 (2009) 179–93.

Resseguie, James L. *The Revelation of John: A Narrative Commentary*. Grand Rapids: Baker, 2009.

Rice, George E. "Apostasy as a Motif and Its Effect on the Structure of Hebrews." *Andrews University Seminary Studies* 23 (1985) 29–35.

Rogal, Samuel J. "John Wesley's Arminian Magazine." *Andrews University Seminary Studies* 22 (1984) 231–47.

Rosner, Brian S. "'Drive Out the Wicked Person': A Biblical Theology of Exclusion." *Evangelical Quarterly* 71 (1999) 25–36.

Rosscup, James E. "A New Look at 1 Corinthians 3:12: 'Gold, Silver, Precious Stones.'" *Master's Seminary Journal* 1 (1990) 33–51.

Ryrie, Charles C. *Balancing the Christian Life*. Chicago: Moody, 1969.

———. *So Great a Salvation: What It Means to Believe in Jesus Christ*. Chicago: Moody, 1997.

Sailhammer, John H. *The Pentateuch as Narrative: A Biblical-Theological Commentary*. Grand Rapids: Zondervan, 199.

Sanders, E. P. *Paul and Palestinian Judaism: A Comparison of Patterns of Religion*. Philadelphia: Fortress, 1977.

Sapaugh, Gregory P. "A Call to the Wedding Celebration: An Exposition of Matthew 22:1–14." *Journal of the Grace Evangelical Society* 5 (1992) 10–34.

Sauer, R. C. "A Critical and Exegetical Re-examination of Hebrews 5:11–6:8." PhD diss. University of Manchester, 1981.

Schaff, Philip, ed. *The Creeds of Christendom*. 3 vols. Reprint. Grand Rapids: Baker, 1998.

―――. *History of the Christian Church*. 8 vols. Scribner, 1882–1910. Reprint, Peabody: Hendrickson, 2006.
Schnackenburg, Rudolf. *The Johannine Epistles*. New York: Crossroad, 1992.
Schreiner, Thomas R. "Circumcision." In the *Dictionary of Paul and His Letters*, edited by Gerald F. Hawthorne et al., 137–39. Downers Grove: InterVarsity, 1993.
―――. "Did Paul Believe in Justification by Works? Another Look at Romans 2." *Bulletin for Biblical Research* 3 (1993) 131–55.
―――. *Faith Alone: The Doctrine of Justification*. Five Solas Series. Grand Rapids: Zondervan, 2015.
―――. *1, 2 Peter, Jude*. New American Commentary 37. Nashville: Holman, 2003.
―――. "Justification Apart from *and* by Works: At the Final Judgment Works Will *Confirm* Justification." In *The Role of Works at the Final Judgment*, edited by Alan P. Stanley, 71–98. Grand Rapids: Zondervan, 2013.
―――. "Perseverance and Assurance: A Survey and a Proposal." *Southern Baptist Journal of Theology* 2 (1998) 32–62.
―――. *Romans*. 2nd ed. Baker Exegetical Commentary on the New Testament. Grand Rapids: Baker, 2018.
―――. *Run to Win the Prize: Perseverance in the New Testament*. Wheaton, IL: Crossway, 2010.
Schreiner, Thomas R., and Ardel B. Caneday. *The Race Set Before Us: A Biblical Theology of Perseverance and Assurance*. Downers Grove: InterVarsity, 2001.
Schremer, Adiel. "Thinking about Belonging in Early Rabbinic Literature: Proselytes, Apostates and 'Children of Israel,' or: Does It Make Sense to Speak of Early Rabbinic Orthodoxy?" *Journal for the Study of Judaism* 45 (2012) 249–75.
Schuchard, Bruce G. *1–3 John*. Concordia Commentary. St. Louis: Concordia, 2012.
Schweizer, Eduard. "The Testimony of Jesus in Early Christian Community." *Horizons in Biblical Theology* 7 (1985) 77–98.
Seifrid, Mark A. "Justified by Faith and Judged by Works: A Biblical Paradox and Its Significance." *Southern Baptist Journal of Theology* 5 (2001) 84–97.
Sell, Alan P. F. "Augustine versus Pelagius: A Cautionary Tale of Perennial Importance." *Calvin Theological Journal* 12 (1977) 117–43.
Shank, Robert. *Elect in the Son*. Springfield: Westcott, 1970.
―――. *Life in the Son*. 2nd ed. Springfield: Westcott, 1961.
Shepherd, Michael B. "Daniel 7:13 and the New Testament Son of Man." *Westminster Theological Journal* 68 (2006) 99–111.
Shetler, Brian. "Prophet and Profit: John Wesley, Publishing, and the Arminian Magazine." *Methodist History* 53 (2015) 85–100.
Shuger, Debora K. "The Mysteries of the Lambeth Articles." *Journal of Ecclesiastical History* 68 (2017) 306–25.
Silva, Moisés. "Perfection and Eschatology in Hebrews." *Westminster Theological Journal* 39 (1976) 60–71.
―――. *Philippians*. Baker Exegetical Commentary on the New Testament. Grand Rapids: Baker, 1992.
Sittser, Gerald L. "Catechumenate." In the *Dictionary of Christian Spirituality*, edited by Glen G. Scorgie, 340–41. Grand Rapids: Zondervan, 2011.
Smalley, Stephen S. *1, 2, and 3 John*. Rev. ed. Word Biblical Commentary 51. Grand Rapids: Zondervan, 2015.

Smiles, Vincent M. *The Gospel and the Law in Galatia: Paul's Response to Jewish-Christian Separatism and the Threat of Galatian Apostasy*. Collegeville: Liturgical, 1998.

Smit, Peter-Ben. "In Search of Real Circumcision: Ritual Failure and Circumcision in Paul." *Journal for the Study of the New Testament* 40 (2017) 73–100.

Smith, Gregory. "The Doctrine of the Future in the Historical Books." In *Eschatology: Biblical, Historical, and Practical*, edited by D. Jeffrey Bingham and Glenn R. Kreider, 135–56. Grand Rapids: Kregel, 2016.

Smith, John Clarke. "Calvin: Unbelief in the Elect." *Evangelical Quarterly* 54 (1982) 14–24.

Snodgrass, Klyne R. "Justification by Grace—to the Doers: An Analysis of the Place of Romans 2 in the Theology of Paul." *New Testament Studies* 32 (1986) 72–93.

———. "Parable." In the *Dictionary of Jesus and the Gospels*, edited by Joel B. Green et al., 591–601. Downers Grove: InterVarsity, 1992.

———. *Stories with Intent: A Comprehensive Guide to the Parables of Jesus*. Grand Rapids: Eerdmans, 2008.

Snyder, C. Arnold. *Anabaptist History and Theology: An Introduction*. Kitchener, ON: Pandora, 1995.

———. "The Influence of the Schleitheim Articles on the Anabaptist Movement: An Historical Evaluation." *Mennonite Quarterly Review* 63 (1989) 32344.

Soulen, R. Kendall. *The God of Israel and Christian Theology*. Minneapolis: Fortress, 1996.

Sparks, Kenton L. *God's Word in Human Words: An Evangelical Appropriation of Critical Biblical Scholarship*. Grand Rapids: Baker, 2008.

Sprinkle, Joe M. "The Rationale of the Laws of Clean and Unclean in the Old Testament." *Journal of the Evangelical Theological Society* 43 (2000) 637–57.

Stanglin, Keith. *Arminius on the Assurance of Salvation; The Context, Roots, and Shape of the Leiden Debate, 1603–1609*. Brill's Series in Church History. Leiden: Brill, 2007.

Stanglin, Keith D., and Thomas H. McCall. *Jacob Arminius: Theologian of Grace*. Oxford: Oxford University Press, 2012.

Stanley, Alan P. *Did Jesus Teach Salvation by Works? The Role of Works in Salvation in the Synoptic Gospels*. Eugene, OR: Pickwick, 2006.

Staples, Jason A. "What Do the Gentiles Have to Do with 'All Israel'? A Fresh Look at Romans 11:25–27." *Journal of Biblical Literature* 130 (2011) 371–90.

Steenbuch, Johannes Aakjaer. "Anabaptists and the Magisterial Reformation: The Question of Grace and Free Will with Particular Emphasis on the Danish Context." *Baptistic Theologies* 8 (2016) 16–32.

Stein, Robert H. *Jesus, the Temple, and the Coming of the Son of Man: A Commentary on Mark 13*. Downers Grove: InterVarsity, 2014.

Steinmann, Andrew E. "What Did David Understand about the Promises in the Davidic Covenant?" *Bibliotheca Sacra* 171 (2014) 19–29.

Stern, Sacha. *Jewish Identity in Early Rabbinic Writings*. Arbeiten Zur Geschichte Des Antiken Judentums Und Des Urchristentums 23. Leiden: Brill, 1997.

Stevens, Christ S. "Does Neglect Mean Rejection? Canonical Reception History of James." *Journal of the Evangelical Theological Society* 60 (2017) 767–80.

Storms, Sam. *Kept for Jesus: What the New Testament Really Teaches about Assurance of Salvation and Eternal Security*. Wheaton, IL: Crossway, 2015.

Stortz, Martha Ellen. "Pelagius Revisited." *Word & World* 8 (1988) 133–40.
Stott, John R. W. "Must Christ Be Lord to Be Savior?" *Eternity* 10 (1959) 14–18, 36–37, 48.
Strand, Kenneth A. "'Overcomer': A Study in the Macrodynamic of Theme Development in the Book of Revelation." *Andrews University Seminary Studies* 28 (1990) 237–54.
Streett, Daniel R. "Review of *1, 2 Peter, Jude* by Tom Schreiner." *Criswell Theological Review* 1 (2004) 248–50.
———. *They Went Out from Us: The Identity of the Opponents in First John*. Beihefte Zur Zeitschrift Fur Die Neutestamentliche Wissenschaft 177. Berlin: de Gruyter, 2011.
Strelan, Rick. "'Outside Are the Dogs and the Sorcerers . . .' (Revelation 22:15)." *Biblical Theology Bulletin* 33 (2003) 148–57.
Svigel, Michael J. "The Apocalypse of John and the Rapture of the Church: A Re-evaluation." *Trinity Journal* 22 (2001) 23–74.
Tannehill, Robert C. "Israel in Luke-Acts: A Tragic Story." *Journal of Biblical Literature* 104 (1985) 69–85.
Tanner, J. Paul. "The 'Outer Darkness' in Matthew's Gospel: Shedding Light on an Ominous Warning." *Bibliotheca Sacra* 174 (2017) 445–59.
Tanner, Norman P., ed. *Decrees of the Ecumenical Councils Volume Two: Trent to Vatican II*. Washington, DC: Georgetown University Press, 1990.
Taylor, John W. "The Freedom of God and the Hope of Israel: Theological Interpretation of Romans 9." *Southwestern Journal of Theology* 56 (2013) 25–41.
The Teaching of the Twelve Apostles. "The Didache." In *The Apostolic Fathers*, edited and translated by Michael W. Holmes, 32–52. 3rd ed. Grand Rapids: Baker, 2007.
Telfer, William. "Meletius of Lycopolis and Episcopal Succession in Egypt." *Harvard Theological Review* 48 (1955) 227–37.
Tertullian. *On Baptism*. In Ante-Nicene Fathers, vol. 3, translated by S. Thelwall, edited by Alexander Roberts and James Donaldson, 669–79. Christian Literature, 1885. Reprint, Peabody: Hendrickson, 1999.
———. *On Prescription Against Heretics*. In Ante-Nicene Fathers, vol. 3, translated by Peter Holmes, edited by Alexander Roberts and James Donaldson, 243–65. Christian Literature, 1885. Reprint, Peabody: Hendrickson, 1999.
———. *On the Apparel of Women*. In Ante-Nicene Fathers, vol. 4, translated by S. Thelwall, edited by Alexander Roberts and James Donaldson, 14–25. Christian Literature, 1885. Reprint, Peabody: Hendrickson, 1999.
———. *Scorpiace*. In Ante-Nicene Fathers, vol. 3, translated by S. Thelwall, edited by Alexander Roberts and James Donaldson, 633–48. Christian Literature, 1885. Reprint, Peabody: Hendrickson, 1999.
TeSelle, Eugene. "Pelagius, Pelagianism." In *Augustine through the Ages: An Encyclopedia*, edited by Allan D. Fitzgerald, 633–40. Grand Rapids: Eerdmans, 1999.
Thomas, C. Adrian. *A Case for Mixed-Audience with Reference to the Warning Passages in the Book of Hebrews*. New York: Lang, 2008.
Thomas, Robert. "1 Thessalonians." In *The Expositor's Bible Commentary*, vol. 11, edited by Frank E. Gaebelein, 229–98. Grand Rapids: Zondervan, 1978.
Thompson, Leonard L. *The Book of Revelation: Apocalypse and Empire*. Oxford: Oxford University Press, 1990.
Thornhill, A. Chadwick. *The Chosen People: Election, Paul, and Second Temple Judaism*. Downers Grove: InterVarsity, 2015.

Thornton, Dillon T. "Satan as Adversary and Ally in the Process of Ecclesial Discipline: The Use of the Prologue to Job in 1 Corinthians 5:5 and 1 Timothy 1:20." *Tyndale Bulletin* 66 (2015) 137–51.

Thuesen, Peter J. *Predestination: The American Career of a Contentious Doctrine.* Oxford: Oxford University Press, 2009.

Ticciati, Susannah. "The Future of Biblical Israel: How Should Christians Read Romans 9–11 Today?" *Biblical Interpretation* 25 (2017) 497–518.

Tomkins, Stephen. *John Wesley: A Biography.* Grand Rapids: Eerdmans, 2003.

Tongue, D. H. "The Concept of Apostasy in the Epistle to the Hebrews." *Tyndale House Bulletin* 5 (1960) 19–27.

Toussaint, Stanley D. "The Eschatology of the Warning Passages in the Book of Hebrews." *Grace Theological Journal* 3 (1982) 67–80.

Towner, Philip H. *1–2 Timothy & Titus.* IVP New Testament Commentary Series. Downers Grove: InterVarsity, 2010.

Treier, Daniel J. *Introducing Theological Interpretation of Scripture: Recovering a Christian Practice.* Grand Rapids: Baker, 2008.

Trigg, Jonathan D. *Baptism in the Theology of Martin Luther.* Studies in the History of Christian Thought. Leiden: Brill, 1997.

Turner, David L. *Matthew.* Baker Exegetical Commentary on the New Testament. Grand Rapids: Baker, 2008.

Twelftree, Graham. H. "Demon, Devil, Satan." In the *Dictionary of Jesus and the Gospels*, edited by Joel B. Green et al., 163–172. Downers Grove: InterVarsity, 1992.

Van Asselt, Willem J. *Introduction to Reformed Scholasticism.* Reformed Historical-Theological Studies. Grand Rapids: Reformation Heritage, 2011.

Van Asselt, Willem J., and Eef Dekker, eds. *Reformation and Scholasticism: An Ecumenical Enterprise.* Texts and Studies in Reformation and Post-Reformation Thought. Grand Rapids: Baker, 2001.

Vander Hart, Mark D. "The Transition of the Old Testament Day of the Lord into the New Testament Day of the Lord Jesus Christ." *Mid-America Journal of Theology* 9 (1993) 3–25.

VanDrunen, David. "The Protectionist Purpose of the Law: A Moral Case from the Biblical Covenant with Noah." *Journal of the Society of Christian Ethics* 35 (2015) 101–17.

Van Houwelingen, P. H. Rob. "The Epistle to the Hebrews: Faith Means Perseverance." *Journal of Early Christian History* 3 (2013) 98–115.

Vanhoozer, Kevin. "Ascending the Mountain, Singing the Rock: Biblical Interpretation Earthed, Typed, and Transfigured." *Modern Theology* 28 (2012) 781–803.

———. *Biblical Authority after Babel: Retrieving the Solas in the Spirit of Mere Protestant Christianity.* Grand Rapids: Brazos, 2016.

———. *The Drama of Doctrine: A Canonical Linguistic Approach to Christian Doctrine.* Louisville: Westminster John Knox, 2005.

Vanlandingham, Chris. *Judgment and Justification in Early Judaism and the Apostle Paul.* Peabody: Hendrickson, 2006.

Van Leeuwen, Marius, et al., eds. *Arminius, Arminianism, and Europe: Jacobus Arminius (1559–1609).* Brill's Series in Church History 39. Leiden: Brill, 2009.

Venema, Cornelis P. *But for the Grace of God: An Exposition of the Canons of Dort.* 2nd ed. Grand Rapids: Reformed Fellowship, 2011.

Victorinus (of Pettau). *Commentary on the Apocalypse.* In Ante-Nicene Fathers, vol. 7, translated by Robert Ernest Wallis, edited by Alexander Roberts and James Donaldson, 344–60. Christian Literature, 1886. Reprint, Peabody: Hendrickson, 1999.

Von Mosheim, John Laurence. *Historical Commentaries on the State of Christianity During the First Three Hundred and Twenty-Five Years.* 2 vols. Translated and Edited by James Murdock. New York: Converse, 1853.

Vos, Antonie. "The Systematic Place of Reformed Scholasticism: Reflections concerning the Reception of Calvin's Thought." *Church History and Religious Culture* 91–92 (2011) 29–41.

Walser, Georg A. *Old Testament Quotations in Hebrews.* Wissenschaftliche Untersuchungen zum Neuen Testament, 2, Reihe. Tübingen: Mohr Siebeck, 2013.

Waltke, Bruce K. *Genesis: A Commentary.* Grand Rapids: Zondervan, 2001.

———. "The Phenomenon of Conditionality within Unconditional Covenants." In *Israel's Apostasy and Restoration: Essays in Honor of Roland K. Harrison*, edited by Avraham Gileadi, 123–39. Grand Rapids: Baker, 1988.

Walton, John H. *Ancient Israelite Literature in Its Cultural Context: A Survey of Parallels Between Biblical and Ancient Near Eastern Texts.* Grand Rapids: Zondervan, 1989.

———. *Ancient Near Eastern Thought and the Old Testament: Introducing the Conceptual World of the Hebrew Bible.* Grand Rapids: Baker, 2006.

———. *Genesis.* NIV Application Commentary Series. Grand Rapids: Zondervan, 2001.

Walvoord, John F. "Christ's Olivet Discourse on the Time of the End: Prophesies Fulfilled in the Present Age." *Bibliotheca Sacra* 128 (1971) 206–14.

Wanamaker, Charles A. *The Epistles to the Thessalonians.* New International Greek Testament Commentary. Grand Rapids: Eerdmans, 2013.

Ward, Tim. "Sin 'Not Unto Death' and Sin 'Unto Death' in 1 John 5:16." *Churchman* 109 (1995) 226–37.

Warfield, Benjamin B. "Introductory Essay on Augustine and the Pelagian Controversy." In Nicene and Post-Nicene Fathers, vol. 5, translated by Peter Holmes and Robert E. Wallis, edited by Philip Schaff, xiii–lxxi. Christian Literature, 1887. Reprint, Peabody: Hendrickson, 1999.

———. Review of *He That Is Spiritual*, by Lewis Sperry Chafer. *Princeton Theological Review* 17 (1919) 322–27.

Waters, Guy Prentiss. *The Federal Vision and Covenant Theology: A Comparative Analysis.* Phillipsburg, NJ: P & R, 2006.

Watson, Nigel M. "Justified by Faith, Judged by Works: An Antimony?" *New Testament Studies* 29 (1983) 209–21.

Weaver, Rebecca Harden. *Divine Grace and Human Agency: A Study of the Semi-Pelagian Controversy.* Patristic Monograph Series 15. Washington, DC: Catholic University of America Press, 1996.

Wedderburn, A. J. M. "The Problem of the Denial of the Resurrection in 1 Corinthians 15." *Novum Testamentum* 23 (1981) 229–41.

Weima, Jeffrey A. D. *1–2 Thessalonians.* Baker Exegetical Commentary on the New Testament. Grand Rapids: Baker, 2014.

Wesley, John. "A Call to Backsliders." In *The Essential Works of John Wesley*, edited by Alice Russie, 519–31. Uhrichsville, OH: Barbour, 2011.

———. "The Great Privilege of Those That Are Born of God." In *The Essential Works of John Wesley*, edited by Alice Russie, 331–40. Uhrichsville, OH: Barbour, 2011.

———. "Justification by Faith." In *The Essential Works of John Wesley*, edited by Alice Russie, 283–93. Uhrichsville, OH: Barbour, 2011.

———. "On Predestination." In *The Essential Works of John Wesley*, edited by Alice Russie, 699–704. Uhrichsville, OH: Barbour, 2011.

———. "On Sin in Believers." In *The Essential Works of John Wesley*, edited by Alice Russie, 341–51. Uhrichsville, OH: Barbour, 2011.

———. "Predestination Calmly Considered." In *The Essential Works of John Wesley*, edited by Alice Russie, 1103–152. Uhrichsville, OH: Barbour, 2011.

———. "Serious Thoughts upon the Perseverance of the Saints." In *The Essential Works of John Wesley*, edited by Alice Russie, 1153–66. Uhrichsville, OH: Barbour, 2011.

———. "Thoughts on the Imputed Righteousness of Christ." In *The Essential Works of John Wesley*, edited by Alice Russie, 1183–86. Uhrichsville, OH: Barbour, 2011.

———. "Troubles in Georgia; Return to England; Peter Bohler; 'I Felt My Heart Strangely Warmed.'" In *The Journal of John Wesley*, edited by Percy Livingstone Parker, 22–37. Revell, 1903. Reprint, Chicago: Moody, 1951.

Wetzel, James. "Predestination, Pelagianism, and Foreknowledge." In *The Cambridge Companion to Augustine*, edited by Eleonore Stump and Norman Kretzmann, 49–58. Cambridge: Cambridge University Press, 2001.

Wieland, George M. "Roman Crete and the Letter to Titus." *New Testament Studies* 55 (2009) 338–54.

Wilkin, Robert N. "Christians Will Be Judged according to Their Works at the *Rewards* Judgment, but *Not* at the *Final* Judgment." In *The Role of Works at the Final Judgment*, edited by Alan P. Stanley, 25–56. Grand Rapids: Zondervan, 2013.

———. *Confident in Christ: Living by Faith Really Works*. 2nd ed. Denton, TX: Grace Evangelical Society, 2015.

Williams, David J. *1 and 2 Thessalonians*. New International Biblical Commentary. Peabody: Hendrickson, 2000.

Williamson, Paul R. *Sealed with an Oath: Covenant in God's Unfolding Purpose*. New Studies in Biblical Theology 23. Downers Grove: InterVarsity, 2007.

Willis, John T. "Mediating Conditional and Unconditional Promises in the Hebrew Bible." *Restorationist Quarterly* 54 (2012) 39–47.

Wilson, Andrew. "Hebrews 3:6b and 3:14 Revisited." *Tyndale Bulletin* 62 (2011) 247–67.

Wilson, Jack H. "The Corinthians Who Say There Is No Resurrection of the Dead." *Zeitschrift für neutestamentliche Wissenschaft und die Kunde der älteren Kirche* 59–52 (1968) 90–107.

Wilson, Stephen G. *Leaving the Fold: Apostates and Defectors in Antiquity*. Minneapolis: Fortress, 2004.

Wilson-Kastner, Patricia. "On Partaking of the Divine Nature: Luther's Dependence on Augustine." *Andrews University Seminary Studies* 22 (1984) 113–24.

Wolthuis, Thomas. "Jude and Jewish Traditions." *Calvin Theological Journal* 22 (1987) 21–45.

Wong, Daniel K. K. "The Pillar and the Throne in Revelation 3:12, 21." *Bibliotheca Sacra* 156 (1999) 297–307.

Woodbridge, John D., and Frank A. James III. *Church History*. Vol. 2, *From Pre-Reformation to the Present Day*. Grand Rapid: Zondervan, 2013.

Wright, David F. "Justification in Augustine." In *Justification in Perspective: Historical Developments and Contemporary Challenges*, edited by Bruce L. McCormarck, 55–72. Grand Rapids: Baker, 2006.
Wright, N. T. *Justification: God's Plan and Paul's Vision*. Downers Grove: InterVarsity, 2009.
———. *Paul: In Fresh Perspective*. Minneapolis: Fortress, 2005.
Yamauchi, Edwin M. "Magic in the Biblical World." *Tyndale Bulletin* 34 (1983) 169–200.
Yarbrough, Robert W. *1–3 John*. Baker Exegetical Commentary on the New Testament. Grand Rapids: Baker, 2008.
Yinger, Kent L. *Paul, Judaism, and Judgment according to Deeds*. Society for New Testament Studies Monograph Series 105. Cambridge: Cambridge University Press, 1999.
Zacolli, Christopher. "'And So All Israel Will Be Saved': Competing Interpretations of Romans 11:26 in Pauline Scholarship." *Journal for the Study of the New Testament* 30 (2008) 298–318.
Zerbe, Gordon. "Jews and Gentiles as People of the Covenant: The Background and Message of Romans 11." *Direction* 12 (1983) 20–28.
———. "Revelation's Exposé of Two Cities: Imperial Rome's Reign of Greed vs. New Jerusalem's Reign of Justice." *Vision* 15 (2014) 52–53.

Author Index

Ambrose (of Milan), 136, 147
Aquinas, Thomas, 149
Arminius, James, xix, 176–82, 193
Ashby, Stephen, 42, 89, 172, 181, 188, 192
Augustine, Aurelius, 130, 133–52, 156, 158–59, 160, 170, 181, 187, 194

Barclay, John, , 59, 61, 63
Bates, Matthew, 40, 238–39
Bauckham, Richard, 37–38, 97–98, 101, 109,
Beza, Theodore, 156, 174–75, 177–78, 187

Caelestius, 135–39
Calvin, John, 151, 156–60, 163, 174–75, 177, 187, 206, 235
Campbell, Alexander, 193
Campbell, Douglas, 54
Campbell, Thomas, 193
Caneday, Ardel, 233, 235–36
Carson, D. A., 28, 47–49, 73, 111, 225–26,
Cassian, John, 141–42
Chafer, Lewis Sperry, 199–201, 204–05, 208
Clement (of Alexandria), 122–23, 129
Clement (of Rome), 114–15
Cotelier, J. B., 114
Cranmer, Thomas, 162
Crouteau, David, 45

Davis, Kenneth R., 165

Dunn, James D. G., 53, 55, 85, 215, 219–20, 231

Eaton, Michael, 91–93, 210,
Episcopius, Simon, 182

Fee, Gordon, 53, 64–65, 70, 75, 77, 107, 224, 228
France, R. T., 35, 39

Gomarus, Franciscus, 179
Gottschalk (of Orbais), 150
Grebel, Conrad, 164
Gregory I, 151
Grotius, Hugo, 187

Harris, Murray, 66, 74

Harrison, Everett, 199, 201
Heiser, Michael, 6, 8, 10, 26, 73
Hodges, Zane, 34, 36, 45, 202, 204–9
Horton, Michael, 159, 206, 216–219, 239

Knight, George W., III, 77

Ignatius (of Antioch), 114–16, 129
Irenaeus (of Lyons), 119–21, 129, 131,

Julian (of Eclanum), 135, 139–40, 143
Justin Martyr, 118–19

Keener, Craig, 47
King, Martha, 74

Knox, John, 156

Luther, Martin, 152–59, 163–65, 167–68

MacArthur, John F. Jr., 202–11
Manz, Felix, 164
Marshall, I. Howard, 3, 13–14, 75–78
McAffee, Matthew, 94
McDermott, Gerald, 8
McKnight, Scot, 89
Moo, Douglas, 18, 60, 95–96
Muller, Richard, 156–57, 172, 174

Newman, Carey C., 72
Novatus, 128–29
Novatian, 124, 126–27, 129–30

Olson, Roger, 126, 128, 172, 174, 182–83, 186, 191–92, 194, 196, 198, 209
Origen (of Alexandria), 122–23
Ortlund, Raymond, 21
Owen, John, 160
Oropeza, B. J., 3, 34, 42, 46, 54, 63, 66–67, 78, 87, 89, 98–99, 108, 113, 150, 152, 180, 186, 195, 219–21

Palmer, Darryl W., 85
Pelagius, 135–41
Picirilli, Robert, 172, 176–77, 179–83
Pinson, Matthew, 152, 172, 187–88, 190–93

Pitre, Brant, 50–51, 88

Ryrie, Charles, 45, 204–8, 211

Sanders, E. P., 53
Schreiner, Thomas, 18, 34, 44, 54–55, 60, 61, 93, 97–98, 100–1, 226, 231–32, 235–36
Schuchard, Bruce G., 106
Snodgrass, Kenneth, 33, 37, 55
Stein, Robert, 44
Stone, Barton, 193
Storms, Sam, 218
Stott, John R. W., 199, 201
Streett, Daniel, 102, 231

Tertullian, 121–22, 129, 132
Thomas, C. Adrian, 53, 89, 91–93, 233, 236,
Towner, Philip, 76

Victorinus, 124
Volf, Judith M. Gundry, 53

Warfield, B. B., 135, 137, 139, 199–201
Wesley, John, 173, 186–93
Whitefield, George, 187, 193
Wilkin, Robert, 34, 36, 43, 207, 210–12, 225, 231
Williams, David, 70
Wright, N. T., 53, 55

Zosimus, 138–39, 141
Zwingli, Ulrich, 163–64

Subject Index

Abraham (Abrahamic), 2, 8–13, 15, 17–18, 28–30, 56–58, 62, 203, 234
Abrahamic Covenant, 11–12
Adam, 4–7, 24, 56–57, 60, 111, 120, 123, 131, 136–37, 143, 145, 165, 168, 175, 179
Adam and Eve, 4–6, 8, 96, 142, 203
Anabaptists, 160, 163–66, 170–71, 174, 186, 226
Anathema, 61
Anglicanism, 161–63, 169–70, 174, 186–88, 193, 201, 226
Antichrist, 102, 105–6, 121
Apostasy, apostates, 1–4, 6–8, 10–13, 19–21, 23, 25, 27–33, 42, 47, 50, 52–53, 60, 63, 65–66, 71, 75, 79–80, 85, 89, 93–96, 101, 106, 110, 113, 116, 119, 121–24, 131–134, 146–47, 149, 154–57, 160–61, 163, 166–67, 169–73, 180–81, 183–84, 186–94, 197–98, 213–14, 216–20, 223, 225–26, 229–32, 235–37, 243–45
Apostolic Fathers, 113–16, 118
Arminian, Arminianism, 42, 57, 60, 89, 93, 160, 163, 166, 172–74, 181, 183–88, 192–93, 197–98, 210, 218–19, 225–26, 233, 235–236
Assurance (of salvation), 52, 55, 57, 69, 74, 107, 111, 147, 151, 155–56, 158, 162, 169, 181, 184, 191, 197–98, 206, 208–9, 214, 225, 229, 237–45
Augsburg Confession, 155, 166

Baptism, 3, 117–18, 122–23, 126, 130–31, 133, 135, 137, 139, 141, 143, 145, 148–52, 154–55, 158–59, 163–65, 170–71, 197, 217, 235–36, 244
Baptist Tradition, 166–67, 173, 193, 198, 203
Beelzebul, 38
Belgic Confession, 160, 179, 183
Believe, belief, 28, 34, 42, 44–46, 50–51, 54–55, 60, 74, 80, 92, 94, 153, 158, 194, 197, 200, 202, 207–08, 232, 234, 239–40
Blasphemy against the Holy Spirit, 38–39

Calvinism (Calvinist), 89, 93, 160–61, 166–67 177, 183, 187–88, 191–93, 197–98, 204, 210, 219, 225, 233, 235
Carnal Christian, 200, 203–4, 219
Christ (Jesus), 3, 32–51, 55, 57, 59–60, 65, 71–72, 74, 76, 84, 86–88, 92, 94 –95, 98, 101–2, 105–6, 111, 119, 155, 201–2, 204, 214, 223, 225, 227–28, 230–34, 239–41, 243–44
Church discipline, 64–65, 86, 166, 244–45
Circumcision, 9, 12, 61, 73, 224

Conversion, 21, 39, 46, 69, 81–82, 110, 133, 163, 165–67, 190–92, 196–198, 200–4, 206–9, 217, 229–30, 235, 238–42
Covenant Theology, 161, 206, 216–17, 237
Covenant, 2–3, 5–11, 19–21, 23–30, 48–49, 54, 56, 58–60, 64, 110, 132, 159, 188, 223–24, 233–34, 236–37

Daniel, 18, 22, 26, 47, 106
David, 15–17, 20, 26, 33, 119, 121, 180–81
Davidic Covenant, 16–18, 30
Day of Atonement, 14
Day of the Lord, 69
Decian persecution, 127–28
Diocletian persecution, 127
Didache, 114–16
Dispensationalism, 199, 203
Divine Image, 4

Election, 43, 58–59, 72, 89, 142–44, 149, 151–53, 155–58, 162–63, 165, 167, 169, 172–73, 176–80, 182–83, 185, 188, 190–93, 195, 225, 238
Elijah, 3, 9, 22
Epistle of Barnabas, 114, 116–117
Eternal Security, 157, 167, 197–98, 211, 216, 218
Ex opere operato, 154
Exodus event, 2–3, 8–9, 12, 17, 21–22, 28–30, 43, 91, 99, 224
Ezekiel, 18, 23–24, 119

Faith, 9–10, 13, 19, 21, 27–30, 32–35, 37–38, 40–44, 49–50, 52–57, 59–64, 66–67, 70, 73–74, 76–83, 86–88, 90–100, 106, 108–121, 124–28, 131–33, 140–42, 144–50, 151–60, 162–63, 165–71, 178, 180–82, 184, 186–201, 204–5, 207–12, 218–19, 223–45
Fall of Adam, 4–7, 137, 142, 175–76, 180

False teachers, 15, 30, 39, 42–43, 47, 61–62, 71, 73–74, 76, 78–81, 84, 88, 97–98, 100–2, 104–5, 111–13, 115–16, 119, 121, 132, 155, 220, 225, 229–30, 233, 238
Federal Vision, 236–37
Final Judgment, 29, 36, 42, 53, 55, 64, 81, 83, 104, 106, 108–9, 115–16, 182, 196, 225–27, 229, 233, 244
Formula of Concord, 153, 155
Free Grace Movement, 207–11, 219, 225, 231, 233

Gehenna, 35, 40, 131, 210
Grace, 6–7, 27, 41–42, 51, 53, 56, 63, 82, 110–11, 122–23, 131–34, 136–37, 139–56, 158–60, 165, 168–70, 179–81, 183–85, 188, 190, 192, 195, 204, 207, 209–11, 217, 224–225, 232, 236–37, 239, 243, 246

Haggai, 13, 22,
Heidelberg Catechism, 160, 183
Holy Spirit (Spirit), 3, 6, 25–29, 38–39, 42, 45, 47, 49, 55–57, 60–63, 66, 72–74, 76–77, 80–82, 86–87, 92, 106–7, 111–12, 120, 122, 131, 133, 141, 145–46, 149, 157, 159–160, 162–63, 165–66, 169, 184–85, 189, 191, 193, 199–200, 208–10, 217, 223, 225, 227, 234

Isaac, 8, 58, 234–35, 238–39, 242
Israel, 2–3, 6–37, 40, 43, 47–48, 51, 54, 57–59, 69, 72, 79, 85, 90–92, 95, 99–100, 116, 120, 122, 132–33, 159, 203, 223–25, 234, 237

Jacob, 8–9, 12, 58, 144, 203, 234
Jeremiah, 13, 22
Judas (Iscariot), 41, 43, 46, l49, 86, 103, 106, 154, 181, 205, 233
Justification, 37, 40, 50, 52, 55–57, 60–61, 63, 81–82, 89, 91, 96–97, 111, 142, 145–46, 148–52,

154–55, 157–58, 165–66, 168–70, 182, 190–92, 194, 196, 198–99, 201, 204, 207–9, 226–27, 231, 238–39

Kingdom of God (of heaven), 38–39, 50, 61, 65, 67, 88, 115, 120, 166, 225, 227

Lambeth Articles, 162
Lapsarianism, supra, infra, 173, 175–76, 178, 180
Lapsed, 65, 125–30, 218
Lutheranism, 152, 158
Lord's Supper, 65, 86, 104, 108, 126, 235, 244
Lordship Salvation, 194–212

Martyrdom, 40, 43, 110, 127,
Mosaic Covenant, 12–18, 21–23
Moses, 2–3, 8–9, 12, 18–21, 28, 58, 78, 85, 91–92

New Covenant, 3, 6, 10, 17–18, 22–23, 26–29, 37, 41, 43, 55, 57, 61–62, 72, 80, 85, 90, 92, 94, 97, 132, 159, 217, 223–24, 227, 231–37
Noah, 6, 11, 19, 35–36, 121–22, 203
Noahic Covenant, 11
Novatian Schism, 124–32

Old Covenant, 10, 20–21, 23, 25–28, 58, 132, 159, 223–24, 234, 236
Olivet Discourse, 35, 42–44, 48, 71, 88, 116, 243
Original Sin, 131, 139–45, 149, 156, 165, 168

Paul, 3, 9, 18, 29, 31, 40, 47, 49, 52–84, 86, 88, 92, 96–97, 108, 111–12, 116, 120, 136, 144, 155, 178, 199–200, 207, 221, 223, 225, 230, 232–34, 239–44
Parables, 33–38, 50, 55
Pelagianism, 27, 134–41, 151–52, 165, 178, 180, 184, 186
People of God (God's people), 2, 7–13, 19, 23, 26–27, 29, 40, 42, 53, 61, 65, 78, 85, 95, 102, 105, 109–10, 112, 115–16, 156–57, 159, 195, 234–37, 239, 244
Predestination, 56, 72, 135, 140–42, 144–45, 147, 149–50, 152–53, 157, 161–62, 169, 172–75, 177, 179, 187, 204,
Prevenient Grace, 42, 180, 188, 190, 193, 197
Priest, 12, 14, 20, 41, 62, 79, 86, 91–92, 107
Protestant Reformation, 96, 146, 149–67, 182, 188, 192–93, 196, 201, 239

Reformed, 5, 42, 55, 59–60, 72, 89, 93, 144, 156–63, 165–66, 169, 171–80, 182–85, 187, 192–93, 195, 197–98, 200, 204–6, 209, 211, 216–19, 226, 231, 233, 235–37
Remonstrants, 182–84, 187–88, 193, 198
Regeneration, 27, 111, 123, 142, 145–46, 148–50, 154, 157–58, 160, 165–166, 170–71, 183, 185, 192, 197, 200, 209, 217
Repentance, 15, 24, 29, 45, 47, 81–82, 94, 111–12, 120, 123, 133, 144, 153–54, 156–57, 160, 178, 189, 191, 196–98, 200–1, 204–8, 242
Restorationist Movement, 193
Resurrection, 11, 18, 23, 41–43, 45, 52, 54, 56, 62, 66–67, 72, 77, 81–82, 99, 106, 109–11, 114–16, 133, 148, 151, 155, 158, 210, 226–27, 232, 238, 240, 243
Roman Catholicism, 148–49, 167–70

Sacraments, (Sacramentalism), 96, 145, 148, 150–56, 158–59, 163, 168–71, 183, 185, 192, 239
Satan, 3, 5, 8, 11, 34, 38–40, 47, 52, 64, 67, 76, 81, 86, 105, 109–10, 112, 120, 123–24, 147, 184, 227, 242
Second Temple Judaism, 3, 53
Semi-Pelagianism, 134, 140–42, 186,

Sermon on the Mount, 39
Shepherd of Hermas, 114, 116–18
Simon Magus, 86–87
Simon Peter, 41–42, 44, 47–49, 64, 78, 84, 86–87, 95, 98–101, 111–12, 130, 180, 221, 223, 225, 230–33
Sodom and Gomorrah, 19, 30, 100, 123
Synod of Dort, 160, 173, 182–86

Tabernacle/temple, 4, 6, 8, 14, 16–18, 22, 26–29, 42, 47, 62, 71–72, 107, 109, 122
Theological Method, 1, 175, 214–16

Thirty-Nine Articles, 162–63
Trent, (Council of), 149, 167–70
Tribulation, 43, 50–51, 88, 108, 110, 117
TULIP, 161

Unpardonable Sin, 38–39

Warning Passages, 89–94, 210, 217–19, 229–31, 235
Wesleyan, 57, 172–73, 186–93
Westminster Confession, 160, 163
Wilderness wanderings, 21, 29, 120

Scripture and Ancient Documents Index

OLD TESTAMENT

Genesis

1:2	26
1:26–28	4
2:15	5
2:16–17	5
2:19–20	4
3:1	5
3:4–5	5
3, 5–7	5
3:8,	6
3:15	5–6, 8, 17
5:24	23
9:5–6	11
9:11	11
11:1–9	11
12:1–2	11
15:1–6	11
15	11–12
15:7–17	11
15:18–19	12
17:5	11
17:11–14	12
29:–30	12
37–47	12
41:38	26

Exodus

1:7–14	12
4:22–23	16
6:6–7	8, 110
12:12	12
19:5	8, 12
19:6	12
20:1–21	13
31:3	26
31:14–15	15
34	19
34:7	13
35:31	26

Leviticus

4:2, 22	14
5:17–18	14
10:1–2	86
16	14
16:16	14
23:29–30	15
26	13
26:9–14	8

Numbers

1	9
11:29	26
14:18	13
14:28–30	9
15:22–41	14
15:30–31	38, 104
18:22	104
27:18	26
33:4	12

Deuteronomy

4:26–27	13
4:36–38	13
5:2–5	13
5:9	13
9:10	8
10:4	8
13	15, 25
18:16	8
24:16	13
28–30	18
29:18–20	38
30:14	18
31:6,	8, 22
31:16–17	22

Judges

14:19	26
16:20	26
21:6	15

Ruth

4:18–22	17

1 Samuel

11:6	26
16:13	26
26	16

2 Samuel

5:1–4	16
6:6–7	86
6:12–23	16
7:1–3	16
7:14–15	17
7:12–16	16
12	33
16:14	26

1 Chronicles

17:13	17
17:11–14	16
28:6	16

2 Chronicles

26:21	15

1 Kings

11:1–2,	17
14:10	15
19	8
19:15–18	9

2 Kings

2:11	23
14:6	13

Job

19:25–27	23

Psalms

19:13	104
23:6	23
41:9	47
51:11	26
73:24	23

Isaiah

5:1–7	48
10:20–21	8
56:3–8	9
57:7–8	21

Jeremiah

2:19–21	48
3:6	21
3:8	22
23:5	6
29:10	22
Jer 31:30	13
31:33–34	18
42	8

Lamentations

5: 21–22	18

Ezekiel

3:16–21	23
11:19–20	18
15:1–8	48
16:31–34	21
18:19–20	13
18:19–32	23
18:24	189
33:1–11	23
36:25–27	18
37:1–23	18

Daniel

4:8	26
5:11–14	26
7	106
12:1–3	18

Hosea

1:9	22
2:18–20	22
4:12	21
9:1	21
10:1–2	48

Habakkuk

2:4	54

Zeph

3:13	9

Haggai

1:3–4	22
2:4–9	23

Zech

8:11–12	9
9:9–13	6
13:7	41

NEW TESTAMENT

Matthew

3:7–10	48
5:29–30	40
6:14	40
7:15–23	220
8:12	35
10:32–33	40
11:26	40
12:31–32	38
12:48–50	36
13:1–23	33
13:19	33
13:21	230
13:44–45	40
16:17–19	41
16:25	40
18:6	40
18:23–35	37
19:28	95
21:18–22	48
21:33–43	37
22:1–14	37
22:13	35
24:9–12	42
24:13	42
24:24	42, 230
24:36–39	36
24:45–51	36
25	243–44
25:1–13	35
25:14–30	35
25:15–17	35
25:30	35
25:31–46	36
25:38–40	44–45, 36
26:14–16	47–48, 41

Mark

3:22–30	38
4:1–20	33
4:15	33
8:38	40
10:29–30	225
11:12–14	48

Mark (continued)

11:20–25	48
13:13	42
13:22	42
14:17	41
14:27	41

Luke

1:3	85
8:4–15	33
8:11	33
9:24	40
9:62	40
12:8–9	40
14:16–24	37
17:2	40
17:32	40
18:8	42
20:9–18	37
21:19	42
22:3–6	41
22:30	95
22:31–32	41
22:47–48	41

John

1:7	45
1:22–23	46, 48
2:23–24	46, 230
3:1–21	45
4:1–38	45
6:64	46
6:66	46
6:70	47
10:11–15	45
10:25–29	45
11:1–45	45
13:18	47
13:21	47
13:26	47
14–16	45
15,	48
15:16	48
15:26–16:4	48
16:1–3	48
17	41
17:9	45
17:12	47
20:30–31	45
21:15–19	41

Acts

1:1	85
2:2–3	27
5:1–11	85, 104
7:2–4,	11
8:4–24	86
14:22	88
16:1–20	75
17:4	68
20:28–32	88
20:29–30	230
29–30	81

Romans

1:16	54
1:17	54
2:12–16	55
3	56
4	56
5	56
6–7	56
7	178
8	56, 82
8:3–4	56
8:11	82
8:22–23	56
8:28–29	190
8:30	56
8:31–39	57
9	178
9–11	57
9:1–5	58
9:6	58
9:27–29	9
11	120, 233
11:1	59
11:1–5	9
11:17–22	49
11:17–24	59
11:25	58
11:26	58

16:20	5

1 Corinthians

1:12–13	64
2–3	199, 204
3:1	199
3:3–4	64
3:9	82
3:10–15	53, 220, 225
4:7	144
5:1	64
5:5	64
5:6–8	3
5:9–13	65
6:1–2	67
6:9–10	65
6:19	82
10	223
10:1–3	3
10:1–13	66
10:6	223
10:11–12	30
11	104, 223
11:30	65
11:32	65
15	82
15:2	66
15:17	66

2 Corinthians

6:1–2	67
6:16	82
12:7	147
13:5–6	67

Galatians

1:6	62
1:6–7	61
1:8–10	224
2:4	61
3:1	62
3:1–5	62
4:8–11	62
4:11	224
5:2–3	62
5:3–4	63
5:4	224
5:13–14	63
5:21	63
6:11–12	62

Ephesians

1	72
1:13–14	72

Philippians

1:6	73, 77
1:12–18	73
1:21	73
1:27	73
2:12–13	73
3:1–3	73
3:7–14	73
3:17–19	73

Colossians

1:21–23	74
2:8	74
2:16–17	74
2:20–21	74
3:1–2	74

1 Thessalonians

1:9	68
1:2–9	68
2:13–16	68
3:1–5	68
4:3–4	68
4:9–12	69
4:13–18	69
5	69
5:2	69
5:3–6	69
5:7	69
5:11	70

2 Thessalonians

1:6–10	79
2:1–2	71
2:2	69

2 Thessalonians (continued)

2:7	47
2:8	71

Phlm

1–25	74–75
1	75
23–24	75

1 Timothy

1–2	76–77
1:3	88
1:9–20	189
4:15–16	77
4:16	88

2 Timothy

1–2	77–79
1:15	88
2:19–3:5	79

Titus

1–2	75

Hebrews

2:1–4	90
3:6	94
3:14	94
3:7–4:13	91
4:1–11	30
4:1	224
4:14	41
4:14–17	91
5:11–12	90
5:11–6:12	91–92
6	160, 231
6:4–6	189
6:4–9	220
6:6	38
7:25	41
10:19–39	92
10:25	90
10:32–34	90
11	21
12:14–29	92
13:3	90
13:23	90

James

1:2–4	95
1:12	95
1:12–13	96
2:14–26	96
2:24	96
5:7	95
5:19–20	96

1 Peter

1:5	99
1:17–19	99
2:12	98
2:21–22	98
3:13–14	98
4:1–5	99
4:12–13	98
4:16	98
5:10	99

2 Peter

1:3–11	99
1:16–21	100
2:1–22	220
2:1–2	230
2:1	100–2
2:22	155
3:1–10	100

1 John

1:1–3	102
1:8	103
2:18–19	47, 102
2:19	220, 230
2:22–23	103
2:26	103
2:28	104
3:9	103
4:2–3	103
5:16	104

2 John

5-6	105

3 John

1-15	105-6

Jude

1-3	97
4	97, 230
5	30
6-8	30
12	97
14-15	98
16	97
17	97
22-23	97

Revelation

1:1-3	106
1:7	106
1:12-20	107
2-3	107-9
2:10	108
2:10-11	228
3:5	107
3:10	108-9
7:5-8	95
12:9	5
20	124
20:2	5
21:7-8	110
21:12	95

EARLY AND MEDIEVAL CHRISTIAN WRITINGS

Aquinas

Summa Theologica
Of Perseverance, Questions 137.1-4
    149
Necessity of Grace, Questions 109.1-10
    149

Augustine

Against Julian, 3.57.	143
City of God	
1.27	145
13.4	145
14.16-19	143
Confessions	136
On Baptism of Infants	143
On Faith and Good Works, 14.21	146
On Free Will	136
On Nature and Grace	136
On the Predestination of the Saints	141, 144

On the Gift of Perseverance

1	146
4-7	147
10-11	148
19	148
20	147
25	148
33	146
34	148
35-40	144
39	148
41	144
48-49	147
51	148
54	144
57-60	148

On the Merits and Remission of Sins

I.40.24-30	145
To Simplicianus 2.16	143-44
Treatise on Rebuke and Grace 39	147

Barnabas

4:13-14	116
5.4	117

1 Clement

27.1	114
28.1	115
28.2-4	115

2 Clement

19.3	115

Clement of Alexandria

The Stromata, 7.16   123
Who is the Rich Man that Shall be Saved?
Chapter 40   123

Cyprian

Exhortation to Martyrdom, 11.4   131
On the Advantage of Patience, 9.24   132
On the Unity of the Church
1.4–5   130
1.20–21   131
On Works and Alms, 8.2   131
To Fidus, On the Baptism of Infants, 58.5   131
To Florentius, 68.8–10   130
To Jubaianus, 72.20–21   132
To Magnus, 75.16   131
To Pompey, 73.7   131–32
To Rogatianus, 6.2–3   131–32
To the Presbyters and Deacons, 5.2   132
Didache, 16.5   116

Hermas

Commandment, 4.3, 31.1–7   117–18
Parable, 8.6, 72.3   117
Parable, 8.6, 72.4–6   117
Vision, 2.2, 6.7–8   117

Ignatius of Antioch

To the Ephesians, 16.2   115
To the Philadelphians, 3.3   116

Irenaeus

Against Heresies
4.21–25   119
4.26.1–5   119
4.27.2   120
4.27.4   120
4.41.1–2   120
4.41.3   120–21
5.28–29   121

Justin Martyr

Dialogue with Trypho
Chapter 47   119
1.219   119

Origen

Commentary on John, 6.17   123
Commentary on Matthew
11.24   123
13.27   123
On First Principles
1.6.3   123
1.8.3   123
3.6.6   123
3.8   123

Victorinus

Commentary on the Apocalypse, 20.1–3   124

Tertullian

On Baptism, Chapter 8   122
On Prescription Against Heretics, Chapter 3   122
On the Apparel of Women, 1.2   122
Scorpiace, Chapter 6   122

www.ingramcontent.com/pod-product-compliance
Lightning Source LLC
Chambersburg PA
CBHW071234230426
43668CB00011B/1425